KERUX COMMENTARIES

PHILIPPIANS

———

KERUX COMMENTARIES

PHILIPPIANS

A Commentary for Biblical Preaching and Teaching

THOMAS MOORE
TIMOTHY D. SPRANKLE

Herbert W. Bateman IV
EDITOR

Kregel
Ministry

Philippians: A Commentary for Biblical Preaching and Teaching

© 2019 by Thomas Moore and Timothy D. Sprankle

Published by Kregel Ministry, an imprint of Kregel Publications, 2450 Oak Industrial Dr. NE, Grand Rapids, MI 49505-6020.

Unless otherwise indicate, the translation of the New Testament portions used throughout the commentary is the authors' own English rendering of the Greek.

All Scripture quotations, unless otherwise indicated, are from the New American Standard Bible® (NASB), Copyright © 1960, 1962, 1963, 1968, 1971, 1972, 1973, 1975, 1977, 1995 by The Lockman Foundation. Used by permission. www.Lockman.org

The Hebrew font, NewJerusalemU, and the Greek font, GraecaU, are available from www.linguistsoftware.com/lgku.htm, +1-425-775-1130.

All photos are under Creative Commons licensing, and contributors are indicated in the captions of the photos.

ISBN 978-0-8254-5835-4

Printed in the United States of America

19 20 21 22 23 / 5 4 3 2 1

Contents

FINAL EXHORTATIONS (4:2–9)

PAUL'S JOY BECAUSE OF THEIR GIFT (4:10–23)

EDITOR'S PREFACE TO THE SERIES

The Kerux Commentary series, unlike other commentaries written for preachers, joins experts in biblical exegesis with experienced communicators of biblical truth. Together they bring a heightened refinement in the handling of the Bible. Every volume emphasizes text-based truths that bridges from the context of the original hearers and readers to the twenty-first-century world. The name, *kerux* (KAY-rüxs) captures the aim of the series. Just as a *kerux* was one who proclaimed the official announcement of the king, so the forty-five volumes in this series will enable the preacher or teacher to accurately and authoritatively communicate the message of our divine King.

Every volume presents preaching units that offer *exegetical*, *theological*, and *homiletical* material to guide preachers and teachers to accurately interpret the Bible and ultimately engage today's world.

EXEGETICAL ANALYSIS	➡	THEOLOGICAL FOCUS	➡	PREACHING/ TEACHING STRATEGY

Solid *exegetical analysis* of the biblical text reveals the literary-theological movement of every biblical passage. The exegetical authors (trained experts in interpretation) engage the biblical text by interacting with original languages that shed light on interpretation (e.g., syntax, grammar, structure), hermeneutical issues relevant to a given passage (e.g., genre analysis), and pertinent secondary literature. From the exegetical analysis is derived a theological focus. The gnomic truths of a passage—those truths that transcend time and culture—emphasize the *theological focus* of each preaching unit. Following the careful exegetical analysis and insightful theological synthesis, homiletical authors (trained experts in preaching) offer suggestions for communicating the text. Based on the popular "big idea" preaching model, every preaching unit offers *preaching strategies*, contemporary connections, suggestions for creative presentation, illustrations, and more. These tools help the preacher and teacher effectively proclaim Scripture.

Kerux commentaries are written for trained pastors and teachers who speak regularly, who have some knowledge of Greek and Hebrew, and who spend a significant time preparing to preach and teach God's Word. As a result, each volume offers:

- a detailed introduction and outline.
- a summary of all preaching sections with their primary exegetical, theological, and preaching ideas.
- preaching pointers that join the original historical context with the contemporary one.
- insights from the Hebrew and Greek text.
- a thorough exposition of the text.
- sidebars of pertinent information and historical background.
- appropriate charts and photographs.
- a theological focus to passages.

- a contemporary big idea for every preaching unit.
- present-day meaning, validity, and application of a main idea.
- creative presentations for each primary idea.
- key questions about the text for study groups.
- lists of books and articles for further reading.

Many thanks to Jim Weaver, Kregel's former acquisition editor, who conceived of this commentary series and further developed it with the team of Jeffrey D. Arthurs, Robert B. Chisholm, David M. Howard Jr., Darrell L. Bock, Roy E. Ciampa, and Michael J. Wilkins. Much appreciation is extended to Dennis and Paul Hillman, whose thirteen-year tenacious commitment to the series contributed to Kerux becoming a reality. Finally, gratitude is extended to the two authors for each Kerux volume, the outside reviewers, editors, and proofreaders, and Kregel staff who suggested numerous improvements.

—Herbert W. Bateman IV

AUTHOR'S PREFACE

The apostle Paul would appreciate my experience working on this commentary: It was a joy. For the better part of a year, Philippians has been in my bones. I have meditated on Jesus's humiliation, Paul's situation, and the Philippians' participation in gospel ministry. I have taken comfort in God's promise to complete the work he's started in his church. And I've embraced my part in divine-human partnerships to imitate Jesus.

I am grateful for my local church as I've turned Tom's exegetical insights into preaching material. Leesburg Grace provided a testing ground for the Preaching Ideas and Creative Elements. Much of what I suggested, I tried. Some illustrations connected better than others.

Regardless, every preacher must do some reworking for his given context. There is no such thing as a ready-made sermon.

My prayer, however, is that in the following pages you will encounter material that will aid you in developing meaningful, truthful, and relevant sermons from Philippians. More personally, I pray your love (and joy) abound as you discern how to inspire your congregation with God's Word.

—Timothy D. Sprankle
Warsaw, IN (July 2019)

OVERVIEW OF ALL PREACHING PASSAGES

Philippians 1:1–8

EXEGETICAL IDEA
The Philippians' longstanding partnership in spreading the gospel caused Paul to thank God for them.

THEOLOGICAL FOCUS
Working together for spreading the gospel causes believers to thank God for one another.

PREACHING IDEA
Linking arms with fellow Christ-followers leads to deep gratitude.

PREACHING POINTERS
Paul opened with a formal greeting and friendly note of thanksgiving, using an epistolary form familiar to the readers. The exegetical section introduces key terms and major themes, highlighting the rich ministry partnership Paul shares with them. The joyful tone and affectionate prayer shine against the backdrop of Paul's imprisonment, a circumstance known by his audience. If the Philippians struggled with anxiety for Paul's plight, his greeting calmed their fears. If they worried about a suppression of the gospel, his greeting eased their concerns. God had not left them alone in Christian service. Chains were no impediment to God's work. In fact, God used chains—the human chain—the linking of arms between fellow Christ-followers.

Today people often feel isolated and impeded in their faith journey. Linking arms with fellow Christ-followers lessens these negative feelings. Serving together creates shared experiences, stronger resolve, and sustained impact. Opportunities to link arms abound. Local churches may provide inroads to ministry teams (e.g., youth group), or connections to community organizations (e.g., YMCA), parachurch ministries (e.g., Habitat for Humanity), and global development efforts (e.g., World Vision) to unite believers across denominational lines. Individual Christ-followers may covenant with others to form discipleship groups, neighborhood Bible studies, or community gardens. Of course, modern or ancient partnerships lacking deep gratitude, gospel purpose, and godly affection at times dissolve. This passage reiterates these conditions for successful partnerships, looking to God to sustain lasting links among his people.

Philippians 1:9–11

EXEGETICAL IDEA
Paul prayed that the Philippians would grow in love and godly character so that they would be ready for the return of Christ and ultimately bring honor to God.

THEOLOGICAL FOCUS

Requests to God for growth in love and godly character prepare believers for Christ's return and brings honor to God.

PREACHING IDEA

Talking to God strengthens our ties with others.

PREACHING POINTERS

Paul built on his words of gratitude for the Philippians' partnership with a prayer for their growth. He let his original readers overhear what he talked to God about concerning them: their character formation. While he has already stressed the promise that God will finish what he started in them, he now qualified the promise with a prayer for their increase in love and Christlike living. These words prime the Philippians for an upcoming appeal to imitate Jesus. Paul shared the prayer to encourage his first-century readers to virtuous living and glorious praise until Jesus returns.

Too often contemporary prayers revolve around juvenile requests: more money, easy days, better health, nice weather, and traveling mercies. Followers of Jesus fail to thrive because we have traded the biblical content of prayer for petty goods or personal safety. Setting spiritual growth as a key prayer request for others establishes an important principle: God's people develop character by talking to him. When we intercede for others, our affection for them increases. Greater affection leads to stronger ties and greater interest in their character formation. As Philippians will demonstrate, we do well to ask God for increases of trust, joy, knowledge, fellowship, perseverance, and purity for fellow Christ-followers. This passage recovers how talking to God strengthens our ties to others.

Philippians 1:12–18a

EXEGETICAL IDEA

Paul encouraged the Philippians that his imprisonment had become an opportunity for proclaiming Jesus, and that despite the impure motives of some preachers, he rejoiced that the gospel was being preached.

THEOLOGICAL FOCUS

Hardships in life are opportunities for proclaiming Jesus.

PREACHING IDEA

Roadblocks open new routes to see God at work.

PREACHING POINTERS

When Paul shifted from introduction to present circumstances, he immediately diffused any notion of disappointment. The movement from prayer to imprisonment rings with joy. The exegetical section not only provides historic details of his house arrest and "captive audience" with Caesar's guard, but also the advances in gospel proclamation, even by poorly motivated preachers. Anticipating the concern of his original audience, Paul assured them of his positive outlook based upon God's ongoing work. Their challenge was looking beyond roadblocks to find joy in God's work in the face of current difficulties.

The tendency to fixate on challenging circumstances remains today. We become pathologically nearsighted. Every accident, misfortune, closed door, and unexpected expense can spark panic or stir disappointment. Our gut reaction to setbacks rarely includes rejoicing; more often we respond with doubt, questions, anger, or disbelief. Consider the last time you were caught driving in a construction zone: were you more prone to praise or road rage? And in the weightier matters of life—college and career, marriage and family, financial and physical well-being—roadblocks abound, so the reminder that God has not stopped working is even more critical to believe. This passage directs our eyes to the new routes God opens when we face roadblocks.

Philippians 1:18b–26

EXEGETICAL IDEA
Paul modeled a Christ-centered view of life and death—willing to die and be with Christ, yet confident of release and further ministry, while certain of his ultimate salvation and that Christ's prestige would be advanced through him.

THEOLOGICAL FOCUS
Believers are to exhibit a Christ-centered view of life and death, seeking to advance Christ's prestige in the way they live or die.

PREACHING IDEA
Live fully in the face of death.

PREACHING POINTERS
Paul's imprisonment had created a dilemma: he faced possible execution or acquittal. Either option had potential benefits, and he weighed them out before his original readers. The exegetical section explains this dilemma, including theological clarification on honor/shame, salvation, and personal eschatology. Paul wrote frankly, disclosing his preference for death and being with Jesus, but ultimately yielded to the likelihood of pressing on in ministry. This internal dialogue modeled for the Philippians—who too will face suffering (1:28)—a healthy outlook on mortality and ministry.

Today, we deny death (Becker, 1997). The death sentence hanging over every person is muted by promises of prolonged life. Modern medicine and cosmetic products offer extended life, extended health, and extended beauty. The proliferation of superhero, zombie, and vampire films betray an unwillingness to look death in the eye. Patient-assisted suicide, which will someday be more widespread, tries to ease the sting of dying by granting power to sick people. Sadly, these denials of death prevent it from shaping our priorities. When was the last time you faced your mortality? How does embracing your finitude affect your daily decisions to love, serve, and bring honor to Jesus? This passage encourages us to consider our certain death as motivation to live fully.

Philippians 1:27–30

EXEGETICAL IDEA
Paul exhorted the Philippians to live in a way consistent with their citizenship in God's kingdom—standing together, promoting the message about Christ Jesus, and fearlessly withstanding persecution, realizing that suffering persecution as Christ's representatives in the world was a gift from God.

THEOLOGICAL FOCUS
As citizens of God's heavenly kingdom, believers should stand together, promoting the gospel and fearlessly withstanding persecution from unbelievers.

PREACHING IDEA
Loyal followers of Jesus band together to stand strong.

PREACHING POINTERS
Paul's letter moved from a personal update to pastoral exhortation. He began a series of admonitions to unified, steadfast, selfless living. He wanted his original readers to reflect the work of Jesus, which is the heart of the gospel. The encouragement stemmed from a sober reality: loyal Christ-followers will always face opposition. Their dual citizenship set them against the prevailing values and popular opinion of their neighbors. First-century residents of Philippi showed strong allegiance to Caesar and upheld values of military status and family honor. The original audience of Paul's letter would not have held such values in service of Jesus, resulting in social, religious, and political pressures.

There is no shortage of social pressures against which loyal followers of Jesus stand today. The Western world celebrates independence, self-expression, and consumerism. These values play out in an anything-goes sexual ethic, unfiltered online sharing, and gross personal debt, to name a few. When Christ-followers decide to band together and resist caving to these cultural values, they stand out, often painting a broad target on their backs. How does society respond when Christian teenagers vow to remain sexually pure until marriage? How do the media present the business owner who refuses to provide services for a same-sex wedding? What pressure does a parent feel when refusing to buy his children the latest gadget? This passage remains relevant today where diverse social pressures threaten our collective loyalty to Jesus.

Philippians 2:1–4

EXEGETICAL IDEA
Based on the encouragement, comfort, tender care, and presence of the Spirit God provides for followers of Christ, Paul exhorted the Philippians to make him completely joyful by living in harmony and humbly putting one another first.

THEOLOGICAL FOCUS
Sincere humility that elevates others creates harmony in the church.

PREACHING IDEA
Put others first to sustain strong bonds with fellow Christ-followers.

PREACHING POINTERS
After warning his readers about suffering at the hands of external forces, Paul continued to advocate for resiliency against internal pressures. Disunity threatened his original readers. The quest for personal honor, selfish gain, and diverse goals tempts every believing congregation. Such internal battles do not justify uniformity—a mockery of biblical unity and minefield for control—but call for a shared commitment to reflect Jesus's humble attitude. Paul wanted harmony for his original readers, and he assured them aid from the Holy Spirit as they sought to put others first.

Selfish gain and personal ambition drive Christ-followers today. More platforms for self-promotion are available at the click of a finger than ever before. People can peddle their thoughts like cheap wares on social media, blogs, websites, chatrooms, and YouTube. While we may use these tools to maintain contact with distant relatives and old friends, they are sometimes used to fuel mob mentality and social disruption. Often, the by-product of our communication tools is a sad mix of disconnection, competition, and ambition. Even within the body of Christ, ambition rears its ugly head. How often do loud voices become lobbyists for their niche ministry, trading the big vision of the local church for their pet project? The passage exposes selfish gain and calls for putting others first, to sustain strong bonds as Christ-followers.

Philippians 2:5–8

EXEGETICAL IDEA
Christ modeled a servant attitude when, rather than maintaining his exalted status, he became a man and suffered a humiliating death for others.

THEOLOGICAL FOCUS
Humility is demonstrated when, rather than insisting on our rights, we take the role of lowly servants.

PREACHING IDEA
Climb down the ladder of privilege to reflect the attitude of Jesus.

PREACHING POINTERS
Building on the call to loyalty, unity, and humility, Paul provided another exhortation: to reflect the attitude of Jesus. In one of the most notable and theologically parsed passages of the New Testament, the apostle described Jesus's downward mobility. The exegetical section sheds light on Jesus's glorious preexistence, incarnation, and inglorious death. Paul's description of Jesus's shameful descent would have sounded remarkable to an honor-oriented culture. Climbing down the ladder of privilege and status hinted of scandal in their context.

One of the driving narratives of today is the promise of upward mobility. From a child's earliest days of education, she learns she can achieve whatever she dreams. Educators chart a path of academic success leading to financial reward. Rags-to-riches stories capture our imaginations. Tales of success show how to arrive at the top at any cost, advancing from anonymity to celebrity, from average to extraordinary. Inversely, demotions and downsizing spell death in our personal life and economy. This passage presents a different path, encouraging followers of Jesus to follow his example and climb down the ladder of privilege to reflect his attitude.

Philippians 2:9–11

EXEGETICAL IDEA
God the Father highly elevated Christ Jesus to the highest universal status so that all personal beings—angelic and human—would submit to Christ and openly declare his divine, sovereign authority, and so increase the Father's fame.

THEOLOGICAL FOCUS
Christ Jesus reigns as the supreme Lord of the universe, and will be acknowledged one day by all.

PREACHING IDEA
Jesus's crowning victory beckons our humble loyalty.

PREACHING POINTERS
Paul completed the Christ hymn focusing on God's work of exaltation. Jesus's humble, selfless steps downward are matched by God's sweeping act of vindication: he raised up Jesus and gave him the uppermost name. Jesus Christ, not Caesar, is Lord. To the first-century readers, Jesus's reversal of misfortune served both to exhort Christlike character (2:5) and bring comfort in the face of suffering (1:28). Jesus's victory challenged the imperialistic images and symbols of status broadcast daily in the streets of Philippi. Their challenge was to acknowledge Jesus's victory by submitting to him until his return.

Competition, not humility, drives the Western world to enthrone a winner for every hour, season, and sphere of life. Athletes and coaches aim for personal records, hall of fame status, and team championships. Students pour into their academics to rise to the head of the class. Politicians set their aim on the White House. We hitch our wagons to these exalted figures, who require nothing from us in return. Moreover, many of us strive to make a name for ourselves. Sadly, personal victories are short-lived; worldly triumphs do not last. This passage begs us to acknowledge the exaltation of Jesus: his crowning victory beckons our humble loyalty.

Philippians 2:12–18

EXEGETICAL IDEA
Paul exhorted the Philippians, as God motivated and empowered them, to strive to become a spiritually mature, holy community as they headed toward the future salvation God would bring to completion, and to rejoice with him in their mutual sacrificial service to God.

THEOLOGICAL FOCUS

God motivates and empowers believers to strive to become a spiritually mature, holy community as they head toward the future salvation God will bring to completion.

PREACHING IDEA

Keep working a plan to become spiritually fit.

PREACHING POINTERS

Transitioning from the Christ hymn, Paul completed his exhortation section with a series of three more imperatives to live like citizens of God's kingdom, not Caesar's. He called the first-century audience to finish strong in their spiritual commitments to personal growth, communal life, and evangelistic witness. Their motivation to live God-pleasing lives has both internal and external factors. Internally, Paul promised them God-given energy to work out their salvation. Externally, Paul promised them that Jesus will return and justify his labors. In either case, the first-century audience should avoid the pitfall of spiritual idleness.

Followers of Jesus today need a revival of focused, spiritual energy. We are distracted and depleted. We expend our energies on too many mindless and distracting tasks. We manage email, count calories, transport children to extracurricular events, and fill our DVRs with more shows we can watch in a weekend. Even the demands of daily life—cooking and cleaning, commuting and working, paying bills, returning phone calls, and answering e-mails—can sap our energy, leaving our spiritual lives underdeveloped. Becoming spiritually fit should be our chief aim, but it requires a plan and discipline to follow. Often the more urgent tasks take priority. This passage motivates us to keep working a plan to become spiritually fit.

Philippians 2:19–30

EXEGETICAL IDEA

The Philippians were to receive and honor two proven, sacrificial servants of Christ from Paul: Timothy and Epaphroditus.

THEOLOGICAL FOCUS

We should value followers of Jesus who demonstrate sacrificial service for the church.

PREACHING IDEA

Give kudos to those who take risks for Jesus.

PREACHING POINTERS

Paul shifted from moral exhortation to traveling arrangements, sharing with his original readers upcoming plans to see them again. Prior to his arrival, however, the Philippians would receive two familiar ministry partners who had risked their lives: Timothy and Epaphroditus. The exegetical section reveals Paul's reinforcement of the Christ hymn while giving updates on these two commendable servants. Their humility and sacrifice deserve recognition. Moreover, Paul alleviated any worries his first-century readers experienced concerning Epaphroditus's delayed return.

Today we can learn a lesson on commending those who take risks for Jesus. Our world has no shortage of role models. Children exalt heroes from TV and movie screens. Famous athletes and star singers shape cultural trends in dress, language, and politics. Parents, teachers, and coaches serve as personal examples to emulate. The challenge is choosing the right kind of role model, who risks her security, comfort, and reputation to make Jesus famous. Not only does Paul consider himself a risk-taker and worthy role model, but he also gives kudos to two ministry partners who risked their life for Jesus.

Philippians 3:1–6

EXEGETICAL IDEA
Paul's warning against Judaizers emphasized that Christ-followers are God's true people because they worship and serve God under the power and direction of the Holy Spirit; they trust only in Jesus the Messiah, who secured their justification; and they do not seek justification through keeping the Law.

THEOLOGICAL FOCUS
God's true people are those who worship God under the power and direction of the Holy Spirit, who trust only in Jesus the Messiah for justification, and who do not seek justification through keeping the Law.

PREACHING IDEA
Don't trust an impressive résumé to secure good standing with God.

PREACHING POINTERS
The tone of Paul's letter takes a turn in chapter 3. The exhortation to copy Jesus's humble, self-giving, sacrificial attitude (as modeled by Timothy and Epaphroditus) contrasts sharply with a warning about Judaizers. Although the original readers may not have directly encountered the legalism Paul criticized, they were no strangers to poorly motivated preachers and cultural pressures. Imminent threat or not, Paul considered it relevant to remind his first-century audience of the happy fact of their new identity in Christ. They don't earn good standing with God by birthright or obedience, but receive it by trusting Jesus.

We are no less affected by moralism in today's church. The specific deeds we deem holy and perverse have a more modern dress, but the tendency to encode some acts as tolerable and others as egregious follows the same old line of logic. We ban certain genres of music (e.g., rap) and make allowances for others (e.g., country). We condemn some content in movies (e.g., sex and language) but justify "lesser" sins (e.g., violence and greed). Moreover, we praise people who take short-term mission trips or practice evangelism, but give little recognition to the volunteer who replaces the trash-can liner or sanitizes the nursery toys. This passage strongly challenges our misplaced trust in an impressive religious resume for good standing with God.

Philippians 3:7–11

EXEGETICAL IDEA
Paul pursued a personal relationship with Jesus as the only way to have a truly right standing before God at the final judgment and to experience the future bodily resurrection.

THEOLOGICAL FOCUS
A personal relationship with Jesus is the only way to have a truly right standing before God at the final judgment and to experience the future bodily resurrection.

PREACHING IDEA
Dump everything that disrupts you from knowing Jesus better.

PREACHING POINTERS
Building off his warning about would-be Jewish moralists, and echoing imagery from the masterful Christ hymn, this passage makes it clear: intimacy with Jesus was Paul's greatest aim, for it was the only means to right standing with God. Though his religious resume is impressive, Paul deemed it—along with every other accomplishment, comfort, or worldly pursuit—dispensable. The original readers would have heard the edge in Paul's rhetoric, as he crassly threw their cultural values into the garbage heap. They prized social status, religious performance, and family lineage, but he willingly pitched his own in the trash.

Our culture does not put a premium on knowing Jesus better. We are conditioned to pursue success, security, and comfort with greater loyalty than knowing him. Busyness in the church can serve as a substitute for knowing Jesus better. Managing our social lives with the myriad of recreational activities, family obligations, and friend groups can distract us from knowing Jesus better. Even all our grandiose (or misguided) thoughts about Jesus may inhibit us from knowing him better. This passage inspires us to dump everything that disrupts us from knowing Jesus better.

Philippians 3:12–16

EXEGETICAL IDEA
The Philippians were to agree with Paul and to pursue the ultimate goal: full intimacy with Jesus in a resurrection body in the age to come.

THEOLOGICAL FOCUS
Believers are to pursue the ultimate goal: full intimacy with Jesus in a resurrection body in the age to come.

PREACHING IDEA
Always take one more step as you strive to become like Jesus.

PREACHING POINTERS

Paul fixed his focus forward in this passage on his forthcoming resurrection and glory. His earthly life was interrupted by a heavenly calling that drove him ever forward. Athletic imagery colors these verses with sweat and vigor, as the exegetical section explains. While the apostle's comments are deeply personal—evident in several first-person pronouns—he invited his original readers to join the marathon. His race was their race; they are spiritual siblings pursuing resurrection and glory together. Perhaps, legalism loomed in the background; however, the passage more clearly encourages followers of Jesus to always take one more step as they strive to become like Jesus.

Today, the idea of striving after Jesus tends toward one of two ends on the human-effort spectrum. On the one hand, followers of Jesus treat salvation as a works-based project. They burn themselves out striving for perfection at home, work, church, and community. On the other hand, an errant understanding of grace discourages some believers from any spiritual effort. The unbreakable promise of heaven renders them of little earthly good. Perfection and passivity constitute the poles of our pursuit of Jesus; his people often pinball between the two. God's calling in our lives embraces the tension of our gritty pursuit and glorious ending.

Philippians 3:17–4:1

EXEGETICAL IDEA

The Philippians were to follow Paul's pattern of living a Christlike life of humility, self-denial, and sacrificial service while they waited for Jesus to return and complete their redemption by giving them resurrection bodies like his.

THEOLOGICAL FOCUS

Believers should follow the apostolic pattern of living a Christlike life of humility, self-denial, and sacrificial service while they wait for Jesus to return and complete their redemption by giving them resurrection bodies like his.

PREACHING IDEA

Follow in the footsteps of people who align their lives with God's kingdom.

PREACHING POINTERS

Paul capped a series of personal affirmations about striving toward Jesus with an exhortation to imitate the apostle and others who align their lives with God's kingdom. The lifestyle of a believer is described with echoes from the Christ hymn—humility preceding the glory of their resurrection bodies. The exegetical section will show this transformation hinges on Jesus's return. In the meantime, Paul warned his original audience to remain steadfast amid "enemies of the cross," an uncertain group of opponents. In any case, their challenge was to follow Paul's footsteps, not those who aligned their lives with earthly ends.

Today we are swayed by many fads, famous people, and faith options that do not align with kingdom values. We emulate parents and teachers, friends and celebrities, media and marketers whose peddle self-indulgence and shameful gain. We buy sleek products to secure social capital. The fear of shame silences our religious convictions (e.g., marriage as a covenant between male and female). We are terribly impressionable people, modifying our behavior based upon our current company. The footsteps we choose to follow become critical in our spiritual formation. This passage appeals to our need to follow in the footsteps of people who align their lives with God's kingdom.

Philippians 4:2–5

EXEGETICAL IDEA
The Philippians were to live together in unity, being deeply satisfied with the Lord in every circumstance, exhibiting a humble, gracious spirit to all people.

THEOLOGICAL FOCUS
Believers are to live together in unity, being deeply satisfied with the Lord in every circumstance, exhibiting a humble, gracious spirit to all people.

PREACHING IDEA
Resolve disagreements before they wreak havoc on harmony and happiness.

PREACHING POINTERS
Paul moved toward his conclusion, transitioning from the topic of external opposition to internal tensions. An interpersonal squabble in the church lingered between two women, Euodia and Syntyche (4:2). The nature of their disagreement was not stated, but given the fact Paul addressed them by name in his letter and asked for a mediator (4:3), it suggested that the matter was disruptive to the community. Here, Paul put the unity principle to the test. The original readers surely had awareness of the tension between these important female figures. Resolving their differences would not only prove beneficial to harmony and happiness in the Philippian church; it would also demonstrate Christlike meekness to a watching world.

Settling disagreements in our day is no simple matter. The lack of civility makes tense conversations toxic. People are trigger-happy on social media, willing to lambaste anyone who reflects an opposing view. Political discourse in America has devolved into name-calling and posturing. And under the banner of tolerance, our culture—overly sensitive and quick to take offense—has effectively banned moral disagreement. Followers of Jesus—whose names share a place in the book of life—should resolve their differences with gentleness. Sadly, when tensions arise among believers, we often descend into the same stubborn discord. The passage appeals to our need to resolve disagreements before they wreak havoc on harmony and happiness.

Philippians 4:6–9

EXEGETICAL IDEA
Instead of worrying, the Philippians were to lay out their concerns before God in prayer and to focus on godly virtues, following Paul's sacrificial, Christlike lifestyle, so that they may experience the peace God gives.

THEOLOGICAL FOCUS

A lifestyle of laying out one's concerns before God in prayer, thinking about godly virtues, and following a sacrificial, Christlike lifestyle leads to experiencing God's peace.

PREACHING IDEA

Keep God ever on your mind to calm your restless heart.

PREACHING POINTERS

Having dealt with interpersonal conflict, Paul transitioned to the life of the mind. His awareness of the Lord's nearness serves as a hinge. Paul's original readers had many reasons for anxiety: the apostle's plight, Epaphroditus's health, opposition, suffering, and misguided teaching all threatened them. Until Jesus returned, they were sure to feel tensions as citizens of heaven among Roman enthusiasts. Paul wrote to assure them that a greater peace than Caesar's was available. However, to feel Christ's peace, they would have to fix their minds on God.

Reasons for unrest abound today. Marketers prey on the fear of being left out. Media fuels the fear of disease, crime, and political scandal. Medical talk and research makes people instantly squeamish (just ask people how they feel when searching their symptoms on WebMD!). And followers of Jesus live in a pluralistic society where religious truth claims come across as oppressive. Cries of intolerance and accusations of hate plague the Western church; persecution has pushed the church underground in many other areas. In such a climate, our anxieties take on a life of their own, filling our minds with soul-squelching chatter. This passage implores followers of Jesus to silence the clamor of restless thoughts by keeping our minds ever on God.

Philippians 4:10–13

EXEGETICAL IDEA

While he delighted in their material provision, Paul had learned to be satisfied in life (experiencing spiritual/emotional well-being and peace) in any circumstance (having much or little) through his relationship with Christ and the strength he provided.

THEOLOGICAL FOCUS

Spiritual/emotional well-being and peace comes through a personal relationship with Christ and the strength he provides in every life situation.

PREACHING IDEA

Satisfaction starts by learning to say: "Whatever God gives is good enough!"

PREACHING POINTERS

Thanking the Philippians for their financial support was one of Paul's key purposes for writing the letter. However, his "Thank you" went beyond a word of gratitude. The exegetical section explains how Paul reframed the discussion, turning his appreciation into a theological primer on contentment in God's supply of inner calm and external needs. His first-century audience may have overvalued their financial gift or underestimated how God provides material goods and internal strength in crisis situations. Paul's "Thank you" was not a backhanded rebuke, but another reminder of God's part in the partnership with his people who proclaim Jesus.

Contentment seems less common than entitlement in the Western world. We assume our most basic needs will be met by employers or government aid, giving little credit to God for his abundant supply. Lack of bread and milk sparks a visit to overstocked grocery stores more often than prayer for daily supply. When our old cars, clothes, and computers wear out, we rush to retailers (online or local) to acquire new goods. Whether we pay cash or finance, it is easy to remove God from the receipt. This passage reminds us that all our assets ultimately come from him, so we must find satisfaction in him, learning to say: "Whatever God gives is good enough!"

Philippians 4:14–23

EXEGETICAL IDEA
The Philippians' material aid to Paul was a spiritual investment and act of worship that would bring spiritual reward and provision from God.

THEOLOGICAL FOCUS
Christian giving is a spiritual investment and act of worship that brings spiritual reward and provision from God.

PREACHING IDEA
God stamps his seal of approval on generous living.

PREACHING POINTERS
Paul continued to convey his appreciation for the Philippians' generosity. Their most recent gift through Epaphroditus—one of many previous donations—showed revived concern for Paul and the expansion of the gospel. The exegetical section will demonstrate how Paul looked beyond the material side to the spiritual, seeing their offering as a God-pleasing sacrifice. If the original readers had mistaken his comments about contentment as a slight, Paul assured them of his gratitude, magnified by the apostle's understanding of their future reward. Paul closed his letter with a final reminder to his readers that their gracious heavenly Father has riches in store for them. Glory is the stamp of approval awaiting generous followers of Jesus.

Generosity should mark today's church as well. There is no shortage of causes and needs to give to: building programs, short-term trips, homeless shelters, camp scholarships, clean water wells, utility relief, and the general church budget. Followers of Jesus will give an account for how they steward, spend, and share their monetary resources. Our wallets are windows into our worship; sacrificial giving pleases God. And knowing the Western church comprises the wealthiest people on the planet only adds to the urgency of giving to good causes and clear needs. This passage speaks directly to the financial opportunities knocking at the doors of the church.

ABBREVIATIONS

GENERAL ABBREVIATIONS

A.D.	*anno Domini* (in the year of our Lord)
B.C.	before Christ
B.C.E.	before the Common Era
C.E.	Common Era
Eng.	English
HB	Hebrew Bible
LXX	Septuagint (the Greek OT)
NT	New Testament
OT	Old Testament

TECHNICAL ABBREVIATIONS

ca.	circa
ch(s).	chapter (s)
cf.	*confer*, compare
col(s)	column(s)
d.	died
ed(s).	editor(s), edited by, edition
e.g.	*exempli gratia*, for example
et al.	*et alii*, and others
etc.	*et cetera*, and so forth, and the rest
f(f).	and the following one(s)
i.e.	*id est*, that is
idem	the same
lit.	literally
n(n).	note(s)
p(p).	page(s)
repr.	reprinted
rev.	revised by
s.v.	*sub verbo*, under the word
v(v).	verse(s)
vol(s).	volume(s)

EXTRABIBLICAL SOURCES

Apocrypha

Tob	Tobit
Jdt	Judith
Wis	Wisdom of Solomon
Sir	Wisdom of Jesus the Son of Sirach (Ecclesiasticus)
Bar	Baruch
Add Dan	Additions to Daniel
Bel	Bel and the Dragon
1 Macc	1 Maccabees
2 Macc	2 Maccabees
1 Esd	1 Esdras
3 Macc	3 Maccabees
2 Esd	2 Esdras
4 Macc	4 Maccabees

Dead Sea Scrolls

1QM	Milhamah or War Scroll

Old Testament Pseudepigrapha

1 En.	1 Enoch (Ethiopic Apocalypse)

Other Sources

	Barn.	Barnabas
	b. Meg.	Babylonian Talmud Megilla
Epicetus	Diatr.	Diatribai (Dissertations)
Eusebius	Hist. eccl.	Ecclesiastical History (Historia ecclesiastica)
Heliodorus	Aeth.	Aethiopica
Irenaeus	Haer.	Against Heresies (Adversus haereses)
Isocrates	Trapez.	Trapeziticus (Or. 17)
Josephus	Ag. Ap.	Against Apion
	m. 'Abot	Mishnah Abot
Origen	Princ.	First Principles (De Principiis)
Philodemus	Lib.	De libertate dicendi
Pliny the Elder	Nat.	Natural History (Naturalis historia)
Polybius	Hist.	The Histories (Historicus)
Qur'an	Ibrahim	Abraham
Seneca	Lucil.	The Epistulae Morales ad Lucilium
Strabo	Geogr.	Geography (Geographica)
Tertullian	Pud.	Modesty (De pudicitia)

SERIES

AB	Anchor Bible
BECNT	Baker Exegetical Commentary on the New Testament
NICNT	New International Commentary on the New Testament
NIDNTT	*The New International Dictionary of New Testament Theology*
NIDOTTE	*The New International Dictionary of Old Testament Theology*
NIGTC	New International Greek Testament Commentary
PNTC	Pillar New Testament Commentary
TNTC	Tyndale New Testament Commentaries
WBC	Word Biblical Commentary
WUNT	Wissenschaftliche Untersuchungen zum Alten und Neuen Testament

REFERENCE

ABD	*The Anchor Bible Dictionary*
BDAG	W. F. Bauer, W. F. Arndt, F. W. Gingrich, and F. W. Danker, *A Greek-English Lexicon of the New Testament and Other Early Christian Literature*. 3rd ed.
BDF	F. Blass, A. Debrunner, and R. W. Funk, *A Greek Grammar of the New Testament and Other Early Christian Literature*
DNTB	*Dictionary of New Testament Background*
DPL	*Dictionary of Paul and His Letters*
EDNT	H. Balz and G. Schneider, eds., *Exegetical Dictionary of the New Testament*
GGBB	D. B. Wallace, *Greek Grammar Beyond the Basics*
HALOT	L. Koehler, and W. Baumgartner, *Hebrew and Aramaic Lexicon of the Old Testament*
ISBE	*International Standard Bible Encyclopedia*
LSJ	H. G. Liddell, R. Scott, and H. S. Jones, *A Greek-English Lexicon*. 9th ed.
MHT	J. H. Moulton and N. Turner, *A Grammar of New Testament Greek: Volume III Syntax*
MM	J. H. Moulton and G. Milligan. *The Vocabulary of the Greek Testament: Illustrated from the Papyri and Other Non-literary Sources.*
TCGNT	B. Metzger, ed., *A Textual Commentary on the Greek New Testament*, 2nd ed.
TDNT	G. Kittel and G. Friedrich, eds., *Theological Dictionary of the New Testament*
TLNT	C. Spicq, *Theological Lexicon of the New Testament*

TRANSLATIONS

CSB	Christian Standard Bible
ESV	English Standard Version
KJV	King James Version
LXX	Septuagint
NA[28]	Novum Testamentum Graece: Nestle-Aland, 28th Revised ed.
NASB	New American Standard Bible
NCV	New Century Version
NET	New English Translation
NIV[84]	New International Version
NKJV	New King James Version
NLT[SE]	New Living Translation
NASB[95]	New American Standard Bible
NRSV	New Revised Standard Version
RSV	Revised Standard Version
UBS[5]	United Bible Society's Greek New Testament, 5th Revised ed.

INTRODUCTION

Author: The apostle Paul

Provenance: Paul wrote while under house arrest in Rome

Date: A.D. 62

Occasion for Writing: Paul sent Epaphroditus back to Philippi, reported about the spread of the gospel, encouraged the Philippians to stand firm, and confronted disunity.

Readers: Paul planted the church in Philippi on his second missionary journey (Acts 16). Since that time they had partnered with him in spreading the gospel.

Genre: Epistle (Letter)

Historical Setting: Philippi, founded ca. 356 B.C. by Philip II of Macedon (father of Alexander the Great). Philippi was made an official Roman colony that honored Caesar Augustus in 42 B.C. The Roman imperial cult that honored the emperor as "Benefactor" probably dominated the religious scene. Paul planted a church made up of mostly Gentiles.

Emphasis: Paul wrote to encourage the church to stand firm and united in the midst of opposition.

AUTHORSHIP OF PHILIPPIANS

Authenticity

Philippians claims to have been written by the apostle Paul (1:1), and there are no good reasons for doubting its authenticity. The consensus is that this is a genuine letter from him. Its themes and situations ring true to what we know of Paul's ministry. Scholars have typically discussed two particular issues regarding authorship.

A Hymn of the Early Church?

Scholars debate whether Paul wrote the "hymn" of 2:6–11 or whether he was quoting an existing hymn of the early Judean church. Discussions focus mainly on the unusual vocabulary and rhythmic style of the hymn. Most believe that it was composed at an earlier time, either by Paul himself or by someone else. Some see it as a hymn of the early church, perhaps originally in Aramaic, that Paul quotes (e.g., Martin, 1997; Martin and Dodd, 1998). A minority view is that as Paul was writing Philippians and meditating on the example of Christ, he heightened the elegance of his writing and composed the text at that time (Fee, 1992, 29–46). The arguments on both sides of the debate are evenly balanced, and some feel that neither view can be proven conclusively (Carson and Moo, 2005, 499–503). Whether Paul is the hymn's original author or not, and whether he composed it while writing the letter or inserted it, this is an exquisite description of Christ's humility, death, and exaltation.

The Apostle Paul by Rembrandt van Rijn (ca. 1657)
Courtesy of Crisco 1492

A Composite Letter?

Some scholars have argued that the epistle was not originally one letter from Paul, but represents a compilation from two or three of his letters to the Philippians. A typical proposal is that three separate letters—(a) a thank-you note (4:10–20), (b) friendly encouragement (1:1–3:1;

4:4–9; 4:21–23), and (c) a warning against opponents (3:2–4:3)—have been "cut and pasted" by an editor (see Collange, 1979; Perkins, 1991; Reumann, 2008). Williams summarizes a number of partition theories (2002, 49). Advocates point to the alleged "rough transitions" in the letter as it presently stands. For example, many note that 3:1 fits nicely with 4:4 and that 3:2–4:3 seems like an insertion. They note the abrupt move from warm encouragement (3:1, "Rejoice in the Lord") to warning (3:2, "Beware the dogs"). Further, the opening expression in 3:1, "finally" (τὸ λοιπόν) sounds like Paul was ready to close the letter. So this is taken as evidence that a later editor has "pasted" 3:2–4:3 onto another letter at 3:1.

The arguments for the composite theory are unconvincing. The fact that scholars cannot agree on the extent of the supposed original letters and that some of the suggestions are mutually contradictory reveal how subjective these arguments can be. Watson concludes that scholars have misunderstood epistolary conventions or have understood them in an unnecessarily restricted sense (2003, 176). Recent studies using rhetorical or text-linguistic analysis argue for the unity of the epistle, though see the critique by Bockmuehl of such studies on both sides (1998, 22–24).

Arguments for unity include (1) the repetition of common themes and verbal parallels that occur in sections of the letter. For example, the repeated occurrence of the verb "to think" (φρονεῖν: 1:7; 2:2 [2x], 5; 3:15 [2x], 19; 4:2, 10 [2x]) throughout, or the parallels between the example of Christ in 2:6–11 and the example of Paul in 3:7–11. (2) The letter as it stands is understandable and in keeping with the usual stylistic fluidity of Hellenistic "family" letters (Alexander, 1989). (3) All extant manuscripts contain the whole letter. There is no manuscript evidence for two or three originally separate letters. (4) No one has demonstrated a convincing purpose for cutting and pasting such letters together. What motive would an editor have had? And why would an editor not smooth out the "rough transitions?" Suggesting that Philippians is a composite letter due to its rough features does not solve the perceived problem. It only shifts the problem of organization from Paul to the supposed editor. (5) The term in 3:1 (τὸ λοιπόν) may be rendered "in addition" instead of "finally" (cf. 1 Thess. 4:1). In the end, it is best to regard Philippians to be a single original letter from Paul.

PLACE AND DATE OF WRITING

Paul was "in chains" when he wrote Philippians (1:7, 13, 17). This could refer to imprisonment or house arrest, perhaps chained to a Roman soldier, which was common (Rapske, 1994, 31, 169, 173, 181; DNTB, 828; Wansink, 1996, 46–47). He expected to be released and to come to Philippi (1:19, 24–26; 2:23–24), though there was a chance he could be executed (1:20–23). He did not state where he was imprisoned. The Philippians knew his location, for they had sent Epaphroditus to attend to his needs (2:25–30). The place of his imprisonment had a "praetorium" (1:13). In Rome this would refer to the Praetorian Guard, an elite detachment of Roman soldiers loyal to the emperor who functioned as his personal troops and bodyguards. Outside Rome, *praetorium* would refer to the headquarters of the provincial governor, especially an imperial governor who had troops under his command such as in Caesarea (DNTB, 176, 995).

Also close to Paul as he wrote were "those from Caesar's household" (4:22), a phrase denoting mainly slaves and former slaves who served a wide range of functions from domestic service to professionals (e.g., doctors and educators), and to bureaucrats who served in the imperial administration throughout the provinces (DPL, 83; DNTB, 1001). Another phrase Paul used, "most of the brothers in the Lord" (1:14), suggests the presence of an established church at Paul's location.

The book of Acts records three imprisonments of Paul: a brief imprisonment in Philippi (16:23–40), a two-year imprisonment in Caesarea (23:23–26:32), and a two-year imprisonment in Rome (28:16–31). In addition, Paul stated that he was "in prison more frequently" than the false apostles threatening the Corinthians (2 Cor. 11:23). According to *1 Clement* 5:6, Paul was imprisoned seven times. So he endured imprisonments for which we have no details. Scholars usually note three possible locations for Paul's imprisonment when he wrote Philippians—Rome, Caesarea, and Ephesus.

Rome

The traditional view is that Paul wrote Philippians during his Roman imprisonment described in Acts 28. This view accounts for Paul's mention of the Praetorian Guard, those from Caesar's household, and the existence of an established church. The view that Paul was writing from Rome goes back at least to the second-century A.D. Marcionite Prologue, which states: "The Philippians are Macedonians. Having received the word of truth, they persevered in the faith and did not accept false apostles. The apostle commends them, writing to them from prison in Rome" (Bruce, 1988, 142).

Some scholars argue that Rome is unlikely due to its distance from Philippi—perhaps as much as 1,200 miles by land (Carson and Moo, 2005, 504), or eight hundred miles by land and sea. This may be a problem because of the several trips between Paul and the Philippians presupposed in the letter. First, there had to be a trip from Paul to Philippi to inform them that he was already imprisoned or else headed there; then a trip from Philippi for Epaphroditus to bring Paul their gift (2:25); then another trip to Philippi for them to hear about Epaphroditus's illness (2:26); finally, another trip from Philippi with news of their concern for Epaphroditus (2:26). In other words, four 800–1,200-mile journeys are presupposed—each taking perhaps as long as two months (Silva estimates four to seven weeks, 2005, 5–6). If we allow two months per journey, this is only eight months, and Paul's first Roman imprisonment lasted two years (Acts 28:30).

These trips are not really as big a problem as some scholars have thought. The number of journeys implied can be reduced if Epaphroditus became sick while en route to Rome and a companion immediately returned to Philippi with the news, and if Paul, when hearing of this, assumed their concern for him. He did not have to wait to hear from the Philippians to know that they were concerned for Epaphroditus (Garland, 2006, 179). Llewelyn suggests that the Philippians may have learned of Paul's dispatch from Caesarea to Rome while he was en route and that Epaphroditus may have already been in Rome when Paul arrived (1995).

Caesarea

As an alternative to Rome, some suggest that Paul wrote Philippians during his two-year imprisonment at Caesarea (Acts 23:23–24:27). Located on the Mediterranean coast, Caesarea was the center of the Roman administration of Palestine. Herod's palace was located there with a guard that would fit the designation "Praetorian" (Acts 23:35). As the imperial headquarters, there would have been "those from Caesar's household." Like Rome, Caesarea is far from Philippi (1,000 miles), though with a two-year window, this is not a problem.

A possible weakness of the Caesarea designation, however, is that there is no evidence of a sizable church in Caesarea. Also against Caesarea may be the facts of his legal case. Paul still had the opportunity to appeal to Caesar (Acts 25:11), so it is not clear that while in Caesarea, Paul would have thought that he might be put to death by the Roman government (Phil. 1:21–23). In reply to this last point, some suggest that in Philippians 1:21–23, Paul may have been thinking not of the Roman courts, but of the Jews who wanted to kill him (Acts 21:31, 36; 22:22; 23:30; 25:3, 24; 26:21). Further, Rapske states that while the provincial Roman governor was strongly counseled by Roman law to grant an appeal to the emperor, he was not bound by law to do so

(*DNTB*, 216–17). Of the three options usually mentioned for the place of writing, this is the least popular among scholars.

Ephesus

In recent decades, this view has gained support. Paul spent nearly three years at Ephesus during his third missionary journey (Acts 20:31). There is no record of Paul being imprisoned there, but he does say that he "fought wild beasts in Ephesus" (1 Cor. 15:32). He also writes of his afflictions in Asia—that he "despaired even of life" and that he "had a sentence of death" from which he was rescued (2 Cor. 1:8–10). "Fought wild beasts" and "sentence of death" are likely metaphorical, and these words may imply imprisonment or other sufferings. Supporters of this view note that the term "praetorium" can refer to the residence of any provincial governor (Matt. 27:27; Mark 15:15; John 18:28, 33; 19:9; Acts 23:35) and that "those of Caesar's household" can refer to slaves or freedmen in imperial service in numerous cities. The major argument in favor of Ephesus, though, is the distance between Ephesus and Philippi—these two cities are only one hundred miles apart. For some scholars, this makes the presupposed trips between Paul and the Philippians more plausible.

Against Ephesus, critics reply that no evidence exists for applying the term "praetorium" to the governor's palace in Ephesus; it was in a *senatorial*, not an *imperial* province. Also, some scholars point out that on this view Paul would have written Philippians around the same time he wrote 1–2 Corinthians and Romans, when he was concerned about the collection for the churches in Judea (1 Cor. 16:1–4; 2 Cor. 8–9; Rom. 15:25–28). They think it strange that Paul talks about the collection in those three letters but makes no mention of it to the Philippians. Others note that there is no explicit record that Paul was actually imprisoned at Ephesus. In particular, there is no direct evidence of a prolonged imprisonment necessitated by the multiple trips between Paul and the Philippians.

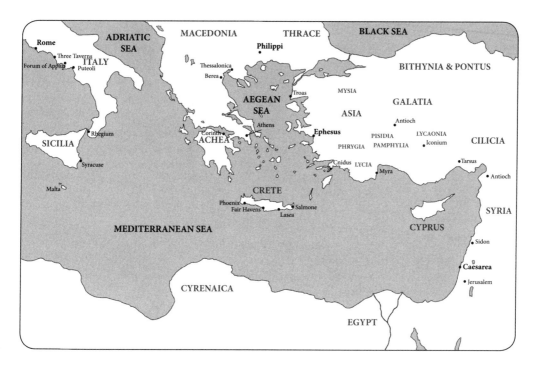

At present, there is no consensus among scholars. Many believe it is impossible to decide the issue. A good case can be made for Rome (the traditional view) or for Ephesus. Fewer support Caesarea. We will assume the traditional view that Rome is the place of origin, since the distance between Rome and Philippi does not seem to be a problem if Paul was imprisoned for two years. The place of origin determines the date of Paul's writing: If he wrote from Ephesus, the date is A.D. 52–55; Caesarea, A.D. 57–59; Rome, A.D. 60–62. Due to the travel reflected in the letter, Paul would likely have written Philippians nearer the end of the latter two terms (Hemer, 1989, 275).

A decision on *where* Paul was imprisoned does not greatly affect the interpretation of Philippians. The important point is to know that he was in prison and that this determined his present reality and relationship with the Philippians. His prison letters have additional gravity and urgency because he was incarcerated (Nebreda, 2011, 250).

OCCASION FOR WRITING

Nearly all of Paul's letters were occasional—written for the particular situations and needs of the recipients at the time of writing. Each letter addressed a specific occasion, determining much of what Paul said and the way he said it. So each letter revealed certain details about what was going on with Paul and with the recipients at the time he wrote. We can say something about Paul's circumstances and those of the church at Philippi by noting what he wrote in Philippians.[1]

Paul's Circumstances

Paul was imprisoned where there was a praetorium (1:13) and believers who were "from

---

1   For criteria on mirror-reading polemics in Paul's letters, see Barclay, 1987. For mirror-reading moral issues, see Gupta, 2012.

Caesar's household" (4:22). His imprisonment had served for the advancement of the gospel and had caused the brethren around him to become bold in their witness for Christ (1:13–14). Some of those preaching were motivated by rivalry toward Paul, but others by love toward him (1:15–18). He faced the possibility of execution, but he expected to be released and to come to Philippi (1:19–26). Epaphroditus had arrived from the Philippians with their gifts to minister to Paul's needs (2:25; 4:18). As the Philippians had heard, Epaphroditus had become ill to the point of death, but God spared him. Paul was now sending him back and wanted them to receive him with joy and honor (2:26–30). Paul hoped to send Timothy to them soon (2:19) and to come shortly himself after his case was resolved (2:24).

The Philippians' Circumstances

The Philippians were experiencing threats of intimidation and persecution from opponents of the gospel (1:27–30). In the face of such opposition, disunity among the believers was a threat. Selfish ambition, conceit, grumbling, and arguing may have been present (2:2–3, 14). An argument existed between two of the leading women in the church who had colabored with Paul—Euodia and Syntyche (4:2–3). Disunity and lack of humility among the believers had the potential to harm their witness to the world around them (2:14–16).

The church also needed to beware of false teachers (3:2–3), though they were not yet present. Paul also called the Philippians' attention to "enemies of the cross of Christ" (3:18–19). Scholars debate the precise identity of these groups. The false teachers (3:2–3) were most likely Jewish-Christian false teachers who advocated circumcision and keeping at least parts of the Old Testament law as necessary for justification. The "enemies of the cross" may refer to the same group or perhaps immoral Gentiles.

Purpose for Writing

Paul's long-term partnership with and affection for the Philippians was reason enough to write. He was keeping in touch from prison and reassuring his extended family (cf. Alexander, 1989, 95). His sending Epaphroditus back to them provided the specific occasion to write about several things. The contents of the letter suggest that he had primarily a twofold purpose in writing—first, to inform and encourage them with news of his circumstances and plans; second, to address several issues regarding their circumstances.

First, he wrote to encourage them by providing news from his imprisonment. After letting them know that he thanked God for their partnership and was praying for them (1:3–11), he reassured them that the gospel was advancing despite his imprisonment (1:12–18a) and let them know of his prospects for the near future—that he expected to be released and to come to them (1:20–26). He assured them that their representative Epaphroditus had executed his task well in ministering to his needs (2:25–30). He also commended Timothy, whom he would send shortly (2:19–23). And he let them know that he too hoped to visit soon (2:24). He also informed them of the joy he felt when he received their financial support (4:10, 14–20) while at the same time assuring them of his contentment in his circumstances (4:11–13).

Second, he wrote to encourage them and direct them toward Christian thinking and behavior as he confronted several issues among them. Through his own example, he urged them to find joy in what matters—the progress of the gospel (1:12–18a) (Thielman, 2005, 309, 321). By explaining how he viewed the prospects of being executed or released, he showed them how they should view the possibility of death (1:18b–24). He exhorted them to live as citizens of the kingdom, worthy of the gospel, standing firm in one Spirit and in unity as they suffered for Christ (1:27–30). He exhorted them to replace selfish ambition, conceit, grumbling, and arguing with putting others first in humility and unity (2:1–16). He urged them to rejoice with him (2:18; 3:1), to beware of false teachers, and to follow his example in pursuing intimacy with Christ (3:2–21). He called on two of the leading women of the church to heal the rift between them (4:2–3). And he gave general exhortations for thinking and behavior (4:4–9). As Still summarizes it, Paul called them to live in such a way that, together, they all could glorify God and advance the gospel as they awaited Christ's return (2012, 66).

READERS TO WHOM PAUL WROTE

Paul wrote to believers in the church at Philippi, a church he planted on his second missionary journey in Acts (Acts 15:36–18:22).

Beginning of the Church

Luke recorded Paul's founding the church in Philippi in Acts 16:11–40. On the second missionary journey, in response to Paul's vision of a "man of Macedonia" (Acts 16:9), Paul, Silas, Timothy, and Luke went to Philippi. On the Sabbath, they went outside the city gate to a place of prayer near the riverside. There they shared the gospel with a group of women who had gathered. Luke first described the conversion of Lydia, a "worshipper of God" (σεβουμένη τὸν θεόν). This designation refers to Gentiles who had become followers of the God of Israel and had attached themselves loosely to the Jewish community, but who had not officially converted to Judaism and did not keep the entire law (Schürer, 1986, 3:161–69). The Lord opened Lydia's heart to believe the gospel. After she and her household were baptized, Lydia persuaded Paul and his companions to stay with her.

Luke then described how Paul and Silas cast a spirit of divination out of a slave girl. Acts 16:16 uses the term "python spirit" (πνεῦμα πύθωνα), perhaps indicating that she channeled the oracles of Apollo, the Python god. Paul and Silas were imprisoned because of their actions, but the Lord miraculously released them when an earthquake caused the prison doors to open and

their bonds to unfasten. As a result, the Philippian jailer and his household believed in Christ and were baptized. With these conversions, the church at Philippi was born. This was the first European church in the Acts narrative, and so

Priestess of Delphi by John Collier (1891)
Courtesy of DcoetzeeBot

represented a milestone as the gospel spread to an entirely Gentile, Roman setting.

It is not clear how long Paul and his team stayed in Philippi on their foundational visit, but presumably it was not too long. While Paul, Silas, and Timothy went on to evangelize Thessalonica, Berea, and Athens (Acts 17:1–34), they apparently left Luke at Philippi. This is implied by the "we sections" in Acts (where the narrative is written using the first person plural "we" and so presented as a firsthand report by Luke). The first "we section" in Acts ends at Philippi (Acts 16:17) and the second "we section" begins there (20:5), suggesting that Luke may have stayed at Philippi rather than traveling with Paul in Acts 17:1–20:3, a period of about seven or eight years. If Luke did remain at Philippi during this time, he would have become an important member of the church there.

During the third missionary journey (Acts 18:23–21:16)—the bulk of which included a stay in Ephesus that lasted nearly three years (Acts 19:1–41; 20:31)—Paul sent two of his helpers, Timothy and Erastus, to Macedonia (Acts 19:22). They likely revisited the church in Philippi. After Paul left Ephesus, he traveled through Macedonia encouraging the churches before going to Greece (Acts 20:1–2; cf. 2 Cor. 2:12–13; 7:5). Again, Philippi would have been one of the Macedonian cities he visited. After a three-month stay in Greece, Paul returned through Macedonia and sailed for Troas from Philippi (Acts 20:3–6). His goal was to reach Jerusalem by Pentecost with a monetary gift for the relatively poor Jerusalem church (Acts 20:16; 1 Cor. 16:1–4; 2 Cor. 9:1–5; Rom. 15:25–29). This collection from the Gentile churches on the mission field was in recognition of their spiritual debt to the mother church in Jerusalem. Once Paul arrived in Jerusalem, he was arrested in the temple and spent two years imprisoned in Caesarea (Acts 24:27). After his appeal to Caesar and subsequent transfer to Rome, Paul spent two years there under house arrest in which he was able to receive visitors (Acts 28:30). Paul probably wrote Philippians during his Roman imprisonment.

Paul's Longstanding Partnership with the Philippians

The Philippians partnered in a special way to support Paul in his missionary work. This is evident from several statements in his letters. Paul noted that they had been his partners "from the first day until now" (Phil. 1:5), which suggests their financial support from the time he planted the church. He also noted that two ladies, Euodia and Syntyche, labored side by side with him in the gospel along with Clement and other fellow workers at the Philippian church (Phil. 4:2–3). They continued to support Paul when he left Philippi and went to Thessalonica (Phil. 4:15–16). Their financial partnership with him was unique. In 4:15 Paul states, "no church partnered with me in the matter of giving and receiving except you only." When Paul stayed for a year and a half at Corinth (Acts 18), he accepted no money from the Corinthians, but he was supported by gifts from "the brothers from Macedonia" (2 Cor. 11:7–9). The Philippians' generosity was not limited to providing for Paul's personal needs. They set an example of sacrificial giving to support the collection for the Jerusalem church that Paul raised during the third missionary journey (2 Cor. 8:1–5). Paul's statement that "their extreme poverty overflowed in a wealth of generosity" (8:2) confirms that the Philippian believers were not wealthy, though there may have been some, like Lydia, who lived above a subsistence level (*DNTB*, 1001–3).

When Paul was imprisoned in Rome, the Philippians sent one of their own, Epaphroditus, to minister to him during his imprisonment (Phil. 2:25–30) and to bring material gifts from the church (Phil. 4:18). It had apparently been sometime since their last gift (Phil. 4:10). All of this explains why Paul considered them "fellow partakers of grace" in his imprisonment and in the defense and confirmation of the gospel (Phil. 1:7). And it explains Paul's affection for

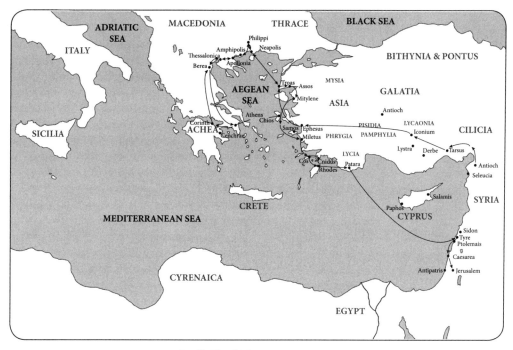

Paul's Third Missionary Journey

them (Phil. 1:8). Clearly Paul enjoyed a special friendship and partnership with the believers at Philippi. There is no evidence of conflict between Paul and the Philippians similar to that evident in, say, his letters to the Galatians or Corinthians. Sampley writes, "Of all the Pauline churches, this one seems to have given Paul the least grief and the greatest joy" (1980, 62). As he wrote Philippians, he rejoiced at the partnership they shared since the founding of the church.

HISTORICAL SETTING

A Roman Colony

Philippi was a city in eastern Macedonia settled by immigrants from Thrace. The modern city Krenides is located near its ruins. In 360 B.C., colonists from Thasos annexed it and named it Krenides ("springs") due to its many springs of water. In 356 B.C., they asked Philip II of Macedon, the father of Alexander the Great, to defend them against Thracian tribes. Because of

the nearby gold mines in the Pangaion Mountains, Philip was happy to take over the area. He founded a new city just west of Krenides, named it after himself, and settled new colonists there.

Rome took control of the city in 168–167 B.C. when the Roman general Luciua Aemilius Paullus defeated the Macedonians and divided Macedonia into four districts. Philippi was part of the eastern district. After a Macedonian revolt in 148 B.C., the Romans consolidated the four districts into one province, with Thessalonica as the capital. From 145 to 130 B.C., the Romans built a strategic stone-paved military road, the Egnatian Way, which connected Byzantium to Dyrrhachium on the Adriatic Sea. In 42 B.C., Philippi was the site of a famous battle. Mark Antony and Octavian (later known as Augustus Caesar) defeated Brutus and Cassius, who in 44 B.C. had assassinated Julius Caesar. After this battle, Mark Antony enlarged the city to include about 730 square miles including the port city Neapolis (modern Kavala) ten miles south. He made it a Roman Colony and resettled it with veteran soldiers who had lost their lands in Italy. Their presence helped to "Romanize" the local population (*DNTB*, 961).[2] In 31 B.C., Octavian, who had taken the name Julius in honor of Julius Caesar, defeated Mark Antony at the Battle of Actium and renamed the city after himself: *Colonia Iulia Augusta Philippensis* ("the colony of the Philippians of Julius Augustus"). Octavian resettled the city once again, this time with Italian colonists and veterans of Legion XXVIII and of the Praetorian Cohort. In the two resettlements by Mark Anthony and Octavian, probably between 1,000 and 3,000 Roman colonists joined the native Greek and Thracian population in Philippi.

Octavian granted Philippi the *ius italicum* (Italian law), an honor that made it Italian soil with a Roman form of administration, law, and judicial procedure, and exempting its citizens from land taxes. Those who possessed citizenship in the colony were citizens of Rome. The city's administration, layout, style, and architecture reflected that of Rome. All of this created a distinctively Roman city in eastern Macedonia loyal to Octavian.

In Acts 16:12, Luke called Philippi "a leading city of that district of Macedonia, a colony" (πρώτη μερίδος τῆς Μακεδονίας πόλις, κολωνία).[3] It was not *the* leading city of Macedonia; Thessalonica was the capital and Amphipolis was the largest city. But it was the most important city in eastern Macedonia, and it was an important stopping point on the Egnatian Way. Paul used the Egnatian Way when he traveled from Neapolis to Philippi, to Amphipolis, to Apollonia, and to Thessalonica (Acts 16:11–12; 17:1).

Augustus von Prima Porta, Courtesy of Soerfm

Population

By the time Paul arrived (ca. A.D. 49), nationalities at Philippi included primarily Macedonians and Romans, but also Greeks from Thasos and southern Greece, Thracians, and immigrants from Egypt and Asian Minor. Philippi was relatively small, with perhaps around 10,000 inhabitants in the mid-first century (Pilhofer, 1995,

---

2   See Nebreda (2011, 147–61) for the "Romanization" of both the western and eastern parts of the empire (in particular, Philippi) through cultural change. This consisted of implementing a common language (Latin), construction of roads to facilitate commerce, introduction of a "higher" Roman culture, redistribution of land and creating *coloniae* in foreign areas, ruling via a pacific form of government, subtle challenges to local and ethnic identities, and *urbanitas* (attitudes of exclusivity and snobbery).

3   This reading is supported by important manuscripts and defended by Metzger and Aland in *TCGNT*, 395.

1:74; Oakes, 2001, 46). The smallish size may have contributed to a stronger sense of "community" in the city (De Vos, 1999, 238–44). Many were Roman citizens who identified themselves as "Roman" (cf. Acts 16:21). Yet the majority were noncitizens. The population included landowners, slaves, peasant farmers, tradesmen, merchants, and agricultural workers. While a significant number were Roman and spoke Latin (the official language), Greek was the common language of the marketplace and surrounding area. Oakes estimates that perhaps 40 percent of the people were Roman citizens (2001, 50). While De Vos believes that the church consisted largely of Roman citizens (1999, 251), Oakes argues that most were not. He thinks the believers came largely from among the city's service groups, slaves, and poor (2001, 59–70).

Religion

Inscriptions, shrines, and coins have been found at Philippi honoring numerous gods, especially Isis, Bacchus/Dionysus, Silvanus, and the Thracian Horseman, among others. Most commentaries assume that Philippi was a syncretistic city in the mid-first century A.D., but Bormann argues that the presence of many of these cults cannot be demonstrated prior to the mid-second century A.D. The Roman imperial cult, which deified the emperor and his family members—honoring him as Benefactor—was dominant throughout the first century (Bormann, 1995, 61–67). Excavations have revealed two unspecified temples that most scholars believe to be imperial cult temples (De Vos, 1999, 249). In Neapolis, an inscription, probably from the mid-first century A.D., calls one Cornelia Asprilla a "priestess of Livia Augusta" (Caesar Augustus's wife) (Pilhofer, 2000, II: 2–3).

Christians would have faced certain challenges in this socio-religious environment. Withdrawal from participation in the imperial cult or from any of the traditional cults would have triggered opposition from the general population and perhaps local authorities. It may have caused them to lose their jobs. They would have had to leave some guilds, civic organizations, or social clubs where idolatry or other immoral practices occurred (De Vos, 1999, 264, 272; Oakes, 2005, 310–14). In the first-century Roman world, religious functions were intertwined with everyday life.

Imagine the opposition you might face from family, friends, customers, and others if, for religious reasons, you declined to participate in numerous basic celebrations and customs of your culture—Thanksgiving, Christmas, Fourth of July, office parties, Friday night football games, singing the national anthem, and so on. Though you might not be arrested, people would notice, and you would become an "outsider."

In working out his social makeup of the church, Oakes estimates its size to be maybe one hundred (2001, 169–70). Verhoef estimates the size to be around thirty-three (2013, 22). While speculative, such numbers remind us that the first believers in the city constituted a very small percent of the population.

Jewish Presence

Philippi likely had only a small Jewish population in Paul's day. Scholars debate whether Philippi had a synagogue. For other cities in Acts, Luke stated that Paul entered the *synagogue* and preached to the Jews (Acts 13:5, 14; 14:1; 17:1, 10, 17; 18:4). But for Philippi, Acts 16:13 mentions only a "place of prayer" (προσευχὴ) outside the city gate next to the river. The debate is whether "place of prayer" denotes a synagogue—as it does in the papyri and the writings of Philo and Josephus. Some scholars argue that it does (Schürer, 1979, 2.439f, 445; Schnabel, 2004, 1153), but others doubt this (Fitzmyer, 1998, 585; Pervo, 2009, 402). Some have thought that since Luke only mentioned Paul finding women gathered there (16:13), Philippi must have lacked the ten Jewish men required to have a synagogue (Bruce, 1990, 358; cf. *m. 'Abot* 3:6; *b. Meg.* 23b). But Paul and his coworkers may have simply come across a women's prayer meeting.

The only archaeological evidence for a synagogue is an inscription mentioning one from the late third or early fourth century A.D. (Koukouli-Chrysantaki, 1998, 28–35). But this may not be relevant to the first century. Even if Philippi had a synagogue, the Jewish presence in the city was minor. This would mean that the church at Philippi had few, if any, Jews. There are a few allusions to the Old Testament in the letter (e.g., Job 13:16 in 1:19; Isa. 45:23 in 2:11; Deut. 32:5 in 2:15; Exod. 15–17, Num. 14–17 in 2:14). This would be expected because of Paul's background. But his use of the Old Testament in the letter was minimal, suggesting a largely Gentile church.

THEOLOGICAL EMPHASES OF PHILIPPIANS

The inspiring and motivating nature of this letter is due especially to several prominent theological themes—each relevant today.

Doctrinal Emphases

The Preexistence and Deity of Christ

Paul described Christ Jesus as "existing in the form of God" (2:6) prior to his "being born in the likeness of men" (2:7). This refers to the timeless, preincarnate existence of the Son of God. "In the form of God" refers to the fact that prior to becoming man, he manifested the outward, visible appearance of God. He visibly revealed God's glory and majesty (cf. Heb. 1:3). The implication is that Jesus Christ himself is fully divine. Further, he is also "equal to God" (2:6). This refers to his equality with the Father in divine essence, status, privilege, power, and glory.

The Self-Emptying and Self-Humbling of Christ

Paul described how the preexistent Son of God "emptied himself" (2:7), a concept explained by what follows: "taking the form of a slave," and being born in the likeness of men." Without giving up his divine essence, the preincarnate Christ set aside the visible appearance of his glory and the divine privileges of his status by becoming a human being, a lowly slave. Once he became a human being, he "humbled himself," being obedient to God to the extent of suffering a humiliating death on a Roman cross (2:8).

The Exaltation of Christ

In 2:9–11, Paul described how God highly exalted Christ after his voluntary self-humiliation. He bestowed on him the name that is above every name, "Lord." This is the title used of Yahweh in the LXX, the name that he shares with no one else (Isa. 42:8). Christ, who preexisted in divine glory but humbled himself, has now received from the Father a position and name that only God may possess. Every knee in the universe will bow in submission and every tongue will acknowledge that Jesus Christ is Lord (cf. Isa. 45:23). He occupies the highest position of authority in the universe. Paul's understanding of the high status of Christ in Philippians agrees with his statements about Christ's status elsewhere (e.g., Rom. 9:5; 1 Cor. 8:6; Col. 1:15–16).

God's Work of Sanctification in Believers

God is the one who works in believers' lives. He provides grace, peace, and mercy (1:2; 2:27). He has begun a good work in them and will bring it to completion (1:6). He makes them able to stand firm with one Spirit, not being frightened of persecution (1:27–28). He is working in them as they work out their own salvation (2:12–13). Their righteousness, which is through faith in Christ, comes from God (3:9). He has called them upward to receive the prize when Christ returns (3:14; cf. 3:21). He sends his peace to guard their hearts and minds (4:6–7). As believers practice what Paul teaches about the Christian life, the God of peace will be with them (4:9). He is pleased when they give sacrificially toward the work of the gospel, and will supply all of their needs according to his riches (4:18–19). All glory and praise will be to God when their lives are filled with the fruit of righteousness, which comes through Christ (1:11). God supplies the initiation, calling, power, resources, and motivation for followers of Christ. And he will see that they reach the goal he has for them.

Unity in the Church

Paul presupposed that Christian unity is based on the theological reality that together believers are "in Christ." The phrases "in Christ," "in the Lord," or "in him" (plus variations) occur twenty-one times. They denote believers' identity as those who belong to Christ and are united with Christ. Christ is the one through whom and in whom they enjoy God's saving blessings. Each use may have a specific force: (1) to denote *identity* as Christians: believers are saints "in Christ Jesus" (1:1; 4:21); (2) to denote *union* with Christ: found "in him" (3:9); (3) to describe *the sphere or cause of relations* to one another: believers are to welcome a brother "in the Lord" (2:29), and to be of one mind "in the Lord" (4:2); (4) to denote *the sphere or cause of actions*: believers are confident "in Christ" (1:14), glory "in Christ Jesus" (1:26; 3:3), are confident to act "in the Lord" (2:24), rejoice "in the Lord" (3:1; 4:4, 10), and stand firm "in the Lord" (4:1); (5) to denote the *object of actions:* hope "in the Lord Jesus" (2:19); (6) to describe the *sphere, cause, or means of God's actions* on behalf of believers: he encourages believers "in Christ" (2:1), calls them upward "in Christ Jesus" (3:14), guards their hearts and minds "in Christ Jesus" (4:7), makes them able "in him who strengthens" (4:13), and fulfills their needs according to his riches "in Christ Jesus" (4:19) (cf. Campbell, 2012, 67–199; Best, 1955, 1–33; *DPL,* 433–36). Believers' existence together "in Christ" determines everything about them—how they see themselves, how they act, how they relate to one another (Marshall, 1993, 138–44).

Practical Emphases

Practical Unity among Christians through Humility

The doctrinal "in Christ" unity of believers has practical implications. In the midst of persecution, believers are to stand firm in one Spirit with one mind and to live in harmony with one heart and purpose (1:27–2:2). They are also to do all things without grumbling or arguing, and so shine as stars in the world (2:14–15). The means for achieving harmony is by cultivating the character quality of humble concern for others and putting others' interests above their own (2:3–4).

Paul reinforced this attitude by presenting several examples of what humility that leads to harmony looks like. The chief example is Christ (2:5–11), but also Timothy, Epaphroditus (2:20–30), and even Paul himself (2:17). In contrast to these positive examples, Paul also noted the negative examples of the rival preachers who minister from envy and rivalry (1:15–17), the false teachers (3:2–3), and the enemies of the cross who set their minds on earthly things (3:19). Unity and harmony require that believers follow the positive examples Paul set forth, especially that of Christ.

The Humility of Christ as a Paradigm for the Christian Life

In 2:6–8, Christ is a *paradigm* for Christian humility, self-sacrifice, and service for others. He is the supreme example of what Paul meant by, "Do nothing from rivalry or conceit, but in humility regard others to be more important than yourselves. Let each one of you not merely look to his own interests, but also to the interests of others" (2:3–4).

The Pursuit of Knowing Christ as the Center of the Christian Life

For Paul, to live was Christ (1:21) and his all-encompassing goal was to know Christ (3:8). In the Old Testament, knowing God came through his acts of self-revelation and consisted of entering into a personal relationship with him that he had made possible (*NIDNTTE* 2:579). Significantly, for Paul, it was now knowing *Christ* that was the center and goal of his life. Christ occupies the place Yahweh held in the

Old Testament (Marshall, 1993, 147). Knowing Christ begins with a personal encounter in which Christ "apprehends" believers (3:12), who then leave their past lives.

OUTLINE

Paul's letter to the Philippians may be divided into six major sections and preached in eighteen sermons.

REPORT OF GRATITUDE AND PRAYER FOR THE PHILIPPIANS (1:1–11)

- Report of Gratitude for the Philippians (1:1–8)
- Prayer for Spiritual Growth (1:9–11)

A CHRIST-CENTERED VIEW OF CIRCUMSTANCES AND LIFE (1:12–26)

- Viewing Every Circumstance as an Opportunity for Proclaiming the Gospel (1:12–18a)
- A Christ-Centered View of Life and Death (1:18b–26)

EXHORTATIONS TO STEADFASTNESS AND UNITY (1:27–2:30)

- Standing Firm in Unity as Citizens of God's Heavenly Kingdom (1:27–30)
- A Plea for Unity (2:1–4)
- Christ's Example of Humble Service (2:5–8)
- God's Elevation of Christ (2:9–11)
- Working Out Your Salvation (2:12–18)
- Two Christlike Servants (2:9–30)

PURSUING CHRIST, NOT THE LAW: A WARNING AGAINST FALSE TEACHERS (3:1–4:1)

- The True People of God (3:1–6)
- The Surpassing Value of Knowing Christ (3:7–11)
- Pursuing the Ultimate Goal (3:12–16)
- Imitating Good Examples (3:17–4:1)

FINAL EXHORTATIONS (4:2–9)

- Living Together in Unity (4:2–5)
- Experiencing the Peace of God (4:6–9)

PAUL'S JOY BECAUSE OF THEIR GIFT (4:10–23)

- Learning to Be Content (4:10–13)
- The Meaning of Christian Giving (4:14–23)

SUGGESTED SOURCES

Erickson, M. J. 2013. *Christian Theology*. 3rd. ed. Grand Rapids: Baker Academic.

Evans, C. A., and S. E. Porter, eds. 2000. *Dictionary of New Testament Backgrounds*. Downers Grove, IL: InterVarsity Press.

Fee, G. D. 1994. *God's Empowering Presence: The Holy Spirit in the Letters of Paul*. Peabody, MA: Hendrickson.

Freedman, D. N. 1992. *The Anchor Bible Dictionary*. 6 vols. New York: Doubleday.

Grudem, W. 1994. *Systematic Theology*. Grand Rapids: Zondervan.

Hawthorne, G. F., R. P. Martin, and D. G. Reid, eds. 1993. *Dictionary of Paul and His Letters*. Downers Grove, IL: InterVarsity Press.

REPORT OF GRATITUDE AND PRAYER FOR THE PHILIPPIANS (1:1–11)

Philippians 1:1–11 consists of Paul's greeting to the Philippian believers (1:1–2), his opening thanksgiving for them (1:3–8), and his prayer for them (1:9–11). His affection and concern for the Philippians is apparent from the beginning of the letter. The introductory thanksgiving plays an important role in introducing the main themes of the letter, setting the tone for what Paul wanted to say, and revealing his pastoral concern (Schubert, 1939, 77; Arzt-Grabner, 2010, 156). Further, the opening thanksgiving gives us a glimpse into Paul's heart for his converts, and it reveals the crucial nature of thanksgiving to God and affection for those with whom we partner in the gospel.

This major section, Report of Gratitude and Prayer for the Philippians (1:1–11), is broken into two preaching units: Report of Gratitude for the Philippians (1:1–8) and Prayer for Spiritual Growth (1:9–11).

Philippians 1:1–8

EXEGETICAL IDEA
The Philippians' longstanding partnership in spreading the gospel caused Paul to thank God for them.

THEOLOGICAL FOCUS
Working together for spreading the gospel causes believers to thank God for one another.

PREACHING IDEA
Linking arms with fellow Christ-followers leads to deep gratitude.

PREACHING POINTERS
Paul opened with a formal greeting and friendly note of thanksgiving, using an epistolary form familiar to the readers. The exegetical section introduces key terms and major themes, highlighting the rich ministry partnership Paul shares with them. The joyful tone and affectionate prayer shine against the backdrop of Paul's imprisonment, a circumstance known by his audience. If the Philippians struggled with anxiety for Paul's plight, his greeting calmed their fears. If they worried about a suppression of the gospel, his greeting eased their concerns. God had not left them alone in Christian service. Chains were no impediment to God's work. In fact, God used chains—the human chain—the linking of arms between fellow Christ-followers.

Today people often feel isolated and impeded in their faith journey. Linking arms with fellow Christ-followers lessens these negative feelings. Serving together creates shared experiences, stronger resolve, and sustained impact. Opportunities to link arms abound. Local churches may provide inroads to ministry teams (e.g., youth group), or connections to community organizations (e.g., YMCA), parachurch ministries (e.g., Habitat for Humanity), and global development efforts (e.g., World Vision) to unite believers across denominational lines. Individual Christ-followers may covenant with others to form discipleship groups, neighborhood Bible studies, or community gardens. Of course, modern or ancient partnerships lacking deep gratitude, gospel purpose, and godly affection at times dissolve. This passage reiterates these conditions for successful partnerships, looking to God to sustain lasting links among his people.

REPORT OF GRATITUDE FOR THE PHILIPPIANS
(1:1–8)

LITERARY STRUCTURE AND THEMES (1:1–8)

Paul's opening greeting wished the Philippians grace and peace from God the Father and Christ (1:1–2). Paul then expressed his gratitude (1:3–8) and let them know that he thanked God as he prayed for them with joy (1:3–4). He was thankful for two reasons: (1) because they had partnered with him in spreading the gospel since their conversion; and (2) because (causal participle) he was confident that God would complete the work he had begun in them (1:5–6). It was only right for him to feel this gratitude and confidence because they were in his heart and were participants with him in his imprisonment and defense of the gospel (1:7). His heartfelt affection for them came from Christ Jesus (1:8).

Introductory Greetings (1:1–2)
Expression of Gratitude (1:3–8)

EXPOSITION (1:1–8)

Letters in the ancient world typically began with the name of the writer, then the recipients, followed by a greeting. Paul first identified himself and Timothy in relation to their ministry for Christ (slaves), and then the Philippians in relation to their covenant status in Christ (saints). He wished all of them, together with their leaders, the grace and peace that came from God and Christ (1:1–2).

After this greeting, Paul expressed his gratitude to God and affection for them because of their longstanding participation with him in spreading the gospel (1:3–8). Paul reported his gratitude to God for the recipients and his prayer for them (1:3–4). He thanked God for

them (1) because of their continued participation with him in the gospel from the first day to the present (1:5), and (2) because he was confident that God would complete the work he had begun in them (1:6). It was right for him to think this because of the deep affection of Christ for them that moved through him, and because they were partners with him in defending the gospel (1:7–8).

Introductory Greetings (1:1–2)

Paul (with Timothy) wished all the Philippian believers, including their leaders, the unmerited favor and well being that came from God and Christ to them through the gospel.

> *1:1.* Δοῦλοι is rendered "slaves" (CSB, NLT), "servants" (NIV, ESV, NRSV, KJV), or "bondservants" (NASB, NKJV). Most translations render ἁγίοις with "saints," though NIV and NLT use "God's holy people." Ἐπισκόποις is rendered "overseers" (NIV, ESV, CSB, NASB) or "bishops" (NRSV, KJV, NKJV). The latter term should not cause readers to think of the office that developed later in the second century—an individual with authority over multiple churches.

1:1. Paul identified himself and Timothy as cosenders of the letter, but Paul was the sole author, as seen by the fact that he wrote in the first person singular. Later, he will refer to Timothy in the third person (2:19). Perhaps listing Timothy as a cosender strengthened his authority in their eyes and prepared for his upcoming mission (2:19–24) (Cousar, 2009, 23f). The Philippians knew Timothy, for he was with Paul at the founding of the church. Timothy became Paul's traveling companion after they met at Lystra on the second missionary journey (Acts 16:1–4).

Paul did not use the authoritative title "apostle" as he did in most of his letters. This was probably due to his close relationship with the Philippians. Instead, he referred to himself and Timothy as "slaves" (BDAG s.v. "δοῦλος" 2bβ, p. 260). Since perhaps 20 percent of the people in Philippi were literal slaves (Oakes, 2001, 49), Paul likely expected his readers to think of the normal concept of slave in the Roman world—those who were owned by, dependent upon, and served a master. He used it as a title of submission and humility. Paul's concept of slavery here was positive, and we should not read into this usage a negative dehumanizing concept (as in American slavery). He was under constraint to serve Christ. One of Paul's major themes in this letter will be the need for Christians to follow Christ's example of taking the lowly position and becoming a slave for others (2:7; cf. Matt. 20:27). So he began the letter exemplifying the attitude he wanted the Philippians to have (Hansen, 2009, 39).

Slave and Servant: Harris notes the important difference between the English renderings "servant" and "slave." A servant gives service to someone, but a slave belongs to someone (2001, 18). A person may be a slave in the outward, literal sense—owned by a master. Or he may be a slave in the spiritual, metaphorical sense—inwardly devoted to a master (Harris, 2001, 27). Paul may have had in mind here both senses (Cohick, 2013a, 24).

Paul and Timothy were slaves "of Christ Jesus" (Χριστοῦ Ἰησοῦ). Paul may have meant that they belonged to Christ (possessive genitive) or that they served Christ (objective genitive). Either way, they were subject to his authority. They had been commissioned by him and represented him. They lived to serve him, were at his disposal, and would give an account to him.

Paul called the recipients of the letter "saints" (BDAG s.v. "ἅγιος" 2dβ, p. 11), literally, "holy ones." A "saint" is not a special kind of super-spiritual believer. All believers are saints. Its background is found in the Old Testament, where Israel was set apart to be a "holy nation," a "people for God's possession" (Exod. 19:5–6). The designation refers not so much to the ethical character of believers as to the fact that they are God's elect, called into a covenantal relationship with him—consecrated to God (*NIDNTTE* 1:130)

Saint: Theologian Karl Barth wrote this perceptive statement about the meaning of Paul's use of the designation *saints*: "'Holy' people are unholy people who nevertheless as such have been singled out, claimed and requisitioned by God for his control, for his use, for himself who is holy. Their holiness is and remains in Christ Jesus" (1962, 10).

The Philippians were God's holy people in as much as they were "in Christ Jesus" (ἐν Χριστῷ Ἰησοῦ). "In Christ" or an equivalent expression, was Paul's favorite phrase for describing the sphere of believers' existence as God's people and the means by which they were God's people.

Paul's address to "all" (πᾶσιν) the saints have hinted at his concern for their unity revealed in the letter. He was writing to *all* of them as saints and they needed to recognize their fundamental unity as God's people (Garland, 2006, 189). Yet Paul singled out the church leadership in his opening greeting—overseers and deacons. This is the only time in Paul's letters when he did so. Overseers were responsible for the spiritual oversight of the church. The specific duties of deacons were less clear, but they may have overlapped with overseers in some respects (Clarke, 2008, 70). Perhaps deacons worked with the overseers especially in administering practical social needs in the church (Martin and Hawthorne,

2004, 10–11). Paul's singling out the leaders of the church put the onus on them to lead the congregation in responding to his letter.

1:2. While the standard greeting for letters in the Greek world was simply "greetings" (χαίρειν; cf. Acts 15:23), Paul transformed the greeting into a theological blessing: "Grace to you and peace from God our Father and the Lord Jesus Christ." "Grace and peace" refer specifically to blessings that flow from the Father and from Christ on the basis of Christ's saving work. "Grace" (BDAG s.v. "χάρις" 2c, p. 1079) denotes an undeserved gift—the full scope of unmerited favor God lavishes upon believers in Christ (cf. Eph. 1:6–8; *NIDNTTE* 4:653–61). "Peace" (BDAG s.v. "εἰρήνη" 2a, p. 288) with God and with others is the experience of wholeness and well-being, resulting from having been justified by faith and reconciled to God and to others through Christ (Rom. 5:1, 11; Eph. 2:14–17; *NIDNTTE* 2:111–17; *EDNT* 3:394–97). Together as a regular greeting in Paul's letters, grace (the cause) and peace (the effect) represent a summary of the gospel blessings for believers. Significantly for the Philippians, living in a Roman colony, Paul blessed them with the peace from God freely given in Christ, not the peace of Rome (*Pax Romana*) imposed through conquest.

Expression of Gratitude (1:3–8)

Paul affectionately thanked God for the Philippians because they were his longtime partners in spreading the gospel and because he was confident that God would complete his work of bringing them to spiritual maturity.

1:3–4. Paul chose to regularly "give thanks" (BDAG s.v. "εὐχαριστέω" 2, p. 415, customary present) for the Philippians, rather than to complain in his circumstances. He found plenty to be thankful for while he was in prison. Thanksgiving, together with praise, depicts the essence of believers' covenantal relationship with God (Pao, 2002, 20–85). It is a God-centered act of worship acknowledging him to be all-powerful and good. Notably, Paul expressed his gratitude for the *people* God had brought into his life— for all he had done, was doing, and would do in their lives. He gave thanks to "my God" (τῷ θεῷ μου). The phrase "my God" reveals the deep, intimate relationship Paul enjoyed with the Father that came about through his Damascus Road encounter with Christ and his subsequent personal experience of God's grace, provision, and protection in the years since.

The occasion of Paul's giving thanks was "upon my every remembrance of you" (ἐπὶ πάσῃ τῇ μνείᾳ ὑμῶν) "always in my every prayer" (πάντοτε ἐν πάσῃ δεήσει μου). "Remembrance" (μνεία, BDAG s.v. "μνεία" 2, p. 654) included both Paul's remembering them and mentioning them in prayer. This suggests that he remembered and prayed for them frequently, including thanking God for them.

Paul understood how important it was to pray for the spiritual growth of all believers in the churches he planted. From his letters it is clear that prayer was a central part of his ministry. The words "all of you" (πάντων ὑμῶν) may be Paul's way of stating that whatever arguments were present in the church, he was concerned for each individual there. He will emphasize this with the words "all of you" several times (1:4, 7 [2x], 25; 2:17, 26; cf. 1:1; 4:21).

Paul thanked God in his every prayer for them, when he was "making" (ποιούμενος, BDAG s.v. "ποιέω" 7a, p. 841, temporal participle) "prayer" (δεήσει) "with joy." Prayer is delightful rather than burdensome when speaking to God with thanksgiving and joy. This is the first of five occurrences of the noun "joy" (BDAG s.v. "χαρά" 1, p. 1077) (1:4, 25; 2:2, 29; 4:1). Paul chose to be joyful rather than bitter in his imprisonment. In reporting his continual thanksgiving and prayer with joy for the Philippians, Paul likely intended to set an example for them. Believers are to thank God for partners in ministry.

Joy in the Christian Life: A major emphasis in Philippians is that the Christian life can be characterized by joy, no matter one's situation. Joy, for Paul, was not dependent on circumstances. More than a mood or emotion, it is an *attitude* that can be chosen, so Paul will feel free to command it later (2:18; 3:1; 4:4). Christian joy is rooted in the absolute confidence that the Lord is for you and at work in you, and that he will bring you to complete maturity and salvation in Christ. It is a product of your relationship with the Lord in the midst of life's circumstances, a fruit of the Spirit (Gal. 5:22).

1:5. Κοινωνία is rendered "partnership" (NIV, ESV, CSB, cf. NLT), "fellowship" (KJV, NKJV), "participation" (NASB), or "sharing" (NRSV).

1:5. Paul stated the first reason why (BDAG s.v. "ἐπί," p. 6) he gave thanks—because of their "partnership in the gospel." "Partnership" or "association," "communion," "fellowship," "close relationship" (BDAG s.v. "κοινωνία" 1, p. 552–53). This and related words occur six times in this letter (1:5, 7; 2:1; 3:10; 4:14, 15). "Partnership in the gospel" refers to their close connection with Paul in spreading the gospel of Jesus (Ware, 2005, 167; Ogereau, 2014a, 259–60). The gospel partnership reflected in Philippians consists of a three-way bond between Paul, the Philippians, and Christ (Fee, 1995, 13). Christ was the center of their partnership, and their common commitment to him was the reason they were partners in the gospel.

The Philippians' partnership with Paul included their financial support (4:14–15), as well as their own ministry of evangelism in Philippi (1:27; 2:15; 4:3) and prayer (1:19). Later, he will mention several of their number whom he considered coworkers (2:25; 4:2–3). On a broader level, partnership also included their sharing with Paul in God's grace in the defense and confirmation of the gospel (1:7), in the gift of the Spirit (2:1), and in sharing the sufferings of

Christ (1:30; 3:10) (Fee, 1995, 84; Hansen, 2009, 48–49). Paul felt deeply connected to the Philippian believers who had joined with him in his life's calling.

The "gospel" ("God's good news to humans" BDAG s.v. "εὐαγγέλιον" 1a, p. 402) was a central concern in Philippians. It occurs nine times (1:5, 7, 12, 16, 27 [2x]; 2:22; 4:3, 15), more than in any of Paul's other letters. Paul did not have to explain the content of the gospel, for its content was not an issue here, and the Philippians were not only in agreement with Paul about the gospel, but were partners in it. Paul's use of the term in this letter referred not merely to the *content* of the gospel message, but also the *activity* of sharing it—evangelism (Garland, 2006, 193). "From the first day" (ἀπὸ τῆς πρώτης ἡμέρας) likely refers to the time of their conversion when Paul and his coworkers planted the church (Acts 16). Their partnership in the gospel had continued from that day. The gift Epaphroditus delivered to Paul was only the most recent evidence of their long-standing partnership with him.

1:6. Ἐπιτελέσει is rendered "bring/carry to completion" (NIV, ESV, NRSV, CSB, cf. NKJV), "perfect" (NASB), or "perform" (KJV).

1:6. Paul stated the second reason why (πεποιθὼς, causal participle) he gave thanks as he prayed with joy—because he was convinced that (ὅτι) "he who began" (ὁ ἐναρξάμενος) a good work in you will carry it on to completion until the day of Christ Jesus." "Convinced" (πεποιθὼς, BDAG s.v. "πείθω" 2b, p. 792) is one of Paul's favorite words in this letter (1:6, 14, 25; 2:24; 3:3, 4). "Confidence, like joy, surfaces often in Philippians" (Hellerman, 2015, 24). "Carry to completion" (ἐπιτελέσει) means that God will finish what he has begun in them (BDAG s.v. "ἐπιτελέω" 1, p. 383). Paul's confident expectation of a bright future for the believers was based on God's past and present work in them.

Previously (1:5) Paul had focused on *their* work of partnering in the gospel. Now he focused on *God's* work in them as they partnered in the gospel. The "good work" (ἔργον ἀγαθόν) God was doing in the Philippians refers broadly to his work of grace in their lives from the time of their conversion—including his impartation of new life in Christ, his bringing them to spiritual maturity, and his provision of a resurrection body when Christ returns (2:13–14; 3:21). In all of this, God was at work in them (1:6; 2:13), and would bring it to completion. Paul was encouraging the Philippians by reminding them of what God had already done and was doing, and by looking forward to what he would yet accomplish in their lives.

God's work in them would continue "until the day of Christ Jesus," a reference to the second coming. At that time, believers will receive their resurrection body (3:21) and God's sanctifying work in them will be completed.

> *1:7.* Καθώς, which joins verse 7 to verse 6, is left untranslated by NIV, ESV, NRSV, and CSB. KJV and NKJV assume a comparative force ("even as/just as"). NASB assumes a causal sense ("for"). Φρονεῖν is rendered "to think" (NRSV, CSB, KJV, NKJV) or "to feel" (NIV, ESV, NLT, NASB). The phrase τὸ ἔχειν με ἐν τῇ καρδίᾳ ὑμᾶς has two accusative nouns (με and ὑμᾶς), either of which may be the subject. NRSV translates, "because you hold me in [your] heart." But the other option is found in most translations: "because I have you in [my] heart" (NIV, ESV, CSB, NLT, NASB, KJV, NKJV). Δεσμοῖς is rendered "chains" (NIV, KJV, NKJV) or "imprisonment" (ESV, NRSV, CSB, NLT, NASB).

1:7. Paul stated the reason why (BDAG s.v. "καθώς" 3, p. 494) he thought and felt the way he expressed in 1:3–6—because "it is right" (ἐστιν δίκαιον) for him to think this about all of them. When Paul said, "it is right," he meant

this was the only fair and appropriate thing for him to think (BDAG s.v. "δίκαιος" 2, p. 247). "To think" refers not only to thinking, but also feeling, discerning, judging—an activity of the intellect and a movement of the will (BDAG s.v. "φρονέω" 1, p. 1065; *NIDNTTE* 4:620). Fowl suggests the translation, "to exercise judgment" (2005, 28–29). It was right for Paul to form this judgment about them. He will use this term at several points in the letter to exhort the Philippians in their own thinking, feeling, and judgment (1:7; 2:2 [2x], 5; 3:15 [2x], 19; 4:2, 10 [2x]).[1] "This" (τοῦτο), likely refers back to all of 1:3–6, but especially to the confidence of 1:6. Paul once again drew attention to the entire church with "about all of you" (cf. 1:1, 4). Again he may have been hinting at the unity that needed to be evident among them. Paul embraced all of them and he wanted all of them to embrace one another.

Paul stated two reasons why it was right for him to think this about them. The first reason (διὰ + infinitive τὸ ἔχειν) was "because I have you in my heart." In biblical thought, the "heart" (BDAG s.v. "καρδία" 1, p. 508–509) is the center of the emotions, understanding, and will—the center of one's physical, spiritual, and mental life (*TDNT* 3:611–13; *NIDOTTE* 2:306; *NIDNTTE* 2:623–27). To say, "I have you in my heart" is to say, "I have great affection for you" (cf. v. 8). It was only right for Paul to be confident that God would complete his work in them because he has great affection for them in his heart.

The second reason (ὄντας, causal participle) why it was right for Paul to think this about them is because of their partnership with him—"since both in my imprisonment and in the defense and confirmation of the gospel, you all are fellow partners with me of grace." For the first time, Paul mentioned his "chains" or "imprisonment" (δεσμοῖς, BDAG s.v. "δεσμός" 1, p. 219) (cf. 1:13, 14, 17).

---

1 Paul used φρονεῖν more than any other New Testament author (ten times in Philippians, thirteen times elsewhere in Paul's letters, three times elsewhere in the New Testament).

Paul underscored that his partnership with the Philippians included his "defense" or "the act of making a defense" (BDAG s.v. "ἀπολογία" 2b, p. 117) and "confirmation" or "validation" (BDAG s.v. "βεβαίωσις," p. 173) of the gospel. This referred to Paul defending the gospel at his upcoming legal hearing (cf. Acts 22:1; 25:16; 2 Tim. 4:16). He saw his trial as more a defense *of the gospel* than of himself. Personal vindication was not important; vindication of the gospel was. Once he was acquitted, as he expected (1:25–26), this would be a confirmation of the validity of the gospel (Collange, 1979, 47–48). Or if he should be condemned and executed, his faithful witness unto death would confirm its validity (1:20).

The Philippians (*all* of them—fourth occurrence in these opening verses) were "fellow-partakers" (συγκοινωνούς, BDAG s.v. "συγκοινωνός," p. 952) with Paul "of grace." Paul referred here to the grace (gift) of serving Christ with him. They shared in his apostolic ministry, which was God's "grace" given to him (Rom. 1:5; 1 Cor. 3:10; Gal. 2:9; Eph. 3:2, 7–8) (Martin and Hawthorne, 2004, 27). Because they had teamed with him in spreading the gospel, they shared this "grace." This included their standing with him as financial contributors and in their suffering the same opposition, which had been "granted" (the verb ἐχαρίσθη is related to the noun χάρις) to them on behalf of Christ (1:29–30). The privilege of sharing all of this with Paul was God's grace to them.

> **Major Themes Introduced in Paul's Thanksgiving**: Paul's introductory thanksgiving (1:3–8) introduced several themes that will be important in the letter (cf. Watson, 1988, 64; Cousar, 2009, 28). For example, *joy* (1:4, 18, 25; 2:2, 17, 18, 28, 29; 3:1; 4:1, 4, 10), *partnership* (1:5, 7; 2:1; 3:10; 4:14, 15), *chains/imprisonment* (1:7, 13, 14, 17), *gospel* (1:5, 7, 12, 16, 27; 2:22; 4:3, 15), *thinking/judging* (1:7; 2:2 [2x], 5; 3:15, 19; 4:2, 10), *affection/love* (1:8, 9, 16; 2:1, 2, 12; 4:1), *all of you* (1:4, 7, 8, 25; 2:17, 26; cf. 1:1; 4:21), *the day of Christ* (1:6, 10; 2:16; 3:11, 20–21).

1:8. Paul strengthened (γάρ) his statement that he "has them in his heart" (1:7) with an appeal to God. "God is my 'witness'" (BDAG s.v. "μάρτυς," p. 619) was a rhetorical formula found in both Jewish and Greco-Roman literature testifying to the character or inner motives of the person (Novenson, 2010). Paul affirmed that God can testify of his sincere character and of the truthfulness of what he was saying (cf. Rom. 1:9; 2 Cor. 1:23; 1 Thess. 2:5, 10). He was not exaggerating, nor was he flattering them in order to keep the support coming. He truly had a deep affection for them. "How I long" (ὡς ἐπιποθῶ) denotes Paul's intense desire to see them and to be with them in person (cf. 1:25; 2:24). Calvin appropriately writes, "We long after the things that are dear to us" (1965, 231). In 4:1 Paul called them his "beloved and *longed for* brethren." He had a deep desire to continue working with them in spreading the gospel—including direct personal contact with them.

Paul longed for them with the "affection" (σπλάγχνοις, BDAG s.v. "σπλάγχνον" 3, p. 938) of Christ Jesus. "Of Christ Jesus" (Χριστοῦ Ἰησοῦ, subjective genitive) denotes Christ as the one who shows affection for them through Paul (Hellerman, 2015, 29). Paul's affection for the Philippians was not merely because of what they did for him—their support of his ministry. Rather, if he longed for them with Christ's affection, there was a deeper cause and motivation for the affection within him (cf. Bockmuehl, 1998, 65). This was the deepest possible affection.

THEOLOGICAL FOCUS

The exegetical idea (the Philippians' long-standing partnership in spreading the gospel caused Paul to thank God for them) leads to this theological focus: Working together for spreading the gospel causes believers to thank God for one another.

This passage is about deep relationships among those who work together for the spread of the gospel. These relationships cause us to thank God for one another. Paul had long enjoyed partnering with the Philippians (it had been perhaps ten to twelve years since Paul had planted the church there). Their partnership, denoted by the key words "partnership" (κοινωνία, 1:5) and "fellow-partakers" (συγκοινωνούς, 1:7), provides important background for what Paul wrote throughout the letter.

Paul's partnering with them meant that he regularly prayed for them with joy. He thanked God for them. He felt deep affection for them—the very affection of Christ. He was also concerned about their spiritual lives and the spiritual health of the church.

Ultimately, our relationships with others in the church and in serving Christ together cannot remain on a merely human level. We are in a three-way bond with Christ, ourselves, and others. Our affection and care for others must derive from Christ loving them through us and loving us through them. Partnership in the gospel creates a deep connection for experiencing life and service to Christ together. We are in Christ; Christ is in us. His love is in us. He extends his love to others through us.

PREACHING AND TEACHING STRATEGIES

Exegetical and Theological Synthesis

Paul enjoyed a meaningful partnership with the Philippians. Unlike other readers who questioned his authority (e.g., Corinth), the Philippians demonstrated genuine concern and financial support toward Paul. Despite his internment, joy and gratitude mark the opening and ending of his letter. Indeed, Philippians is a discourse among friends.

In addition to its affectionate tone, the epistolary greeting stands out for several stylistic and theological reasons. Paul frontloaded the letter with key terms, addressed church leaders by honorary titles, and granted to Timothy and himself the modest label "slave of Christ." These choices foreshadow both the christological heart of the letter (2:5–11), as well as the ethical

refrain for harmony (2:3, 14; 4:2). For Paul knew the "saints" he wrote to were prone to selfish ambition.

Paul was not an advocate for gospel ministry as a soloist. His missionary journeys and body of letters showcased his practice of linking arms with other gifted and committed followers of Jesus. From his first journey with Barnabas and John Mark (Acts 13) to his closing years with Timothy and Luke (2 Tim. 4:11), Paul proclaimed the gospel as a team player. His ministry labors emphasized the good news of Jesus, not personal bylines or church headlines. By linking arms with other believers in gospel ministry, Paul set a precedent for deep gratitude and lasting impact.

Preaching Idea

Linking arms with fellow Christ-followers leads to deep gratitude.

Contemporary Connections

What does it mean?

Linking arms is a powerful metaphor for partnership in Christian service. It places ministry in the context of a friendship or a team. In a partnership, both people or parties benefit from sharing their strengths and resources for a common purpose. While Paul does not write to individualistic Westerners of the twenty-first century, his collaborative model of ministry could not be more relevant.

We live in a culture of do-it-yourself (DIY) spirituality. An endless stream of Christian literature, podcasts, and blogs has given every follower of Jesus her personal choice in how to develop spiritually. Ironically, DIY spirituality lacks two of the key ingredients to Pauline formation: God and fellow Christ-followers.

The impulse to place ourselves at the center of the world is endemic. The very existence of voluntourism—which is not an evil exclusive to Christian short-term mission projects, but also humanitarian aid—exposes the tendency for individuals to flaunt their good deeds for social-media praise. Selfishness likely drives more aid and relief work than most of us would want to admit. In *When Helping Hurts* (2009), Fikkert and Corbett warn that the lasting impact of such trips is marginal at best, and often damaging.

If Paul ever suffered the delusion of being indispensable, years of imprisonment surely knocked it out of him. While others proclaimed the gospel in wider circles (and some for impure motives), Paul accepts the limits of his prison quarters. And the back-and-forth correspondence with the Philippians remind him his ministry is not limited by his reach. He linked arms with others and gratefully watched God continuing to work.

Is it true?

Is it true that linking arms in Christian service leads to deep gratitude? It certainly has the *potential* to increase our affection for others. The apostle Paul happily gave credit to colaborers in Philippi (2:14; 4:2). Of course, partnerships, like all team projects, may be hijacked by a strong ego or lethargic personality. They are upset by poor communication and unclear expectations. And they may lack God's favor. Thus, linking arms cannot be claimed as a foolproof means to deep gratitude or lasting impact.

However, the apostle Paul's legacy remains an outstanding testimony of the power of linking arms in Christian service. Partnerships counteract the sense of isolation tied to DIY spirituality; shared mission provides a sense of companionship. It also helps us transcend ourselves. Linking arms emphasizes personal strengths, knowledge, and abilities, reducing the effect of our personal weaknesses and limitations. A good partnership makes everyone better. Instead of laboring out of jealousy, rivalry, and one-upmanship, partners serve with joy, gratitude, and humility.

Christian colleges and mission agencies—founded and funded by linking arms—stand as a testimony. Christian publishers link arms with authors of various doctrinal backgrounds. Hospitals, community food banks, adoption agencies, and campus ministries each rely on linking arms with likeminded believers to make the gospel known. Even individual missionaries, local church leaders, and stay-at-home mothers maintain their vitality by linking arms with others. Lasting fruits rarely result from lonely service.

Now what?

So is Christian service destined to fail if it does not rely on partnerships? Does every gospel labor require a company of saints? Must a local church link arms with another church or community group to enjoy any success? No. While the text illustrates the power of teamwork, it does not invalidate individual acts of ministry and obedience.

Nevertheless, the precedent for lasting impact through linking arms should not be ignored. In an age where evangelicalism does not receive the benefit of the doubt, but has earned a reputation for being "irrelevant" and "extreme," partnerships paint an alternative picture: followers of Jesus affectionately allied in good faith (Kinnaman and Lyons, 2016). Those who link arms in Christian service value humility more than credit, community more than isolation, lasting impact more than short-lived fame. They recognize God's mission transcends their individual goals and local church aims; God is their primary partner. This is a paradigm shift, which is the first step in linking arms with others in Christian service.

After making the paradigm shift, individuals, congregations, and community organizations must honestly assess their areas of giftedness and connect themselves with others who share similar goals but have different resources and experiences. Partnerships thrive on mutuality. Each party contributes from its pool of strengths—time, money, facilities, or personnel. A spiritual gifts test or asset map proves helpful at this stage.

Asset Mapping: Community Asset Mapping is a powerful tool developed by John McKnight and Jody Kretzmann from DePaul University. Rather than approaching people as "needy" and serving as a service provider, Asset-Based Community Development [ABCD] recognizes all people have strengths (i.e., "assets") that they can employ to link arms with others. For free resources, see https://resources.depaul.edu/abcd-institute/Pages/default.aspx.

Finally, partnerships require the right attitude. Healthy relationships can neither be faked nor forced. Shared experiences develop trust over time. Grateful prayers nurture genuine affection. The background of Philippians and Paul's opening prayer illustrate this essential attitude of honesty, patience, gratitude, and prayer.

Linking arms will not happen overnight, but this passage may begin a paradigm shift for Western churches. The sermon might prove most helpful if it surfaces the need to link arms with other Christ-followers in readily accessible ways. Consider encouraging younger mothers to connect with older mothers for encouragement in parenting; experienced teachers to coteach with junior instructors in youth or children's ministry; eager servants to join a seasoned hospitality team in the church to extend a culture of welcome.

Creativity in Presentation

A live illustration may prove helpful in demonstrating the power of partnerships. On the stage place a large sofa and attempt to move it alone. Then invite several others on stage to transport the couch with ease. A more humorous illustration would pit the lone preacher against a group of congregants in a contest of Tug of War or Red Rover. Close the service with an invitation to stand and link arms with a neighbor for the benediction. These illustrations show how linked arms lighten the load, magnify strength, and increase solidarity.

A clip from end of *The Lego Movie* (2014), directed by Phil Lord, would also drive home the point, where Emmet, the unlikely hero, convinces a mismatched crew of specialists to work as a team. The refrain from the movie's theme song brings home the point: "Everything is awesome. Everything is cool when you're on a team." *The Avengers* (2012) or *Remember the Titans* (2001) also paint a memorable picture of teammates succeeding by overcoming selfish ambition and linking arms. "ABCD in 3 Minutes" is an educational YouTube clip—not flashy but effective—about local churches working as community partners. Each media resource tells the story of the sum being greater than the individual parts.

Real stories of churches establishing ministry partnerships abound. Sweney (2011) chronicles Perimeter Church's transition from megachurch in Atlanta to model church in linking arms. Breathe Partners, a parachurch organization, links stateside churches with Haitian counterparts to give, pray, and serve. I have two colleagues whose congregations link arms for an annual trip to serve with their partner church in Haiti for a week. And a movement is stirring—both in country and abroad—to bring the "C" back into the YMCA. Chaplains, spiritual directors, and Christian emphasis teams in various YMCAs have reached out to churches, inviting them into a loose partnership, offering spiritual courses, community prayer, or vacation Bible school opportunities for thousands of non-Christians who grace their doors weekly. My local YMCA chaplain recently told me, "We have the mission field; the church has the workers. I'm trying to bring them together." Hearing a live testimony from a Christian community leader could create a powerful application to the sermon.

The key point to reiterate is this: Working together for spreading the gospel causes believers to thank God for one another. Linking arms with fellow Christ-followers leads to deep gratitude.

- Link arms as ministry partners, not position-holders (1:1–2).

- Link arms in gratitude for God and others (1:3–6).

- Link arms affectionately, in spite of circumstances (1:7–8).

DISCUSSION QUESTIONS

1. In what ways did Paul's history with the Philippians determine his attitude toward and relationship with them?

2. What things do true spiritual partners who share kingdom work have in common?

3. In what practical ways can you express gratitude for spiritual teammates/partners and be a channel of Christ's love for them?

4. What are the true partnerships in your church and in your personal life? Where are they strong? Where are they weak?

5. What are some practical steps for improving partnerships in your church for maximum kingdom effectiveness? What is the first step you need to take to strengthen partnerships in the gospel?

6. How might the reputation of evangelicalism shift if local churches spent more time forging partnerships than acting as soloists or waging turf wars?

Philippians 1:9–11

EXEGETICAL IDEA
Paul prayed that the Philippians would grow in love and godly character so that they would be ready for the return of Christ and ultimately bring honor to God.

THEOLOGICAL FOCUS
Requests to God for growth in love and godly character prepare believers for Christ's return and brings honor to God.

PREACHING IDEA
Talking to God strengthens our ties with others.

PREACHING POINTERS
Paul built on his words of gratitude for the Philippians' partnership with a prayer for their growth. He let his original readers overhear what he talked to God about concerning them: their character formation. While he has already stressed the promise that God will finish what he started in them, he now qualified the promise with a prayer for their increase in love and Christlike living. These words prime the Philippians for an upcoming appeal to imitate Jesus. Paul shared the prayer to encourage his first-century readers to virtuous living and glorious praise until Jesus returns.

Too often contemporary prayers revolve around juvenile requests: more money, easy days, better health, nice weather, and traveling mercies. Followers of Jesus fail to thrive because we have traded the biblical content of prayer for petty goods or personal safety. Setting spiritual growth as a key prayer request for others establishes an important principle: God's people develop character by talking to him. When we intercede for others, our affection for them increases. Greater affection leads to stronger ties and greater interest in their character formation. As Philippians will demonstrate, we do well to ask God for increases of trust, joy, knowledge, fellowship, perseverance, and purity for fellow Christ-followers. This passage recovers how talking to God strengthens our ties to others.

PRAYER FOR SPIRITUAL GROWTH (1:9–11)

LITERARY STRUCTURE AND THEMES (1:9–11)

Paul reported what he prayed for the Philippians ("this I pray"). His prayer consists of two requests, each followed by a purpose or result (Wiles, 1974, 208). First, he prayed that their love may abound even more in knowledge and discernment (1:9). The purpose/result of their love abounding in knowledge and discernment would be that they will approve what is excellent (1:10a). Second, he prayed that they may be pure and blameless for the day Christ returns, that is, that they may be filled with the fruit of righteousness (1:10b–11a). The purpose/result of their being filled with the fruit of righteousness would be that God will be glorified and praised (1:11b).

Prayer for Love to Increase (1:9–10a)
Prayer for Spiritual Maturity (1:10b–11)

EXPOSITION (1:9–11)

Paul continued the opening of his letter by specifying what he was praying for the Philippians. As he summarized the major content and themes of his prayers, he introduced some basic concerns the letter would address (Wiles, 1974, 206–207). His prayer focused on the Philippians' growth in spiritual maturity so that they would be ready for the return of Christ. By providing an agenda for spiritual growth, this prayer report shows believers how to pray for one another.

The culture at Philippi presented certain challenges to spiritual growth for this small band of Jesus followers. First, the dominant religious-political force was the Roman imperial cult, which deified the emperor. They would face pressure to return to the idols and civil/religious practices from which they had turned in order to serve God (cf. 1 Thess. 1:9). Second, Roman culture valued public honor, recognition, status, and accomplishment. But these disciples would have to learn to live by a new set of values. They required a new definition of what is honorable and to be esteemed. They would have to think differently about ideals such as love, greatness, humility, service, honor, and shame. Christians were to be known for their love (cf. John 13:35) as well as their pure and blameless lives. But living such lives in this culture required wisdom and discernment from the Lord.

Paul's prayer speaks to the growth in spiritual maturity needed by the Philippians. He prays for their love to abound in spiritual discernment, so that they will approve what is excellent. He also prays that they will be pure and blameless for the day Christ returns. All of this will lead to God being glorified and praised. The prayer provides an agenda for spiritual growth, and it fills out some of what Paul meant when he said that he was confident God would complete the good work he had begun in them until the day of Christ (1:6).

Prayer for Love to Increase (1:9–10a)

Paul prayed that God would make their love for him (God) and for all people to increase, along with the wisdom that comes from the Spirit, so that they have godly perspectives and attitudes in all matters of life as they follow Christ.

1:9. Ἐν can denote sphere: "that your love may abound *in* knowledge" (NIV, CSB, NASB, KJV, NKJV) or association: "that your love may abound *along with* knowledge" (ESV, NRSV). Αἰσθήσει is rendered "discernment" (ESV, NASB, NKJV, CSB), "judgment" (KJV), "insight" (NIV, NRSV), or "understanding" (NLT).

1:9. Paul returned to what he stated in 1:4—that he regularly prayed for his partners in the gospel. "And this 'I pray'" (προσεύχομαι, iterative or customary present, depicting repeated or regular prayer) indicates that he would now give the content of what he regularly prayed. The first request of his prayer (ἵνα) is "that your love may abound still more and more." "Love" (BDAG s.v. "ἀγάπη," 1a, p. 6) focuses not so much on an emotion, as placing a high value on someone else, on favoring them (*EDNT* 1:9). It is "the ultimate theological word both to describe God's character and to articulate the essence of Christian behavior" (Fee, 1995, 98).

> **"Love" (noun [ἀγάπη]; verb [ἀγαπάω]) as a Christian virtue**: "Love" terminology appears frequently in the LXX. It is used of the relationship between spouses, family members, and friends. Notably it is used of God's love for his people (Deut. 7:8; Jer. 38:3 [Eng. 31:3]; Hos. 11:4) and in the two love commandments—love for God and neighbor (Deut. 6:5 and Lev. 19:18). Jesus cited these as the two greatest commandments (Matt. 22:37–40). Paul used the noun seventy-four times, including four times in Philippians (1:9, 16, 2:1, 2), and the verb twenty-nine times (none in Philippians). For Paul, love began with God. His love has been poured into believers' hearts through the Spirit (Rom. 5:5) (*EDNT* 1:10). It is the primary "fruit of the Spirit" (Gal. 5:22) and the essence of the "law of Christ" (Gal. 6:2 with Gal. 5:14). Paul famously described love in 1 Corinthians 13:4–7.

Paul prayed for their love to abound. "Abound" (περισσεύῃ, BDAG s.v. "περισσεύω" 1aδ, p. 805) is a favorite verb Paul used to depict the rich abundance of the Christian life. "Still more and more" (ἔτι μᾶλλον καὶ μᾶλλον) suggests that love was present in the Philippian church. But Paul prayed that God would make it increase. Paul did not specify *for whom* he wanted their love to abound. A parallel prayer in 1 Thessalonians 3:12 specifies the objects,

"Now may the Lord make you increase and abound in love for one another and for all." Since Paul did not specify an object here, we should think of love in a comprehensive sense—love for God and for all people. Paul might have had in mind the love they exhibited as they spread the gospel (Hellerman, 2015, 30–31), but it was not limited to this.

Paul wanted their love to abound "in (ἐν) knowledge and all discernment." He wanted spiritual perception and discernment to accompany their increasing love. Biblical love increases as spiritual knowledge and moral understanding increase. To love biblically, believers must love what God loves. This takes knowledge and discernment—two concepts closely related as seen by the fact that a single preposition "in" (ἐν) governs the two nouns.

> **Paul and Knowledge**: "Knowledge" (γνῶσις, ἐπίγνωσις) is not merely knowledge *about* persons or things, but also the knowing that comes through *experience* or *relationships* (Hellerman, 2016, 32). Paul's concept of knowledge came from the Old Testament, where to know God meant to "enter into the personal relationship he himself makes possible" (*NIDNTTE* 1:579). Knowledge begins with the fear of the Lord and comes through revelation from him (Prov. 1:7; 2:5). It includes knowledge of his will (Acts 22:14; Rom. 2:18; Col. 1:9), the law (Rom. 7:1), and the truth, the gospel (1 Tim. 2:4; 2 Tim. 2:25). Knowledge consists of personal recognition and reception of the God's Word, and obedience to it (*NIDNTTE* 1:582; *EDNT* 2:25). It comes through the Spirit who indwells believers (1 Cor. 2:12–14). Goodness, purity, faith, and godliness should accompany knowledge (Rom. 15:14; 2 Cor. 6:6; 8:7; Titus 1:1).

The first noun, "knowledge" (ἐπιγνώσει, BDAG s.v. "ἐπίγνωσις," p. 369), is a compound term. Elsewhere, Paul used the related compound verb (ἐπιγινώσκω) to denote a fuller knowing at the second coming (1 Cor. 13:12).

But here, the noun seems to be equivalent to the uncompounded form "knowledge" (γνῶσις) in Romans 15:14 and 1 Corinthians 1:5 (*TDNT* 1:707). It denotes a *personally experienced knowledge* of God that comes through revelation and relationship. Spiritual growth in love requires increasing in a deeper personal knowledge of God and his ways. To avoid overintellectualizing the term, Hellerman suggests the translation, "perception" or "insight" (2015, 32).

The second noun, "discernment" (αἰσθήσει), occurs only here in the New Testament. It frequently occurs in Proverbs (LXX) to denote moral understanding based on experience, a practical application of understanding, a perception basically equivalent to "wisdom" (BDAG s.v. "αἴσθησις," 2, p. 29 *TDNT* 1:188). Fowl suggests the translation, "moral understanding" (2005, 32). Compare Hebrews 5:14, where the mature have their faculties (αἰσθητήρια)—their capacity for discernment—trained to distinguish between good and evil. When Paul prayed for "all" (πάσῃ) discernment, he was praying for discernment on a broad scale—the ability to make right moral decisions in every kind of situation.

Paul was praying that the Philippians' love may discriminate between what is good and evil, between what honors God and does not honor God. Without knowledge and discernment in a variety of circumstances, a mere increase of love will not be helpful. Godly love agrees with increasing discernment. The Philippians were not to indiscriminately love everything, as though the love that comes from God is undiscerning and tolerant of evil. Carson writes of our present-day culture: "Without the constraints of knowledge and insight, love very easily degenerates into mawkish sentimentality or into the kind of mushy pluralism the world often confuses with love" (1992, 126).

Knowledge and discernment properly inform love so that it is godly. Followers of Christ are to love what is good and right. "Hate what is evil; cling to what is good" (Rom. 12:9; cf. Amos 5:15). In order to love what is good and right, believers must possess the knowledge and discernment that comes through the Spirit. Compare Paul's similar prayer in Colossians 1:9, "that you may be filled with the knowledge (ἐπίγνωσιν) of his will in all wisdom (σοφίᾳ) and *spiritual* (πνευματικῇ) insight (συνέσει)."

> *1:10.* Τὰ διαφέροντα is rendered "the things that are excellent" (ESV, NASB, KJV, NKJV), "what is best" (NIV, NRSV), or "what really matters" (CSB, NLT). The phrase εἰς ἡμέραν Χριστοῦ may express goal—"for the day of Christ" (NIV, ESV) or extension of time—"until the day of Christ" (NLT, NASB, KJV, NKJV), "in the day of Christ" (NRSV, CSB).

1:10a. Paul stated the purpose or result (εἰς)[2] of his first request (1:9). The increasing love for which he prayed is not an end in itself. Love abounding more and more in knowledge and all discernment is for the purpose or result of approving what is excellent. Paul wanted the Philippians to know what to approve and what not to approve, what to love and what not to love, what matters and what does not matter. "Approve" (δοκιμάζειν, BDAG s.v. "δοκιμάζω" 2, p. 255) in this context has the idea of drawing a conclusion about the worth of something on the basis of testing it. He wanted them to approve of "what is excellent" (τὰ διαφέροντα). He meant those things that from a biblical perspective are "superior, worth more than something else" (BDAG s.v. "διαφέρω" 4, p. 239). Their love was to abound with knowledge and discernment so that they approve of the perspectives, attitudes, beliefs, motives, activities, and actions that are most essential and advantageous to following

---

2 Purpose denotes intention; result denotes outcome. BDAG states that "in many cases, purpose and result cannot be clearly differentiated, and hence ἵνα is used for the result that follows according to the purpose of the subject or of God" (s.v. "ἵνα" 3, p. 477).

Christ—the very things that growing in spiritual maturity entail. These are the things Paul will address in the letter.

Garland (2006, 195) describes three possible applications to what Paul had in mind with the phrase "approve things that are excellent." (1) Discerning between *what is true and what is false*. For example, believers need to know the ethical teaching of the New Testament and to approve those behaviors that are godly and good. (2) Discerning between degrees of *what is good and what is better*. Recognizing the most essential things necessary for walking with Christ will involve choosing the best among a number of acceptable and good options. (3) Discerning between *things that matter and things that do not*. For example, Paul believed that the progress of the gospel mattered more than his imprisonment. We can recognize these most essential things when God causes our love to abound in knowledge and all discernment.

Prayer for Spiritual Maturity (1:10b–11)

Paul also prayed for God to increase their spiritual maturity and godly character so that they would be ready for judgment when Christ returns, and so ultimately bring honor to God.

1:10b. Paul's second request (ἵνα) was that the Philippians become pure and blameless—he wanted God to make them spiritually mature and godly in character. Then they would be ready for judgment when Christ returns.

Paul used two terms to describe his desire for their spiritual maturity and godly character. "Pure" (εἰλικρινής) occurs only here in his letters, though the related noun "purity, sincerity" occurs three times (1 Cor. 5:8; 2 Cor. 1:12; 2:17). It means "morally sincere, without hidden motives or pretense" (BDAG s.v. "εἰλικρινής," p. 282). Paul was thinking either of pure motives

in interpersonal relationships among believers (Fee, 1995, 102) or of purity before God at Christ's return (Hellerman, 2015, 33). "Blameless" (ἀπρόσκοποι), in Paul's only other use of it, denotes giving no offense, not causing someone else to stumble (1 Cor. 10:32). In Acts 24:16 it refers to a clear, blameless conscience. So here it could refer to being blameless because one has not given offense or caused someone else to stumble (as in 1 Cor. 10:32), or to being blameless because one has not stumbled (as in Acts 24:16), or perhaps to both of these ideas (cf. BDAG s.v. "ἀπρόσκοπος" 1, p. 125).

Growth in spiritual maturity and godly character would prepare the Philippians for Jesus's return. "The day" (ἡμέραν) "of Christ" (Χριστοῦ) refers to his second coming (BDAG s.v. "ἡμέρα" 3bβ, p. 438). In 1:6, Paul expressed his confidence that God would complete the work he had begun in them until the day of Christ. Now he revealed that this is what he was praying for. His focus was on the day the Philippians would stand before Christ "for" judgment. He wanted them to be ready for it. He had set his eyes on that goal and he wanted the Philippians to do likewise. Focusing on the return of Christ provides motivation for present godliness. With "pure and blameless" Paul was not suggesting that believers may obtain sinless perfection in this life. But he was saying that as God works in them, they can live morally pure lives in their preparation for the day Jesus returns.

1:11. Paul further explained his statement in 1:10b. He desired that on the day of Christ the Philippians would be "filled" (BDAG s.v. "πληρόω" 1b, p. 828)[3] with the fruit of righteousness." "Filled with the fruit of righteousness" expresses what Paul meant by "pure and blameless" (Fee, 1995, 103). But scholars debate the meaning of "righteousness" (δικαιοσύνης,

---

3 The perfect tense participle "filled" (πεπληρωμένοι) is stative, portraying the continuing resultant state of an action completed in the past (*GGBB*, 573–75). It reflects the perspective of the future day of Christ, when the existing results of God's prior work in the believer through Christ will be evident.

BDAG s.v. "δικαιοσύνη" 3a, p. 247) and its relation to "fruit. (1) "Fruit of righteousness" could mean, "the fruit that *comes from* believers' righteous standing before God." In this case "righteousness" (right standing) is the source of the ethical fruit in believers' lives. The ethical fruit consists of such things as love, humility, unity, and so on. (2) Or "fruit of righteousness" could mean, "the fruit that *consists of* righteousness." In this case "righteousness" refers not a right standing before God, but to ethical righteousness—godly character and right behavior. On this view, "righteousness" identifies what the fruit is—again, such things as love, humility, unity, and so on.

Either view is possible. Both express Paul's theology. Because of the immediate context, we lean toward (2). Paul used the biblical imagery of a tree loaded with fruit to depict believers in whom God has accomplished his work of producing spiritual maturity and holiness in their lives (cf. Ps. 1:3). "Fruit" (καρπόν) refers to ethical characteristics and behavior, and reflects the result of a process over time in which God works in believers to make them more like Christ (cf. 1:6; BDAG s.v. "καρπός" 1b, p. 510). Paul prayed that the fruit that comes from living rightly will be increasingly evident in their lives in the present age in preparation for the age to come. The passive voice "be filled" shows that this fruitfulness is the result of God's work in the believer.

Paul described the source and means of this fruit. It is the fruit (of righteousness) "that is through Jesus Christ." "Through" (διὰ) indicates agency (Campbell, 2102, 247). Jesus is the one who produces this fruit in the lives of his disciples. Grammatically, the phrase "that is through Jesus Christ" (τὸν διὰ Ἰησοῦ Χριστοῦ) connects to "fruit" (καρπόν), not "righteousness" (δικαιοσύνης). This is because the article "that" (τόν), which begins the relative clause, agrees in gender with "fruit (καρπόν), not "righteousness" (δικαιοσύνης). So the fruit (righteous character and behavior) produced in the lives of the Philippians would come not though self-effort, but through the work of Christ in them. Paul was most likely thinking of the work Christ accomplishes in believers by means of the presence of the Spirit.

The ultimate purpose or result (εἰς) for which Paul prayed is that Christ's work in the Philippians would be "to the glory and praise of God." "Glory" (δόξαν) refers to "honor as enhancement or recognition of status or performance" (BDAG s.v. "δόξα" 3, p. 257). "Praise" (ἔπαινον) refers to "the act of expressing admiration or approval" (BDAG s.v. "ἔπαινος" 1, p. 3571). Paul was thinking of the glory and praise that would arise *for* God ("God" is the object of glory and praise) as a result of what he had accomplished in the Philippians' lives (cf. Eph. 1:6, 12, 14). The chief end of God's purposes in redemption is that he be honored in all creation because of what he has accomplished in believers. This is why believers should pray for and pursue growth in holiness. The good work that God has begun in them—that he will complete (1:6)—will ultimately bring honor to him. This note of praise provides a suitable ending, not only to the prayer, but also to the introduction of the letter (1:3–11). Paul began the introduction with thanksgiving (1:3). He ended it with praise (O'Brien, 1991, 82).

THEOLOGICAL FOCUS

The exegetical idea (Paul prayed that the Philippians would grow in love and godly character so that they would be ready for the return of Christ, and ultimately bring honor to God) leads to this theological focus: Requests to God for growth in love and godly character prepare believers for Christ's return and brings honor to God.

Paul's prayer shows us how to pray for the Spirit's work in our lives and the lives of others so that we will be ready for Christ's return. It sets an agenda for our pursuit of a mature Christian character. The Holy Spirit has inspired and preserved a number of Paul's intercessory prayers for the benefit and instruction of the church—to teach us how to pray and to show us what to pursue.

The assumption in Paul's prayer is that God is at work in believers—bringing to completion the process of redemption he has begun (1:6). This process will continue until the second coming. Until then, God is at work in us through the Spirit, conforming our character to Christ's. As with all the intercessory prayers in Paul's letters, this text reveals that prayer for growth in spiritual maturity is a necessary means God uses to make us like Christ.

PREACHING AND TEACHING STRATEGIES

Exegetical and Theological Synthesis

Philippians 1:9–11 compliments Paul's grateful reference to God's work in the Philippian church (1:6). The spiritual task God started—evident in their holy standing (1:1) and gospel partnership (1:5)—he promised to finish at the second coming of Jesus.[4] Theological certainty inspired Paul's eloquent intercession. He asked God to develop Christlike character in his people, resulting in praise of God.

Paul's emphasis on character formation and Jesus's second coming eludes modern prayers. Followers of Jesus today may give lip service to growth in love and patience, but blameless living and purity sound like prudish requests. The phrase "fruits of righteousness" may spark debate about the forensics of salvation, but it is less likely to inspire living aligned with God's standard. Wisdom and insight are nearly impossible in the deluge of data we drink from daily. And the return of Jesus feels less imminent than the speculation sure to surround our talk of it.

Our prayers have lost focus. We have made them too immediate, inward, and private. We ask for God's blessing on upcoming surgeries and traveling mercies. We do not ask for his Spirit to make our lives abound in love and resound with praise. And we've relegated our conversations with God to our closets, quiet times, or polite dinner blessings. The encouragement that prayer evokes when we make our talks public is powerful. Because Paul wanted to encourage the Philippians' growth in character—a good work God started—he brought them into his conversation with God.

Preaching Idea

Talking to God strengthens our ties to others.

Contemporary Connections

What does it mean?

What does it mean to talk to God? Does talking with God require exalted speech or special knowledge? How does it strengthen ties to others? Let's be clear: There is no special dialect or vocabulary required to talk to God. Every follower of Jesus has bold access to God because Jesus provided it through his death, resurrection, and exaltation (Heb. 4:14–16). Eloquence is unnecessary. Although Jesus teaches his disciples a model prayer (Matt. 6:9–11), it serves as a starting point for prayer, not the final word on what a believer can or cannot say.

Likewise, Paul's epistolary prayers provide a model. He records his talks with God as a form of encouragement to his readers. When we talk to God about others, we should not feel shy to tell others about it. We can let others know *that* we prayed and *what* we prayed. Telling someone we prayed for their self-control, for example, may lead to her redoubled effort in exercising self-control. Empathy and encouragement are outgrowths of prayers made public.

Talking to God about others is one form of prayer called "intercession." These prayers build a three-way tie between God, the praying person, and beneficiary of prayer. People will

---

4   Paul often blends divine sovereignty with human responsibility in this letter. God energizes us, but we work out our salvation (2:12–13). God provides, but we deem his provision "good enough" (4:11–13).

often request intercessory prayer when facing a crisis, decision, or difficult circumstance. When we talk to God about others we acknowledge God has the power to act where we are limited. This is not only true in crises but also in character growth. He is ultimately responsible for making us like Jesus.

Is it true?

Is it true that talking to God strengthens our ties with others? Does prayer really change relationships and improve others' circumstances? It is true that God uses prayer to make changes. He changes people's situations and their attitudes. He grants wisdom and gives daily bread. He heals relational wounds and provides timely answers. He certainly uses prayer in spiritual growth, but character formation is slow and fitful. At any point, prayers may seem ignored and development delayed. We must take a long-term view of character development.

C. S. Lewis provides a caution against short-term views of others' character in his classic, *Mere Christianity* (1996, 177–84). Not knowing a person's present struggles or personal background, we are not able to judge fairly. Nor do we know how much worse off someone might be without God's gradual transformation.

Measuring either increases in character formation or relational connectedness is tricky business. We cannot chart increases of love and discernment like a child's height (or aging man's waist). However, relationships with others do strengthen over time if we faithfully talk to God about them. Character does develop over time if we make it a matter of ongoing conversation with God. If patience and perseverance undergird our prayers, the three-way bond between us, God, and fellow Christ-followers is sure to strengthen.

Now what?

Is Paul's prayer for the Philippians the final word on spiritual growth? Are we expected to publicize all our intercessory prayers? The invitation to pray is open to all believers; theological depth is not a prerequisite. However, Paul sets an example by bringing the Philippians into his thoughtful, theological, growth-focused conversation with God.

When our understanding of God's work in others matures, the content of our prayers for them shifts. Rather than asking God to grant them general blessings and soothe their passing cares, we should petition him to magnify the fruit of the Spirit in their lives. Then our conversations with God should spill into communication with others. Sadly, we are often quicker to give advice to a friend than to talk to God about her needs. Bonhoeffer is adamant about the order: we should talk to God about others before we talk to others about God. He writes (1954, 36), "[S]piritual love will speak to Christ about a brother more than to a brother about Christ."

Finally, we must show caution: Prayer is a sensitive topic, and many people rate themselves poor in prayer. The least helpful thing to do is offer Paul's prayer as a shaming device. Marketing and social media keep most people on the lesser side of comparisons all day long. Paul's conversation with God should inspire us to pray, not simply expose our miserable petitions.

Creativity in Presentation

Consider illustrating the power intercession with a humorous skit.

Lead Character: A person opens prayer for several people.

The Interceder: Someone in the group agrees to pray for each person's request.

The Group: Each person in the group presents a request with a look of concern on their face.

The Interceder: As a request is made, the "interceder" bows his head, nods, grunts, and sighs, but utters no words but "Amen." The response is always a polite but confused "Thank You."

Lead Character: A person offers a closing prayer—something to the effect of: "Father, I am glad we can talk to you and use words. And

I pray you will help this man learn to use his. Amen."

The parental bedtime prayer is somewhat equivalent to Paul's epistolary one. A typical bedtime prayer from a mother and father not only begs God for his protection in the night watches, but also asks him to turn his little girl into a godly woman. The child who daily hears his parents' prayer for honesty is primed for honesty. A request to several parents for a sample bedtime prayer to read during the service could have dramatic effect. Consider asking them to explain how praying for their children strengthens their affection for them.

Personal testimonies of intercessory prayers help reinforce the homiletical idea. I attended a wedding where both maternal grandmothers had talked with God for decades about their grandchildren, asking for purity and wisdom in choosing a spouse. These women glowed with affection for their grandkids. I heard an elderly woman from my church tell a mother she daily asked God to restore the younger woman's prodigal son. The other woman immediately teared up. Hospital rooms often showcase prayers of recovery and encouragement for patients in the form of cards. Consider finding an example or two of people in your church recently covered in prayer and letting them share how God used the affirmation to uphold their spirit.

Finally, a printed or downloadable prayer card could help people adapt Paul's words as they talk to God during the week. The card could remind people to pray specifically for the spiritual growth of a few, fellow Christ-followers. In fact, closing the sermon with a few minutes to group people together to pray could illustrate the power of Paul's prayer and strengthen ties among fellow Christ-followers.

> **Pauline Prayers for a Prayer Guide**: The following list of Pauline prayers is not exhaustive, but illustrates the common themes in Pauline prayers: Romans 15:13, 30–33; Galatians 6:18; Ephesians 1:17–21; 3:14–21; Colossians 1:9–12; 1 Thessalonians 3:11–13; 2 Thessalonians 3:16; Philemon 4–7.
>
> In addition to occasional requests for boldness and deliverance, Paul regularly asks God to increase love, knowledge, and faith for his readers. In other words, Christian spiritual maturity and character formation head his list of intercessions.

The point to stress is this: Paul showed how to pray for growth in spiritual maturity while looking forward to Christ's return. Talking to God strengthens our ties to others.

- Talk with God about others' growth (1:9–10a).

- Talk with God about his glory (1:10b–11).

DISCUSSION QUESTIONS

1. How do you let others know that you have prayed for them? When was the last time someone told you that, and what they prayed for you?

2. How does God use prayer to improve your relationship with other believers? Who are people you pray with regularly? Who would you like to pray with more?

3. What does it mean practically for Christian love to be discerning? Can you give some examples of discerning love?

4. What things are prevalent in culture that believers should approve or disapprove? How does spiritual discernment enable us to know what to love or what not to love?

5. Where do you gain spiritual discernment? How can you increase in spiritual discernment?

6. What specific examples of moral purity do you see in the church? What are examples moral impurity or areas in which believers need improvement?

FOR FURTHER READING

Butler, P. 2006. *Well Connected: Releasing Power, Restoring Hope through Kingdom Partnerships*. Colorado Springs: Authentic.

Carson, D. A. 2014. *Praying with Paul: A Call to Spiritual Reformation*. 2nd ed. Grand Rapids: Baker Academic.

Steindl-Rast, D. 1984. *Gratefulness, The Heart of Prayer: An Approach to Life in Fullness*. Ramsey, NJ: Paulist.

Sweney, C. 2011. *A New Kind of Big: How Churches of Any Size Can Partner to Transform Communities*. Grand Rapids: Baker Books.

A CHRIST-CENTERED VIEW OF CIRCUMSTANCES AND LIFE (1:12–26)

After his opening greetings, thanksgiving, and prayer report (1:1–11), Paul gave a brief report on how things were with him in prison. He reassured the Philippians that the gospel was advancing *through* his imprisonment, despite the impure motives of some of the preachers in Rome (who opposed him personally), and he rejoiced that the gospel was being preached (1:18b–26). Then he spoke about his future prospects, contemplating the possible outcomes of his upcoming trial. He could be condemned and executed or he could be acquitted and released. And he was okay with either. He was willing to die and be with Christ or to continue in ministry, so long as Christ is exalted in his body (1:18b–26). In all, Paul modeled for the Philippians a Christ-centered view of circumstances and life as he thought of his present imprisonment and what the future may bring. His passion for Christ and the gospel take center stage in his report.

This major section, A Christ-Centered View of Circumstances and Life (1:12–26), is broken into two preaching units: Viewing Every Circumstance as an Opportunity for Proclaiming the Gospel (1:12–18a) and A Christ-Centered View of Life and Death (1:18b–26).

Philippians 1:12–18a

EXEGETICAL IDEA
Paul encouraged the Philippians that his imprisonment had become an opportunity for proclaiming Jesus, and that despite the impure motives of some preachers, he rejoiced that the gospel was being preached.

THEOLOGICAL FOCUS
Hardships in life are opportunities for proclaiming Jesus.

PREACHING IDEA
Roadblocks open new routes to see God at work.

PREACHING POINTERS
When Paul shifted from introduction to present circumstances, he immediately diffused any notion of disappointment. The movement from prayer to imprisonment rings with joy. The exegetical section not only provides historic details of his house arrest and "captive audience" with Caesar's guard, but also the advances in gospel proclamation, even by poorly motivated preachers. Anticipating the concern of his original audience, Paul assured them of a positive outlook based upon God's ongoing work. Their challenge was looking beyond roadblocks to find joy in God's work in the face of current difficulties.

The tendency to fixate on challenging circumstances remains today. We become pathologically near-sighted. Every accident, misfortune, closed door, and unexpected expense can spark panic or stir disappointment. Our gut reaction to setbacks rarely includes rejoicing; more often we respond with doubt, questions, anger, or disbelief. Consider the last time you were caught driving in a construction zone: Were you more prone to praise or road rage? And in the weightier matters of life—college and career, marriage and family, financial and physical well-being—roadblocks abound, so the reminder that God has not stopped working is even more critical to believe. This passage directs our eyes to the new routes God opens when we face roadblocks.

VIEWING EVERY CIRCUMSTANCE AS AN OPPORTUNITY FOR PROCLAIMING THE GOSPEL (1:12–18a)

LITERARY STRUCTURE AND THEMES (1:12–18a)

This section consists of two parts. First, Paul asserted that his imprisonment, perhaps contrary to their expectation, had actually served to advance the gospel in Rome (1:12). This had resulted in (1) the whole praetorium guard and other imperial servants now knowing that he was a prisoner because of his faith in Christ; and (2) most of the believers in Rome now emboldened to preach the gospel without fear (1:13–14). Second, Paul elaborated on the motives of those preaching: Some of the believers preached Christ out of envy and rivalry toward him. But others preached from an attitude of good will and love toward him (1:15–17). Either way, Paul rejoiced that Christ was being proclaimed (1:18a).

The Proclamation about Jesus Continues (1:12–14)
Motives for Preaching (1:15–18a)

EXPOSITION (1:12–18a)

Paul reported on his circumstances. His report focuses on the advance of the gospel rather than his personal inconveniences or suffering. He gave no details on how he was arrested, how he was being treated, or what his needs were. Since he was consumed with the gospel of Christ, his personal report—how it was going with him—was about this.

Paul encouraged the Philippians by letting them know that the proclamation of Jesus was actually advancing *through* his imprisonment.

Even if some were preaching out of envy and rivalry (toward him), he rejoiced that the gospel was advancing. With this outlook Paul provided an example for his readers in their circumstances. They were experiencing some of the same struggles he was (1:30), and he was modeling the proper response. Every circumstance in life—including hardships—was an opportunity for the gospel to advance.

The Proclamation about Jesus Continues (1:12–14)

Paul encouraged the Philippians by explaining how his imprisonment had become an opportunity for proclaiming Jesus.

> *1:12.* The generic ἀδελφοί is rendered "brothers" (ESV, CSB), "brethren" (NASB, KJV, NKJV) or "brothers and sisters" (NIV, NLT). "Beloved" (NRSV) is less appropriate. The adverb μᾶλλον, as in 1:9, 23; 3:4, can mean *more* in the sense of "to a greater or higher degree" (NASB "greater progress"). Or it can mark an alternative to something, meaning *rather*—"instead" (KJV), "really" (ESV), "actually" (NIV, NRSV, CSB, NKJV).

1:12. Paul began his report by asserting that his imprisonment, rather than hindering the spread of the message about Jesus, had actually provided an opportunity for spreading it. This had resulted in two outcomes. (1) The message had spread throughout the imperial guard and to others in the emperor's service that he was imprisoned because of his commitment to Christ. (2) The believers in Rome had begun to share the message more boldly because of his imprisonment.

He opened by expressing his desire. "I want" (BDAG s.v. "βούλομαι" 2aδ, p. 182) you "to know" (γινώσκειν, BDAG s.v. "γινώσκω" 6c, p. 200) highlights what Paul was about to report. While he used the masculine plural "brothers" (ἀδελφοί, also in 1:14; 3:1, 13, 17; 4:1, 8, 21), he meant "brothers and sisters" (all the believers in the church), for in 4:1–2, he again used "brothers," then proceeded to address two women. In the ancient world, kinship based on the same paternal line formed the tightest bond among same-generation relationships (Hellerman, 2015, 41). So his use of "brothers and sisters" for believers reflected their very close relationship in Christ. In addition, the family metaphor reflects an important theological reality: since we have been "adopted" through Christ (Eph. 1:5) and are all "sons of God through faith" in him (Gal. 3:26), we are now spiritual "brothers and sisters" to one another (cf. Mark 3:31–35).

Paul reported on his situation ("my circumstances/what has happened to me" [τὰ κατ᾽ ἐμέ], lit., "the things concerning me"). The same phrase occurs in two other Prison Epistles (Eph. 6:21 and Col. 4:7). Paul was referring in a general way to the circumstances of his imprisonment.[1] He wanted them to realize that what had happened to him had actually (μᾶλλον can denote degree, "more," or in this context, a comparative sense, "rather," *EDNT* 2: 382) turned out for the advancement of the message about Jesus. This is the opposite of what they would have expected. They may have thought that Paul's imprisonment was a serious setback in his ministry. But he reassured them that rather than proving a hindrance, his imprisonment had resulted in the gospel's "advance" (προκοπήν, BDAG s.v. "προκοπή," p. 871). By "advance of the gospel," Paul was referring to the spread of the message about Jesus through evangelism, as 1:13–18 will make clear. He reframed the circumstances of his imprisonment so that the readers would gain a new perspective. What men intend for evil, God sovereignly intends for good. Hardships in life are opportunities for proclaiming Jesus.

Paul's Circumstances in His Imprisonment: There were several types of incarceration in the Roman world, ranging from severe, dungeon-like conditions to light confinement in a barracks or house. More serious crimes generally resulted in more severe incarceration. In general, Roman citizens (like Paul) fared better than noncitizens, and the wealthy fared better than the poor. Imprisonment without chains was usually a concession to high status. Paul's first imprisonment in Rome (Acts 28:16–31) was of the lighter kind. He was able to rent his own apartment, a privilege available only to a few. Since food provided by officials was enough barely to survive, he likely ate food brought to him by friends on the outside. Though perhaps chained to a guard, Paul was able to read and to entertain visitors and openly preach Jesus and expound the Scriptures (Rapske, 1994, 227–42; *DNTB*, 827–30).

1:13. Δεσμούς is rendered "chains" (NIV, NLT, NKJV) or "imprisonment" (ESV, NRSV, CSB, NASB). The Greek word order is awkward (τοὺς δεσμούς μου φανεροὺς ἐν Χριστῷ γενέσθαι, "my imprisonment evident in Christ has become"). "In Christ" (ἐν Χριστῷ) may connect grammatically with the subject (δεσμούς)—"my imprisonment in Christ has become evident," (NASB, KJV), or with the predicate (φανεροὺς γενέσθαι)—"it has become evident that my imprisonment is in (or for) Christ" (NIV, ESV, NRSV, CSB, NLT, NKJV).

Πραιτωρίῳ is rendered "praetorian guard" (NASB), "palace guard" (NIV, NLT, NKJV), or "imperial guard" (ESV, NRSV, CSB).

---

1   On the basis of the similar phrase in the Greek text of Acts 22:4; 25:14, which clearly refers to Paul's legal matters, Turner suggests that the phrase here refers to Paul's case in the courts (MHT 3:15).

1:13. Paul explained a first result (ὥστε) of his imprisonment. It had become "evident" (φανερούς) or "visible," "plainly to be seen," "clear" (BDAG s.v. "φανερός," 1, p. 1048) to those aware of his case that he was a prisoner, not because of criminal activity or politics, but because he was a follower of Christ. His imprisonment was the result of "his Christian faith and missionary activities" (Hellerman, 2015, 44).

He stated the extent to which his imprisonment for the cause of Christ had become evident: "throughout the whole praetorium and to all the rest" (ἐν ὅλῳ τῷ πραιτωρίῳ καὶ τοῖς λοιποῖς πᾶσιν). The "praetorium" (πραιτωρίῳ) refers to Caesar's elite personal guard. During Paul's house arrest in Rome (Acts 28:16–31), imperial guards would have rotated every four hours. Paul would have been able to explain repeatedly why he was in prison, the nature of the charges against him, and why he was a follower of Christ. It was a golden opportunity for witnessing to a "captive audience." Paul could reinterpret his imprisonment for every guard he encountered. He could let them know that while he might be "in chains," more importantly he was "in Christ." Gradually the reason for Paul's imprisonment would have become known throughout the elite troops. His imprisonment was evidence of the change that Christ had brought about in his life—now he was a slave and prisoner of Christ (Bockmuehl, 1998, 75).

The "whole" (ὅλῳ) praetorium does not necessarily mean that every individual soldier had heard Paul's story. But it had spread widely throughout the guard as a whole. "All the rest" (λοιποῖς πᾶσιν) likely refers to those imperial officials and others who were familiar with Paul's case, but who were not soldiers of the praetorium guard. All who had heard of Paul, the prisoner, had heard that he was in prison because he was a follower of Christ. What an opportunity for the gospel to go forward among some of the most powerful people in the empire! Houlden comments: "In getting himself put in prison, and in Rome above all,

he has acted the Trojan horse, entering into the very heart of the Gentile world to which Christ had dispatched him as an apostle" (1977, 58).

While Paul did not try to get himself arrested, he did appreciate the good that had resulted. He did not speak here of conversions to Christ among the guard. Whether any of them became believers we do not know. But he will reveal at the end of the letter that some in the service of Caesar were believers, for he sent greetings from the "saints" in "Caesar's household" (4:22). It is possible that some or all of these "saints" became believers as a result of Paul's imprisonment. At any rate, he wanted his readers to understand how this obstruction in his life had turned out to serve God's purpose. They should be encouraged. Paul was able to look at his imprisonment this way because he focused on Christ above all else in every circumstance. In the same way, he wanted his readers to look at the trials in their lives as opportunities for the message about Jesus to go forward and for God to receive glory.

Praetorium: Assuming that Paul was writing from Rome, "praetorium" refers to Caesar's elite guard, consisting in Paul's day of about 9,000 soldiers. Originally the term referred to a *location*, to a general's tent or a camp headquarters. Later, it was used of a governor's palace (Matt. 27:27; Mark 15:16; John 18:28, 33; 19:9; Acts 23:35). By Paul's day, it commonly referred to Caesar's personal troops and bodyguards (*DNTB*, 995). Because it is parallel to the later phrase "and to all the rest," Paul was referring to people, not a place (Lightfoot, 1953, 99–104). Cohick describes this elite guard as the "Secret Service and Navy Seals rolled into one" (2013, 45).

1:14. Ἐν κυρίῳ is connected with the preceding ἀδελφοι, "brothers in the Lord" (CSB, KJV, NKJV), or the following participle πεποιθότας, "have become confident in the Lord" (NIV, ESV, NRSV, NASB). Δεσμοῖς may be a dative of cause, "have become confident because of my imprisonment/chains" (NIV, NLT, NASB), or of means, "have become confident *through* my imprisonment/chains" (ESV, NRSV, KJV, NKJV). Τόν λόγον is rendered "the word" (ESV, NRSV, NASB, KJV, NKJV), "the gospel" (NIV), or "the message" (CSB, NLT).

1:14. Paul explained a second result (καί) of his imprisonment and how it had served to advance the gospel in Rome. It had emboldened most of the brothers (and sisters, see 1:12) to speak the word fearlessly. "Most of the brothers" (τοὺς πλείονας τῶν ἀδελφῶν) refers to the church as a whole. "The word" (τὸν λόγον) refers to the message about Jesus, as Paul will make clear in 1:15–17 with the phrases "preach/proclaim Christ." The majority of believers had been stirred up to bold witness as a result of Paul's imprisonment.

The reason why the majority spoke the gospel fearlessly is because they "have become confident" (BDAG s.v. "πείθω" 2a p. 792, causal participle) "in the Lord" (ἐν κυρίῳ). Christ and his work in their lives was the source of these brothers' confidence.

The immediate cause or means by which they had become confident in the Lord was through Paul's "imprisonment" (τοῖς δεσμοῖς, dative of cause [NIV, NLT, NASB] or means [ESV, NRSV, KJV, NKJV]). Paul did not suggest that they lacked bold witness before his imprisonment (Hellerman, 2015, 46), but now they dared "all the more" (περισσοτέρως) to speak "without fear" or "without a cause to be afraid" (BDAG s.v. "φόβως," p. 15). "Dare" (τολμᾶν, "to have courage, be brave enough," BDAG, s.v. "τολμᾶν" α, p. 1010) suggests that preaching Christ was dangerous in Rome. Fee notes that "this probably reflects the historical situation in Rome in the early 60s, when Nero's madness was peaking and the church there had begun to fall under suspicion, as Nero's pogrom against

them just a couple of years later bears witness" (1995, 116). Fearless witness on the part of Paul had ignited passion for fearless witnessing in the hearts of others. This has often been the case in church history. When the threat increases, the Lord stirs up the hearts of his people so that along with the threat, there is an increase in bold proclamation of Christ.

Motives for Preaching (1:15–18a)

Paul elaborated on those in Rome who were boldly preaching: while some were preaching with ill will toward him, and others with good will, in both cases, he rejoiced that the message about Christ was proclaimed.

1:15. Paul elaborated ("some indeed," τινὲς μὲν καί) on the second result of his imprisonment, that it had served to advance the gospel in Rome so that most of the brothers dared to speak the word fearlessly. He identified two groups of believers who were proclaiming Christ. Both are part of the "brothers." "They preach" Christ (BDAG s.v. "κηρύσσω" 2bβ, 543). To "preach Christ" is to preach the good news about Christ. What distinguished the two groups was not their gospel, but their motives toward Paul.

Those of the first group ["some" (τινὲς μέν)] preached "out of envy and rivalry" (διὰ φθόνον καὶ ἔριν).[2] "Envy" (φθόνον) expresses the resentment one feels from not having the advantages another enjoys (BDAG s.v. "φθόνος," p. 1054; *NIDNTTE* 4:602). "Rivalry"(ἔριν) denotes engagement in strife, discord, and contention (BDAG "ἔρις," p. 392). Paul did not state why they resented him. Since he had not founded the church at Rome, perhaps they followed a different leader and considered Paul a rival (Bruce, 1983, 43). Perhaps they saw Paul as an intruder on their territory (Hellerman, 2015, 48) or as a threat to their power base (Flemming,

---

2 In both occurrences in this verse, διά with the accusative indicates the (motivating) cause of the preaching (BDAG s.v. "διά" B2a p. 225).

2009, 69). This would not be the first or last time that fellow members of the one body of Christ created factions based on personalities (compare the situation reflected in 1 Corinthians 1:12). Hellerman notes, "Envy was a common theme in an honor culture in which males vigorously competed with one another for acclaim in the public arena" (2015, 47). Whatever their reason, the first group resented Paul.

Those of the second group ["others" (τινὲς δέ)] preached Christ out of "good will." By this Paul meant their goodwill toward himself (BDAG s.v. "εὐδοκία" 1, p. 404). They considered him not a rival, but a friend.

1:16. NIV, ESV, NRSV, CSB, NLT, and NASB begin with a description of those favorable toward Paul, the last group mentioned in 1:15 ("the latter out of love"). This follows the earlier Greek manuscripts and the NA28/UBS5 text, creating a chiastic AB/BA pattern in 1:15–17. KJV and NKJV, following later manuscripts reflecting the Majority Text, refer first to the first group mentioned in 1:15, "the former . . . from selfish ambition" (AB/AB pattern). We will follow the NA28/UBS5 text.

1:16. Paul continued to elaborate, by contrasting the attitudes of the two groups of preachers identified in 1:15. First, he described the last group mentioned (we will call them the "good preachers"). Then in 1:17, he will describe the first group from 1:15 (the "bad preachers"). The result is a literary device (chiasmus) containing an AB/BA pattern:

A   bad preachers (1:15a)
    B   good preachers (1:15b)
    B' good preachers (1:16)
A' bad preachers (1:17)

The chiasm serves to highlight A, the bad preachers' motives (Fee, 1995, 118–19).

The good preachers (οἱ μέν) preached Christ "out of love" (ἐξ ἀγάπης). Their motive included their love for Paul, as the contrast with 1:17 ("thinking to cause affliction in my imprisonment") makes clear. But the object of "love" may be broader, including also love for God, for the lost, for the world, and for the gospel (Harmon, 2015, 123–24). The reason that they preached out of love is because they "knew" (εἰδότες, causal participle) he was "appointed for the defense of the gospel." "Appointed" or "destined" (BDAG s.v. "κεῖμαι" 3, p. 537) refers to God's sovereign appointment of Paul. Specifically, God put his apostle in this place at this time in order to present the gospel to the highest levels of society. The good preachers understood that the gospel was on trial, and Paul had been appointed by God to present an oral "defense" (ἀπολογίαν) of it, in this case, before Caesar (BDAG s.v. "ἀπολογία" 2b, p. 117). And while he was on the inside, they wanted to do their part by preaching on the outside.

1:17. Ἐριθείας is rendered "selfish ambition" (NIV, NRSV, NLT, NASB) or "rivalry" (ESV, CSB), while ἀγνῶς is rendered "sincerely" (NIV, ESV, NRSV, CSB) or "pure motives" (NLT, NASB). θλῖψιν ἐγείρειν is rendered "stir up/cause trouble" (NIV, CSB), "afflict" (ESV), "increase suffering" (NRSV), "make chains more painful" (NLT), or "cause distress" (NASB).[3]

1:17. In contrast (οἱ δέ) to the good preachers who loved Paul, the bad preachers, mentioned first in 1:15, "proclaimed" (καταγγέλλουσιν) Christ "out of selfish ambition, not from pure motives." The change of verb from "preach" (κηρύσσουσιν) in 1:15 to "proclaim" (both here and in 1:18) is purely stylistic; no difference in meaning is intended. "Selfish ambition" or "self-interest" (ἐριθείας) refers to conduct determined by selfishness (BDAG s.v. "ἐριθείας," p.

---

3 KJV and NKJV (1:16) have "add affliction," which follows D2 K Ψ 𝔐 in reading a different verb, "to bring upon, inflict" (ἐπιφέρειν).

392; *EDNT* 2:52). It suggests the bad preachers' desire to exalt themselves and their ministry at the expense of Paul (thus "rivalry" in ESV, CSB). In 2:3 Paul will exhort the Philippians to do nothing out of "selfish ambition" (ἐριθείαν).

Paul stated that they did not preach from "pure motives" (BDAG s.v. "ἀγνῶς," p. 14). If they were preaching Christ with pure motives, their only concern would be to see people accept the gospel and to see Christ exalted. Instead, they also wanted to exalt themselves and further their own reputations at the expense of Paul. Their personal envy and rivalry with him contaminated their motives in preaching. Envy, rivalry, and selfish ambition existed in the first-century church, as it unfortunately still does today.

These bad preachers were "thinking" (οἰόμενοι with a component of tentativeness), that they would cause Paul distress in his imprisonment (BDAG s.v. "οἴομαι," p. 701). He did not specify what type of "distress" (θλῖψιν, BDAG s.v. "θλῖψις" 1, p. 457). It could be physical, emotional, or both. They may have thought their preaching the gospel would cause him to suffer harsher treatment in his imprisonment, or cause Caesar to look unfavorably on Paul at his trial (Winter, 1994, 93–95), or that they could antagonize him by furthering their own ministry and influence while he was stuck in jail. They may have seen this as their time to shine, now that Paul was out of the way (Hansen, 2009, 74). Whatever their exact intent, they clearly were

envious and wanted to build themselves up while adding to Paul's frustration as he heard of their activity and success.

Their "tentative thinking" (οἰόμενοι) contrasts with the good preachers' "knowing" (εἰδότες) in 1:16. Those who loved Paul *knew* he was appointed for the defense of the gospel. They correctly interpreted his imprisonment. Their understanding was accurate and sure. But these only *thought* (imagined) that they would be able to cause Paul distress by their preaching. They failed to understand that Paul was encouraged because he saw God's sovereign purpose being fulfilled through his imprisonment. Paul would not allow their efforts to get to him. On the contrary, he rejoiced that they were preaching the gospel!

1:18a. Paul concluded with a rhetorical question: "What then" (τί γάρ) or "What does it matter" (BDAG, §299 [3]; BDAG s.v. "τί" 1aβ, p. 1007). His question introduced a conclusion to his description of the situation. "Only that" (πλὴν ὅτι) drives home a single point: Those thinking they would cause him distress failed, for he *rejoiced* that Christ was proclaimed. His joy was due to the fact that the gospel was being preached. "In every way, whether by false motives or true" refers to the different motives of the two groups. Paul could affirm the message of the "bad" preachers even if he could not affirm their motives. "False motives" or "pretense" (πρόφασις) refers to an ostensible,

Good Preachers	Bad Preachers
Boldness through Paul's imprisonment	Boldness through Paul's imprisonment
Preach Christ	Preach Christ
Because of goodwill	Because of envy and rivalry
Out of love	Out of selfish ambition, not sincerely
Know that Paul is appointed	Think they will cause him distress
True motives	False motives
Paul rejoices that the gospel is preached	Paul rejoices that the gospel is preached

*The "Good Preachers" and "Bad Preachers" (Phil. 1:14–18) (Adapted from Thielman, 1995, 61)

but not true, reason (BDAG s.v. "πρόφασις" 2, p. 889). Mark 12:40 applies "false motives" (πρόφασις) to religious hypocrites. The "bad" preachers of 1:17 had false motives because in appearance they desired to magnify Christ, but their hidden motive was to cause Paul distress. "True motives" (ἀλήθεια) are those whose appearance agrees with reality (BDAG s.v. "αλήθεια" 3, p. 42). There was no pretense in the "good" preachers. They loved Paul and preached Christ sincerely as they stood with him in his imprisonment.

Paul chose to "rejoice" (χαίρω) or "to be in a state of happiness and well-being" even when others were out to harm him (BDAG s.v. "χαίρω" 1, p. 1074). Christ and the gospel matter! This is the first of eight occurrences of the important verb "rejoice" in Philippians (1:18; 2:17, 18, 28; 3:1; 4:4[2x], 10). Paul demonstrated that joy is an attitude believers can choose. As long as Christ is being proclaimed, Paul would not allow the impure motives of some of the preachers rob him of joy. This does not suggest that the animosity of others did not hurt. Rather, Paul was able to count personal attacks against him as less important than the progress of the gospel. In this, Paul set an example for the Philippians. He yielded his "right" to be treated with respect and willingly participated in the sufferings of Christ. He refused to dwell on how others had hurt him in order to focus on the greater good being achieved. The gospel was advancing and this was what really mattered (1:10). Paul's example challenges all believers to respond to "opponents" similarly.

THEOLOGICAL FOCUS

The exegetical idea (Paul encouraged the Philippians that his imprisonment had become an opportunity for proclaiming Jesus, despite the impure motives of some preachers, and he rejoiced that the gospel was being preached) leads to this theological focus: Hardships in life are opportunities for proclaiming Jesus.

This passage is about how we choose to view our circumstances—especially those that are physically or emotionally unpleasant. We must learn to view every negative circumstance in life not as an obstacle, but as an opportunity for the gospel about Jesus to advance. As believers, we must choose to reframe how we view our situation. Thielman states: "When difficult, even life-threatening, circumstances face us, we should take Paul as our example and look for how God might be working in such circumstances to advance the gospel either in our own lives or in the lives of others" (1995, 64).

When we learn to look at every circumstance as an opportunity for proclaiming the message about Jesus, we have a new way to deal with adversity. We can demonstrate the reality of the gospel through our rejoicing in the midst of suffering. We can show others how God accomplishes his purposes, not in spite of suffering, but through suffering. We can speak of his sovereignty and love. Every difficulty or challenge in life is a divine opportunity to speak of God's goodness and to proclaim Christ.

PREACHING AND TEACHING STRATEGIES

Exegetical and Theological Synthesis

Paul made it plain and clear: Imprisonment has neither stopped God from advancing the gospel nor stolen his joy. He could maintain his confidence because he had witnessed God change the lives of Caesar's guards, as well as embolden other followers of Jesus in Rome. Paul even saw through the poorly motivated preachers who tried to exploit his chains for their selfish aims. Paul did not write to support evangelistic pragmatism—*Anything goes as long as Christ is preached*—but to model a healthy, Christlike attitude in adversity for the Philippians to mimic.

Of course, Paul was no wide-eyed optimist. His positive outlook was an outgrowth of prayer (1:9–11), personal struggle (1:18b–26), and meditations on Christ Jesus (2:5–11). Moreover, Paul accepted God's providence in his imprisonment with clear evidence. He watched God transform lives up close in Caesar's household. He heard of God transforming lives abroad. That God opens new routes through roadblocks is an embodied experience, not a hollow slogan.

Adverse circumstances invite a reality check. They allow us to assess our attitude, long-term focus, and view of God. Paul's circumstances may not directly parallel problems in our congregations, but his mindset in adversity applies today. To Paul, God was the central character; the advance of the gospel, his primary goal. A theocentric-view of life keeps disappointment from impeding our faith journey. God still speaks and works in spite of our roadblocks.

Preaching Idea
Roadblocks lead to new routes to see God at work.

Contemporary Connections

What does it mean?
A roadblock metaphorically stands for any situation, circumstance, or object that slows us down or sets us back in our service for God. We may not all be preachers like Paul, but we proclaim Jesus in our parenting, as loving neighbors, through our integrity at work, or as faithful friends. Impediments to personal ministry, likewise, come in all shapes and situations: a sudden change of address, loss of job, medical issue, federal law, religious persecution, or death of a loved one.

Roadblocks may appear to interrupt God's work in his people. Legal changes may hurt a Christian daycare's funding. A major home repair may threaten a family's plan for short-term missions. A wrecked knee may sidetrack a student athlete from a career in sports. However, none of these roadblocks impedes God. He is not restricted to a single path for financing and faithfully proclaiming Christ Jesus. Although

his timing in revealing new routes to us may stretch our patience, we must not count his slowness as absence.

Is it true?
Is it true that roadblocks lead to new routes to see God at work? Certainly, this truth is verified in Scripture, history, and personal experience. Persecution in Jerusalem spread the gospel to broader regions (Acts 8:1). Paul's first encounter with the Philippians resulted from a closed door in Asia Minor (16:7). His audience with Caesar followed an imprisonment in Jerusalem (25:12). Oppression from state churches in Europe led to early migration to North America. The underground church in Asia expands despite political barriers. And, on a personal level, my wife's two grueling labors prompted us to pursue international adoption for our third child.

Philippians provides one more illustration of God's redemptive use of suffering. Exodus and exile bookend the Hebrew Scriptures. Jesus embodied the Suffering Servant (Mark 10:45). Paul later warned his Philippian readers of the inevitability of suffering (1:28), experienced in his and Epaphroditus's service (2:27). In God's economy, however, suffering often precedes vindication and exaltation (e.g., Rom. 8:28–30; 2 Cor. 4:17; Phil. 2:5–11). New routes and fresh starts do not always manifest immediately, but God's sovereign hand eventually surfaces.

Now what?
Should we seek out roadblocks, hardships, and suffering? Should we be suspicious when life goes smoothly, expecting disaster to strike at any moment? Of course not. We are not called to live as masochists or cynics but to maintain trust in God's work, even if life turns sour.

We encounter bad circumstances often enough without having to seek them out as a badge of our faithfulness. In a pluralistic world, professors antagonize students who confess faith in Jesus, coaches show fewer leniencies to athletes with moral convictions, and colleagues dismiss followers of Christ for their conservative views. And not all roadblocks are personal attacks. Active church members lose loved ones, face bankruptcy, and watch their children wreck their lives with substance abuse. These scenarios are all too common.

Paul modeled a healthy outlook as he faced roadblocks. His trust in God and transforming power of the message about Christ Jesus anchored his joyful attitude. His focus transcended his troubles. If prison walls and rival preachers could not dampen his joy, neither should we let a stalled car or negligent parent dampen ours.

What allows one to stay resilient in the face of roadblocks is veering from a victim mentality to confidence in God's continued work. Identifying ways God continues to transform others—emboldening them, answering their prayers, levering their generosity—shifts our eyes from our personal suffering to his kingdom agenda. Noting former adverse circumstances that God used for growth spurts—a breakup, a layoff, a surgery—builds confidence. And this theological lens not only grants perspective, but also guards us from rushing through roadblocks. New routes take time to develop; patience is advised.

Creativity in Presentation

The illustration for this sermon can begin in the parking lot or church hallways. Orange cones or yellow tape may block traffic from certain entrances and direct people to enter a different way. If the facilities do not allow for much creativity in devising alternative routes, one may procure a few construction signs to set on the stage. These visual aids will surface the angst virtually every driver feels when encountering roadblocks.

Notable figures in history may serve as case studies of how God opens new routes through roadblocks. Charles Colson's part in the Watergate scandal landed him in prison. While this was a self-imposed roadblock, it certainly opened new routes for ministry through writing, speaking, and advocacy in Prison Fellowship. Comedian Michael Jr. struggled with dyslexia throughout his childhood, but credits the disability for his quick wit, which God has used to reach national audiences. (You can find his story on YouTube, shared from the TEDx Stage in Reno, Nevada.) The roadblock of a broken spine has built a platform for Joni Eareckson Tada to inspire followers of Jesus through writing, painting, and radio broadcast.

On a personal note, I have several friends who experienced major roadblocks. Friends from college battled infertility for years. It kept them from work in international missions, but later resulted in their adopting multiple children. An elder from my church lost a management job and faced unemployment in his mid-fifties. After six months of searching, God landed him in a counseling program, where he earned a graduate degree and started a new, fulfilling vocation. Similar stories abound in any congregation, and a live or recorded "road block" testimony may prove effective.

The sermon should stress this: Hardships in life are opportunities for proclaiming Jesus. Roadblocks lead to new routes to see God at work.

- Roadblocks don't stop Paul and others from preaching (1:12–13).

- Mixed motives don't stop Paul from rejoicing (1:15–18a).

DISCUSSION QUESTIONS

1. How can negative circumstances actually enhance your opportunity for Christian witness? How have you learned to look at circumstances this way?

2. What is the proper biblical attitude toward other Christian denominations or groups with whom you have differences, but who preach the true gospel?

3. When other Christians oppose you, how can you set aside personal feelings and rejoice in (and even pray for) their ministries? How can you get there emotionally?

4. What is the proper biblical attitude toward other Christians who oppose you in various ways—for example, by spreading lies or rumors, holding grudges, undermining your church or ministry?

5. What painful situation has God worked through in your life for good purposes? How long before you saw the good outcome?

6. What is your first response to a roadblock?

Philippians 1:18b–26

EXEGETICAL IDEA
Paul modeled a Christ-centered view of life and death—willing to die and be with Christ, yet confident of release and further ministry, while certain of his ultimate salvation and that Christ's prestige would be advanced through him.

THEOLOGICAL FOCUS
Believers are to exhibit a Christ-centered view of life and death, seeking to advance Christ's prestige in the way they live or die.

PREACHING IDEA
Live fully in the face of death.

PREACHING POINTERS
Paul's imprisonment had created a dilemma: He faced possible execution or acquittal. Either option had potential benefits, and he weighed them out before his original readers. The exegetical section explains this dilemma, including theological clarification on honor/shame, salvation, and personal eschatology. Paul wrote frankly, disclosing his preference for death and being with Jesus, but ultimately yielded to the likelihood of pressing on in ministry. This internal dialogue modeled for the Philippians—who too will face suffering (1:28)—a healthy outlook on mortality and ministry.

Today, we deny death (Becker, 1997). The death sentence hanging over every person is muted by promises of prolonged life. Modern medicine and cosmetic products offer extended life, extended health, and extended beauty. The proliferation of superhero, zombie, and vampire films betray an unwillingness to look death in the eye. Patient-assisted suicide, which will someday be more widespread, tries to ease the sting of dying by granting power to sick people. Sadly, these denials of death prevent it from shaping our priorities. When was the last time you faced your mortality? How does embracing your finitude affect your daily decisions to love, serve, and bring honor to Jesus? This passage encourages us to consider our certain death as motivation to live fully.

A CHRIST-CENTERED VIEW OF LIFE AND DEATH (1:18b–26)

LITERARY STRUCTURE AND THEMES (1:18b–26)

This section consists of five parts. First, Paul asserted that he would continue to rejoice, for he was confident that his imprisonment would result in his final salvation through their prayer and the Spirit enabling him to stand firm in Christ (1:18b–19). Second, the reason for his confidence was because of his expectation that Christ would be exalted in his body—whether through life (acquittal) or death (execution) (1:20). Third, Paul explained why either outcome from his trial—life or death—would exalt Christ: Living meant he would live for Christ and have effective ministry; dying meant he would gain more intimacy with him (1:21–22). Fourth, Paul explained how he was torn between two competing options. Going to be with Christ was far better for him personally, but to remain in ministry was more necessary for the Philippians' spiritual growth (1:23–24). Fifth, because he was convinced of this, Paul knew that he would be acquitted and continue in ministry for their spiritual progress, so that they would exult in Christ when he was released and returned to them (1:25–26).

Joy and a Confident Future (1:18b–19)
Christ Exalted by Life or Death (1:20)
On Living and Dying (1:21–22)
Torn between Living and Dying (1:23–24)
Paul's Confidence in Acquittal and Release (1:25–26)

EXPOSITION (1:18b–26)

Having described the advance of the gospel in Rome (1:12–18a), Paul became more personal. He reflected on what the future may hold. Execution was possible. But whether he was executed or set free, he knew that through their prayers and through the Spirit enabling him to stay true to Christ, both he and his gospel would be finally vindicated. Christ would be glorified. As far as the court date before Caesar, Paul's greater desire was to die and be with Christ. While this seems remarkable, it should be no surprise. If the goal of his life was to know Christ intimately, to die was to gain more intimacy with him. Death was the means for the ultimate goal of his life to be realized. But Paul also knew that he needed to remain in ministry to help his converts grow spiritually. Torn between these two options, he was convinced that he would be released from prison. When he rejoined them, they would have reason to glory in Christ because of his deliverance. Even in this personal reflection, his concern was for the advance of the gospel—specifically with its progress in their spiritual lives.

Confidence in God's Sovereignty: Underlying all that Paul said in this section was his total trust in God's control and care during his imprisonment. He knew that God was for him and was working out the plan for his life. Through this personal reflection, Paul modeled a Christ-centered view of life and death, willing to die and be with Christ or to continue in ministry, so long as Christ was exalted in his body. His intent was not merely to let the Philippians know how he approached life and death, but to show them how they were to think about their lives and deaths as Christians (cf. Wansink, 1996, 112–19).

Joy and a Confident Future (1:18b–19)

Paul will continue to rejoice because he was confident that through the Philippians' prayers for him and the Spirit enabling him to stand firm in Christ, he would receive final salvation.

1:18b–19. Χαρήσομαι is rendered "I will rejoice" (ESV, CSB, NASB, KJV, NKJV) or "I will *continue to* rejoice" (NIV, NRSV, NLT). Σωτηρίαν is rendered "deliverance" (NIV, ESV, NRSV, CSB, NLT, NASB, NKJV), or "salvation" (KJV). In the phrase ἐπιχορηγίας τοῦ πνεύματος, the genitive πνεύματος may be objective, "God's provision of the Spirit" (NIV) or subjective, "help from the Spirit" (CSB, cf. NLT). Some translations are ambiguous—"supply/provision of the Spirit" (NASB, KJV, NKJV). "Help of the Spirit" (ESV, NRSV) reflects a subjective genitive.

1:18b. Paul turned from describing his present rejoicing in the advance of the gospel (1:12–18a) to assert his continued joy as he contemplated what was in store for him. "Yes, and" (ἀλλὰ καί) introduces Paul's point with emphasis (BDF §448 [6]). The context suggests ongoing joy: "I will continue to rejoice" (Hansen, 2009, 77; Hellerman, 2015, 57).

1:19. The reason why (γάρ) he would continue to rejoice is because he knew that this would "turn out for . . . [his] salvation." "I know" (οἶδα) reveals Paul's absolute confidence in God. "This" (τοῦτο) refers back to all of 1:12–18, the progress of the gospel around Paul. "Turn out" (ἀποβήσεται) refers to the resultant state or condition after Paul's trial (BDAG s.v. "ἀποβαίνω," 2, p. 107). Salvation (σωτηρίαν) would be the result no matter the verdict. Though most English versions have "deliverance," suggesting a reference to being set free from prison, Paul likely meant "eternal salvation" or "final vindication" (BDAG s.v. "σωτηρία" 2, p. 985–86) This was how he used the word (σωτηρίαν) every other time it occurred in his letters (including Phil. 1:28; 2:12). Paul was confident that, no matter

the outcome of his appearance before Caesar, God would work out everything for his final salvation and vindication on the last day.

The means (διά) by which God would provide this salvation is "through . . . prayers and the supply of the Spirit of Jesus Christ." The way Paul linked "prayers" and "the supply of the Spirit" (both nouns are joined using one preposition διά and one article τῆς) suggests that they are closely connected. Paul would receive the "supply of the Spirit" in answer to their prayers (Hansen, 2009, 79). This "supply" (ἐπιχορηγίας) "assistance," "support" of the Spirit probably refers to the Spirit's supplying power to Paul, which would enable him to testify boldly during his trial, staying true to Christ and the gospel (BDAG s.v. "ἐπιχορηγία," p. 387). In response to the Philippians' prayers, the Spirit would empower Paul.

Paul referred to the Holy Spirit as "the Spirit of Jesus Christ." This reflects the close association of the Spirit and Christ (cf. Rom. 8:9; Gal. 4:6; 1 Peter 1:11). Christ lives in believers through the presence of the Spirit. Whatever the outcome of his trial, Paul knew that the Holy Spirit, the Spirit of Christ, was with him and would strengthen him in answer to the prayers of the Philippians. The ultimate result would be vindication in God's heavenly court.

Christ Exalted by Life or Death (1:20)

Paul expressed his confident expectation that at his trial the prestige of Christ would be advanced in the world by his bold testifying—either through his successful defense of the gospel and acquittal, or through his staying true to Christ and the gospel unto execution and death.

1:20. Κατά, which connects 1:20 to 1:19, is rendered "according to" (NASB, KJV, NKJV), "as" (ESV), or left untranslated (NIV, NRSV, and CSB). Αἰσχυνθήσομαι is rendered "be ashamed" (NIV, ESV, CSB, NLT, KJV, NKJV) or "put to shame" [disgraced] (NSRV, NASB). Παρρησία is rendered "courage" (NIV, ESV) or "boldness" (NRSV, CSB,

NASB, KJV, NKJV, cf. NLT). Μεγαλυνθήσεται is rendered "will be exalted" (NIV, NRSV, NASB), "will be honored" (ESV, cf. NLT), "highly honored" (CSB), or "will be magnified" (KJV, NKJV). Σώματί μου is rendered "my body" in most translations, but "my life" in NLT ("body" understood as a figure of speech to represent the whole self or life).

1:20. The reason (BDAG s.v. "κατά" 5δ, p. 512) for Paul's confidence ("I know" in 1:19) was "because of [according to] . . . eager expectation and hope." "Eager expectation" (ἀποκαραδοκία) or "confident expectation" or "unreserved waiting" (*TDNT* 1:393) along with "hope" (ἐλπίς) reflect certainty. Paul expressed the highest degree of certainty about the future, a "vehement and unshakable expectation" (Fee, 1995, 135; cf. *EDNT* 1:132). Paul was not guilty of wishful thinking. He possessed an intense, certain expectation of what would surely happen (cf. Thielman, 1995, 77) based on the reality that God sovereignly controls of all history—including the future. He was confident of what the future holds because he trusted in God.

The content (ὅτι) of Paul's eager expectation and hope was "that in no way will I be put to shame, but with all boldness, now as always, Christ will be exalted in my body, whether through life or through death." This contains two contrasting parallel (ἀλλά) statements: a negative statement of what will *not* happen and a positive statement of what *will* happen. Paul would "in no way" (ἐν οὐδενί, denoting manner) "be put to shame" (αἰσχυνθήσομαι) or "disgraced" (BDAG s.v. "αἰσχύνω" 2, 30). The disgrace to which he referred is disgrace *before the Lord* should he fail to stand boldly and proclaim Christ at his trial (cf. Ware, 2005, 204). But he knew that he would not suffer disgrace. Rather, Christ would be exalted in him whether he lived (acquittal and release) or died (execution). He was confident that by God's empowerment, he would testify of Christ faithfully so that his commitment to Christ would be honored and the gospel vindicated. Then ultimately, at the final judgment, he would not experience disgrace due to a failure to testify faithfully at his trial.

Paul knew that "with all boldness, now as always, Christ will be exalted." In this context, "boldness" (παρρησία) refers to Paul's outspoken, plain preaching and testifying of Christ (Eph. 6:19; cf. BDAG s.v. "παρρησία" 2, p. 781; *NIDNTTE* 3:659; Marrow, 1982, 445). He would openly and authoritatively set forth the gospel when he appeared before Caesar. He would "tell it like it is" (Osiek, 2000, 43). Paul knew that God had appointed him and brought him to Rome for this task. With "now as always" (ὡς πάντοτε καὶ νῦν), Paul looked just ahead to his trial. It was the moment for which he had been waiting. The opportunity for bold proclamation was at hand. Throughout his career, Paul had faithfully proclaimed the gospel, and Christ had been magnified. He was confident that the same would be true when he appeared before Caesar.

Jesus, not Paul, is the one who would be exalted. "Will be exalted" (μεγαλυνθήσεται) means that Jesus will be "held in greater esteem." "The prestige of Christ will be advanced" due to Paul's witness (BDAG s.v. "μεγαλύνω" 2, p. 623). Paul switched from the first person ("In no way will I be ashamed") to the third person ("Christ will be exalted"). He did not say, "I will exalt Christ," lest that very confidence exalt himself (Lightfoot, 1953, 91). This reflects Paul's humility. If Christ would to be magnified in Paul, God would be the one who will do it.

Christ would be exalted in Paul's body, whether through life or through death. "In my body" (ἐν τῷ σώματί μου) denotes both the means and location of Christ's exaltation. He would be exalted whatever happened to Paul's body. If Paul was released, Christ would be exalted because Paul was acquitted. If Paul was executed, Christ would be exalted through his faithful witness unto death. Either way, Christ would be magnified. Paul cared more about proclaiming before Caesar that Christ was Lord than he did about whether he personally lived or died.

On Living and Dying (1:21–22)

Paul explained why either outcome from his trial—life or death—would advance Christ's prestige in the world: acquittal meant he would live to serve Christ and engage in effective ministry; dying meant he would gain more intimacy with Christ.

1:21. Paul explained (γάρ) the last part of 1:20, why Christ would be magnified "whether through life or through death." He alternated between the possibilities of life (acquittal) and death (execution) in 1:21–24 (Flemming, 2009, 73):

Life (21a)	To live is Christ
Death (21b)	To die is gain
Life (22a)	If I am to live on in the flesh, this will mean fruitful labor for me
Death (23b)	Having the desire to depart and to be with Christ
Life (24)	But to remain in the flesh is more necessary for your sake

The maxim, "To me to live is Christ and to die is gain," expressed Paul's personal feelings about what living versus dying meant to him. If acquital and release came, he would continue to live for Christ and exalt him. Paul will expand on "to live is Christ" in 3:7–14.

In the possibility of death, he did not say in this verse what the "gain" (κέρδος) was. But in 1:23 he said he desired to depart and to be "with Christ." And later in 3:8, using the related verb, Paul said that he regarded all things to be garbage in order that he

"may gain (κερδήσω) Christ." We may presume then that the "gain" in 1:21 is greater intimacy with Christ (BDAG s.v. "κέρδος," p. 541). If Paul's life on earth consisted of a single-minded pursuit of Christ, then finally to be *with* Christ would mean that he had achieved his goal. Death is not the end but a beginning, a transformation point. "One becomes more after death, not less" (Kraftchick, 2007, 204–5). Death is gain because it means increased intimacy with Christ.

> *1:22*. Σαρκί is rendered "flesh" by most translations, but "body" by NIV. Αἱρήσομαι is rendered "choose" (NIV, ESV, CSB, NASB, KJV, NKJV) or the softer "prefer" (NRSV). Οὐ γνωρίζω is rendered "I do not know" (NIV, NRSV, CSB, NLT, NASB) or "I do not make known" (ESV, NKJV). Syntactically, τί αἱρήσομαι may form a dependent clause modifying γνωρίζω: "And which I shall choose I do not make known" (most English translations). Alternately, it may form an independent clause and be translated as a question followed by an answer: "And which shall I choose? I do not make known" (NIV; BDF § 368; MHT 3:117). Some early manuscripts (𝔓⁴⁶ B 2464) read the aorist subjunctive (αἱρήσωμαι) instead of the future indicative, indicating a deliberative question ("And which should I choose?").

1:22. Paul continued to explain (δέ signals an expansion of 1:21, Hellerman, 2015, 67) how he felt about the possible outcomes of his trial with a conditional (if . . . then) statement. While the prospect of dying and gaining more intimacy with Christ was appealing (1:21b), Paul acknowledged that if (εἰ δέ) he was acquitted and released, this would mean effective ministry for him. "To live in the flesh" (τὸ ζῆν ἐν σαρκί) means that Paul would continue to live in his present physical body. If Paul was acquitted and released, then he would engage in more effective ministry. "Fruitful labor" (καρπὸς ἔργου) or "gain from the labor" (BDAG s.v. "καρπός" 2, p. 510) refers to an extension of his missionary work (Martin and Hawthorne, 2004, 57)—both planting new churches and strengthening believers in existing churches. Paul modeled a positive outlook and willingness to embrace further ministry. If he was writing from Rome, he had been in prison for nearly four years. For him, release led not to retirement, but to continuing his labors for the gospel on the outside. Apostolic ministry had always meant difficulty (1 Cor. 15:30; 2 Cor. 4:8–11; 6:4–10; 11:23–29). But when Paul contemplated further ministry, suffering was not his focus. He focused on the positive results: "fruitful labor"—the spiritual benefit that God would bring to peoples' lives through his ministry (Hansen, 2009, 85).

Yet the Apostle Paul presented a dilemma (hypothetically, as if he had a choice) in order to express his inner struggle ("and which I will choose I cannot make known"). This does not suggest that he actually had a choice in the outcome of his trial. His future (acquittal or execution) would be decided for him. Paul used the verb "choose" (αἱρήσομαι, BDAG s.v. "αἱρεω" 2, p. 28), which was appropriate, for he wanted to set an example of Christlike thinking for the Philippians (Wansink, 1996, 97). As he looked at the situation from the perspective of what he would personally desire (to go to be with Christ) and from the perspective of what was needed in the church (to continue in ministry), a dilemma presented itself.

Paul could not tell which option he would choose. The negated Greek verb (οὐ γνωρίζω) can mean, "I do not know" (BDAG s.v. "γνωρίζω" 2, p. 203) and many English versions translate it that way. But the other seventeen times Paul used this verb, it meant, "to reveal" or "to make known" (BDAG s.v. "γνωρίζω" 1, p. 203), and it is better to stay with Paul's regular meaning here—"I cannot tell" (ESV, NKJV). Paul saw good reasons for choosing either option (expressed in 1:23–24). He could not tell the Philippians which he would pick, perhaps because he knew that his preference (to die and

be with Christ in heaven) conflicted with God's purpose for him (to continue in ministry) (Hellerman, 2015, 68).

Torn between Living and Dying (1:23–24)

Paul felt torn between the possible outcomes of his trial, for personally he thought it best to die and be with Christ in heaven, yet he knew that his acquittal and continued ministry would help them grow as followers of Jesus.

1:23–24. The verb Συνέχομαι is variously rendered "be torn" (NIV, NLT), "be hard pressed" (ESV, NRSV, NASB, NKJV), or "be pressured" (CSB). Some translations (ESV, NRSV, NASB) begin the final clause with "for" (reading γὰρ, found in 𝔓⁴⁶ ℵ 1 A B C 076 6 33 81, regarded genuine by Fee, 1995, 139, n. 1). Others omit "for" and render, "which is far better" (NIV, CSB, NLT, KJV, NKV). Σαρκὶ is rendered "flesh" (ESV, NRSV, CSB, NASB, KJV, NKJV) or "body" (NIV).

1:23. The reason why (explicative δέ, Reumann, 2008, 223) Paul could not tell which he would choose was because he was "hard pressed between the two [choices]." "Hard pressed" or "torn" (συνέχομαι) reflects the pressure Paul felt because of what he desired and what he knew was more necessary (BDAG s.v. "συνέχω" 5, p. 971). The reason (ἔχων, causal participle) he was torn is because he had "the desire to depart and to be with Christ." "Desire" (ἐπιθυμίαν) usually represents sinful desire in the New Testament, but here represents a longing for good things (BDAG s.v. "ἐπιθυμία" 1b, p. 372). To "depart" (ἀναλῦσαι, euphemism for dying) and "be with Christ" was the more appealing option for Paul.

Being "with Christ" was Paul's way of referring to the *intermediate state*—the period of time between a believer's death and the bodily resurrection at the second coming. To be "with" (σὺν) Christ describes the conscious, joyful, ongoing state of *proximity and association with*

(Campbell, 2012, 219, 222–23) the ascended and reigning Christ in heaven that begins immediately after a believer's death (cf. Luke 23:43; BDAG s.v. "σύν" 1aγ, p. 961). Nowhere did Paul offer a detailed description of the intermediate state. He only said it consists of being "with Christ" and being "absent from the (present mortal) body (2 Cor. 5:6, 8)." The reason (γάρ) Paul preferred to die and be with Christ is that it was "much better indeed" (πολλῷ μᾶλλον κρεῖσσον; cf. BDAG s.v. "κρείττων" 2a, p. 566). He would instantly realize the his goal of intimacy with Christ that began at his Damascus Road conversion (Acts 9).

While Paul desired to die and be with Christ, the intermediate state is not the ultimate stage of redemption. He made it clear that believers still wait for Jesus to return (1:6, 10; 2:16) to receive their resurrection bodies (3:20–21). Then "we will always be with (σύν) the Lord" (1 Thess. 4:17). The resurrection at the *parousia* (= coming) was the ultimate stage of redemption for Paul (1 Cor. 15:22–28, 50–57).

1:24. Paul desired to die and be with Christ, "but" (δέ) the other option, to remain, was more necessary for the Philippians' sake. To "remain" (ἐπιμένειν) "in the flesh" (τῇ σαρκὶ) means to stay alive in the present mortal body (BDAG s.v. "ἐπιμένω" 1, p. 375). Paul knew that this was what the Lord had chosen (1:25–26; 2:24). "More necessary" (ἀναγκαιότερον) reflects what God had determined to be necessary for Paul—the advance of the gospel and spiritual growth of his converts. His remaining alive would benefit them spiritually, and this rightly took precedence over his personal preference. Paul explained, "for your sake" (δι' ὑμᾶς) in 1:25 where he speaks of the Philippians' "progress and joy in the faith."

Paul's Confidence in Acquittal and Release (1:25–26)

Because Paul was convinced that the Philippians needed further teaching and encouragement from him to grow spiritually, he knew that he would be acquitted at his trial and released from prison so that when he returned to Philippi, the Philippians would exult and take pride in what Christ had done for him.

> *1:25*. Τῆς πίστεως is rendered objectively, "the [Christian] faith" (NIV, ESV, CSB, NASB) or subjectively, "of [your personal] faith" (NRSV, NLT, KJV, NKJV).

1:25. Because Paul was "convinced" (πεποιθώς, causal participle) of this—that staying alive was more necessary for the Philippians (anaphoric τοῦτο)—he "knew" (οἶδα) that he would "remain and continue with them all." He "knew" he would be acquitted and released (BDAG s.v. "οἶδα" 1e, p. 693). And he willingly "placed his confidence" in God's resolution to his dilemma described in 1:23–24 (BDAG s.v. "ποίθω" 2b, p. 792). His purpose for describing the dilemma had been to express his personal longing and to show his readers how to think about the choice of life or death as followers of Christ. Paul did not say *how* he knew that he would be released. Perhaps their need of his further ministry had simply led him to the conviction that it was God's will to deliver him (Bockmuehl, 1998, 94). Or perhaps he knew this through direct revelation from the Lord.

Paul likely used two verbs "remain" (μενῶ) and "continue with" (παραμενῶ) for emphasis (Silva, 2005, 75). He would continue to partner with them in the ministry of the gospel and encourage them in their walk with Christ. "With you all" (cf. 1:1, 4, 7, 8) once again shows that he was concerned for all of those in the church. If there were divisions, he was not favoring one group over another.

Paul's purpose (εἰς) for continuing with them was for their "progress and joy in the faith." Previously, Paul had used the term "progress" (προκοπήν) in 1:12, where he spoke of the "advance" of the gospel in Rome. Here he was concerned about its advance in the lives of the Philippians. He was thinking of the spiritual growth he wanted to see in their lives (BDAG s.v. "προκοπή," p. 871). For example, Paul wanted them to improve in areas he wrote about: love with knowledge and discernment (1:9–10), standing together without fear (1:27–28), unity and humility (2:1–11), doing all things without grumbling or arguing (2:14), knowing Christ in the power of his resurrection and in his suffering (3:10), keeping focused on the prize of God's upward call (3:12–14), and so on.

Paul's linking of "progress" and "joy" (both are governed by the article τήν and both are modified by the genitives "your" and "of faith") shows that they are connected. Spiritual progress includes experiencing "joy" (BDAG s.v. "χαρά" 1, p. 1077). "The faith" likely refers to the gospel's content, what Christians believe (Martin and Hawthorne, 2004, 63). Paul wanted to see them grow in spiritual maturity and joy as they continued in the faith—as followers of Christ.

1:26. Καύχημα is rendered "boasting" (NIV, NRSV), "glory" (ESV), "confidence" (CSB, NASB), "pride" (NLT), or "rejoicing" (KJV, NKJV). The two prepositional phrases, "in Christ Jesus" (ἐν Χριστῷ Ἰησοῦ) and "in me" (ἐν ἐμοὶ), may be joined to the subject or to the predicate. Some connect "in Christ Jesus" to "boasting"—"boasting in Christ Jesus" (NIV, ESV, NRSV, NLT). Others connect it to "abound"—"may abound in Christ Jesus" (CSB, NASB, KJV, NKJV). Some connect "in me" to "boasting"—"proud confidence in me" (NASB), "rejoicing for me" (NKJV). Others connect it to "abound"—"overflow on account of me" (NIV), "in me you may have ample cause to glory" (ESV), "because of me your confidence may grow" (CSB). NRSV renders ἐν ἐμοὶ to denote association ("with me")—"that I may share abundantly in your boasting."

1:26. Paul's ultimate purpose (ἵνα) for remaining and continuing with them was "so that . . . [their] boast may abound in Christ Jesus on account of . . . [him] through . . . [his] coming to . . . [them] again." "Boast" (καύχημα) denotes "the act of

taking pride in something or that which constitutes a source of pride" (BDAG s.v. "καύχημα" 1, p. 537). This boast is not negative, related to arrogance. As Fee states, the Greek word "has to do first with putting one's full 'trust or confidence in' something or someone and thus, second, in 'glorying' in that something or someone" (1995, 154–55). Here Paul spoke of the Philippians' ("your" [ὑμῶν] subjective genitive) boast. He was thinking of their pride and exultation in what Christ had done for Paul when he was released from prison and returned to them. Later he will say that the Philippians will be the cause of *his* boast on the day of Christ (2:16; cf. 2 Cor. 1:14).

Paul's purpose was that their boast may "abound" (περισσεύῃ, cf. 1:9). The sphere in which he intended for their boast to abound was "in Christ Jesus" (ἐν Χριστῷ Ἰησοῦ). Some connect "in Christ Jesus" with the noun "boast"—"boast in Christ Jesus" (Bockmuehl, 1998, 95; Martin and Hawthorne, 2004, 63). But Greek word order favors connecting it with the verb "abound"—"boasting may abound in Christ Jesus" (Reumann, 2008, 230). Either way, Christ is the ultimate reason for their boast (Hansen, 2009, 92).

The immediate occasion for their boast would be "in me" or "on account of me" (ἐν ἐμοί) (Reumann, 2008, 230). Paul would not be the object of their boast; he would provide the occasion for their boast. This occasion would occur "through" (διά) Paul's coming to the Philippians. "Coming" (παρουσίας) refers to Paul's return to Philippi after his release (BDAG s.v. "παρουσία" 2a, p. 780). When he arrived, they would glory in his acquittal. They would have great delight and pride in Christ.

Paul was finished with his report on how things were going with him. He began with his concern for the progress of the gospel in Rome (1:12); he concluded with his concern for their progress and joy in the faith (1:25). He had demonstrated a Christ-centered approach to life—his imprisonment, his future, and his desires. In this way he provided a model for his readers so that they were encouraged to center their lives on Christ and the gospel.

THEOLOGICAL FOCUS

The exegetical idea (Paul modeled a Christ-centered view of life and death, willing to die and be with Christ, yet confident of release and further ministry, while certain of his ultimate salvation and that Christ's prestige would be advanced through him) leads to this theological focus: Believers are to exhibit a Christ-centered view of life and death, seeking to advance Christ's prestige in the way they live or die.

Like Paul, our desire should be that Christ is magnified every moment we live in these earthly bodies. This applies to the way we live and the way we die. In both cases, we are to point others to the glory of Christ. Following Christ as Lord means we learn to look at life this way: "to live is Christ." A Christ-centered view of life means that our lives consist of loving, serving, pursuing, honoring, and exalting Christ. God sovereignly arranges every circumstance, including seeming obstacles, so that we might pursue this purpose. Magnifying Christ becomes the determining factor in choices within our control (Where will I live? What will I do? Who will I marry? What kind of husband or wife, mother or father, brother or sister, friend or coworker will I be?) and circumstances beyond our control (How will I respond to this?).

Following Christ as Lord means that we learn to look at death this way: "to die is gain." If Christ is our focus and goal, death is gain because it places us in his direct presence. A Christ-centered view of death means that death is a point of transition into a greater, more intimate relationship with Christ.

PREACHING AND TEACHING STRATEGIES

Exegetical and Theological Synthesis

What is central to Philippians 1:18b–26 is that Paul's life-or-death dilemma does not disqualify

him from honoring Jesus. The same joy he expressed at the advance of the gospel (1:12–18a) carried into his reflection on mortality and ministry. Execution or acquittal awaited him, and both options had their appeal. Death offered him a more intimate audience with Jesus; life meant more fruitful service. In either case, Paul rejoiced at the chance to point to Jesus, making Christ's story the focal point of his life and death.

Paul's theological insights on death prove helpful for Westerners who are prone to overlook their mortality. In this brief passage, Paul developed a theology of personal salvation, which included reward and fellowship with Jesus. While many Christ-followers speak vaguely of "dying and going to heaven," Paul's picture of death included the notion of entering Jesus's presence and receiving honor. Final judgment, glory, and cosmic renewal are tied to the day of Christ, not one's death.

Considering our mortality need not be morbid. Paul used it as motivation for joy, confidence, hope, and ministry. Facing death with hope of vindication and fellowship with Christ fuels a buoyant attitude. Our lifestyle should prepare each of us for our death sentence. Whether pressing on or facing death, we must choose to live fully.

Preaching Idea

Live fully in the face of death.

Contemporary Connections

What does it mean?

What does it mean to live fully in the face of death? First, we acknowledge each one of us will die. For some, death is imminent—the expected end of a battle with cancer or likely outcome of a tour of military duty. For others, death remains distant—a by-product of time and natural decay. In any case, thanks to Adam and Eve, we each have a death sentence. And following death is judgment (Heb. 9:23), which should sober us.

Second, the reality of death inspires

self- reflection: *Did my life matter? Did I make a difference? Did I make the most of my time?* It is common for those near to death to ask these questions, share their joys, and air out their regrets. Universally, people wish they had spent more time with loved ones and less time pursuing selfish gain. Followers of Jesus wonder if their life and service evoked God's pleasure.

Fortunately, believers do not have to wait to the end of life to steel ourselves against regret. True discipleship implies a daily death sentence. Jesus called his followers to deny themselves and daily bear their cross (Luke 9:23). Paul wrote, "I die daily" (1 Cor. 15:31). For those daily committed to living fully, to pointing with their words and deeds to Jesus, their death sentence will merely sound like an encore to an entire life of sacrifice. Until their final breath, their greatest joy is the opportunity to see others formed into Christlikeness.

Is it true?

Is it true that we can live fully in the face of death? Certainly, untimely deaths and fatal accidents claiming the lives of loved ones produce grief. Each person responds to tragedy differently; we must give space for people to grieve in their own time.

And yet, in the face of death, God's people have historically proclaimed their trust in him. The Scriptures recount numerous stories of people facing death with bold faith. David spent years on the run from King Saul, chronicling his desire to exalt God in the face of death throughout the Psalms. Jeremiah's death sentence did not turn the volume down on his prophetic preaching. Daniel and his contemporaries braved furnaces and lions' dens while maintaining a powerful testimony. Stephen told the story of Jesus even while his opponents threw stones at him.

Modern-day death sentences have likewise led followers of Jesus to tell his story. In her book, *In the Presence of Enemies* (2010), missionary Gracia Burnham recounts her year-long captivity in a Philippine jungle with her husband Martin. The couple had lived in the country for nearly two decades prior to being taken hostage. During their rescue attempt, her husband was killed. Despite her losses, Gracia continues to tell the story of Jesus's faithfulness in her books and speaking engagements.

Now what?

Should followers of Jesus seek out death? Should they welcome martyrdom to bolster their witness? No. God does not call us to throw caution to the wind, but to be conscientious of our limited lifespan. We must not accept Western culture's denial of death. Our mortality should motivate sacrificial ministry, not justify a life of fear and consumption. (Consider the cultural refrain YOLO—"You Only Live Once"—as justification for all sorts of indulgence.)

Given our limited lifespan, followers of Jesus should resolve to make the most of their time in imitating Jesus and telling others about him. It does not magically happen on the deathbed, if we have not made a practice of witnessing in the workplace, at the dinner table, and about the neighborhood. David Brooks, in *The Road to Character* (2016, xi), calls these eulogy virtues—character traits nurtured over a lifetime. Living fully starts today.

To make imitation of Jesus and evangelism defining features of our lives—eulogy virtues—we begin by daily committing ourselves to the tasks. We yield ourselves to God in the morning through prayer. We give God access to our schedule. We seek opportunities to tell others of his goodness at various points of the day. We bind ourselves to others who follow Jesus and rejoice when hearing their stories of ministry. A procession of days given to imitating Jesus and telling others about him shapes a path to a gainful—regret-free, God-honoring, peace-filled—death.

Creativity in Presentation

Consider opening the sermon by reading a recent obituary (any one will do) to the congregation. Use it as a prompt for personal reflections on your mortality. Stress the reality that everyone dies. Then offer your own, handcrafted obituary stating the virtues you hope summarize your life. At some point in the sermon, distribute half-sheets of paper to the members of the congregation to encourage them to draft their own eulogy.

Both *Voice of the Martyrs* magazine and Maier's updated version of *Foxe's Book of Martyrs* (2016) are flush with powerful testimonies of people who gave their lives to tell the story of Jesus. Richard Wurmbrand's classic, *Tortured for Christ* (1998), powerfully models how a death sentence could not silence him. These examples awaken the North American church to the plight faced by her persecuted brothers and sisters across the globe. While they may not intersect with the daily realities of your congregation, they may inspire their daily prayers for God's purposes and protection.

It is more likely we know fellow believers who have faced terminal cancer or other life-threatening diseases, only to amplify their talk of Jesus. They often share their stories on CaringBridge or Facebook pages, which could be mined for inspiring quotations in the sermon. A friend of my parents battling Lou Gehrig's disease self-published a book entitled *Nobody Tells a Dying Guy to Shut Up* (Chilcoat, 2009), which perfectly models the apostle Paul's ethos.

Ultimately, the emphasis of the sermon should be: Believers exhibit a Christ-centered view of life and death, seeking to advance Christ's prestige in the way they live or die. Therefore, we should live fully in the face of death.

- Living fully in the face of death leads to rejoicing (1:18b–20).

- Living fully in the face of death leads to exaltation (1:21).

- Living fully in the face of death leads to a dilemma (1:22–26).

DISCUSSION QUESTIONS

1. How can this attitude of living for Christ become a greater reality in your life?

2. How do you get to the place where you agree with Paul's view of death?

3. Can you describe someone you have known who has glorified Christ in the *way* they have died (or the *way* they approached their own death)? How can that be a lesson for you?

4. What is the theological relationship between God's sovereign will and our human responsibility to pray?

5. When you pray for yourself or others, do you focus more on telling God what you want him to do, or on agreeing with what he intends to do? Why is the latter important?

6. Based on keeping a journal for a month, how have interruptions or negative events been God's orchestrated moments in your life?

7. How do you envision Jesus receiving honor at your funeral?

8. What examples of death-denying do you witness in our culture?

FOR FURTHER READING

Erickson, M. J. 2013. *Christian Theology*. 3rd ed. Grand Rapids: Baker Academic. Pages 1070–86. "Individual Eschatology."

Grudem, W. 1994. "Death and the Intermediate State." In *Systematic Theology*. Grand Rapids: Zondervan, 810–27.

Rapske, B. M. 2000. "Prison, Prisoner." Pages 827–30 in *Dictionary of New Testament Backgrounds*. Edited by C. A. Evans and S. E. Porter. Downers Grove, IL: InterVarsity Press.

Wumbrand, R. 1998. *Tortured for Christ*. Bartlesville, OK: Living Sacrifice.

EXHORTATIONS TO STEADFASTNESS
AND UNITY (1:27–2:30)

After Paul brought the Philippians up to date with how things were going on his end (1:12–26), he moved to exhortation. The basic exhortation of the letter (1:27) introduces a larger series of exhortations (1:27–2:18) that form the heart of Paul's concern. He will exhort the Philippians to stand together as citizens of God's heavenly kingdom (1:27–30), to be of one heart and mind putting each other first (2:1–4), to have the same servant attitude of humility and service that Christ exhibited (2:5–11), and to hold fast the word of life (2:12–18). With the repeated exhortations (seven imperative verbs in 1:27–2:18) and the inspiring example of Christ, Paul is like a general exhorting his troops or a coach motivating his team to compete well and be victorious in representing Christ in Philippi (cf. Martin and Hawthorne, 2004, 66–67).

This major section, Exhortations to Steadfastness and Unity (1:27–2:18), has six preaching units: Standing Firm in Unity as Citizens of God's Heavenly Kingdom (1:27–30), A Plea for Unity (2:1–4), Christ's Example of Humble Service (2:5–8), God's Elevation of Christ (2:9–11), Working Out Your Salvation (2:12–18), and Two Christlike Servants (2:19–30).

Philippians 1:27–30

EXEGETICAL IDEA
Paul exhorted the Philippians to live in a way consistent with their citizenship in God's kingdom—standing together, promoting the message about Christ Jesus, and fearlessly withstanding persecution, realizing that suffering persecution as Christ's representatives in the world was a gift from God.

THEOLOGICAL FOCUS
As citizens of God's heavenly kingdom, believers should stand together, promoting the gospel and fearlessly withstanding persecution from unbelievers.

PREACHING IDEA
Loyal followers of Jesus band together to stand strong.

PREACHING POINTERS
Paul's letter moved from a personal update to pastoral exhortation. He began a series of admonitions to unified, steadfast, selfless living. He wanted his original readers to reflect the work of Jesus, which is the heart of the gospel. The encouragement stemmed from a sober reality: Loyal Christ-followers will always face opposition. Their dual citizenship set them against the prevailing values and popular opinion of their neighbors. First-century residents of Philippi showed strong allegiance to Caesar and upheld values of military status and family honor. The original audience of Paul's letter would not have held such values in service of Jesus, resulting in social, religious, and political pressures.

There is no shortage of social pressures against which loyal followers of Jesus stand today. The Western world celebrates independence, self-expression, and consumerism. These values play out in an anything-goes sexual ethic, unfiltered online sharing, and gross personal debt, to name a few. When Christ-followers decide to band together and resist caving to these cultural values, they stand out, often painting a broad target on their backs. How does society respond when Christian teenagers vow to remain sexually pure until marriage? How do the media present the business owner who refuses to provide services for a same-sex wedding? What pressure does a parent feel when refusing to buy his children the latest gadget? This passage remains relevant today where diverse social pressures threaten our collective loyalty to Jesus.

STANDING FIRM IN UNITY AS CITIZENS OF GOD'S HEAVENLY KINGDOM (1:27–30)

LITERARY STRUCTURE AND THEMES (1:27–30)

As part of the the central exhortation part of the letter (1:27–2:18), this section (a single sentence in the Greek text) consists of six ideas, each building on the previous one. First, Paul exhorted them to live out their heavenly citizenship in a manner worthy of the gospel (1:27a). Second, he stated the purpose for the exhortation: so that he may hear that they were standing firm in one Spirit (1:27b). Third, using two parallel participles, he explained the means by which they were to stand firm in one Spirit: by contending with one mind side by side for the gospel and by not being intimidated by those who opposed them (1:27c–28a). Fourth, Paul asserted that their contending and not being intimidated would be a double sign—a sign of destruction for their opponents, but of their salvation (1:28b). Fifth, he stated that this was from God. God had granted them not only to believe, but also to suffer for Christ's sake (1:28c–29). Finally, with another participle Paul stated that the means by which they were suffering was by having the same conflict that they saw him have and now heard that he was having (1:30).

> ### Citizens of God's Kingdom (1:27a)
> ### Standing in Unity (1:27b)
> ### How to Stand (1:27c–28a)
> ### A Double Sign (1:28b)
> ### The Gifts of Belief and Suffering (1:28c–29)
> ### The Same Conflict as Paul (1:30)

EXPOSITION (1:27–30)

Paul turned to exhortation—to what he wanted the Philippians to do. Many scholars agree that this paragraph provides the basic exhortation of the letter (Watson, 1988, 79). Paul exhorted them to live worthy of their calling as citizens of a heavenly kingdom, standing together in one Spirit, with one mind striving together for the gospel. Here we first learn that the Philippians were facing opposition similar to what Paul faced in Philippi. Paul wanted to encourage them toward Christlike living in an unbelieving world. He reframed the way they were to think about both opposition (a gift from God) and their own steadfastness (a sign of the opponents' destruction and of their salvation).

Citizens of God's Kingdom (1:27a)

Paul exhorted the Philippians to live in the non-Christian culture of Philippi in a manner consistent with their identity as citizens of God's kingdom.

1:27. Μόνον is typically rendered "only" (ESV, NRSV, NASB, KJV, NKJV). The NIV ("whatever happens"), NLT ("above all"), and CSB ("just one thing") provide more "oomph." Πολιτεύεσθε is rendered by most translations without any hint of political nuance: "conduct yourselves" (NIV, NASB, cf. NKJV); "live your life" (NRSV, CSB, cf. ESV). But NLT brings out the political nuance of the word ("live as citizens of heaven"). The majority of translations understand ἐν ἑνὶ πνεύματι to be a reference to the human spirit, parallel to "one mind" in the following phrase (ESV, NRSV, CSB, NLT, NASB, NKJV). But the revised NIV understands πνεύματι to refer to the Holy Spirit. Μιᾷ ψυχῇ is rendered "one mind" (ESV, NRSV, CSB, NASB, KJV, NKJV), "one purpose" (NLT), or "one man" (NIV).

1:27. To highlight the basic imperative, Paul began with "only" (μόνον). Barth suggests rendering it emphatically, "Just one thing!" (1962, 45). The basic exhortation, which will be explained by the rest of the paragraph, is: "live out your [heavenly] citizenship in a manner worthy of the gospel of Christ." Many recent commentators emphasize this by challenging the usual translation of the imperative "conduct yourselves" or "live your life" (BDAG s.v. "πολιτεύομαι" 3, p. 846). They argue that in the context of Philippians, Paul intended to bring out the word's political connotation. It derives from the Greek word for "city" or "city-state" (πόλις) and is related to the noun Paul used in 3:20, usually translated "citizenship" or "commonwealth" (πολίτευμα).

When Paul wrote elsewhere that believers were to live "worthily" (ἀξίως, Eph. 4:1; Col. 1:10; 1 Thess. 2:12), he used the verb "walk" (περιπατέω).[1] But Paul's choice of "live your life" (πολιτεύεσθε), seems more intentional, perhaps because of the privileged status Philippi enjoyed as a Roman colony. While we do not know whether any of the believers were Roman citizens (an elite status) like Paul was (Acts 16:37–38; 22:25–29; 23:27), they would have been able to appreciate the political overtones of the term. In view of Paul's statement in 3:20 that they were members of a heavenly "commonwealth" (πολίτευμα), his use of the verb here likely had a political connotation. He meant that his readers must live as citizens of heaven in the midst of a Roman city. They were a colony of Christians planted in Philippi. They must be loyal first of all to Christ and to conduct their lives according to the gospel, the standards of their commonwealth (Thielman, 1995, 93; Flemming, 2009, 85).

Heavenly Citizenship and Roman Citizenship: Paul's letters addressed the need for believers to be good citizens, specifically to respect civil governments as God's appointed agents for social good (Rom. 13:1–14). More generally, believers were to pray for civil leaders so that they may live quiet, peaceful, and godly lives (1 Tim. 2:1–2). Philippians complements these ideas by emphasizing that believers' primary citizenship is in God's kingdom, where their first loyalty lies (1:27; 3:20).

Some have understood Paul to mean that believers should reject their Roman citizenship (De Vos, 1999, 281). But Paul said nothing about that. Others have understood Paul to be emphasizing believers' responsibility to balance a dual allegiance, one in the earthly city and another in the heavenly (Lincoln, 1991, 100–101). But Paul's point in this letter was not allegiance to an earthly kingdom. Instead, he emphasized that their real commonwealth was in heaven (3:20). They were part of God's kingdom, over which Jesus rules. Paul would agree that Christians should be good citizens of their respective countries, but that was not his concern here (cf. Fowl, 2005, 61). Rather, he wanted them to know that while they presently lived in a Roman colony, they belonged to a heavenly one.

The manner in which the Philippians were to live out their citizenship was "in a manner worthy (αξίως) of the gospel of Christ." Elsewhere he said believers were to "walk" (= live) in a manner worthy of their calling (Eph. 4:1), worthy of the Lord (Col. 1:10), and worthy of God (1 Thess. 2:12). "Worthy of the gospel" does not mean that they deserved salvation. Paul meant that they must live a "gospel-influenced lifestyle," a life that was in line with the ethics promoted by the message about Christ Jesus. As citizens of heaven, Philippian believers must live in a manner necessary for those whose lives had been transformed and were being transformed by God (BDAG s.v. "ἀξίως," p. 94). Paul will explain what this entails in the rest of

---

1 Paul used this verb about thirty times in his letters to denote the "walk" of the Christian life. He also regularly used "live" (ζάω).

1:27–2:18. The attitude and behavior of Christ in 2:5–8 provide a noteworthy example of the "gospel lifestyle."

"The gospel of Christ" (τοῦ εὐαγγελίου τοῦ Χριστοῦ) could mean the gospel *about* Christ (objective genitive), the gospel *proclaimed by* Christ (subjective genitive), or both. Since for Paul, Christ was both the author and the object of the gospel, it is probably not crucial to distinguish between the two (*TDNT* 2:731).

Standing in Unity (1:27b)

Paul intended for the Philippians to stand together as citizens of God's kingdom promoting the gospel about Christ in Philippi.

The purpose or result (ἵνα) for their living out their citizenship worthy of the gospel was so that, whether Paul came and saw them or remained absent, he may hear things about them (1:27b). Paul expected to hear good news about how his friends were living. This would be true whether he came and saw them in person (1:26; 2:24), or whether he heard about them before he arrived—probably from Timothy who he was sending to bring him news of them (2:19).

The content (ὅτι) of what Paul expected to hear is that they were "standing firm in one Spirit." "Stand firm" suggests the image of a soldier refusing to break rank, but instead holding his ground in battle (Geoffrion, 1993, 55; Krentz, 1993, 119–21). They must not retreat or give ground as they contended for the faith against opponents of the gospel. The fact that Philippi was founded as a colony of military veterans and that, situated on the Egnatian Way, Roman armies would have passed through, might suggest the Philippians would appreciate the military imagery of this verb (Hellerman, 2015, 79).

In this case they were to stand firm "in one Spirit" (ἐν ἑνὶ πνεύματι). Scholars debate the referent of "Spirit." Most translations render it "in one spirit," understanding Paul to refer to the human disposition. And many commentators argue that the phrase denotes the Philippians' unified corporate human spirit, a common disposition and purpose in the community (Martin and Hawthorne, 2004, 70). If this is right, the phrase is parallel to the immediately following "with one mind" and means basically the same thing.

But the revised NIV renders it "in one Spirit," referring to the Holy Spirit. If this is right, the phrase denotes the sphere in which believers are to stand firm. We prefer this view because (1) Paul used the phrase "in one Spirit" elsewhere (1 Cor. 12:13; Eph. 2:18), and these usages clearly refer to the Holy Spirit; (2) in the other texts where Paul used the preposition "in" (ἐν) with the verb "stand firm," he denoted the *sphere* in which they were to stand firm: stand firm "in the Lord" (Phil. 4:1; 1 Thess. 3:8), stand firm "in the faith" (1 Cor. 16:13).

Believers can achieve and maintain unity in the church only through the presence and power of the Holy Spirit, as they stand firm in the one divine Spirit. This agrees with other statements Paul made about the presence of the Holy Spirit in believers as the key to unity in the church (cf. 2:1; 1 Cor. 12:13; Eph. 2:22; 4:3–4) (Fee, 1995, 166).

> **Keys for Living as Citizens of God's Kingdom in an Ungodly Society (1:27–29):**
> 1. Live worthy of the gospel—adhering to its moral and ethical (Christlike) guidelines.
> 2. Stand firm in unity, united in the realm of and empowered by the one Spirit.
> 3. Contend together for the Christian faith with a common purpose and aim.
> 4. Do not be intimidated by opponents of Christianity.
> 5. Expect to suffer persecution—a gift from God and a sign of your salvation.

How to Stand (1:27c–28a)

Paul explained that the Philippians were to evangelize their community without being intimidated by the opposition of non-Christians in Philippi.

Paul clarified how they were to stand firm in one Spirit with two parallel participles (adverbial participles of means) that follow: (1) "with one mind contending side by side for the faith of the gospel," and (2) "not being intimidated in any way by those who oppose" (1:27c–28a). The first way they were to stand firm in one Spirit was by "contending side by side" (συναθλοῦντες). This suggests a military image of fighting side by side in battle (BDAG s.v. "συναθλέω," p. 964), or an athletic image of a team working together as one (Martin and Hawthorne, 2004, 71), or of gladiators fighting side by side in an amphitheater (Lightfoot, 1953, 106). "Contending" implies that living worthy of the gospel consists of a strenuous effort, and that believers do not struggle alone (Flemming, 2009, 87). They will "contend" for the gospel through active evangelism—offering reasonable arguments for their faith in Christ, and living godly lives as they "shine as lights" in the community (2:15) (Keown, 2009, 109–24). In 4:3, Paul will use the same word of coworkers who contended alongside him for the gospel.

They were to contend "with one mind" (μιᾷ ψυχῇ). This could denote the Philippians' feelings and emotions (BDAG s.v. "ψυχή" 2c, p. 1099). But more likely, it denotes a common purpose or aim (Fee, 1995, 166). They were to contend together "for the faith" (τῇ πίστει, dative of advantage) "of the gospel" (BDAG s.v. "πίστις" 2c, p. 219). This refers to "the faith, that is, the gospel" (genitive of apposition). Paul wanted them to defend the validity of what was believed about Christ: the Christian doctrine and the Christian lifestyle. Note that Paul presented the Christian fight positively—it was not *against* non-Christians; it was *for* the gospel (Thurston and Ryan, 2005, 69).

1:28. Πτυρόμενοι is rendered "frightened" (NIV, ESV, CSB), "intimidated" (NRSV, NLT), or "terrified" (KJV, NKJV). The NASB "alarmed" may be too soft. Ἔνδειξις is rendered "sign" (NIV, NLT, NASB), "clear sign" (ESV), "evident token" (KJV),

or "proof" (NKJV). "Evidence" (NRSV, CSB) may be too soft.

1:28a. The second way they were to stand firm in one Spirit was by "not being intimidated in any way by those who oppose you." "Intimidated" (πτυρόμενοι) or "frightened" is found only here in the New Testament. It was used in Greek literature of animals being startled by a loud noise, in particular of horses being spooked in battle (BDAG s.v. "πτύρω," p. 895). It also was used of the surprise that could occur when one received unexpected misfortune, such as the panic felt when receiving a diagnosis of a terminal illness (see examples in Holloway, 2001, 117–18). Paul wanted to hear that his readers were not spooked, panicked, or intimidated by the opponents of the gospel they were facing.

"Those who oppose you" (τῶν ἀντικειμένων) refers to opponents of the gospel in Philippi. Although Paul did not identify them, the Philippians knew who they were. They were not the Judaizers Paul will warn against in chapter 3 (as argued by Martin and Hawthorne, 2004, 72; Silva, 2005, 82–3). More likely, these were non-Christians—perhaps including Roman authorities—who were trying to intimidate them (Fee, 1995, 167). This fits with what Paul said in verse 30—that they were experiencing the "same struggle" they saw him have and now heard that he has. In Philippi, Paul experienced persecution from non-Christians and was dragged before the Roman magistrates there (Acts 16:19–24). When he wrote the letter he was in Roman custody.

The Christians in Philippi were a tiny minority. Their religious and social beliefs differed from those around them. They would have faced pressure to conform to religious and cultural norms from family, friends, neighbors, coworkers, and potentially, the authorities. Oakes argues that followers of Christ would have faced especially economic pressure, such as being kicked out of trade guilds and losing jobs. Perhaps they would find it difficult to get work because of their "strange beliefs." They also may have been called before the magistrates because they were Christians (Oakes, 2001, 89–96).

A Double Sign (1:28b)

The Philippians' firm commitment to their faith and refusal to be intimidated by unbelievers was a double sign—a sign that God would eternally condemn unbelievers and a sign that he would eternally save believers.

Paul stated, "This is for them a sign of destruction, but of your salvation." "This" (ἥτις) likely refers to all of 1:27b–28a—standing firm, contending side by side, and not being intimidated (Fee, 1995, 168). "Sign" (ἔνδειξις) occurs only three other times in the New Testament (Rom. 3:25, 26; 2 Cor. 8:24), where it means, "proof" or "demonstration." Here it means, "something that points to or serves as an indicator of something"—an omen (BDAG s.v. "ἔνδειξις" 1, p. 332). The sign would have a double significance.

First, the sign (the Philippians standing firm without being intimidated) would be "for them (the opponents) a sign of destruction." The Philippians' opponents, not the Philippians, were the ones to be destroyed. "Destruction" (ἀπωλείας) refers to eternal destruction at the final judgment, its normal meaning in the New Testament (Rom. 9:22; 2 Thess. 2:3; 1 Tim. 6:9; Matt. 7:13; John 17:12; Acts 8:20; Phil. 3:19; Heb. 10:39; 2 Peter 2:1, 3; 3:7, 16; Rev. 17:8, 11 cf. BDAG s.v. "ἀπώλεια" 2, p. 127). Paul did not indicate that the opponents would necessarily perceive this sign (Bockmuehl, 1998, 101). It was a sign he wanted his *readers* to perceive, even if the opponents did not.

Second, the sign would be a sign "of your salvation." "Your" presents a subtle contrast. While destruction is *for* the opponents, salvation *belongs to* the Philippians (see *GGBB*, 143–44, dative of disadvantage contrasts with genitive of possession). If the opponents' eternal destruction was certain, the believers' eternal salvation was even more certain, for they already possessed their salvation. As in 1:19, "salvation" (σωτηρίας) refers to vindication at the final judgment.

Paul's pointing out this sign was significant. Coming out of a pagan environment, the Philippians may have been predisposed to think that their suffering was a negative omen. Perhaps they assumed suffering meant that God was displeased with them or that they had done something wrong. But Paul said just the opposite—it was a positive sign of their salvation. When the church stands firm and does not wilt in the face of persecution, that itself becomes a sign of the final destinies of both persecutors and believers.

The Gifts of Belief and Suffering (1:28c–29)

God had given the Philippians not only the privilege of daily trusting in Christ for salvation, but also the privilege of suffering persecution as his representatives in the world.

1:28c–29. Referring back to all he had said in 1:27b–28b, Paul stated, "And (τοῦτο) that [is] from God" (1:28c)." God's sovereign plan for believers includes not only their faith, but also their being persecuted for their faith. Paul explained why the opposition they faced was from God: "because/for (ὅτι) to you it has been granted for the sake of Christ" (1:29). "To you" (ὑμῖν) is in an emphatic position in the Greek sentence. Paul was emphasizing what had been given *to the believers*. "It has been granted" (ἐχαρίσθη) has God as the implied subject (BDAG s.v. "χαρίζομαι" 1, p. 1078). God had graciously given believers two privileges: *believing* in Christ and *suffering* for the sake of Christ.

Two gifts are in view (to believe, to suffer), but Paul emphasized the latter, since he elaborated on that gift in 1:30. The first gift, "to believe" (BDAG s.v. "πιστεύω" 2aβ, p. 817) includes more than just the act of faith at conversion. Paul was thinking especially of an ongoing trust in Christ throughout the Christian life (customary present tense). Both initial faith and ongoing faith in Christ are from God. The second gift, "to suffer"

(BDAG s.v. "πάσχω" 3aβ, p785), likewise refers to ongoing suffering. In this context it refers specifically to enduring opposition from those who are hostile to Christ and the gospel. Paul was not addressing the general topic of the suffering of Christians in a fallen world (see Rom. 8:17–30). He was referring to the trials and persecution endured by the Philippians due to the fact that they are Christians. "To suffer" is an active, not passive concept, as the athletic "struggle" in verse 30 demonstrates (Hellerman, 2015 85). This is part of the participation of Christ's sufferings Paul will mention in 3:10.

The phrase, "for the sake of Christ/him," occurs twice. The repetition emphasizes believers' connection with Christ. "For the sake of" (ὑπέρ) denotes the *reason why* when used with verbs of suffering (BDAG s.v. "ὑπέρ" 2, p. 1031). Believers suffer opposition because they have chosen to identify with and to serve Christ. The idea is not that believers' suffering achieves something for Christ, or that they suffer instead of Christ (argued by Martin and Hawthorne, 2004, 75). Rather, they suffer because they are identified with Christ (Hansen, 2009, 102). They represent him in the world.

Paul wanted to encourage his readers by reframing how they looked at suffering, persecution, or harassment. *Suffering* for Christ, like *faith* in him, is a gracious gift from God. When believers encounter opposition because they are Christians, it does not mean that God has abandoned or forgotten them. On the contrary, it is a gracious gift from God—a part of knowing Christ in his sufferings. When believers live for Christ, they suffer with him, and to this they are called. Calvin comments:

> Oh, if this conviction were fixed in our minds, that persecutions are to be reckoned among God's benefits, what progress would be made in the doctrine of godliness! And yet, what is more certain than that it is

the highest honour of the Divine grace, that we suffer for His name either reproach, or imprisonment, or miseries, or tortures, or even death, for in that case He decorates us with His insignia. (1965, 243)

On the other hand, believers are not to view suffering as a virtue, something to be sought and accomplished for Christ. It is simply the outcome of a life devoted to serving Christ and following him (Nebreda, 2011, 211–12).

The Same Conflict as Paul (1:30)

The suffering the Philippians were experiencing was the same persecution from unbelievers they saw Paul endure in Philippi and now heard that he endured in prison in Rome.

> *1:30.* The circumstantial participle ἔχοντες is rendered "engaged in" (ESV), "having" (CSB, KJV, NKJV) or "experiencing" (NASB). It may be causal, denoting the reason why suffering has been given—"since you are going through" (NIV); "since you are having" (NRSV).

1:30. Paul elaborated on the gift of suffering for Christ's sake that God had granted the Philippians. They were suffering by "having" (ἔχοντες, circumstantial participle of means)[2] the "same conflict" they saw Paul experience and now heard that he was experiencing. Paul used "conflict" or "struggle against opposition" (BDAG s.v. "ἀγών 2, p. 17) four other times in his letters (Col. 2:1; 1 Thess. 2:2; 1 Tim. 6:12; 2 Tim. 4:7). He depicted the Christian life and ministry as a struggle against opposition—either a military battle (Geoffrin, 1993, 80–81; Krentz, 1993, 126) or an athletic competition (Reumann, 2008, 273–74, 294). This was an appropriate image for the constant toil and wrestling that Paul engaged in as he carried out his apostolic ministry of preaching the gospel,

---

2. "Having [ἔχοντες] the same conflict" may also express cause or result of the infinitive "to suffer."

planting churches, opposing false teachers, enduring persecution, and caring for the saints. And the Philippians were experiencing it, too. To spread the message about Jesus is to struggle against all that opposes Jesus.

The Philippians were experiencing the "same conflict" they saw Paul have (when he was with them in Philippi) and that they now "heard" he had (in prison in Rome). Some in the church had seen Paul and Silas beaten and imprisoned (Acts 16:11–40). "And now 'hear' that I have" refers to the news they will have received through Epaphroditus and will hear as they read the present letter (BDAG s.v. "ἀκούω" 1, p. 37).

Because the Philippians participated with Paul in sharing the message about Jesus, they shared "the same conflict." This does not necessarily imply that they were experiencing opposition in exactly the same form as Paul—being beaten and thrown into jail. But it is possible, if not probable, that they were at least facing harassment and threats from the authorities as well as from pagan neighbors. The primary point is that the struggles they faced were joined to Paul's personal struggles as part of the apostolic struggle for the gospel message about Christ Jesus (Hawthorne and Martin, 2004, 77).

Paul presented himself as a model for how to interpret and respond to suffering because of the gospel. We need to learn to view the Christian life and its struggles from the apostolic perspective. To participate in the shared and lived out message is to participate in the sufferings of Christ. It is to stand firm amidst opposition from the world. It is a sign of our coming salvation. All of this is a gracious gift from the Father.

THEOLOGICAL FOCUS

The exegetical idea (Paul exhorted the Philippians to live in a way consistent with their citizenship in God's kingdom—standing together, promoting the gospel, and fearlessly withstanding persecution, realizing that suffering persecution as Christ's representatives in the world was a gift from God) leads to this theological focus: As citizens of God's heavenly kingdom, believers should stand together, promoting the gospel and fearlessly withstanding persecution from unbelievers.

The ethics and values of God's kingdom will clash with the ethics and values of our earthly culture. We are to stand together in a hostile environment, knowing that we are citizens of God's heavenly commonwealth. We are to recognize where our primary citizenship and loyalties lie, and we must not be afraid of those who would seek to intimidate us. In the face of persecution or even martyrdom, we are to stand firm in the faith, contending for the gospel. Following Christ includes not only living as he lived but also, if necessary, suffering as he suffered. This is the life that is in line with (worthy of) the gospel. We should expect opposition and suffering because of who we are in Christ.

PREACHING AND TEACHING STRATEGIES

Exegetical and Theological Synthesis

The major thrust of Philippians 1:27–30 is an exhortation to stand firm as followers of Jesus against the pressures of society at large. Believers in Philippi comprised a small fraction of the population, driven by opposing loyalties and different values. Paul underscored the importance of unity, helped along by the Holy Spirit. Not only does unity build confidence for fellow Christians; it also subverts the plot of the opponents, whose eventual defeat is sure to come. As Paul earlier stated: God's people and purposes are sure to prevail, but not without pressure in the process.

Loyalty to Jesus does not guarantee life free from pressures. If anything, the journey of faith promises troubles will come. Followers of Jesus live with dual citizenship and competing loyalties. We swear allegiance to a risen King, not local figureheads. The good news we preach strikes a different chord than the latest headlines, medical findings, political opinions, educational promises, and shopping deals regularly impressed on us.

Society endlessly aims to press followers of Jesus into its mold. Resistance intensifies the pressure. But God intends the pressure to push his people together in unity. A common enemy (e.g., principalities and powers) often crystalizes the resolve of a people. Rather than shrinking away at the societal pressures to conform to culture, the passage calls God's people to resist in a strong, shared loyalty to Jesus.

Preaching Idea

Loyal followers of Jesus band together to stand strong.

Contemporary Connections

What does it mean?

What does loyalty to Jesus look like? Loyalty means trust, commitment, and allegiance to another. A loyal spouse does more than avoid adultery; he pledges himself to faithful love and service in the marriage. A loyal employee does more than clock her time at work; she engages her daily business with honesty, integrity, and understanding of the company's mission. Similarly, a loyal follower of Jesus moves beyond the sinner's prayer and compulsory church attendance; he surrenders his whole self—will, emotions, time, energy, and resources—to imitating Jesus, encouraging his people, and telling others about him.

Moreover, this exhortation to loyalty has a corporate component. Fidelity to Jesus should mark the body of Christ more than denominational preferences and worship styles. Sadly, Western Christianity has a reputation for infighting and division over secondary issues. Churches tout external differences (seeker-sensitive, progressive, KJV-only, intergenerational, missional) or theological approaches (Reformed, Baptist, Pentecostal) as their unifying element. But uniformity is a cheap substitute for unity. God's people must rediscover loyalty to Jesus and love for neighbor as our primary calling.

Is it true?

Is it true that banding together to stand strong helps us remain loyal to Jesus? Yes, but not without a challenge. Throughout history God has called his people to reject the religious influences of its pagan neighbors. Abram left his homeland. Gideon destroyed a family altar. Elijah confounded the prophets of Baal. Paul defied Roman authorities. And none of these heroes of the faith acted alone, but banded together with spouse, siblings, soldiers, and other loyal saints.

Ironically, the pressure to conform not only comes from the outside, but often most harshly from within a faction of one's own people. Jesus felt the ire of the Pharisees. Peter faced the scorn of religious authorities in Jerusalem.

Extending beyond the pages of Scripture, figures from church history emerge who withstood opposition and showed loyalty to Jesus: John Tyndale, Joan of Arc, Dietrich Bonhoeffer, and Martin Luther King Jr. While we often credit individuals for their loyalty, these people always banded with others. Their loyalty to Jesus cost them comfort, reputation, and, sometimes, their very lives. However, acts of loyalty do not always proceed so dramatically. Loyalty to Jesus may motivate a follower of Jesus to cancel his cable service, avoid consumer debt, or allot two hours a week to community service. These smaller practices of nonconformity in the name of loyalty often raise eyebrows of extended family members, coworkers, and peers.

Now what?

Should followers of Jesus emblazon their loyalty to Jesus on banners and buildings? Should non-conformity drive their public identity? No: Followers of Jesus must show discernment in how they differ from society. If we are primarily known for how we don't fit in (or worse, what we are against), we have failed to display our driving purpose: loyalty to Jesus. We must not let nonconformity (or uniformity) become its own cause, for it will breed moralism, not transformation.

Spiritual formation writers lift the veil on unseen forces constantly shaping us. Indeed, in one way or another, we are constantly being formed. To ignore cultural forces—from Amazon to Disney to the fast-food industry to public education to Wall Street—is to ensure the dilution of our loyalty to Jesus. We must learn to ask what societal pressures are pinching us: *How does the media shape our fears? How does advertising affect our appetite? How do our neighbors influence our attitude?*

Finally, we must understand loyalty to Jesus as something greater than managing personal appearances. Our faith commitment may show up on our Facebook profile, Twitter feeds, weekly calendar, car bumpers, and t-shirts. But we cheapen loyalty when we reduce it to words. True loyalty must also be evident in our fidelity to (1) Christ's body, (2) financial contribution to kingdom causes, and (3) spiritual character demonstrated in moments of tension or seasons of joy. We must ask ourselves: *How evident is* my *loyalty to Jesus in these three areas? How evident is* our *(group) loyalty in these three areas?*

Creativity in Presentation

While the following idea could stir up unhealthy controversy in many patriotic churches in the United States, try setting a Christian flag and a national one on either side of the pulpit (or, perhaps, they're already there). At the beginning of the sermon, invite people to stand and pledge their allegiance to the Christian flag. Then, while they remain standing, quietly move the national flag from beside the pulpit to the perimeter of the auditorium. Acknowledge our dual citizenship, but emphasize our higher loyalty to heaven.

> I pledge allegiance to God's kingdom and to the kingdom for which Jesus suffered, one

kingdom, ruled by God, with liberty and justice for all.

Since marital fidelity serves as a good analogy for loyalty, consider reading a marital vow to the congregation to repeat. The marriage? The congregation and Jesus, their beloved bridegroom. While this exercise could feel a bit campy, you could follow it with several scenarios where your fidelity is tested. After each one, pose the question: Did you stay loyal? At the close of the sermon, you may come back around to the vow, but this time read it from Jesus's perspective, assuring the congregation he has remained loyal to his beloved bride.

Tests of Marital Loyalty
1. You did not receive a reply to your prayer request as quickly as you wanted.
2. You feel like you're doing the greater share of the chores around the house.
3. Other religious suitors (like Buddha) are promising moments of peace, quiet, and nirvana.
4. You realize you've been cranky, distant, and unlovable.
5. You had different plans for your bonus money, vacation week, and weekend.

Hacksaw Ridge (2016), the inspiring, true story directed by Mel Gibson, chronicles the resolve of Desmond Doss, whose loyalty to God inspires his pacifism in the Second World War. During his military training, he refuses to bear arms, resulting in fierce opposition from fellow soldiers. Doss's speech during the court-martial scene powerfully conveys his loyalty to God. Another real-life example captured in film is Martin Luther King's sermon in *Selma* (2014), directed by Ava DuVernay, where the congregation echoes his chorus: "No more! No more! No more!"

Personal stories of loyalty-at-a-cost can be effective. As a matter of conviction, I have resolved not to pay for television or use Facebook.

For years I (Tim) have faced questions and criticism from church and family members for a personal conviction to reduce distractions from my life. (I have not applied the same logic to ESPN radio.) Author Andy Crouch, in *The Tech-Wise Family* (2017, 29), encourages ten such countercultural commitments that sound "almost Amish" but certainly help grow a family's loyalty to Jesus. Many Christians commit their vacation time and large sums of money to volunteering or mission trips. Their rejection of the American dream does not always earn applause from the secular world. Having personal examples or testimonies of these kinds woven into the sermon gives it relevance.

In short, the sermon should stress this: As citizens of God's heavenly kingdom, believers should stand together, promoting the message about Jesus and fearlessly withstanding persecution from unbelievers. We should band together to stand strong as loyal followers of Jesus.

- Be loyal to Jesus (1:27a).

- Let's band together (1:27b).

- Let's stand strong (1:28–30).

DISCUSSION QUESTIONS

1. Which is ultimately healthier for the church and for believers—to live in a culture friendly to Christianity or hostile to it? Why?

2. What are the main difficulties you will face if you try to obey Christ in the non-Christian environment you encounter?

3. What resources do you have for being able to stand firm in obedience to Christ in the midst of persecution or harassment for your beliefs?

4. Why are unity and community so important in a hostile environment? What can believers accomplish together that they cannot accomplish alone?

5. What do the following words from Bonhoeffer's *The Cost of Discipleship* mean to you?

   > Cheap grace is grace without discipleship, grace without the cross, grace without Jesus Christ, living and incarnate. Costly grace is the treasure hidden in the field; for the sake of it a man will gladly go and sell all that he has. It is the pearl of great price to buy which the merchant will sell all his goods. It is the kingly rule of Christ, for whose sake a man will pluck out the eye which causes him to stumble. . . . Such grace is *costly* because it calls us to follow, and it is *grace* because it calls us to follow *Jesus Christ*. It is costly because it costs a man his life, and it is grace because it gives a man the only true life. (1947, 47)

6. How has cheap grace caused the church to become lethargic and lose its prophetic voice in today's culture? What is the value of Bonhoeffer's concept of costly grace?

7. How does culture aim to shape you in the following areas: sexuality, materialism, use of technology, security, ethics, politics, and view of humanity?

8. In what ways do you feel pressure from within the church to adopt certain moral convictions, ministry philosophy, or traditions?

9. What is the difference between unity and uniformity?

Philippians 2:1–4

EXEGETICAL IDEA
Based on the encouragement, comfort, tender care, and presence of the Spirit God provides for followers of Christ, Paul exhorted the Philippians to make him completely joyful by living in harmony and humbly putting one another first.

THEOLOGICAL FOCUS
Sincere humility that elevates others creates harmony in the church.

PREACHING IDEA
Put others first to sustain strong bonds with fellow Christ-followers.

PREACHING POINTERS
After warning his readers about suffering at the hands of external forces, Paul continued to advocate for resiliency against internal pressures. Disunity threatened his original readers. The quest for personal honor, selfish gain, and diverse goals tempts every believing congregation. Such internal battles do not justify uniformity—a mockery of biblical unity and minefield for control—but call for a shared commitment to reflect Jesus's humble attitude. Paul wanted harmony for his original readers, and he assured them aid from the Holy Spirit as they sought to put others first.

Selfish gain and personal ambition drive Christ-followers today. More platforms for self-promotion are available at the click of a finger than ever before. People can peddle their thoughts like cheap wares on social media, blogs, websites, chatrooms, and YouTube. While we may use these tools to maintain contact with distant relatives and old friends, they are sometimes used to fuel mob mentality and social disruption. Often, the by-product of our communication tools is a sad mix of disconnection, competition, and ambition. Even within the body of Christ, ambition rears its ugly head. How often do loud voices become lobbyists for their niche ministry, trading the big vision of the local church for their pet project? The passage exposes selfish gain and calls for putting others first, to sustain strong bonds as Christ-followers.

A PLEA FOR UNITY (2:1–4)

LITERARY STRUCTURE AND THEMES (2:1–4)

Philippians 2:1–4 is a single independent Greek sentence. It begins with four parallel "if" clauses denoting benefits God provides for Christ-followers. These four benefits provide a fourfold premise for Paul's exhortation. The main verb is the imperative, "make complete" my joy (2:2a). The next clause explains what will make Paul's joy complete—that they are of the same mind (2:2b). Then follows a series of participle clauses that explain how they can be of the same mind: by having the same love, being united in spirit, focusing on one goal, doing nothing according to selfish ambition or conceit, regarding one another as more important, and looking to the interest of others (2:2c–4).

Four Benefits God Provides for Christ-Followers (2:1)
Paul's Joy in Their Unity (2:2a–b)
Achieving Christian Unity (2:2c–4)

EXPOSITION (2:1–4)

In 1:27 Paul exhorted the believers to live out their citizenship worthy of the message about of Christ. This is the fundamental exhortation of 1:27–2:18. He wanted to hear that they were standing firm in unity, contending for the faith, and not intimidated by opponents. The threat was from unbelievers *outside* the church. Now Paul continued to describe what it meant to live as citizens in a manner worthy of the gospel of Christ. But in this paragraph he transitioned to the threat that could come from *within* the church. Division from within could threaten their ability to withstand opposition from without. So Paul exhorted them to live humbly in harmony with one another.

Four Benefits God Provides for Christ-Followers (2:1)

As a fourfold premise for his exhortation that follows, Paul stated four benefits God provides for Christ-followers: encouragement, comfort, tender care, and the presence of the Spirit.

> *2:1.* Most English translations preserve the fourfold *if*-clause structure. But NLT renders the *if*-clauses as questions. Παράκλησις is rendered "encouragement" (NIV, ESV, NRSV, CSB, NLT, NASB) or "consolation" (KJV, NKJV). Παραμύθιον is rendered "consolation" (NRSV, CSB, NASB) or "comfort" (NIV, ESV, NLT, KJV, NKJV). NIV and NLT specify that the comfort comes from *God's* love. Κοινωνία is rendered "sharing" (NRSV, NIV), "participation" (ESV), or "fellowship" (CSB, NLT, NASB, KJV, NKJV). Σπλάγχνα is rendered "tenderness" (NIV, cf. NLT), "affection" (ESV, CSB, NASB, NKJV), or "compassion" (NRSV). Οἰκτιρμοί is rendered "compassion" (NIV, NASB, cf. NLT), "sympathy" (ESV, NRSV), or "mercy" (CSB, KJV, NKJV).

2:1. Paul opened with a consequence (οὖν) of what it meant for the Philippians to live out their citizenship worthy of the gospel standing firm in unity (1:27–30). He will exhort them to live humbly in harmony with one another (2:2–4). But as a fourfold premise for the exhortation (εἴ + indicative, *GGBB*, 690–94), he first listed four benefits God had provided believers through Christ and the Spirit. Together they would enable and motivate believers to live together in harmony.

Paul's first premise (εἴ) was that there is "encouragement" (παράκλησις) "in Christ." "In Christ" (ἐν Χριστῷ) denotes both the sphere in which believers find encouragement, and the cause of their encouragement

(Campbell, 2012, 105). It comes from their unity with him. "Encouragement" refers to lifting the spirits of others (BDAG s.v. "παράκλησις" 3, p. 766). Paul just stated that the Philippians shared in Christ's sufferings (1:29–30). Now he states that they shared in his encouragement and comfort (Fee, 1995, 179–80). God does not exempt believers from suffering. But he does lift their spirits and provide comfort in the midst of it.

> **God's Provision for Enabling Harmony in the Church (2:1)**
>
> Paul described four benefits, often channeled to us through *other* believers, that God provides Christ-followers. These enable us to live in humility and harmony with one another.
> 1. Encouragement in Christ—Unity with one another in Christ lifts believers' spirits.
> 2. Comfort from love—The love of God and Christ comforts believers.
> 3. Sharing of the Holy Spirit—Believers share the indwelling presence and life of the Spirit, along with fruit, gifts, and wisdom from him.
> 4. Affection/compassion—Believers experience tender concern and care from God and Christ.

Paul's second premise (εἴ) was that there is "comfort" (παραμύθιον) "from love." We should not sharply distinguish "comfort" from the previous noun "encouragement" (*TDNT* 5:820–21). The term refers to "that which offers encouragement, especially as consolation" (BDAG s.v. "παραμύθιον," p. 769). Paul used "encouragement" (παράκλησις) and "comfort" (παραμύθιον) nearly synonymously.

This comfort is attained "from love." Paul was referring to the love of God and of Christ that believers experience, sometimes directly (cf. Rom. 5:5; 2 Cor. 13:14) (Fee, 1995, 180–81). But note that often they experience God's love when it is expressed through other believers, and that the love believers express for one another ultimately comes from God (cf. Gal. 5:22; Col. 1:8; 2 Tim. 1:13). When believers love one another in Christ, they share God's love and so become channels of his comfort.

Paul's third premise (εἴ) was that there is a "sharing/fellowship of the Spirit."[3] "Sharing" (κοινωνία) denotes a "close association involving mutual interests and sharing, association, communion, fellowship, close relationship" (BDAG s.v. "κοινωνία" 1, p. 552). Previously Paul used this word to refer to the partnership he and the Philippians enjoyed in the gospel (1:5). He will use it again in 3:10 to refer to sharing in Christ's sufferings. Here it is clear that Paul's partnering with the Philippians was more than an evangelistic enterprise; it was a sharing of the Holy Spirit. "Sharing of the Spirit" suggests both that the Spirit brings about sharing (subjective genitive), and that the Spirit is the one whom Christians share (objective genitive) (Fee, 1995, 181; Reumann, 2008, 297, 303).

Because believers are in Christ, they share the one Spirit and are united. "In one Spirit all were baptized into one body, and all were given one Spirit to drink (1 Cor. 12:13). The Spirit indwells believers individually and corporately (Rom. 8:9; 1 Cor. 3:16; 6:19). Together, they share in the life, fruit, insight, power, and gifts of the Spirit. By this common experience of the Spirit, they experience "an ever-deepening fellowship" with one another (Harris, 2005, 941).

Paul's fourth premise (εἴ) was that there is "affection and compassion." He previously used "affection" (σπλάγχνα) in 1:8 to refer to the "affection" of Christ Jesus (BDAG s.v. "σπλάγχνον," p. 938), which was the basis and source of his own longing for the Philippians. "Compassion" (οἰκτιρμοί) refers to a "display of concern over another's misfortune" (BDAG s.v. "οἰκτιρμός," p. 700). Paul used the same term to speak of the "mercies" of God (Rom. 12:1) and

---

3   The parallel expression in 2 Corinthians 13:14 confirms that Paul is referring to the Holy Spirit.

to call God the Father of "mercies" (2 Cor. 1:3). Together, "affection" and "compassion" include both the inner feelings for others and the outward expression of those feelings.

Whose affection and compassion did Paul mean? There are no qualifying words such as "in Christ" or "in the Spirit" in this clause. Since Paul has already spoke of Christ's affection, and since elsewhere he referred to God's mercies, he likely refers first of all to the affection and compassion of God and of Christ (Martin and Hawthorne, 2004, 85). But in Colossians 3:12, using both terms, Paul exhorted believers to "put on . . . a heart of compassion." And Paul had already said that he longed for them all with the affection of Christ Jesus (Phil. 1:8). So "affection" and "compassion" may refer secondarily to believers' feelings toward one another (Fee, 1995, 182; Hansen, 2009, 110). By demonstrating affection and compassion, believers can be channels of God's affection and compassion.

These four premises are defining and motivating truths. Christians receive encouragement that comes from being joined to Christ; they experience comfort from the love of God and Christ; they experience deep fellowship with God and one another in the Holy Spirit; and they receive God's affection and compassion. These realities come both directly from God and through his people. What an encouraging statement of the spiritual benefits to be enjoyed in Christ and to be experienced in his body!

Paul's Joy in Their Unity (2:2a–b)
Based on the benefits just noted, Paul exhorted the Philippians to make him completely joyful by uniting around common goals for living together as Christians.

2:2. Τὸ αὐτὸ φρονῆτε is rendered "same mind' (ESV, NRSV, NASB), "like-minded (NIV, KJV, NKJV), "thinking the same way" (CSB), "agreeing wholeheartedly with one another" (NLT). Σύμψυχοι is rendered "one in spirit" (NIV), "in full accord" (ESV, NRSV, KJV, NKJV), "sharing the same feelings" (CSB), "working together with one mind" (NLT), "united in spirit" (NASB). Τὸ ἕν φρονοῦντες is rendered "of one mind" (NIV, ESV, NRSV), "focusing on one goal" (CSB), or "one purpose" (NLT, NASB, KJV, NKJV).

2:2a. Paul gave an exhortation based on the fourfold premise of 2:1: "make my joy complete." "Make complete" (πληρώσατε) suggests bringing to completion what is already begun (BDAG s.v. "πληρόω" 3, p. 828). Paul noted that he prays for them with joy (1:4). Now he urged them to fill up his joy. Again Paul let the Philippians know that he was not a detached apostle, but rather a spiritual father who wanted his children to walk in maturity. Their spiritual well-being would bring joy to his heart.

Paul explained (ἵνα) what it would take to make his joy complete: "that you are of the same mind." This was his primary concern. "To be of the same mind" (τὸ αὐτὸ φρονῆτε) refers to their seeking the same goals in unity. He wanted them to have common goals for living together as Christians. The example of Christ (2:5–11) will illustrate the mindset Paul desired. He did not mean that everyone must always have the same opinion about all matters. Such a demand would create conflict! The idea is that they were to cultivate a oneness in their collective thinking, attitude, and will (*TDNT* 9:233; *EDNT* 3:439).

Achieving Christian Unity (2:2c–4)
Five ways the Philippians were to unite around common goals for Christian living were by loving others with the love they had received from God; cultivating a harmonious spirit; being committed to one goal: a Christlike servant heart; not exhibiting self-promotion or conceit but thinking of others as more important; and being attentive to the needs of others.

2:2b. The first way they could unite around common goals for Christian living was by having "the same love" (τὴν αὐτὴν ἀγάπην).

They were to share with others the same love that they had experienced from God (2:1). This love is outward-focused. As Fee says, "Love begins when someone else's needs are more important than my own" (1995, 185). Paul will move in that direction in the next verse.

The second way they could unite around common goals for Christian living was by being "united in spirit" (σύμψυχοι). This word occurs only here in the New Testament, meaning "harmonious," "in full accord," "of one mind," or "together as one person"—a unity in feeling, thought, and action (BDAG s.v. "σύμψυχος," p. 961; *EDNT* 3:291). In 1:27 Paul exhorted them to contend for the gospel "with one mind/soul/spirit" (μιᾷ ψυχῇ). Now he urged them to cultivate a harmonious spirit in all matters of community living.

The third way they could unite around common goals for Christian living was by "thinking the *one thing*" (τὸ ἓν φρονοῦντες). This is "virtually synonymous" (Hellerman, 2015, 99) with the previous imperative in 2:2a, "think the *same thing*" (τὸ αὐτὸ φρονῆτε). If there is a distinction, "the same thing" emphasizes their general unity and harmony around a common goal. "The one thing" emphasizes the oneness of the goal. They were to be "focusing on one goal" (CSB) or "intent on one purpose" (NASB). Contextually, the single goal was to "have this mindset among yourselves which also [was] in Christ Jesus" (2:5)— the servant heart described in 2:6–8.

2:3. Ἐριθείαν is rendered "selfish ambition" (NIV, NRSV, NKJV), "selfishness" (NASB, cf. NLT), "rivalry" (ESV, CSB), or "strife" (KJV). Κενοδοξίαν is rendered "conceit" (ESV, NRSV, CSB, NKJV; cf. NIV, "vain conceit"; NASB, "empty conceit" or "vainglory" (KJV). NLT has "impress others." Ταπεινοφροσύνη is rendered "humility" (NIV, ESV, NRSV, CSB, NASB, cf. NLT) or "lowliness of mind" (KJV, NKJV). Ἡγούμενοι ὑπερέχοντας is rendered "consider above" (NIV) "count more significant than" (ESV), "regard/think/esteem as

better than" (NRSV, NLT, KJV, NKJV), "consider/regard more important than" (CSB, NASB).

2:3. The fourth way they could unite around common goals for Christian living was by not [acting] according to "selfish ambition" or "conceit." These are two attitudes and motives that destroy unity. In 2:2, Paul focused on their unity of heart and mind around a common pursuit. Now he moved to how they were to think of and act toward others.

Paul already mentioned "selfish ambition" (ἐριθείαν) as a characteristic of the preachers in Rome (1:17). It denotes self-seeking and the desire to promote one's own well-being or agenda at the expense of others (BDAG s.v. "ἐριθεία," p. 392; cf. *TDNT* 6:660–61; *EDNT* 2:52). Such a stance is directly opposite of Christ, who emptied himself for the sake of others. Selfishness on the part of individuals is a major stumbling block to unity in the body. When a person thinks only of himself, he cannot follow Christ.

An equally destructive characteristic is "conceit" (κενοδοξίαν). This term comes from the combination of two words "empty" and "glory," and occurs only here in the New Testament. It refers to the glory a person bestows on himself, but without adequate cause—an exaggerated, empty self-evaluation (BDAG, s.v. "κενοδοξία," p. 538), a high opinion of self that is baseless. Paul will contrast this person with Christ's example in the next paragraph. Christ did not promote himself but emptied and humbled himself. Then God exalted him. Those who exhibit "empty conceit" often attempt to exalt themselves by putting down others. The irony of such self-promoters is that they are actually insecure about their worth—therefore the need to seek honor from others.

Paul stated the contrast (ἀλλά) to acting according to selfish ambition and conceit. Instead, they were to be "in humility regarding one another as more important than yourselves." "Humility" is the major personal quality that promotes unity (BDAG s.v. "ταπεινοφροσύνη,"

p. 989). It is the positive, Christlike mindset that regards oneself in the proper way especially in regard to God, but also to others. It is unpretentious, unassuming, and modest. Paul used this noun in a similar way elsewhere (Eph. 4:2; Col. 3:12). Humility allows a person to regard others as more important than himself or herself. In Scripture it is "a mark of moral strength and integrity" (Bockmuehl, 1998, 110). Thurston notes that "humility" would have been a startling word to the Philippians because it was normally applied to slaves, not to the proud citizens of a Roman colony (Thurston and Ryan, 2005, 74).

Humility: Greek writers spoke of "humility" as a negative characteristic to be overcome. But they were thinking of such attitudes as shame and complacency—for example, a slave who saw himself as poor, unfit, and helpless. Humility was an inferiority complex, the opposite of self-confidence and self-respect (*TDNT* 8:1–5; *NIDNTTE* 4:448–49). This is not the positive biblical concept of humility. In Scripture, the humble person sees himself in proper relationship to God, not belittling himself, but seeing himself as dependent. He trusts in God, believing that God hears his prayers (Ps. 18:27; 102:17; Prov. 3:34; 29:23; Isa. 57:15; 66:2). For positive examples, see Moses (Num. 12:3), Paul (Acts 20:19), and especially, Jesus (Matt. 11:29; 2 Cor. 10:1; Phil. 2:6–8). Jesus did not see himself as unfit and helpless. He understood who he was in relation to his Father and, trusting in him, fulfilled his destiny through obedience. Humility is not self-disparagement, but seeing oneself rightly in relation to God and others.

Humility was the attitude in which the Philippians were to "regard one another as more important than" themselves. "Regard" (ἡγούμενοι) means, "to engage in an intellectual process, to think, consider" (BDAG s.v. "ἡγέομαι" 2, p. 434). Paul exhorted believers to focus on others in the Christian community in a conscious way, to give them their due consideration (Fee, 1995, 188).

Instead of being preoccupied with self and selfish desires (What do others think of me? What do I want for myself? How am I doing?), believers are to consider the needs of other Christians.

Though "one another" (ἀλλήλους) only occurs here in Philippians, Paul used this term forty times in his letters (BDAG s.v. "ἀλλήλους," p. 46; *EDNT* 1:63). It usually appears in exhortations of how believers are to treat fellow believers (the "one another" commands). For the truly humble person who has a proper view of his or her worth in God's eyes, "regarding one another" becomes possible. The small world of a mind turned inward becomes enlarged through turning one's attention outward—toward others. Unity within a group becomes possible when individuals become humble and selfless.

Individuals become humble and selfless when they regard others to be "more important" (ὑπερέχοντας) or "to be in a controlling or higher position" than themselves (BDAG s.v. "ὑπερέχω" 2–3, p. 1033). Paul meant that believers were to look at one another as "surpassing" themselves. Not that others are intrinsically more valuable—"better"—but that believers are to consider them "more important" (Fee, 1995, 189). Without putting themselves down, believers are to build each other up, to put each other in first place, and so honor, serve, strengthen, and encourage them (Hansen, 2009, 116).

Hellerman argues that in the honor culture of Roman Philippi, Paul's idea that believers were to consider one another as possessing a superior rank and so to exercise humility in serving them would be a revolutionary concept. For example, a believer of high social status possessing citizenship is to consider a Christian slave to outrank him or her, and so to serve that slave as a brother or sister in Christ who is "more important" (2015, 102). Christian ethics turns the social stratification based on "honor" upside down. In addition, with respect to family honor in the Mediterranean world, epigraphic evidence from Philippi suggests that family members deferred to persons within their kinship groups. But they competed with representatives of other families. When Paul exhorted believers at Philippi to regard others as more important than themselves, they would hear him urging them to treat one another as family, rather than rivals. In Christ they were family (Hellerman, 2009b, 15–25).

"Regard One Another as More Important Than Yourselves" (2:3) Illustrated

In the flow of Paul's argument in Philippians, he provided illustrations of his exhortation:

1:25—Paul was willing to live on in the flesh to serve believers.

2:6–8—Jesus was willing to die for the sake of believers.

2:17—Paul was willing to suffer in order to serve believers.

2:20–23—Timothy was willing to serve believers.

2:27–30—Epaphroditus was willing to die in order to serve believers.

3:18–19—Many served their own belly (negative example!).

2:4. In the first half of the verse, several translations add the word "only" so that "not only" will balance "but also" (ἀλλὰ καί) in the second half (ESV, CSB, NLT, NKJV, cf. NASB "merely"). "Also" (καί) is omitted by NIV, NRSV due to its omission in several important manuscripts.[4] Accordingly, NIV and NRSV do not balance the sentence by adding "only" to the first half of the verse.

2:4. Paul concluded his explanation of how they could unite around common goals for Christian living. The fifth way was by "each one looking not to his own [interests], but indeed all of you to the [interests] of others." This statement also clarified how the Philippians were to regard one

another as more important than themselves (2:3b). They were to be attentive to the needs of others. "Looking" (σκοποῦντες) means, "pay careful attention to, look out for, notice" (BDAG s.v. "σκοπέω," p. 931). "Interests" (NIV, ESV, NRSV, CSB, NLT, NASB, NKJV) does not occur in the Greek text, which literally reads "his own things" (τὰ ἑαυτῶν). "Interests" is commonly added in English versions in order to make clear what "things" Paul meant. It is appropriate to add some word such as "interests," "needs," "concerns." This is also true in the second half of the verse. For the question of whether "only" should be added to 2:4a, "look not *only* to his own interests," or omitted, "not looking to your own interests," see below.

THEOLOGICAL FOCUS

The exegetical idea (based on the encouragement, comfort, tender care, and presence of the Spirit God provides for followers of Christ, Paul exhorted the Philippians to make him completely joyful by living in harmony and humbly putting one another first) leads to this theological focus: Sincere humility that elevates others creates harmony in the church.

Unity in the church is based on the benefits God provides for believers through Christ and the Spirit (2:1). It is built on a common mindset (2:2) and humble relating to one another (2:3–4). We are to love others with the love we have received from God. We are to cultivate a harmonious spirit. We are to be focused on one goal—following the mindset Christ exhibited when he refused to use his divine status to his advantage, but rather emptied himself and became a human with the lowly status of a slave. His purpose was to give himself up in humble service for others in order to achieve their good by providing redemption. In the same way we are not to

---

4 "Also" (καί) is omitted in mostly western manuscripts (D*.c F G it vg^cl Tert) and K. Support for inclusion of καί is found in 𝔓⁴⁶ ℵ A B C D1 L P Ψ, etc. Scribes likely dropped "also" (καί) in the second half in order to balance it with the first half, which lacked "only" (Fee, 1995, 175, n. 8).

promote ourselves, but rather consider others to be more important. And we are to be attentive to their needs.

Paul did not say we must always have the same opinion on any matter. But we are to have a common mindset and united heart, and be devoted to a common pursuit. This theological focus highlights the central importance of unity in the church, and the important role of humility and selflessness for achieving it. A realistic humble attitude and a selfless regard for others on the part of individuals in the church are prerequisite for practical unity.

Look Not to Your Own Interests (2:4): Some English versions (ESV, CSB, NLT, NKJV, cf. NASB) add the word "only"—looking not *only* to his own interests—to avoid suggesting that Paul was saying believers were to show no concern at all for their own interests. "Not *only*" is intended to balance "but *also*." But "only" is not in the original, which reads, "looking not to his own interests." The addition "only" tends to soften Paul's point, which was that believers were to turn away from looking out for their own interests and instead look out for the interests of others. Paul similarly exhorted the Corinthians, "Let no one seek his own [good/advantage], but that of the other" (1 Cor. 10:24).

Other English versions (NIV, NRSV) do not add "only" and omit "also" (καὶ) in the second half. Nevertheless "also" (καὶ) has early and widespread support in the manuscripts and is likely original. Without "only" in the first part of the statement, "but also" (ἀλλὰ καὶ) turns attention away from the first part ("his own interests") and instead toward the second part ("interests of others") (Engberg-Pederson, 2003, 197–204). Its meaning is closer to "but rather" or "but indeed" than "but also" (Hooker, 2000, 500; Bockmuehl, 1998, 113–14). "Each one not looking to his own interests, but *indeed* all of you to the interests of others." Presumably Paul would expect each believer to provide for his or her own basic needs. But the point is to serve others and look out for

their interests first (per the example of Christ in the next section). This builds and maintains unity in the body.

PREACHING AND TEACHING STRATEGIES

Exegetical and Theological Synthesis

Philippians 2:1–4 opens with a central truth: Body life should be marked by comfort, unity, fellowship, and affection woven together by God's Spirit. Even amid external pressures, these theological realities bind the Philippian believers together. This information frames Paul's exhortation, calling his readers to singlemindedness in their attitude, goals, and humble service.

While Paul made humility sound normative, the virtue was not widely accepted in the Roman world. In fact, humility was considered a weakness. Similarly, in the Western world, social Darwinism advocates for rising to the top of the human pyramid. Most of our modern success stories lionize men with giant egos and women with tremendous ambitions. Humility receives less praise than high self-esteem. Customized consumerism, self-help gurus, and public educators feed the belief that there are no little men or women. Everyone can achieve greatness, they argue. The individual reigns, they assert. In such a world, others become an object or obstacle to personal goals, not partners pursuing the advance of God's kingdom.

Life as heavenly citizens, implied in Paul's "stand firm" edict, grows from shared attitudes, shared goals, and unity in the Spirit. The means to this unity is not blind uniformity and unconditional agreement, but something more demanding: love, harmony, a Christlike attitude, denial of self, and service to others (2:2b–4). Thus, to achieve unity (or even glimpse it for a season), a group of motely individualists must band together for the good of one another. Matching T-shirts and a memorable mission statement can only take God's people so far.

Preaching Idea

Putting others first sustains strong bonds with fellow Christ-followers.

Contemporary Connections

What does it mean?

What does it mean that putting others first bonds us with fellow Christ-followers? God envisions his people in groups; salvation has a corporate side. Hellerman (2010, 132) coins the term *familification*. "We are not only justified from our sins in salvation," he argues, "but also brought into the family of God." Followers of Jesus constitute the body of Christ; we serve, suffer, and grow together. Each one's gifts and needs shape the local congregation. Each person matters.

But doesn't it play out that some people's needs are met and others are overlooked? Sadly, too often this is true. For churches that always heed the latest crisis or loudest lobbyist, unity is not evident. These churches settle into appeasement and management strategies, not real unity. And the selfless ones may end up getting ignored or taken advantage of. However, in a healthy community, unity spreads a spirit of mutual encouragement and care. No single person sets the agenda for corporate life; rather, together they embrace the mission of the church: Christlike maturity and goals (Phil. 2:5; Eph. 4:11–16).

Is it true?

Is it true that we should put others first to sustain strong bonds? Yes, people "take one for the team" in all sorts of relational dynamics. In the world of professional sports, a player may accept a cut in salary to make room for more players. In the business world, one may accept an unflattering assignment to move the company forward. Parents often work extra hours or concede personal preferences to satisfy the whole family. (This explains countless viewings of Pixar's *Finding Dory* in my home.)

But "putting others first" can be a slippery metric. If we are keeping an account of selfless deeds, they are not as selfless as we hoped. If we amass them for later leverage, to broadcast how accommodating we are or to grumble about making concessions, we have lost the spirit of selflessness.

Can we ever escape selfishness? Probably not. However, it would be a theological mistake to assume *nothing* we do is good. God, in fact, created us for good works (Eph. 2:10). Jesus assumes our good works will point others to God (Matt. 5:16). Because God's Spirit works within his people, conforming us to the image of Jesus, we should assume selflessness occasionally leaks out. Spiritual formation writers call this "self-forgetfulness," meaning our focus on loving God and others has become so great that we have virtually left ourselves behind.

Now what?

Unity as a goal is misdirected. As a mission unto itself, unity breeds uniformity. On the other hand, directing people's minds to their shared blessings has a centering effect. A good starting point is to celebrate the comfort, unity, fellowship, and affection they share in God's Spirit (Phil. 2:1). Their common allegiance to the person of Jesus likewise begets unity (2:5–11).

Of course, by itself, intellectual agreement will not produce unity. Followers of Jesus must also commit to seeking the good of others. An orientation toward others requires the spade work of confessing one's ego, jealousy, bitterness, gossip, competitiveness, and other attitudes destructive to community. Selfish ambition may show up in the need to have the last word, respected title, or credit for a good idea. Selflessness, however, approaches others in an attitude of love.

Finally, local churches may help foster unity by clarifying and posting their ministry goals. Setting goals need not be viewed as an act of control or playing God. Rather, inviting the congregation to help shape, pray through, and actualize these goals brings ownership. Biblically defined goals revolve around Christian maturity and mission. The church may also provide opportunities for service that do not merely advance the programing of the church, but also foster loving community (e.g., potluck).

Creativity in Presentation

Give the congregation a glimpse into the world of ME. Hold up the two letters *M* and *E*. Work your way through a typical day, from morning until evening, showing how the message "It's all about ME" is ingrained (from the bathroom mirror to social media to advertising to diet). Suggest to them that the ME mentality even hits churches, where we have seats, songs, and sermons that fit ME. Let them know the most unifying fact of ME (flip the first letter over) is WE, which is a whole bunch of MEs (flip the first letter back). Then pose the questions: *How does this reflect God's idea of unity? And what happens when one ME doesn't get what ME wants?* Let them think before saying, *ME leaves.* (These letters can serve as references throughout the sermon, where you keep exchanging the *M* for *W*.)

The Christian faith is built upon Jesus's putting others first to sustain an eternal bond with his people. Other biblical examples have illustrative power, including the Israelites' offering in the wilderness to build the tabernacle (Exod. 36:1–7), or the early church's redistribution of wealth (Acts 4:32–37). David sacrificed his claim to the throne during Saul's reign, keeping Israel from civil war (1 Sam. 24:6). The death of Stephen and James, an ultimate act of selflessness, sparked unity in prayer and mission among God's people (Acts 8:1; 13:1–17).

Personal or historical examples may communicate the truth to the congregation. I (Tim) have worked at a few Christian conferences where the keynote speakers graciously declined their honorarium, donating it to the local church or nonprofit organization. I know a pastor who declined a lucrative offer in product development to lead a fledgling church. In *Who Stole My Church?* (2010), MacDonald records numerous trade-offs younger and older church members made (e.g., music styles) for the betterment of their congregation. Dietrich Bonhoeffer exchanged the comforts of asylum in the United States to lead a remnant of the German church in a unified fight against Hitler.

In any case, the sermon should make this point: Humbly putting others first creates harmony in the church. We should put others first to sustain strong bonds with fellow Christ-followers.

- God bonds with his people (2:1).

- We bond with each other (2:2).

- Putting others first sustains strong bonds (2:3–4).

DISCUSSION QUESTIONS

1. How does our culture view humility? What cultural factors and elements stoke our egos?

2. What steps can you take to make conflict a win-win scenario? What guardrails can you put in place to keep some people from constantly getting run over in conflict?

3. What relationships with others are going well? Why are these going well? What character qualities and behaviors promote healthy relationships?

4. How can the spiritual realities Paul states in 2:1 provide the resources for improving humility and unity in relationships with others?

5. Think of the spheres of relationships you experience in church (e.g., marriage and family, small groups, ministry teams, Sunday worship). What specific steps can you take to promote a deeper sense of common purpose in these relationships?

6. What are some ways you can demonstrate concern for the affairs of others?

Philippians 2:5–8

EXEGETICAL IDEA
Christ modeled a servant attitude when, rather than maintaining his exalted status, he became a man and suffered a humiliating death for others.

THEOLOGICAL FOCUS
Humility is demonstrated when, rather than insisting on our rights, we take the role of lowly servants.

PREACHING IDEA
Climb down the ladder of privilege to reflect the attitude of Jesus.

PREACHING POINTERS
Building on the call to loyalty, unity, and humility, Paul provided another exhortation: to reflect the attitude of Jesus. In one of the most notable and theologically parsed passages of the New Testament, the apostle described Jesus's downward mobility. The exegetical section sheds light on Jesus's glorious preexistence, incarnation, and inglorious death. Paul's description of Jesus's shameful descent would have sounded remarkable to an honor-oriented culture. Climbing down the ladder of privilege and status hinted of scandal in their context.

One of the driving narratives of today is the promise of upward mobility. From a child's earliest days of education, she learns she can achieve whatever she dreams. Educators chart a path of academic success leading to financial reward. Rags-to-riches stories capture our imaginations. Tales of success show how to arrive at the top at any cost, advancing from anonymity to celebrity, from average to extraordinary. Inversely, demotions and downsizing spell death in our personal life and economy. This passage presents a different path, encouraging followers of Jesus to follow his example and climb down the ladder of privilege to reflect his attitude.

CHRIST'S EXAMPLE OF HUMBLE SERVICE (2:5–8)

LITERARY STRUCTURE AND THEMES (2:5–8)

Continuing the exhortation of 2:2–4, Paul exhorted the Philippians to have the same attitude that Christ exhibited (2:5). To illustrate this attitude, Paul included a poetic description of Christ's life. This "Christ hymn" exhibits a V-pattern: 2:6–8 describing his self-emptying and self-humbling, 2:9–11 describing his exaltation. While Christ preexisted in the very form of God (2:6a), he did not consider his equality with God as an advantage to exploit (2:6b). On the contrary, he emptied himself by means of taking the very form of a slave and being made in the likeness of men (2:7a–c). Once he became a man (2:7d), he humbled himself (2:8a) by becoming obedient unto death—even to the extent of a humiliating death by crucifixion (2:8b). We will consider Christ's exaltation (2:9–11) in the next unit.

Christ's Example of Humility (2:5)
Christ's Preincarnate Glory and Status (2:6a)
Christ's Refusal to Use Deity to His Own
Advantage (2:6b)
Becoming a Man (2:7a–c)
Self-Humbling through Obedience to the
Point of Death (2:7d–8)

EXPOSITION (2:5–11)

In 2:3–4 Paul exhorted the Philippians to regard one another as more important than themselves and to look not to their own individual interests, but rather to the interests of others. Now he offered Christ as the supreme example of that attitude and behavior. By following Christ's example, unity in the church was possible. Verse 5 contains the exhortation: "Have this attitude among yourselves which was also in Christ Jesus." Then verses 6–11 contain a dramatic narrative of Christ's self-emptying and subsequent exaltation by the Father. Paul's point was that believers must *follow the example Christ modeled* when he became a man and suffered a horrendous death on a Roman cross

This text, one of the loftiest portraits of Christ in Scripture, is easily the most discussed and debated passage in Philippians. Reumann calls it "the Mt. Everest of Philippians study" (2008, 333). The language poetically intensifies as Paul described the self-emptying of the preincarnate Christ through his incarnation and death. The exposition of this section is necessarily longer than others because of the significant debate concerning the background and meaning of 2:6–8.

Much of the discussion in the scholarly world has focused on the origin of 2:6–11: whether this was a hymn from the early church that Paul quoted, or whether he elevated his prose style and composed it as he wrote the letter. Scholars also discuss the hymn's background: for example, whether it depicted Christ in terms of Isaiah's Servant of the Lord, or whether it compared Christ to Adam. For our purposes, understanding the text in the flow of Paul's argument in Philippians is of primary importance. If this was a hymn from the early church, Paul put his stamp of approval on it by including it here (Hansen, 2009, 132–33). We should interpret it according to its usage in the context of Philippians rather than seeking a "pre-Philippians" context and meaning.

The hymn divides into two parts, revealing a conceptual "V pattern." In 2:6–8, Jesus is the subject who acted. He emptied himself and humbled himself to the point of a humiliating death. The movement of the narrative is downward. In

2:9–11, the movement turns upward. God is the subject who acted. He exalted Christ so all would bow and acknowledge Christ as Lord. The narrative begins with Christ preexisting in the form of God (2:6) and ends with him universally acclaimed to be Lord (2:11). In between, it describes the drama of God's saving action in Christ's incarnation, death, and exaltation. The *depth* to which Christ *humbled* himself (incarnation and death on a cross) is matched by his being *highly exalted* by God. Even more than the devotional benefits of reciting the grand narrative of Christ's preexistence, incarnation, death, exaltation, and lordship, Paul's practical point at this stage in the letter was to provide a model for believers to follow. Christ's choice to humble himself for the sake of others and not insist on his "rights" established a paradigm for the Christian life.

Christ's Example of Humility (2:5)

The Philippians were to be humble servants in their relationships with others just as Christ was a humble servant.

> *2:5.* Φρονεῖτε is rendered, "have the mindset" (NIV), "have the mind" (ESV, NRSV, KJV, NKJV) or "have the attitude" (CSB, NLT, NASB). The plural φρονεῖτε ἐν ὑμῖν is made explicit by NIV ("in your relationships with one another"), ESV ("among yourselves"), and NASB ("in yourselves"). A major translation variant is due to the verb that must be supplied in the relative clause. Most translations supply a verb that makes Christ the one who possessed the desired attitude: "that *was* in Christ Jesus" (NRSV); "that Christ Jesus *had*" (NLT; cf. CSB); "which *was* also in Christ Jesus" (NASB, KJV, NKJV); "the same mindset as Christ Jesus [had]" (NIV). ESV reflects a different understanding of the relative clause: "have this mind . . . which *is yours* in Christ Jesus. In this rendering, "in Christ Jesus" denotes the sphere in which believers live.

2:5. Paul urged the Philippians to "have this attitude among yourselves which also [was] in Christ Jesus." This exhortation formed a bridge between the commands in 2:2–4 and the example in 2:6–11. He previously used the verb "have this attitude" (φρονεῖτε) in 1:7 and twice in 2:2. More than mere intellectual activity, the word denotes thinking, feeling, discerning, acting—a frame of mind. "This" (τοῦτο) points back to the attitude Paul spoke of in 2:2–4. The prepositional phrase "among yourselves" (ἐν ὑμῖν) could be translated "in you" (NRSV, NASB, NKJV) as it was in 1:6 ("you" is plural), but "among yourselves" (ESV) or "in your relationships" (NIV) better emphasizes the corporate nature of Paul's command here. He wanted this attitude to prevail throughout the community of believers. Naturally, it would need to be present within individual believers if it was to be prevalent among the community.

Paul identified the attitude he meant: "which (ὅ) also [was] in Christ Jesus." This pointed forward to the example he was about to narrate. The Greek text lacks a verb in the second half of the statement. Literally, it reads, "Have this attitude among yourselves, which also in Christ Jesus." Scholars debate what verb Paul intended to be supplied. There are two main options, yielding two different ideas. (1) The first option reads, "Have this attitude among yourselves, which also [was] in Christ Jesus" or something similar. In this view, "in Christ Jesus" denotes the person with the attitude Paul was encouraging. He made a direct comparison between the attitude Christ had and the attitude he wanted believers to have. The same attitude that was "in (ἐν) Christ" is to be "in/among (ἐν) you." Most English translations and many commentators prefer this option (Fee, 1995, 200–201; Bockmuehl, 1998, 122–24). The strength of this view is that it naturally prepares for the example of Christ in 2:6–8.

(2) The other option is less common among English translations (preferred by RSV, ESV), but is supported by a significant number of commentators (e.g., Martin and Hawthorne, 2004, 106–109; Silva, 2005, 95–96; Hansen, 2009, 120–21): "Have this attitude among yourselves, which also [you have] in Christ Jesus." In this view, the

phrase "in Christ Jesus" does not denote Jesus's attitude. It denotes the sphere in which Christians live. Supporters of this view note that Paul often used the phrase "in Christ" or equivalent as a technical phrase to denote the sphere of Christian existence. The attitude Paul was encouraging was the one appropriate for believers who had been incorporated into Christ. If this view is correct, Paul was exhorting believers to live up to their position in Christ. "You are in Christ. Now have the appropriate attitude." Many who hold this view still acknowledge that in 2:6–11 Paul presented Christ as an example to follow.

While we prefer option (1), option (2) has capable defenders. Since Paul did not provide a verb in 2:5b, we cannot be certain which one he intended. Both options suit the context, though option (1) seems to better introduce the example of Christ. Both options fit Paul's theology: Christian ethics are dictated by (1) Christ as example, and (2) the fact that believers are in Christ. Hooker argues that Paul's appeal contains *both* ideas—the attitude shown by Christ and the attitude that is therefore appropriate for those who are "in him" (2000, 507). On either view, Paul was going to present Christ as one who exhibited the behavior believers were to follow: Christ humbled himself, so his followers were to humble themselves. Christ did not insist on his "rights," so the Philippians were not to insist on their "rights." Christ sacrificially served others, so they were to sacrificially serve others.

It is important to notice that Paul exhorted believers to have *the same attitude* Christ had. No one can imitate his example by doing precisely what he did. Perhaps it is better to speak of "conforming to Christ's attitude" than to "imitating his example" (Hurtado, 1984, 123). Conforming actually goes beyond mere imitating (Nebreda, 2011, 334). No one else can be the Son of God who willingly becomes man and dies to pay for others' sins. But believers can conform their minds and hearts to his, resulting in humility and sacrificial service in obedience to the Father for the sake of others.

Christ's Preincarnate Glory and Status (2:6a)

Prior to Christ's becoming human (his preincarnate state), he eternally existed as the radiant, visible appearance of God's glory, majesty, power, privilege, and status.

2:6. Some translations render the circumstantial participle ὑπάρχων as concessive—"*although* he existed/was" (ESV, NRSV, NLT, NASB). Others allow it to reflect Christ's prior circumstances: "existing/being" (NIV, CSB, KJV, NKJV). Ἐν μορφῇ θεοῦ is most often rendered "in the form of God" (ESV, NRSV, CSB, NASB, KJV, NKJV), but is also rendered "in very nature God" (NIV) and "he was God" (NLT). Ἡγήσατο is rendered "consider" (NIV, CSB, NKJV), "count" (ESV), "regard" (NRSV, NASB), and "think" (NLT, KJV). Ἁρπαγμὸν is rendered "something to be used to his advantage" (NIV, CSB), "something to be exploited" (NRSV), "a thing to be grasped" (ESV, NASB), "something to cling to" (NLT), or "robbery" (KJV, NKJV).

2:6. Paul transitioned to the Christ hymn, signaled by the opening "who" (ὅς). This hymn (2:6–11) is the most important christological passage in Philippians, and one of the most important in the New Testament. Paul described the career of Christ, from his eternal preexistence in the form of God to his incarnation and death, to his exaltation, and ultimately to his universal acclamation as Lord at the second coming. He told his readers who Christ is, how he has acted, and how God responded. His portrait of Christ showed that it was God's intent to give sacrificially on behalf of others. This aspect of Christ—humble self-sacrifice for the sake of others—provided a model of the attitude believers were to follow. In providing this kind of example, the Christ hymn radically departed from notions of honor and status in other ancient Greco-Roman hymns. Humility was not celebrated in those hymns. Christ turned the idea of what should be considered honorable upside down (see chart below, adapted from Martin and Nash, 2015). Paul's main reason for including this passage was to support his exhortation in 2:5. He described the attitude that Christ exhibited. In addition, the vindication, exaltation, and glorification of Christ in 2:9–11 provided encouragement for believers who were suffering for their faith. It was worth it to follow Jesus, no matter the cost. He is Lord, and he will be universally acknowledged as such.

Theme	Hellenistic Hymns	Philippians 2:6–11
Origin	Described the subject as well-bred, the son of nobility; or, if of low birth, how he overcame this low status to become noble. The hero rose.	Although Christ preexisted in the form of God, he did not use that to his advantage, but willingly lowered himself and took the lowest form, the form of a slave. Christ descended.
Birth	A god was praised because he was born immortal. A man who became a god was praised because he overcame a mortal birth through deification (the mortal became immortal).	Although divine, Christ was born in the likeness of humanity. Instead of a human becoming a god, he was praised because God became a man.
Body	A deified man who ascended from earth to heaven was praised because his body was either transformed into a divine spirit or else left behind altogether.	Christ was praised not because he was a man who left behind a human body to become a divine spirit, but because as God he became human and added a human body.
Virtues	Praised for achieving the heights of human power. The characteristic of humility and the status of being weak, lowly, or a slave were considered obstacles to virtue.	Praised for humbling himself. Weakness, humility, lowliness, and servanthood were considered virtues.
Deeds	Mighty deeds were celebrated. Sacrificial deeds were praiseworthy if they achieved a higher goal, especially for others. But obedience was rarely celebrated. To be obedient meant one was of lower status.	In willingly becoming a slave Christ was obedient to the point of death. Rather than suggesting a low status, obedience was worthy of praise.
Manner of Death	Praised for a noble and honorable death, for example, courage shown in battle.	Praised for what was thought to be the most shameful way to die—execution by crucifixion (reserved for the lowest class of criminals, slaves, insurrectionists).
Honors Bestowed after Death	Praised for things such as famous children or deification—as in the case of the Roman emperors after Julius Caesar. These were normally so honored because in life they had achieved worldly honor and status.	Highly exalted by God to the place of universal honor above all powers. Christ was honored by God because he divested himself of his place of honor and became a lowly slave.
Names/Titles	Reflected titles earned during life, for example, "Olympian," King," Founder" (of a city), "Savior" (of a people).	Given the name that is above every name. Scholars disagree which name is in view: "Jesus" or "Lord."

"Who, existing in the form of God" describes Christ's preincarnate state—his eternal, pre-temporal existence from before the creation of the universe. "Existing" (ὑπάρχων) emphasizes that he continually, eternally existed prior to the incarnation (BDAG s.v. "ὑπάρχω" 2, 1029; Fee, 1995, 203). Most translations render this as a concessive idea: "*although* existing in the form of God." Although Christ was [a], he did not regard [b]. Paul presented Christ's decision to become human as one that might not necessarily follow from his existence in the form of God. Other translations render it simply to reflect Christ's prior circumstances: "existing in the form of God." Christ was [a], he did not regard [b].

What Does the "Preexistence of Christ" Mean?

The "preexistence of Christ" means that the eternal Son of God existed prior to the creation of time and space and prior to his becoming the human Davidic Messiah (Christ). It means more than that he preexisted in the plan, purposes, and mind of God (as we did); even more so, refers to an actual and personal existence. John put it this way, "In the beginning was the Word, and the Word was with God, and the Word was God." (John 1:1). In Jesus's words: "Truly, truly, I say to you, 'Before Abraham was, I AM'" (John 8:58). Paul presupposed or alluded to Christ's preexistence in several texts (Rom. 8:3; 1 Cor. 8:6; 2 Cor. 8:9; Gal. 4:4; Col. 1:16). While preexistence refers to the divine Son's timeless existence before and outside of creation, it does not refer to the preexistence of the human Jesus or of the Christ. It refers to the eternal existence of the Son who willingly took on human flesh in "the fullness of time" (Gal. 4:4) and became the Christ (see further, Byrne, 1997, 308–30; O'Collins, 2009, 248–49; Kärkkäinen, 2013, 178–81).

The major interpretive question concerns Paul's meaning when he spoke of Christ "existing *in the form* of God." The phrase clearly refers to Christ's state prior to the incarnation, otherwise the statements in 2:7 of Christ "being born in the likeness of men" and "being found in appearance as a man" do not follow. But in his preexistent state, what did "in the form of God" mean? In the New Testament, "form" (μορφή) occurs only here and in 2:7 ("taking the *form* of a slave"), and in the longer ending of Mark (16:12).

To begin, we should distinguish the "form of God" from the "image of God." While some have connected Christ existing in the "form" (μορφή) of God and Adam being created in the "image" (εἰκών) of God (Gen. 1:26–27 LXX), they are not the same. Steenburg has demonstrated that "form" (μορφή) denotes the visible, outward appearance or shape, while "image" (εἰκών, translating the Hebrew *ṣlm*) lacks this specific visual connotation (1988, 77–86). In 2:6 Christ's existence "in the form of God" is connected to his "being equal to God." Adam was created "in the image of God," but was not "equal to God." "Form" and "image" are not used synonymously.

In determining what "in the form of God" signifies, we need to consider (1) the meaning of "form" (μορφή), (2) the Old Testament background of God's visible appearances, (3) the Philippians 2:6 context in which Christ is "equal to God," but does not regard this as something to be exploited, and (4) Christ's being both "in the form of God" prior to the incarnation, and "taking the form of a slave" after it (2:7).

(1) In Greek literature outside the New Testament, "form" (μορφή) normally refers to the "outward appearance, the shape" of something (BDAG s.v. μορφή," p. 659), to that which may be perceived by the senses (*TDNT* 4:745), and is observable (Steenburg, 1988, 84–85; Fabricatore, 2010, provides an extensive survey of occurrences of the term). In the LXX, it refers to "outward appearance" (Judg. 8:18; Job 4:16; Isa. 44:13; Dan. 3:19; Wis 18:1). So "in the form of God" means that *in his preexistent state, Christ manifested the outward, visible appearance of*

God. One wrinkle comes when we take into account the fact that God is invisible; he is spirit and does not have a body (Col. 1:15; 1 Tim. 1:17; John 4:24). This leads us to consider the Old Testament background of how God visibly "appeared."

(2) In the Old Testament, the means by which God revealed himself so that he could be "seen" by his people on earth was by revealing his "glory" (LXX, δόξα) (e.g., Exod. 16:10; 24:16; 33:18; 40:34). The outward appearance or "form" of God in the Old Testament was his "glory." This does not suggest that the words "form" and "glory" are equivalent. It only suggests that God appeared through the visible manifestation of his glory. With this background, Christ existing "in the form of God" suggests that prior to the incarnation, he appeared as the glory of God, "the image of sovereign divine majesty" (*TDNT* 4:751; Hellerman, 2015, 110–11). Or, as Hebrews 1:3 puts it: Christ is the "radiance of [God's] glory" (Fowl, 1990, 50–54; 2005, 92–94). A similar but distinctive way to think of God's revelation of himself is to consider his *heavenly* appearance. Bockmuehl argues that Paul used "form" to refer to the visible identifying features of God as he appears in heaven. In this he followed Jewish mystical tradition (cf. Isa. 6:1–4; Ezek. 1:26; 8:2–3; Dan. 7:9). According to Bockmuehl, "the form of God pertains to the beauty of his eternal heavenly appearance" (1997, 21).

(3) In the context of Philippians, "in the form of God" is parallel to, though not synonymous with, his being "equal to God" (2:6b). The two phrases inform one another. Since Paul did not specify how Christ was equal to God, it is unwise to limit this equality to one particular aspect—for example, equal in status but not in essence—unless the context demands it. "Equal to God" may apply to his status, power, privilege, glory, essence, and so on. Christ preexisting "in the form of God" must be understood in a way that is compatible with this equality. This means that while "in the form (μορφή) of God" does not *refer* to the divine essence, it is compatible

with it and may *require* it. Indeed, it is hard to see how Christ can exist "in the form of God," or how he can be the visible manifestation of God's glory, without being divine in nature himself.

(4) Christ's existence "in the form of God" preceded his "taking the form of a slave," "being born in the likeness of men," and "being found in appearance as a man" (2:7). This required a change in form or outward appearance. The preexistent Christ was not man, nor did he exist in the form of man. He was in the form (visible appearance) of God. But at the incarnation, he became man, taking the form (visible appearance) of a slave.

Because the Greek term (μορφή) refers specifically to "form, outward appearance," we prefer the translation of ESV, NRSV, CSB, NASB, KJV, NKJV ("in the form of God") rather than NIV ("in very nature God"). Paul's point was that Christ existed as the visible manifestation of God—of his glory, majesty, power, and status. But it is also true that his being in the form of God implied that he shared the divine essence, so the NIV translation reflects a theologically correct deduction that goes back centuries (e.g., Gregory of Nyssa, *Against Eunomius* IV § 8).

This understanding of "form" (μορφή) can also account for its use in 2:7. If "in the form of God" denotes Christ's outward appearance as the glory of God, then "taking the form of a slave" denotes Christ's outward appearance in suffering humiliation as a man, even a criminal (Hansen, 2009, 137). The "form of God" (μορφῇ θεου) is the form proper to God, as an expression of his glorious divine state. And the "form of a slave" (μορφήν δούλου) is the form proper to a slave, as an expression of his lowly human state (*EDNT* 2:443).

To summarize, Christ existing "in the form of God" refers specifically to his eternal, preincarnate state as the radiant, visible appearance of God's glory, majesty, power, privilege, and status. In the context of 2:6–7 where it is connected to "being equal to God," "form of God" implies that he shares the divine essence.

Christ's Refusal to Use Deity to His Own Advantage (2:6b)

The preincarnate Christ did not consider his equality with God in essence and status to be something he should use for his own advantage.

In showing how Christ was an example of humility, Paul pointed out that, prior to becoming human, Christ did not regard his equality with God as something to exploit. "Regard" (BDAG s.v. "ἡγέομαι" 2, p. 439) connects with the same word in 2:3. Paul exhorted believers to "regard" one another as more important than themselves; here he gave an example of what Christ "did not (οὐχ) regard." The critical phrase "being equal to God" (τὸ εἶναι ἴσα θεῷ) is parallel to, though not synonymous with, "existing in the form of God" in 2:6a. Both phrases describe the preincarnate state of the eternal Son of God. Paul did not specify *how* Christ was equal to God, nor did he limit it to a particular aspect of God. Since Paul did not specify how he was equal to God, we should think of his divine essence, status, privilege, power, glory, and so on (cf. Garland, 2006, 219).

According to the various translations, Christ did not regard his equality with God as: "something to be used to his advantage" (NIV, CSB), "something to be exploited" (NRSV), "a thing to be grasped" (ESV, NASB), "something to cling to" (NLT), or "[an act of] robbery" (KJV, NKJV). Each of these translations is an attempt to render the phrase "did not regard being equal to God God *harpagmon* (ἁρπαγμόν)." This is the only time the term (ἁρπαγμόν) occurs in the New Testament. It does not occur in the Greek Old Testament and rarely in Greek literature outside the Bible. *Harpagmon* may be rendered as an act of robbery, a violent seizure of something; something one claims by gripping or grasping; a piece of good fortune, a windfall, prize, or gain (BDAG s.v. "ἁρπαγμός" 3, p. 133). Related to the meaning of the term (ἁρπαγμόν) is the question of whether Paul was saying (1) that Christ already possessed equality with God but did not regard it as (ἁρπαγμόν), or (2) that

Christ was grasping at equality with God—something he did not yet possess. Over the centuries, scholars have discussed the meaning of this phrase at length (for an extensive survey, see Wright, 1993, 62–90). Here are several popular English translations:

(1) "Did not consider it *robbery* (ἁρπαγμόν) to be equal with God" (NKJV, KJV). The idea is that Christ knew that he was equal to God, and he knew that he possessed this equality, not by an act of aggression or by usurping authority; rather, he possessed it as an inherent right. He knew that his divine status was not something he had seized illegitimately. A weakness with this view is that we expect Paul to give an example of Christ *not* taking advantage of his existing in the form of God (2:6a). But in this view, 2:6b becomes an example of Christ claiming his advantage and status. Paul in effect would be saying, "Have this attitude among yourselves which also was in Christ Jesus, who, existing in the form of God, knew that he was inherently equal to God." This view is not widely held today, but, according to Lightfoot and Wright, was supported by most Latin fathers, including Tertullian, Ambrose, and Augustine (Lightfoot, 1953, 134; Wright, 1993, 73).

(2) "Did not count equality with God *a thing to be grasped*" or "*clung to*" (ESV, NASB, NLT, NET). The idea is that Christ did not regard his equality with God as something to be greedily clutched and held on to. Instead he willingly emptied himself, abandoning (some of) the privileges of being equal with God. This view understands that Christ was always equal to God, but it makes a distinction between Christ's deity and the rights and privileges of that deity. The self-emptying of 2:7 consists not of giving up deity, but of giving up some of the privileges associated with it. The problems with this view are: (a) the language *could* be understood to mean that the preincarnate Christ, though already in the form of God, was not yet equal to God, and did not seek to acquire equality by grasping for it. (b) Or if it is understood to mean

that Christ *was already* equal to God, Paul *could* be saying that Christ decided not to hold on to being equal with God. The self-emptying of 2:7 could refer to his deity in some way. But this idea does not fit with teaching elsewhere in Paul's letters (and in the New Testament) that as a man, Christ remained fully divine. Lightfoot notes that this was the predominate view of the Greek fathers, including Origen, Theodore of Mopsuestia, and Cyril of Alexandria (1953, 135).

(3) "Did not consider equality with God *something to be used to his own advantage*" or "*something to be exploited*" (NIV, CSB, NRSV). This view results from an investigation of the rare idiom "to regard [something to be] ἁρπαγμὸν" in Greek literature. Though there are few linguistic examples, where it does occur, according to Hoover, it does not refer to grasping at something—whether to acquire it or to hold on to it. Rather, it depicts the *attitude one has toward something already possessed*, specifically, whether one will take advantage of it (Hoover, 1971, 118). This sheds light on 2:6b. The preincarnate Christ possessed equality with God. But he did not regard that equality as something to be taken advantage of or exploited. The advantages of this translation are: (a) It takes into consideration the meaning of the Greek phrase elsewhere. (b) It agrees with New Testament theology that Christ did not lay aside any of his divine equality in becoming a man. (c) It agrees with the context of 2:7–8, which states what Christ did—he chose to empty himself (though without any thought of giving up deity) and to humble himself. This view has found support among most, but not all, recent commentators (e.g., Wright, O'Brien, Fee, Thielman, Bockmuehl, Hawthorne [in Martin and Dodd] Hooker, Silva, Fowl, Garland, Hansen, Flemming, Witherington, Cohick, Harmon, Hellerman), and we regard it to be the preferred translation.

To sum up, "who . . . did not regard this being equal to God (ἁρπαγμόν) an advantage to exploit" means that while Christ in his preincarnate state was the visible manifestation of God's glory and equal to God in divine essence and status, he did not regard that equality something he should use to his own advantage. He did not excuse himself from the task the Father had assigned—to become a man and go to the cross. Rather than using his identity and status for his own advantage, he would humble himself and serve others. In this he has provided a model for believers—a model of humble service to benefit others, rather than selfishly hanging on to what they might possess.

This willingness to forego status and privilege would have been unheard of among the gods and great leaders known to the Philippians (e.g., Apollos, Zeus; Alexander the Great, the Roman Caesars). They always used their positions to their own advantage, not to serve others (Hansen, 2009, 146). This kind of voluntary stepping down was also unknown in ancient novels about heroes, which like the culture, valued honor and status (Fisk, 2006, 65, 73). Unfortunately, too often we see the same thing among leaders in today's world, both Christian and non-Christian. But it must not be that way among those who follow Christ.

Becoming a Man (2:7a–c)

Without ceasing to be God, Christ set aside the visible appearance of his glory and the divine privileges of his status by becoming a lowly man.

2:7a–c. Ἐκένωσεν is rendered more literally, "he emptied himself" (NRSV, CSB, NASB), or more figuratively, "he made himself nothing" (NIV, ESV), "he gave up his divine privileges" (NLT), or "made himself of no reputation" (KJV, NKJV). Μορφὴν δούλου, corresponding to μορφῇ θεοῦ in 2:6a, is rendered, "form of a servant/slave" (ESV, NRSV, CSB, NASB, KJV, NKJV) or "humble position of a slave" (NLT), but also "very nature of a servant" (NIV). Ἐν ὁμοιώματι ἀνθρώπων is rendered "in human likeness" (NIV, NRSV), "in the likeness of men" (ESV, CSB, NASB, KJV, NKJV), but also "as a human being" (NLT).

2:7a–c. In contrast to what the preexistent Christ did not do (2:6b), this is what he did do. "But" (ἀλλά) presents a strong contrast: "on the contrary." He did not regard being equal to God an advantage to exploit; on the contrary, he "emptied" (ἐκένωσεν) himself. While Romans 8:3 and Galatians 4:4 focus on God's initiative at the incarnation (God sent his Son), Philippians 2:7 focuses on Christ's initiative (Hooker, 2000, 504).

In the nineteenth century, a misguided attempt to state *what* Christ "emptied himself of" gained popularity. On this view, Christ emptied himself of certain divine attributes (omniscience, omnipotence, omnipresence) and maintained others (love, righteousness, holiness). The theological result of this view is that the human Christ was not fully God. Christ had traded the form of God for the form of a human slave, and in the process given up some of his deity. But the text does not say this. Would it even be possible for God the Son to lay aside some of his divine attributes? In order to understand what Paul meant by "he emptied himself," we should consider two factors: (1) the metaphorical use of "emptied," and (2) the two explanatory clauses that follow—taking the form of a slave, being born in the likeness of men.

(1) *The metaphorical use of "emptied."* Paul used the verb "empty" (κενόω) four other times in his letters (Rom. 4:14; 1 Cor. 1:17; 9:15; 2 Cor. 9:3). Each time, the concept of "emptying" was metaphorical. This suggests that "emptied" in 2:7 also was figurative. It is not that Christ literally emptied himself of something, but that he "poured himself out" (Fee, 1995, 210; Martin and Hawthorne, 2004, 117). He "made himself nothing" (NIV). Wright states:

> [Emptied] does not refer to the loss of divine attributes, but—in good Pauline fashion—to making something powerless, emptying it of apparent significance. The real humiliation of the incarnation and the cross is that one who was himself God,

and who never during the whole process stopped being God, could embrace such a vocation. (1993, 84)

The same thought was expressed using a different metaphor in 2 Corinthians 8:9 ("though he was rich, yet for your sake he became poor"). Paul probably made a play on words with 2:3 by using the verb "emptied." In 2:3 he warned the Philippians not to do anything according to "conceit" (κενοδοξίαν). He was referring to those who might bestow on themselves "empty glory" and who might on their own way. In contrast to that attitude, he said that Christ, who truly existed in glory, "emptied" himself (Martin and Hawthorne, 2004, 117).

But if Christ did not empty himself of divine attributes, and if the verb "emptied" was used metaphorically, meaning he "poured himself out," can we still say that Christ emptied himself of *something*? Lightfoot states that he gave up "the glories, the prerogatives, of Deity . . . the insignia of majesty" (1953, 112). According to Martin, "he who existed eternally in a heavenly station surrendered that high place" (1997, 194). The best way to describe what Christ gave up or surrendered is to consider what Paul said in the two explanatory clauses that followed (2:7b–c).

(2) *Two explanatory clauses.* Paul explained how Christ emptied himself: by "taking the form of a slave" (2:7b), and "being born in the likeness of men" (2:7c). The first clause presented a stark contrast: Christ traded the form of God for the form of a slave (BDAG s.v. "δοῦλος" 1a, p. 260). "Form" (μορφήν) has the same meaning it did in the phrase "form of God" (2:6a). It refers to the shape or outward appearance Christ took as he became a human. He voluntarily moved from the highest and most glorious appearance and status to the lowest. "Slave" should be understood relative to Christ's preexistent glory. Paul was not saying that he became a literal human slave (as opposed to a free man) in Roman society. Christ's "emptying himself" consisted of taking the lowly form of a human

being. This form of existence concealed his true dignity and glory. In this sense, it is correct to say that when Christ became a man, without giving up his deity, he did give up for a time the *visible appearance* (form) of the glory and majesty he still possessed. Further, he set aside the divine *privileges of status and rank* in order to become a lowly human. This is what it meant for him to trade the form of God for the form of a slave. For purposes of Paul's illustrating the exhortation of 2:3–4, this would have been an especially powerful example among the socially conscious Philippians (Witherington, 2011, 143; cf. Hellerman, 2015, 115).

It may be that the slave metaphor simply expresses the extent to which Christ chose to empty himself. Leaving his exalted status and riches in heaven, he opted for a lowly status and life of poverty in Israel (MacLeod, 2001, 320–21). But can we press the metaphor and ask, "Theologically, to whom or what did Christ make himself a slave?" Hurtado says he was a slave to God (1984, 112). Gupta argues that Christ was a "double agent"—as a man he appeared to be a slave to the powers of sin and death, but in reality, as the Son of God, he was the Father's loyal agent who came to subvert these powers (2010, 1).

The second clause, "being born in the likeness of men," confirmed the reality of the incarnation. "Men" (ἀνθρώπων) focuses on his becoming *human*, not specifically *male* (Thurston and Ryan, 2005, 82; cf. BDAG s.v. "ἄνθρωπος" 1, p. 81)). The temporal event of "being born" (aorist participle γενόμενος) contrasts with the eternal state of "existing" (present participle) in the form of God (2:6a). Christ has always existed in the form of God, but in a moment in time, he became a human (compare Paul's same use of the aorist participle, Rom. 1:3; Gal. 4:4).

"In the likeness (ὁμοιώματι) of men" does not suggest that Christ was not fully human and only appeared to be a man. "Likeness" emphasizes what Christ shared in common with us: humanity. "In the likeness of sinful flesh"

(Rom. 8:3) makes the same point—that Christ became human. Elsewhere Paul also employed "likeness" to denote a common experience, or lack of it (Rom. 6:5; 5:14). At the same time, "likeness" seems to indicate that while Christ shared our humanity, he was distinct. While human, he still retained his deity. So "likeness" denotes commonality yet with distinctiveness (BDAG s.v. "ὁμοίωμα" 3, p. 707; cf. Fee, 1995, 213; Hansen, 2009, 152–53). Not only was he divine; he also consistently and fully obeyed God (*TDNT* 5:197). Christ was fully man, but a different kind of man.

To sum up, "he emptied himself" consisted of Christ setting aside the visible appearance of his glory and the divine privileges of his status by becoming a man. In contrast to his preexistent glory, he took the form of a lowly slave. He did this without ceasing to be fully God, although his full glory and majesty were masked for a time. While he chose "to limit himself in the exercise of certain divine prerogatives . . . he never set aside anything essential to his being God" (Fee, 2006, 34).

Self-Humbling through Obedience to the Point of Death (2:7d–8)

Once Christ became a man he humbled himself by obeying God to the extent of enduring a humiliating Roman crucifixion.

> *2:7d–2:8.* Σχήματι . . . ὡς ἄνθρωπος is rendered "in appearance as a man" (NIV, NASB, NKJV), "in human form" (ESV, NRSV, NLT), or "as a man in his external form" (CSB). Γενόμενος is rendered "by (means of) becoming obedient" (NIV, ESV, CSB, NASB; cf. NLT, "*in* obedience) or "and (so) became obedient" (NRSV, KJV, NKJV). The genitive σταυροῦ is rendered "on a cross" (NIV, ESV, NRSV, CSB, NLT, NASB) or "of the cross" (KJV, NKJV).

2:7d. Paul continued the downward movement of the first half of the hymn. "Being found" (εὑρεθεὶς) modifies the main verb of 2:8 ("humbled"), denoting time or circumstance.

"Being found" suggests discovery through observation (BDAG s.v. "εὑρεθείς" 2, p. 412), emphasizing that Jesus's real humanity could be seen by anyone (*TDNT* 7:956). While "being born in the likeness of men" (2:7a) refers to the historical event of Christ's birth, "being found in appearance as a man" refers to the empirical evidence of that event—he was seen to be human (Hansen, 2009, 154). "Appearance" (σχήματι) denotes the form in which something appears (BDAG s.v. "σχῆμα" 2, p. 981). Like the preceding "taking the *form* of a slave" and "being born in the *likeness* of men," it does not suggest that Christ only *appeared* to be human (but was not). Together, these three statements emphasize the reality of Christ's complete humanity, while at the same time retaining his distinctiveness as one who was more than human (Martin and Hawthorne, 2004, 120).

2:8. "He humbled (ἐταπείνωσεν) himself" is parallel to "he emptied himself" in 2:7a:

> Existing in the form of God . . . he *emptied* himself. . . .

> Being found in appearance as a man, he *humbled* himself. . . .

Just as Christ emptied himself when he existed in the form of God, so he humbled himself once he existed as a man. This depicts Christ's voluntary choice to live as a simple peasant (cf. 2:7—"taking the form of a slave"). He did not choose to spend his time on earth as the most exalted of men, though that would have been his right. He made the deliberate decision to take the lowest place. Christ's "whole life was characterized by self-surrender, self-renunciation, and self-sacrifice" (Martin and Hawthorne, 2004, 122). Hellerman suggests "humiliated" rather than "humbled," for the former "signifies action performed in a social context" while the latter "denotes an attitude or state of mind"

(2015, 116; BDAG s.v. "ταπείνοω" 2a, p. 990). Jesus's self-humbling was not just a mental exercise, but also a humiliating public event! Some scholars see an echo of Isaiah's Servant of the Lord, who "poured out his soul to death," in Paul's description of Christ here.

The word "humbled" (ἐταπείνωσεν) echoes Paul's exhortation in 2:3, that "in *humility*" (ταπεινοφροσύνη) believers should regard one another as more important than themselves. Christ provided the model for the attitude and behavior Paul was encouraging. And note, he was not humbled by someone else; he actively humbled himself. In fact, for Christ to serve as a model of the humility Paul was encouraging, he had to humble himself. His example would not be relevant unless it was self-humbling. The counterpart to his self-humbling will be his exaltation by God in the next verse.

"Becoming (γενόμενος) obedient unto death" explains how Christ humbled himself. Paul does not specify *to whom* Christ was obedient (BDAG s.v. "ὑπήκοος," p. 1035). But the following statement, "Therefore also *God* highly exalted him" suggests that he obeyed God the Father. The concept of Christ's obedience to the will of the Father is found elsewhere (Mark 14:36; John 4:34; 6:38; Gal. 1:4; Heb. 5:8; 10:7). "Unto" (BDAG s.v. "μέχρι" 3, p. 644) "death" (θανάτου) denotes the *extent* of Christ's obedience. He obeyed his Father's will all the way to "death" (BDAG s.v. "θανάτο" 1bβ, p. 443). "Even death on/of a cross" denotes the nadir of the downward movement, the extreme measure to which Christ humbled himself. The genitive "cross" (σταυροῦ) which is a "pole to be placed in the ground and used for capital punishment" (BDAG s.v. "σταυρος" 1, p. 941) may refer to the place of his death ("on a cross") or to what produced his death ("of the cross") (*GGBB*, 105). His was not just any death; it was death by crucifixion. "By stressing the manner of Christ's death, Paul stresses the degree of humiliation he suffered" (Kraftchick, 2007, 201).

In the Roman Empire, death by crucifixion was the ultimate humiliation and shame. As a form of capital punishment, the Romans reserved crucifixion for slaves, violent criminals, and unruly elements in rebellious provinces. They carried it out publicly, above all else for its effect as a deterrent. By displaying the naked victims at a prominent place—such as a crossroads or on high ground—they humiliated them (Hengel, 1977, 87). Often their corpses were left on the crosses to be eaten by wild animals until what remained was tossed into a common grave. It was the most shameful death possible.

For Jews, anyone who was crucified was under God's curse (Deut. 21:23; Gal. 3:13). The idea that their Messiah had been crucified was

Christ Crucified by Diego Velázquez (1632)
Courtesy of Crisco 1492

offensive. To Gentiles it was simply foolishness (1 Cor. 1:23). In humbling and humiliating himself, Christ endured the cross, despising its shame (Heb. 12:2). For the early Christians who lived under Roman rule, the shame of the cross was obvious. The cross was a sign of humiliation and rejection. The stigma for early Christians was that the one they followed as "Lord" had been crucified as a rebel, as the lowest form of criminal. This is the extent to which Jesus willingly humbled himself. Instead of insisting on the rights and privileges that were legitimately his, he was obedient unto death—even the shameful death of a Roman cross. In this way he established a paradigm for the lives of would-be Christ-followers: "Whoever does not carry his own cross and come after me cannot be my disciple" (Luke 14:27).

The emphasis on Christ's humiliation would have created a stigma for the Philippian believers. In the midst of their status-conscious culture, they followed one who had been shamefully discredited. But this fact would also be encouraging for those who experienced humiliation themselves. They followed a Savior who had taken the form of a slave and experienced humiliation like them—only more so! The preexistent Son willingly became man to experience shame and humiliation with them! The depth of Christ's humiliation in the first half of the hymn prepares Paul's readers for the height of his exaltation in the second half.

THEOLOGICAL FOCUS

The exegetical idea (Christ modeled a servant attitude when, rather than maintaining his exalted status, he became a man and suffered a humiliating death for others) leads to this theological focus: Humility is demonstrated when, rather than insisting on our rights, we take the role of a lowly servant.

Christ's humility and sacrificial service provide us with a paradigm for the Christian life.

His incarnation consisted of embracing lowly service as a human. In this he has shown us how to put others first. He put us first by (1) not regarding his status as something to be used for his advantage; (2) making himself nothing, taking the form of a lowly slave; (3) humbling himself and obeying God to the point of a humiliating death. He has set the example we are to follow.

Christ's actions in humbling and giving of himself reveal an aspect of the very character of God (Hooker, 2000, 514–15; Fowl, 2005, 96). The extent of his humiliation reveals the extent of God's love and commitment to his people. "If we want to know what God is like . . . God is like Jesus" (Flemming, 2009, 124). Now we too are to love and serve others with the same humility.

Christ's self-emptying and self-humbling is a rebuke to the way the world normally esteems and uses power and status—in particular, in the church. It is not the *possession* of status and power that is wrong, but rather its *misuse* (Hellerman 2003b, 433). Christ used his power and status, not to benefit himself, but to benefit others. In virtually all cultures today, individuals tend to guard their status and power, and use it to their own advantage. But Christ, through his example, calls us to take the humble role of a servant and put the interests of others first. He shows us how to use power and status correctly and in a way that subverts worldly ideas.

PREACHING AND TEACHING STRATEGIES

Exegetical and Theological Synthesis
Philippians 2:5–8 artfully presents Jesus's descent from preexistent glory to criminal death. He chose not to leverage his glorious status but to embrace a servant's role. Not only does the Christ hymn echo Isaiah's Suffering Servant passage (ch. 53), it also contrasts radically with hymns to rival gods of the Greco-Roman world. Paul's presentation of Jesus both inspires the Philippians' praise and illustrates the ideal mindset of a kingdom citizen: willing to climb down the ladder of privilege rather than cling to status.

Jesus exchanges the "form of God" (2:6) for the "form of a slave" (2:7). To a status-sensitive culture, his tradeoff stands out as more than a step down: Jesus inverted the value pyramid of his day. He did not simply ignore distinctions in status, but he redefined them from a divine perspective, preferring humility to honor.

Furthermore, Jesus did not demonstrate mild meekness. More than giving up a spot in line or seat on the bus, Jesus subjected himself to the shameful torture of crucifixion. Clause by clause, the Christ hymn outlines his tragic climb down the ladder to the nadir of human existence. Neither the gospel nor this hymn gives death the final word—he is risen, indeed—but this passage does not allow us to skip lightly over the downward mobility of Christ Jesus.

Preaching Idea
Climb down the ladder of privilege to reflect the attitude of Jesus.

Contemporary Connections

What does it mean?
What does it mean to climb down the ladder of privilege to reflect the character of Christ? First, we recognize the ladder of privilege has different rungs which we inherit at birth. Every human life is subject to uncontrollable conditions. No one choses his family of origin, including birthplace, biology, or economic boundaries. However, God is no stranger to our origins: he knit us in the womb (Ps. 137:13) and brought us forth at appointed times and places (Acts 17:26).

Second, social status is not static. We may choose to climb up or be forced to climb down. And while Western culture champions upward mobility, Scripture consistently admonishes downward motion (e.g., James 1:9; 4:10; 1 Peter 1:7–8). God shows preference for the humble, promising to raise them up. Jesus warns his disciples against power-grabbing, encouraging them to a life of service (Mark 10:41–45).

His tough conversation with the rich young ruler may have been tailor made for the wealthy man, but its principle still applies: status is less important in God's economy than sacrifice.

Third, climbing downward imitates Jesus's example, but does not assure his outcomes. Jesus inverted the social pyramid as an act of obedience to secure salvation for the world. We choose humility as an act of obedience that enriches community. The pursuit of wealth and worldly status leads to rivalry among God's people. The imitation of Jesus—who is the tuning fork for his followers—secures unity in our humility.

Is it true?

Is it true that climbing down the ladder of privilege reflects the character of Christ? The answer depends on the motive and manner of our descent. Followers of Jesus are prone to two ills: the humble brag and legalistic obedience. The humble brag uses our personal sacrifices to shine a spotlight on ourselves. The man who resigns from a formidable job to pursue menial work in hopes of writing a memoir about it has committed a humble brag. The woman who has given her leisure time (a sure sign of status) to volunteering at the local food bank, only to lament how exhausted she is by her service, has committed the humble brag. While the motive to share may not always precede an act of humble service, we must beware of that motive creeping in. Jesus never gave into this temptation. Neither shall we, if we want to reflect his character.

Legalistic obedience likewise fails to capture the attitude of Jesus. Setting menial work, low pay, and marginal social status as the standard for followers of Jesus misses the point. Not every follower of Jesus will climb down the ladder of privilege. In fact, God can make great use of kingdom citizens with wealth and positions of influence. William Wilberforce leveraged his political clout to champion the abolition of slavery. Sacrifice, not status, is at the heart of the exhortation.

> **William Wilberforce**: Wilberforce was an English statesman who tirelessly campaigned for the abolition of slavery in Great Britain. His life spanned from 1759 to 1833. Days before his death, the Slavery Abolition Act of 1833 passed. His commitment to Jesus motivated his political convictions. Search "William Wilberforce" on Wikipedia for fuller treatment of his life.

Now what?

How does a follower of Jesus climb down the ladder of privilege? Are we expected to quit our jobs, sell our goods, and join the lowest ranks of society? No. Wholesale renunciation of our privileges is not wise. Even the apostle Paul claimed his Roman citizenship to make an appeal to Caesar. We must be clear: A downward climb begins with purpose and proceeds with thoughtfulness. Just as the Christ hymn reflected intentional stages, so should our descent.

First, we must acknowledge the privileges we steward. God has given each of a certain degree of status, freedom, and wealth. Whereas culture would push us to accumulate more, we should gratefully accept our lot. Contented people hold privileges loosely, neither guarding them nor hoarding them, but receiving them as a gift from God and relinquishing them when he calls us to.

The next step down the ladder of privilege moves us from grateful stewards to sacrificial servants. Consistent with the character of Jesus is the act of attending to others' needs (Matt. 25:31–46; Mark 10:35–45). While there is no mandate to put ourselves in harm's way for others (i.e., legalistic obedience), the call to service is undeniable. No act of service is too small—from a cup of cold water to an inheritance gift—if it flows from a desire to imitate Jesus.

Creativity in Presentation

For a visual illustration, set an eight- or twelve-foot ladder on the stage. At each step on the ladder, briefly describe an advancement in your career, beginning with early education and advancing to the apex: the author, podcaster, and pastor of a world class megachurch. Then work your way down the ladder, step-by-step, describing Jesus's descent from preexistent glory to shameful death. With the help of a few other hands, flip the ladder over for the remainder of the sermon.

Examples of climbing down the ladder to reflect the attitude of Jesus abound in the business world. A clip or reference to the television show *Undercover Bosses* might prove illustrative. Richard Stearns shares his testimony in *The Whole in Our Gospel* (2009), reporting his transition from making impressive sums of money in the corporate world to steady improvements in the developing world. Frank Blake, former CEO of Home Depot, was known for donning an orange apron and serving customers from the floor in local stores. He modeled his servant leadership and customer service culture after Jesus. A clip from his interview on Andy Stanley's Leadership Podcast (iTunes.com 9/3/15; 10/1/15) provides helpful advice.

David Platt has spurred many followers of Jesus to leverage their privileges for good causes. Two of Platt's five challenges in *Radical* (2010) include sacrifices of time and money. The book nudged me and my wife to adopt a child with special needs from Ethiopia; it inspired several of our friends to support us financially in the process. Other personal examples of sacrifice and downward mobility from within your church context or ministry partnerships will make the message memorable.

Whatever creative means you employ, be sure to emphasize the following: Humility is demonstrated when, rather than insisting on our rights, we take the role of a lowly servant. Therefore, we should climb down the ladder of privilege to reflect the attitude of Jesus.

- Jesus left a model of downward mobility to mimic (2:5).

- Jesus did not leverage his divine and glorious status (2:6).

- Jesus lowered himself to human and slave status (2:7).

- Jesus let himself die a criminal and inglorious death (2:8).

DISCUSSION QUESTIONS

1. How does the idea of privilege bring perspective to recent American debates over immigration and racism?

2. What privileges have you inherited? How can you leverage them for others' good?

3. Where have you seen God humble you in life? What did you learn from the experience?

4. How does the example of Christ in 2:6–8 challenge the notion of leadership you commonly experience in your world (at work or in other places)?

5. What inner qualities must one possess in order to follow Christ's example *from the heart*? What inner qualities would you personally need to develop in order to exhibit the "same attitude" as Christ?

6. What is the most "distasteful" aspect of becoming a "servant" or being treated like one? What change in your thinking is necessary in order to deal with this?

7. What "advantages" in your life will you have the most difficulty "refusing to exploit" if you are to live according to Christ's example?

8. What are some practical ways you can begin to follow Christ's example right now—in your work, family, or other areas?

Philippians 2:9–11

EXEGETICAL IDEA

God the Father highly elevated Christ Jesus to the highest universal status so that all personal beings—angelic and human—would submit to Christ and openly declare his divine, sovereign authority, and so increase the Father's fame.

THEOLOGICAL FOCUS

Christ Jesus reigns as the supreme Lord of the universe, and will be acknowledged one day by all.

PREACHING IDEA

Jesus's crowning victory beckons our humble loyalty.

PREACHING POINTERS

Paul completed the Christ hymn focusing on God's work of exaltation. Jesus's humble, selfless steps downward are matched by God's sweeping act of vindication: He raised up Jesus and gave him the uppermost name. Jesus Christ, not Caesar, is Lord. To the first-century readers, Jesus's reversal of misfortune served both to exhort Christlike character (2:5) and bring comfort in the face of suffering (1:28). Jesus's victory challenged the imperialistic images and symbols of status broadcast daily in the streets of Philippi. Their challenge was to acknowledge Jesus's victory by submitting to him until his return.

Competition, not humility, drives the Western world to enthrone a winner for every hour, season, and sphere of life. Athletes and coaches aim for personal records, hall of fame status, and team championships. Students pour into their academics to rise to the head of the class. Politicians set their aim on the White House. We hitch our wagons to these exalted figures, who require nothing from us in return. Moreover, many of us strive to make a name for ourselves. Sadly, personal victories are short-lived; worldly triumphs do not last. This passage begs us to acknowledge the exaltation of Jesus: his crowning victory beckons our humble loyalty.

GOD'S ELEVATION OF CHRIST (2:9–11)

LITERARY STRUCTURE AND THEMES

This is the second half of the Christ hymn. In response to Christ's self-emptying and self-humiliation, God highly exalted him and gave him the name ("Lord") that is above every name (2:9). The purpose and result of God's exalting Christ and bestowing on him the name above every name was that at the name of Jesus all rational creatures throughout the universe should bow in submission and acknowledge that Jesus Christ is "Lord" (2:10–11a). The ultimate purpose and result (εἰς) for all of this is glory (renown) for God the Father (2:11b).

God's Elevation of Christ (2:9)
Angelic and Human Submission to Christ (2:10)
Universal Acknowledgment of Jesus's Sovereign Authority (2:11a)
God the Father's Fame (2:11b)

EXPOSITION (2:9–11)

The Christ hymn continues. In the first half of the hymn (2:6–8), Christ was the one who acted and the movement was downward, climaxing in his death on a cross. This self-humbling was the example Paul presented as an attitude the Philippians were to follow. But he could not leave the narrative of Christ's career there. In the second half of the hymn, with a dramatic turn, Christ remains the central character, but God is now the one who acted. Christ is the object acted upon, and the movement is upward, climaxing in the universal acknowledgment that Jesus Christ is Lord, to the glory of God the Father. This was

the Father's vindication of Christ who humbled himself. While the exaltation of Christ is unique, Paul may well have wanted to reassure believers through this example that they too would experience vindication by God at the second coming (cf. 3:20–21). In this way, the hymn provided not only a challenge to believers to humble themselves and put others first; it also provided reassurance for believers who were suffering for their faith in Christ (Thielman, 1995, 114; Bockmuehl, 1998, 140–41; Nebreda, 2011, 337–40).

God's Elevation of Christ (2:9)

In response to Christ Jesus's self-humiliation, God vindicated him by elevating him to the highest level in heaven and giving him the appropriate name to his status ("Lord"), a name with more authority than any other in the universe.

2:9. "Therefore also" (διὸ καί) draw an inference or conclusion, connecting God's action in 2:9–11 with Jesus's actions in in the previous verses. This was the proper response to Jesus's emptying and humbling himself. The verbs "highly exalted" and "freely gave" are coordinate (καί), with the latter adding to the former.[1] God's exaltation of Christ included freely giving to him the name that is above every name. "Highly exalted" (ὑπερύψωσεν) occurs only here in the New Testament, being formed by adding a preposition meaning "over and above," or "beyond" (ὑπέρ) the normal word for "exalt" in the New Testament (ὑψόω). In this way it denotes the ultimate super-exaltation—exaltation to the

---

1   Καί may be epexegetical ("even") so that "freely gave" explains "highly exalted;" perhaps translate: "highly exalted him by freely giving" (Fee, 1995, 221; Reumann, 2008, 354).

highest possible level, to "the loftiest height" (BDAG s.v. "ὑπερυψόω," p. 1034). The word occurs also in Psalm 97:9 (LXX), which says that Yahweh is *highly exalted* far above all gods. This does not mean "that Yahweh is on a step higher than other deities, but that He is unique and in a class apart because He is the incomparable One" (Martin, 1997, 242). What is true of Yahweh is true of Christ. He exists in a class by himself.

In 2:6–8 Paul described Christ's downward trek in stages: He emptied himself—he humbled himself—becoming obedient unto death—even death on a cross. But here Paul described God's super-exaltation of Christ as a single event. He did not mention the stages separately: resurrection—ascension—sitting at the right hand of God (but see Rom. 8:34; Eph. 1:20–21). All were included in the one idea "highly exalted." Some have suggested that after God "highly exalted" Christ, he was more divine or closer to the Father than during his preincarnate state (Martin in Martin and Hawthorne, 2004, 125). But this is unlikely. The super-exaltation does not compare Christ's positions before his incarnation and after his ascension. The comparison is with the depth to which Christ humbled himself in 2:8. After his extreme humiliation, God exalted Christ to the highest possible position in the universe so that now he reigns as Lord (Fee, 1995, 221).

God's exaltation of Jesus is evident in the name God gave him. "Freely gave" (ἐχαρίσατο) means that the name God gave Christ was given "graciously as a favor" (BDAG s.v. "χαρίζομαι" 1, p. 1078). This explains the relationship between Christ's self-emptying/self-humbling and God's bestowal of the name. It was a gift rendered, not as payment for Christ's actions, but as approval and vindication (Silva, 2005, 109; Hansen, 2009, 160–61). God was pleased with his Son's voluntary self-sacrifice. So he lavished his favor upon him as a sign of his approval. Paul previously used this same verb in 1:29, stating that God had freely given believers not only the gift of believing in Christ, but also of suffering for his sake.

God gave to Christ the personal "name" (BDAG s.v. "ὄνομα" 1dγ, p. 713) that is above (ὑπέρ) every name. Possession of the name above every other name signifies a status and position above every other being. Though some have argued that the "name" God gave Christ at his exaltation was "Jesus" (2:10), it is more likely that the name was "Lord," as reflected in the climatic acknowledgement in 2:11.

What Changed after God Exalted Christ and Gave Him the Name above Every Name?

When God exalted Christ and gave him the name above every name, he vindicated him after his humiliating death. But Christ did not become more divine. Nor did he draw closer to the Father in a relationship more intimate than they enjoyed prior to the incarnation. But something changed. It was not a change in Christ's *deity*; it was a change in his *function* or *role* in the history of salvation. Now, as the God-man, Christ possesses the name "Lord" and the status as *Davidic King within history* that goes along with it. He reigns as Lord over all—specifically as the *vindicated, exalted Messiah*. This change of role is found in several New Testament texts: "All authority has been given to him" (Matt. 28:18). God has made him "both Lord and Christ" (Acts 2:36). God has appointed him "Son of God in power" (Rom. 1:4). He has "inherited a more excellent name ("Son") than the angels" (Heb. 1:4). Together, these texts speak of Christ's reign as Messiah and Lord after his incarnation and earthly work (cf. Bockmuehl, 1998, 144). Further, he is being increasingly and more widely acknowledged to be "Lord," an acknowledgment that ultimately will be universal (cf. Hellerman, 2010a, 97).

Angelic and Human Submission to Christ (2:10)

The purpose and result of God's elevation of Christ Jesus is that every rational creature throughout the universe—angelic and human—should bow in submission to him, signifying Christ's superior might, sovereignty, and universal majesty.

2:10–11. The aorist subjunctive κάμψῃ (v. 10) is usually rendered "should bow" (NIV, ESV, CSB, NLT, KJV, NKJV; cf. "should bend" NRSV). Likewise the aorist subjunctive ἐξομολογήσηται (v. 11) is rendered "should confess" (ESV, NRSV, CSB, KJV, NKJV), "should acknowledge" (NIV), or "should declare" (NLT). NASB reflects the future indicative ("will bow," "will confess"), which also occurs in Isaiah 45:23 LXX. Most manuscripts contain the aorist subjunctive κάμψῃ ("should bow") in 2:10. Significant manuscripts (A C D F* G K L) switch to the future indicative ἐξομολογήσεται ("will acknowledge") in 2:11. But several of the oldest manuscripts (𝔓⁴⁶ א B) have the aorist subjunctive ἐξομολογήσηται ("should acknowledge"). It is difficult to decide which is original in 2:11. Scribes could have changed Paul's future indicative ἐξομολογήσεται to agree with the aorist subjunctive κάμψῃ in 2:10. Or they could have changed Paul's aorist subjunctive ἐξομολογήσηται to agree with the future indicative ἐξομολογήσεται in Isaiah 45:23. NA28 and UBS5 editors prefer the aorist subjunctive ἐξομολογήσηται because it is found in the major older manuscripts (*TCGNT,* 546). Whether subjunctive or indicative, these verbs express the purpose and result of God's actions in 2:9.

2:10. Paul expressed both the intended *purpose* (intent) and actual *result* (outcome) of God's action in 2:9 (ἵνα) (Collange, 1979, 106). With God's sovereign power, his intended purpose is also the result he accomplishes. His two actions—highly exalting and freely bestowing—elicit two responses on the part of all rational beings: every knee bows (2:10) and every tongue acknowledges (2:11).

"At the name of Jesus" makes it clear that the exalted Christ is the one to be honored. While some identify the name God gave him as "Jesus," the phrase "name of Jesus" (ὀνόματι Ἰησοῦ) likely means "the name Jesus now possesses" (genitive of possession). Jesus has received a new

name from God. The name God gave him was "Lord," as demonstrated in the climactic confession in 2:11. Paul's citation of Isaiah 45:23 LXX, where in context the "Lᴏʀᴅ" (Κύριος, the LXX rendering of Yahweh[2]) is the one before whom every knee bows, also supports this view. God gave to Jesus the name that he (Yahweh) shares with no other (Isa. 42:8). This name indicates divine authority and divine identity. "At (ἐν) the name" denotes the occasion that Jesus would be acknowledged—"that *when* the name of Jesus ("Lord") is mentioned every knee should bow" (BDAG s.v. "ὄνομα" 1dγב, p. 713).

God exalted Christ so that every knee should "bow" (κάμψῃ) before him. Bowing the knee occurs in Scripture as a posture of prayer and worship (Ps. 95:6; Luke 22:41; Acts 9:40; 20:36; 21:5; Eph. 3:14), and as a posture of subjection and homage to a superior (1 Kings 19:18; 1 Chron. 29:20; Isa. 45:23; Rom. 11:4; 14:11; cf. the mock homage in Mark 15:19) (*TDNT* 1:738). Here it refers to every rational creature (angelic and human) paying homage to Christ at his second coming (BDAG s.v. "κάμψῃ" 2, p. 507). To bow the knee before the Lord Christ is to demonstrate submission and acknowledge his superior might, sovereignty, and universal majesty (*NIDNTTE* 1:593; Martin, 1997, 265).

"Every" (πᾶν) knee indicates that all without exception will acknowledge Christ's lordship. "In heaven and on earth and under the earth" indicates the universal scope of the bowing before Christ. This reflects the ancient view of the universe having three "stories" or spheres. Some scholars identify specific beings associated with each sphere. Hofius suggested that those "in heaven" are angels and perhaps demons who dwell in the heavenly realm (Eph. 1:20–21; 3:10; 6:12); "those on earth" are humans living on earth at the return of Christ; and those "under the earth" are departed humans who live in Sheol (1976, 53–54). But perhaps we do not need to specify the particular inhabitants of the three

---

2   In the LXX, "Yahweh" is rendered Κύριος ("Lord") more than 6,100 times (*TDNT* 3:1059).

realms. The full phrase simply describes the universe (Müller, 2002, 109). Paul's point was that *all* rational beings throughout the universe—angelic and human—will bow in submission to Christ. Already in the present age, millions of believers willingly bow their knees before Christ. A partial fulfillment of 2:10–11 is occurring as the gospel spreads. But the worship of the church in the present day is only a foretaste of the universal homage to be given to Christ at his return (Martin, 1997, 266–70; Hansen, 2009, 168).

Universal Acknowledgment of Jesus's Sovereign Authority (2:11a)

The purpose and result of God's elevation of Christ Jesus is also that every rational creature throughout the universe should verbally acknowledge his divine, sovereign authority by openly declaring that he is Lord.

2:11a. God's purpose for exalting Christ was also (καὶ) that every tongue should "acknowledge" (ἐξομολογήσηται), "profess," or "acknowledge," that (ὅτι) Jesus Christ is Lord." This universal acknowledgment provided the climax to the hymn. Only now did Paul reveal the name that Christ received from his Father. The confession, "Jesus is Lord" was one of the earliest confessions of the church. It served as an expression of one's faith and commitment to Christ (Rom. 10:9), and could be uttered only as the Spirit enabled (1 Cor. 12:3). But here every tongue among all rational creatures will *acknowledge* Christ's lordship, his sovereign authority and identity as the Lord. The idea is not that all will bow to Christ in true faith and genuine worship, though many will. On the tongues of unbelievers, it will serve not as an expression of faith, but as an acknowledgment that God has in fact made Jesus Lord.

Some have suggested that this verse implies the whole creation will finally be reconciled to God and express faith in Christ. Paul would then be saying that in the last day all will gladly worship and praise Christ as Lord (e.g., Hofius, 1976, 37–40). This interpretation goes as far

back as Origen (*Princ.* 6.1–2). But this is not what Paul meant, for (1) he stated elsewhere in Philippians that those who opposed the gospel would face "destruction," that is, final judgment (1:28; 3:19). (2) Elsewhere in the New Testament it is clear that not all will repent in the presence of Christ when he returns (Rev. 9:20–21; 16:9, 11). Some will be cast into the lake of fire (Rev. 20:11–15). (3) Isaiah 45:22–24, the text Paul is cited, includes a begrudging acknowledgment on the part of some—verse 24, "all who were enraged against him will come to him and be put to shame" (Bockmuehl, 1998, 146–47; Witherington, 2011, 154). (4) The word commonly rendered "confess," or "acknowledge" does not *necessarily* denote praise or faith, though it regularly implies this in Scripture. It can mean simply to "declare openly in acknowledgment" (BDAG s.v. "ἐξομολογέω" 3, p. 351). Here it denotes the acknowledgment of Christ's sovereign authority by all (*TDNT* 5:214), the recognition of Christ for who he is from a position of homage (*NIDNTTE* 3:510). Compare the statement of the young martyr to the evil Antiochus IV, that he would be punished and forced to confess that Yahweh alone is God:

> But you [Antiochus], by the judgment of God, will receive just punishment for your arrogance. I, like my brothers, give up body and life for the laws of our ancestors, appealing to God to show mercy soon to our nation and *by trials and plagues to make you confess* (LXX, ξομολογήσασθαι) *that he alone is God* (2 Macc 7:36b–37 NRSV).

When Paul wrote that all "confess," he did not mean that all confess their faith in Jesus Christ as Lord. But they do acknowledge that he is Lord. At the second coming, some will gladly and gratefully acknowledge Christ to be their Lord. Others will submit in forced acknowledgment.

Paul's language in 2:10–11, "That every knee should bow . . . every tongue should confess," is a citation from Isaiah 45:22–23:

Turn to me so you can be delivered, all you who live in the earth's remote regions! For I am God, and I have no peer. I solemnly make this oath—what I say is true and reliable: 'Surely *every knee will bow to me, every tongue will solemnly affirm.* (LXX, ξομολογήσηται)' (NET)

This Isaiah text prophesied that every knee would bow to Yahweh, including those who are put to shame (Isa. 45:24). When Paul cited this text in Romans 14:11, he referred to God. But here the "Lord" is now Jesus Christ. God's exaltation of Jesus means that he will receive the universal homage and worship that only Yahweh may receive. Jesus's exalted status is basically equal to Yahweh's (Bauckham, 2009, 208), and matches his status prior to his self-emptying (2:6).

The confession "Jesus Christ is Lord" implies of course that in the first century Caesar was not, but the view that Paul was engaging here in a *direct* anti-imperial polemic (cf. Wright, 2000, 160–83) lacks sufficient evidence to be established (for a critique, see, e.g., Burk, 2008, 309–37; Kim, 2008, 3–71; Cohick, 2013b, 166–82). Better is the view that Paul did not *primarily* direct his statements against the imperial cult, but it was *part* of his message (Fantin, 2011, 40–45). In every age and every culture, the confession, "Jesus Christ is Lord" signifies that no one else is. Further, note that while the scope of Caesar's (or any other human leader) realm is limited, the scope of Jesus's realm is universal.

God the Father's Fame (2:11b)
The universal submission to Jesus and acknowledgment of his divine, sovereign authority will result in God's glorious fame increasing through the universe.

2:11b. The end of verse 11 made sure that the Father has retained his proper position. The ultimate purpose, result, or end (εἰς) for which all rational creatures bow and acknowledge that Jesus Christ is Lord is "to (εἰς) the glory of God the Father." In this context, "glory" (δόξαν) refers to "fame, recognition, renown, honor, or prestige" (BDAG s.v. "δόξα" 3, p. 257). God the Father will be recognized and acknowledged for who he is. This phrase denotes at least the final purpose of 2:10–11 ("that every knee should bow and every tongue confess"). It may also denote the final purpose of 2:9 ("God exalted Christ and freely gave him the name above every name") and perhaps even of 2:7–8 ("Christ emptied himself and humbled himself"). All of these events are, in God's sovereign purpose, directed toward the glorifying of God the Father. Christ's self-emptying, his exaltation, and the universal acknowledgment of his lordship were intended to and in fact result in more glory and fame for the Father. God is honored and glorified when Christ is honored and recognized for who he is. The Father's glory is not diminished by the exaltation of his Son; it is increased.

A New Set of Values: J. Hellerman argues that by exhorting the Philippians to put others first and by including the example of Christ's self-emptying and self-humbling followed by exaltation (2:3–11), Paul reconstructed an alternative worldview and challenged them to adhere to a new set of values opposed to those of the Roman colony Philippi. In a culture preoccupied with public honor and status, Paul used Christ's example to redefine what is honorable. Specifically, the role of a *slave* and the humiliating death of a *cross* are redefined as honorable in God's eyes. As we live out our faith in a culture that values wealth, power, status, and worldly achievement, we must remember that we follow the one who exhibited an alternative set of attitudes and behaviors. We who follow Christ must value humble service and self-sacrifice for the good of others. And if we possess status, power, or wealth, we must use those resources to serve and benefit others (see further, Hellerman, 2003b, 421–33).

THEOLOGICAL FOCUS

The exegetical idea (God the Father highly elevated Christ Jesus to the highest universal status, so that all personal beings—angelic and human—would submit to Christ and openly declare his divine, sovereign authority, and so increase the Father's fame) leads to this theological focus: Christ Jesus reigns as the supreme Lord of the universe, and will ultimately be acknowledged as such by all.

This text is about the universal exalted status Christ received freely from the Father after his humiliation and suffering. He was raised and is seated at the right hand of God, reigning as Messiah (Davidic King) and Lord, the position of supreme authority over creation (Ps. 110:1; Acts 2:34–35; 1 Cor. 15:25–27; Rom. 8:34; Eph. 1:20–22; Col. 3:1; Heb. 1:3–4; 1 Peter 3:22).

God has given Christ Jesus the name that in Isaiah 42:8 he said he shares with no one else: Yahweh (Hebrew name) = "Lord" (LXX Κύριος). This shows that Christ enjoys equal status with the Father. As believers, we willingly bow our knees to Christ and confess him to be Lord. At the second coming, when the name that Jesus was given (Lord) is mentioned, every knee will bow symbolizing submission, and every tongue (of both believers and unbelievers, human and angelic) will openly declare, "Jesus Christ is Lord." This reality should encourage steadfastness and joy in all believers who participate in the spread of the gospel in hostile contexts, and who are suffering for their faith. All creation will eventually acknowledge their Lord.

PREACHING AND TEACHING STRATEGIES

Exegetical and Theological Synthesis

The clear focus of Philippians 2:9–11 is God's intervening action to raise up Jesus and bestow on him the most glorious name. In the second movement of the Christ hymn, God reverses the misfortunes of the executed Christ, exalting him to the highest place. The passage weaves together a reference from Isaiah 45:22–23, language from the imperial cult, and formal elements of Greco-Roman hymns to emphasize the great victory of Jesus. Philippians 2:9–11 makes it clear: God's vindication of Jesus calls for bowing, praising, and indeed, for celebration.

To say "Jesus is Lord" goes beyond simple confession. The Old Testament backdrop sets Jesus's lordship on equal footing with Yahweh. Moreover, the title "Lord" rules out other rulers. Imperialistic claims to sovereignty don't rival Jesus's heavenly status. Thus, to proclaim "Jesus is Lord" is both to affirm his heavenly status and deny all earthly pretenders. Few of us realize the weight of this confession when first praying the Sinner's Prayer. The deeper our understanding of Jesus's glorious name, the greater our sense of loyalty.

Sadly, many will not know the weight of this truth until the second coming of Jesus. Then homage toward Jesus will be a universal and compulsory response. This end-times display of reverence should not be confused with followers of Jesus who have "called on the name of the Lord" for salvation (Rom. 10:9). For citizens of heaven, our confession—Jesus is Lord—is an anthem of trust through the high and low points of life.

Preaching Idea

Jesus's crowing victory deserves our humble loyalty.

Contemporary Connections

What does it mean?

What is Jesus's crowning victory? Is his exaltation a once-for-all-times event or an ongoing, vicarious experience? And what does humble loyalty look like? These are important questions to consider. The Christ hymn emphasizes God's agency in the exaltation of Jesus. The enthronement of Jesus was a single act. Following his resurrection, Jesus ascended into the heavenly realm (Acts 1:12). Authors of Scripture depict Jesus sitting at the right hand of the Father with full authority as his Son (Heb. 1:1–3). The sacrificial work of Jesus is finished (John 19:30; Heb. 10:10–13), but his return will bring to completion God's redemptive program (1 Cor. 15:23–28; Phil. 1:6, 10).

One of the underemphasized theories of atonement is *Christus Victor* (Wright, 2013a, 95). This theological proposition interprets the victory of Jesus over sin, death, and Satan as the central work of his crucifixion and resurrection. Paul makes several boasts of Jesus's triumph over his spiritual opponents, and the cosmic scope of his redemption (Rom. 8:31–39; Eph. 1:10; 3:8–12; 4:8–10; Col. 2:9–15). *Christus Victor* does not invalidate other theories of atonement, but it does capture the reversal of misfortune—from death to life, from victim to victor, from dishonor to glory—both for Jesus and his followers.

In the realm of school, sports, theater, and business, great victories inspire cheers, ovations, applause, and praise. Newly crowned world champions receive bottles of champagne. "Just married" couples inspire dancing, bubbles, kisses, and cake. These momentous occasions call for full-bodied celebration. Is this the same as humble loyalty? Not exactly. Parties naturally follow triumphs, but all earthly celebrations come to an end. Then the hard work of practice, training, and married life must resume. The crowing victory of Jesus is no passing celebration. His exaltation is everlasting. It demands more than a thunderous applause. Corporate worship may acknowledge the crowning victory, but daily obedience to his commands shows humble loyalty.

Now what?

What does humble loyalty to Jesus look like? How expressive should we be in demonstrating our loyalty? How should Jesus's crowning victory affect our spiritual confidence? First, it is important to recognize humility and confidence are not mutually exclusive. Too often we hang our heads in defeat. We grovel in the shadow of our sins, rather than rejoice in the triumph of the empty tomb. Jesus's seat on the heavenly throne does not exempt us from suffering, internal struggle, or discord. He does, however, promise to reverse our misfortunes and help us overcome in our trials (2 Cor. 2:14; 1 John 4:4). In fact, it may be *more* reckless for us to assume failure rather than to accept victory as the logical outcome of our spiritual battles. Sadly, followers of Jesus seem more inclined to concede than celebrate.

Second, we must allow people space to express their loyalty to Jesus differently. Some people show loyalty with a quiet voice; others raise arms and voices in thunderous praise. We must guard against making our shared victory in Jesus a cause for uniformity in expression. The recognition of Jesus's glorious name is more important than the posture we strike.

Third, we cannot limit humble loyalty to Sunday morning worship. Our loyalty must affect the way we love our family, colleagues, and opponents during the week. Our ability to avoid complaining, serve others, and give generously reflect our fidelity. Even the simple disciplines of prayer, Bible reading, fasting, and solitude exemplify our willingness to submit to Jesus. His lofty status should compel us regularly to say, "Here I am, Lord. Your will, not mine, be done."

Creativity in Presentation

To illustrate a victorious celebration, you need to look no further than the latest champion in local or professional sports. For example, the 2016 Cubs (Major League Baseball), 2016 Cavaliers (National Basketball League), and 2018 Philadelphia Eagles (National Football League) each overcame great odds, reversing their fortunes to secure victory. Their win inspired whole cities, evident in parades and T-shirt sales. Consider decorating the church podium with flags, pendants, posters, and swag from a recent championship team.

The ticker-tape parades for the first US astronauts followed a similar script. These national heroes, especially Alan Shepard and Neil Armstrong, helped reverse the fortunes of the United States in the race to space with Russia in the 1960s. A summary of the space race and video clip from the event would capture the spirit of celebration. Handing out bags of confetti to toss out in at a closing song can help the congregation experience the celebration (but be sure to warn the maintenance people or pitch a hand in cleaning up!).

The unlikely victory is stock-in-trade in Hollywood. Any *Rocky* film, especially the climatic boxing match at the end, provides a variation on this theme. *Star Wars* movies often take battles to the eleventh hour, but the Rebels thwart the Dark Side and a celebration ensues. A short clip of any such crowning event may prove effective.

Finally, a short poem by Emily Dickinson (1964), "Success is counted sweetest," explains the way loss and suffering pave the way for greater appreciation in victory. The Christ hymn inspired Dickinson's classic lines. Her text is accessible online. The relevance of any of these examples is seeing how victory inspires a range of responses. The greater the crown or less expected the victory, the more dramatic is the celebration to follow.

The key idea to articulate is this: Christ Jesus reigns as the supreme Lord of the universe, and will ultimately be acknowledged as such by all. Jesus's crowning victory deserves our humble loyalty.

- Jesus won a crowning victory (2:9).

- We will all respond in humility (2:10–11).

DISCUSSION QUESTIONS

1. How important is celebration to corporate worship? What songs or forms lend themselves best to a spirit of celebration?

2. How does Jesus's reversal of fortune challenge the sense of defeat or gloom that covers many believers?

3. Why should God's exaltation of Christ after his self-humbling and self-humbling encourage every believer?

4. What practical relevance does Christ's present position in heaven at God's right hand have for your life today?

5. How does the reality that unbelievers hostile to Christ will one day acknowledge his lordship affect your dealings with or attitudes toward unbelievers?

6. Looking at the Christ hymn as a whole, what value in your culture has Christ subverted?

Philippians 2:12–18

EXEGETICAL IDEA

Paul exhorted the Philippians, as God motivated and empowered them, to strive to become a spiritually mature, holy community as they headed toward the future salvation God would bring to completion, and to rejoice with him in their mutual sacrificial service to God.

THEOLOGICAL FOCUS

God motivates and empowers believers to strive to become a spiritually mature, holy community as they head toward the future salvation God will bring to completion.

PREACHING IDEA

Keep working a plan to become spiritually fit.

PREACHING POINTERS

Transitioning from the Christ hymn, Paul completed his exhortation section with a series of three more imperatives to live like citizens of God's kingdom, not Caesar's. He called the first-century audience to finish strong in their spiritual commitments to personal growth, communal life, and evangelistic witness. Their motivation to live God-pleasing lives has both internal and external factors. Internally, Paul promised them God-given energy to work out their salvation. Externally, Paul promised them that Jesus will return and justify his labors. In either case, the first-century audience should avoid the pitfall of spiritual idleness.

Followers of Jesus today need a revival of focused, spiritual energy. We are distracted and depleted. We expend our energies on too many mindless and distracting tasks. We manage email, count calories, transport children to extracurricular events, and fill our DVRs with more shows we can watch in a weekend. Even the demands of daily life—cooking and cleaning, commuting and working, paying bills, returning phone calls, and answering e-mails—can sap our energy, leaving our spiritual lives underdeveloped. Becoming spiritually fit should be our chief aim, but it requires a plan and discipline to follow. Often the more urgent tasks take priority. This passage motives us to keep working a plan to become spiritually fit.

WORKING OUT YOUR SALVATION (2:12–18)

LITERARY STRUCTURE AND THEMES OF PHILIPPIANS 2:12–18

This unit is structured around three imperatives. (1) In 2:12–13, Paul stated the basic exhortation: Just as they had always obeyed, they were to "work out" their salvation with fear and trembling. He went on to explain that God was the one working in them to bring about what he desired. (2) In 2:14–16, he exhorted them to "do" all things without grumbling or arguing so that they might be blameless children of God in a crooked and perverse generation, in which they shined as lights in the world. This would lead to Paul's personal exultation when Jesus returns, for it would mean that he had not labored among them in vain. (3) In 2:17–18, he depicted his ministry as a sacrificial drink offering that he added to their sacrifice and service to God. In this he rejoiced with them and he exhorted them to "rejoice" and "rejoice with" him.

> ### *Living Out Your Salvation (2:12–13)*
> ### *No Griping or Arguing (2:14–16)*
> ### *Joy in Sacrifice (2:17–18)*

EXPOSITION (2:12–18)

This paragraph concludes Paul's exhortation section to the Philippians that began in 1:27. There he urged them to live as citizens worthy of the gospel of Christ—the governing command of 1:27–2:18. In 2:1–4 he urged them to be of one mind, humbly regarding each other as more important than themselves. Then he exhorted them to have the same attitude Christ exhibited when he emptied and humbled himself—as depicted in the Christ hymn (2:5–11). Now Paul exhorted them to do their part to live out the future salvation God was working in them.

Living Out Your Salvation (2:12–13)

Paul exhorted the Philippians, as God motivated and empowered them, to strive to become a spiritually mature, holy community, with a reverent fear of God, as they headed toward the future salvation he would bring to completion.

2:12. As he did elsewhere (1 Cor. 14:39; 15:58; Phil. 4:1) Paul used "so then (ὥστε) my beloved/ brethren," to draw an inference from the preceding paragraph or section (Moule, 1959, 144). Here is the practical application for those who follow Christ. Paul's inference may come specifically from the Christ hymn (Hansen, 2009, 170, n. 300) or from all he had written since 1:27 (Silva, 2005, 117). Before getting to the exhortation, Paul reminded the Philippians of two things. First, he called them "my beloved" (ἀγαπητοί μου, cf. 4:1), reaffirming his great affection for them (cf. 1:8).

Second, he reminded them of their past faithfulness from the time of their conversion: "just as you have always obeyed" (ὑπηκούσατε). "Just as" (καθώς) introduced the comparison from which Paul would move to an exhortation (BDAG s.v. "καθώς" 1, p. 493). They had consistently obeyed both God and Christ (Hansen, 2009, 171), a reminder that served as encouragement and motivation for them to fulfill the command he was about to give.

Paul expected the Philippians to obey God. "Not only as in my 'presence' (παρουσία) but now much more in my 'absence' (ἀπουσία)" can be taken either with what precedes—"just as you have always obeyed"—(Fee, 1995, 234), or with what follows—"work out your salvation"—(Martin and Hawthorne, 2004). If the former is right, Paul noted that since their conversion, they had always been obedient, both when he was present and especially now in his absence. If the latter, he explicitly exhorted them to work out their salvation now that he was absent. Either way, Paul was concerned with their present character and conduct while he was away.

The basic imperative of the paragraph is, "Work out [κατεργάζεσθε] your own salvation." "Salvation" [σωτηρίαν] refers to the eternal salvation believers are already experiencing, but not yet completely (BDAG s.v. "σωτηρία" 2, p. 896). They will experience a future consummation of salvation, with all of its benefits (for example: eternal life in God's kingdom, freedom from sin and death, joy, God's presence) fully realized, when Christ returns.

Paul's exhortation focused on their present experience and responsibility. They were to "work out" their salvation. "Work out" (κατεργάζ) may also be rendered "accomplish," "achieve," or "bring about" (BDAG s.v. "κατεργάζομαι" 2, p. 531). Paul was not referring to "working *for*" or "earning" salvation. This would contradict his teaching that salvation is by grace through faith, not works (Rom. 4:4–5; 10:10; Gal. 2:16; Eph. 2:8–9; Titus 3:5).[3] He was talking about "continuing to work toward the conclusion of something already begun" (Thurston, 2005, 94).

Believers' future salvation, to be fully revealed when Jesus returns, has ethical implications for the way they live in the present. Paul wanted the Philippians to put forth the effort to carry out ethical behavior that was in keeping with what God had already done and was doing in them through the gospel. He wanted them to be on track with what God would ultimately bring about (1:6).

The command "work out" is plural—directed to the community as a whole. Paul was thinking of how believers related to, cared for, and served one another. This does not rule out the individual application of the command. Each individual was to work out his or her own salvation as part of the community. But it is a corporate exhortation dealing with how believers related to each other (2:1–5, 14–15). Paul wanted the church to become the spiritually mature, holy community that God intended it to be.

They were to work out their own salvation "with fear and trembling." The Old Testament background of "the fear of the Lord," shows that Paul was referring to a reverential fear and awe of God's holiness and majesty (Fee, 1995, 236–37; Reumann, 2008, 410).

The Old Testament Background of Fear and Trembling

In the Old Testament, there is a direct connection between the believer's fear of Yahweh and Yahweh's holiness (Exod. 3:5–6; Exod. 20:20; Ps. 96:9; 111:9–10; Isa. 8:13). The fear of Yahweh is the motive for keeping the law (Lev. 19:14; Deut. 5:29; 17:13; Ps. 103:11; Prov. 1:7) The worshipper could stand before God in both *fear and love* (Deut. 10:12), and in both *fear and trust* (Exod. 14:31) (*NIDNTTE* 4:611). God's holiness could cause both "terror and dread," but also "love and trust" (Waltke, 1992, 20). The terror of God's holiness and wrath toward sin caused sinners to pursue God's mercy. And the reverent fear of a Holy Father caused believers to pursue obedience. This was the "fear and trembling" Paul desired for the Philippians.

2:13. NRSV and CSB add, "enabling you," to make clear that God gives believers empowerment so that they are the ones who will and work (cf. NLT, "giving you").

2:13. Paul provided an explanation (γάρ) for the exhortation in 2:12. Believers were to work out their own salvation, for God was working in them. The "working out" did not rest on believers' ability and efforts, but on God's work

---

3   Paul used this verb twenty times in his letters for accomplishing good or evil (eleven times in Romans, six times in 2 Corinthians), but never in the sense of achieving justification through works (Hellerman, 2015, 13–32).

in them that he would complete (1:6). "He who works" (ὁ ἐνεργῶν) means that God was the one who supplied the power and energy for the work that they were to put forth.

To say that God was the one who "worked" in believers did not excuse them from personal responsibility to put forth the effort to "work out" their own growth. They were to apply themselves in order to accomplish what was required. Paul stated that God was working "in you" (ἐν ὑμῖν, cf. 1:6; 2:5). This refers to God's presence within individuals, and by extension to his presence within the community. He was working in individuals and therefore in the church as a whole.

Work Out Your Salvation: Human Responsibility and Divine Sovereignty (2:13)

Believers must put forth effort to "work out" their salvation (2:13). This highlights human responsibility. But God is the one working in them to provide for the willingness and power on their part (2:14; cf. 1:6). This highlights God's sovereignty. Together, Paul's strategy for spiritual growth (sanctification) presupposes two things: (1) that spiritual growth is part of God's sovereign plan. It is purposed, provided for, and empowered by God; (2) that believers are responsible to cooperate with God's purpose and strive for spiritual growth in community (see Wagner, 2007).

Paul stated what it was that God did in believers: he caused them "to will" or "to resolve" (BDAG s.v. "θέλω" 2, p. 448) and "to work" or "to actively put forth effort" (BDAG s.v. "ἐνεργέω" 2, p. 335). God's working in them not only provided the power to energize personal responsibility, it also created the desire and intent. Believers become willing to work out their own salvation because of God's working in them.

The reason for (BDAG s.v. "ὑπέρ" 2, p. 1031) God's work in believers was "his" own purpose and pleasure. The idea is that believers are to work out their own salvation in accordance with God's sovereign will. He produces both

the willingness and activity in believers to bring about his purposes, including Christlike spiritual fruit in the community. This is in keeping with his divine pleasure and plan for the complete and final salvation of his people.

No Griping or Arguing (2:14–16)

Paul exhorted the Philippians to get rid of all complaining and petty disputes so that they may be a holy community free from accusation, testifying of the gospel of Jesus among unbelievers. At the judgment seat of Christ, their fidelity to the gospel would give Paul reason for exulting in what Christ accomplished through his ministry.

2:14. The second section of this paragraph begins with another imperative: "Do [ποιεῖτε] all things without grumbling or arguing." This is more specific than the general exhortation of 2:12. "All things" (πάντα) is all-inclusive, referring to all of the exhortations beginning at 1:27, and more. "Grumbling" (γογγυσμῶν) refers to "behind the scenes talk, complaint, displeasure, expressed in murmuring" (BDAG s.v. "γογγυσμός," 204). Paul was likely alluding to the Old Testament "grumbling" texts in which Israel murmured against God and against Moses (Exod. 16:7, 8 [2x], 9,12; Num. 17:5, 10). He compared the grumbling among the Philippians to the Exodus generation in order to cause them to understand how seriously God takes complaining. There is no evidence in Philippians that the believers there were grumbling explicitly against God as the Israelites did, but it may be that Paul wanted them to understand that grumbling about leaders or circumstances was ultimately grumbling against God (cf. Silva, 2005, 124).

"Arguing" (διαλογισμῶν) refers to "verbal exchanges that take place when conflicting ideas are expressed: dispute" (BDAG s.v. "διαλογισμός" 3, p. 232–33.). Paul's appeal to Euodia and Syntyche (4:2) will provide evidence of at least some arguing in the church. Grumbling (complaining to yourself or to others) and arguing (petty disputes with others) works against unity, harmony, and humbly putting others first in the community (Martin and Hawthorne, 2004, 143), the very things that Paul was urging them to pursue (2:2–4). Bockmuehl quotes Aquinas: "While you cannot exist without sin, you can exist without grumbling!" (1998, 156).

2:15. Ἀκέραιοι is rendered "pure" (NIV, CSB), "innocent" (ESV, NRSV, NASB), or "harmless" (KJV, NKJV). Ἄμωμα is rendered "without fault" (NIV, NKJV, cf. CSB), "without blemish" (ESV, NRSV), "above reproach" (NASB), and "without rebuke" (KJV). Σκολιᾶς is rendered "warped" (NIV), "crooked" (ESV, NRSV, CSB, NLT, NASB, NKJV). Διεστραμμένης is rendered "crooked" (NIV), "twisted" (ESV), and "perverse" (NRSV, NLT, NASB, KJV, NKJV, cf. CSB). Φωστῆρες is rendered "stars" (NIV, NRSV, CSB) or "lights" (ESV, NASB, KJV, NKJV, cf. NLT, "bright lights").

2:15. Paul stated the purpose (ἵνα) for which they were to do all things without grumbling or arguing: so that they may be "blameless and pure." "Blameless" (ἄμεμπτοι) describes one in whom others find no fault, particularly "faultless of the Mosaic covenant" (BDAG s.v. "ἄμεμπτος," p. 52). Paul will later use this adjective to describe his "blameless" life as a Pharisee who meticulously kept the law prior to his conversion (3:6). "Pure" (ἀκέραιοι) denotes the characteristic of being "innocent as far as evil is concerned" (BDAG s.v. "κέραιος," p. 35). Elsewhere in the New Testament, the same word refers to being "innocent" as doves (Matt. 10:16) and "innocent" regarding evil (Rom. 16:19). Together, these words denote a community that is free from accusation, complaining, fault-finding, personal attacks, bickering, and gossip. To the degree that the Christian community does all things without grumbling or arguing, it will be more blameless and pure.

Paul continued the purpose clause begun in 2:15a by further describing what he wanted to be true of the Christian community: that they would be "children of God without fault." Instead of being "fault finders" (complaining and arguing), they were to be "without fault." Paul was echoing the Song of Moses (Deut. 32:5). Moses told the Israelites that they were "no longer God's children" because they were "blemished children" (LXX, τέκνα μωμητά). Paul reversed that language in order to speak of what the Philippians were to become. If they would do all things without grumbling and arguing, they would be children of God who were "without fault" (ἄμωμα). Paul was not saying they had to be "without fault" in order to *become* children of God; he was saying that *as* children of God they needed to live in a manner befitting their true identity (cf. Hansen, 2009, 181–82). "Children [τέκνα] of God" suggests that believers exhibit characteristics of their heavenly Father (BDAG s.v. "τέκνα" 4, p. 995). The word stresses not merely a family relationship, but family resemblance (Hellerman, 2015, 136).

Continuing to echo Deuteronomy 32:5, Paul stated his desire that the Philippians become faultless children of God "in the midst of a crooked and perverse generation." Whereas Moses accused the Israelites of being a "crooked and perverse generation" (LXX, γενεὰ σκολιὰ καὶ διεστραμμένη), Paul stated that the believers lived in the midst of a "crooked and perverse generation." The phrase no longer referred to God's people, but to the unbelievers in Philippi and beyond. "Crooked" (σκολιᾶς) means, "being morally bent or twisted, crooked, unscrupulous, dishonest" (BDAG s.v. "σκολιός," p. 930). "Perverse" (διεστραμμένης) means, "departed from an accepted standard of moral or spiritual values, crooked, perverted" (BDAG s.v. "διαστρέφω" 2, p. 237). The "crooked and perverse generation" is the unbelieving world in which the church must exist. Unbelievers in the world will grumble, argue, complain, gossip and bicker. But the church must be different.

Paul drew attention to the evangelistic function of the church in society. "Among whom" or "in which" (ἐν οἷς) denotes where believers shined (BDAG s.v. "ἐν" 1, p. 326). "You shine (φαίνεσθε) as stars" echoes Daniel 12:3a (LXX). Daniel prophesied that God's people would shine like stars in the kingdom age. Paul understood that since God's kingdom age had already dawned, believers were shining as stars or producing light now (BDAG s.v. "φαίνω" 1b, p. 1046. "Stars" (φωστῆρες) technically refers to any of the light-giving bodies in the heavens—the sun, moon, and stars (BDAG s.v. "φωστήρ" 1, p. 1073; cf. Gen. 1:14). Just as stars shine physically in a dark sky, so believers shine morally in a dark generation. In this way they will be distinct from their society and be able to reflect the light of the gospel to unbelievers.

2:16. Ἐπέχοντες is rendered as an imperative, "hold fast/firmly" (CSB, NLT) or as an adverbial participle connected to "shine," "holding fast" (NIV2011, ESV, NRSV, NASB, NKJV). KJV renders it as a participle but with the meaning "hold forth" (cf. NIV84). Καύχημα is rendered "boast" (NIV, NRSV, CSB), "proud" (ESV, NLT), "glory" (NASB), or "rejoice" (KJV, NKJV). Ὅτι is rendered "that" (NIV, ESV, NRSV, CSB, NLT, NKJV, KJV) or "because" (NASB).

2:16. Paul explained how the Philippians would shine as lights in the world—by "holding fast the word of life" (ἐπέχοντες, participle of means). The "word of life" (λόγον ζωῆς) is the "word *about* life" (objective genitive, Hansen, 2009, 185) or the "word that *produces* life" (genitive of product, Harmon, 2015, 268), or both. Either way, the phrase refers to the gospel message.

Some dispute the meaning of "holding fast" (ἐπέχοντες). (1) Most understand it to mean, "maintain a grasp on (something), hold fast to" (BDAG s.v. "ἐπέχω" 1, p. 362; Bockmuehl, 1998, 159; Martin and Hawthorne, 2004, 146; Reumann, 2008, 393–94). (2) But others argue that it has an evangelistic sense, "hold forth, present, offer" (LSJ s.v. "ἐπέχω" 2.619; Lightfoot, 1953, 118; Silva, 2005, 126; Ware, 2005, 259–68). Both

meanings find support in the context. The first option agrees with 1:28 (not being intimidated by opponents). The second option agrees with 1:27 (contending together for the faith) and 2:15 (shine as stars in the world). Both ideas are likely present in the verse, if not the word (Fee, 1995, 247). Paul wanted believers to hold to the gospel in their beliefs, behavior, and lifestyle. As they did this they would commend the gospel to unbelievers around them and have opportunities to share it.

Paul's intention (εἰς) for their holding the word of life (and for all of 2:14–16a) was "so that I can boast on the day of Christ." Paul previously used the word "boast" (καύχημα) in 1:26, of the Philippians' exultation in what Christ had done for Paul after he was released from prison and returned to them. Here Paul himself wanted to take pride in the spiritually mature, holy Philippians on the day he stands before the judgment seat of Christ (BDAG s.v. "καύχημα" 1, p. 537; cf. 2 Cor. 1:14; 1 Thess. 2:19). This is not a conceited boast, but rather a joyful exaltation because of what *God* will have done through Paul in the course of his ministry. "In the day of Christ" (1:6, 10) denotes the time when Paul will boast—at the judgment seat of Christ (cf. 2 Cor. 5:10; 1 Cor. 4:1–5; Rom. 14:10–12).

The content (ὅτι) of Paul's boast would be, "*That* I did not run in vain nor labor in vain" (most versions).[4] With "did not run in vain nor labor in vain," Paul used two favorite metaphors to depict his apostolic ministry. The first is "run" (ἔδραμον). While "run" appears in most translations, the term actually conveys the idea of "exerting oneself" as in the case of running a footrace during Roman games (BDAG s.v. "τρέχω" 2, p. 1015). Paul compared his ministry to a race and himself to a runner (cf. 1 Cor. 9:24–26; Gal. 2:2). The second, "labor" (ἐκοπίασα) conveys the idea of "working hard" or "toil" (BDAG s.v. "κοπιάω" 2, p. 558). It was taken from the working class in the Roman Empire

---

4   NASB understands the as the ὅτι clause to denote the reason for his boast: "*because* I did not run."

and perhaps from Paul's personal experience as a tentmaker (cf. 1 Cor. 4:12; 15:10; 2 Cor. 11:23; Gal. 4:11; Col. 1:29; 1 Thess. 2:9; 2 Thess. 3:8). Together, these two images spoke of Paul's strenuous training, toil, and struggle to the point of weariness and exhaustion in ministry.

"In vain" (εἰς κενόν) would mean that his "running" and laboring" were to no purpose—that his ministry accomplished nothing (BDAG s.v. κενός" 3, p. 539). But this will not be the case. The lives of his converts will be reason for exulting in what Christ accomplished through him. They will indicate that all of his strenuous toil paid off (cf. 4:1; 1 Thess. 2:19). Paul did not seem to be in doubt that this would occur. He was confident that God who began a good work in the Philippians would bring it to completion until the day of Christ Jesus (1:6).

Joy in Sacrifice (2:17–18)

Paul rejoiced that his sacrificial service to God—his apostolic suffering in being imprisoned for sharing the gospel—was being added to the Philippians' sacrificial service to God—their partnership in the gospel and lives devoted to Christ—and he exhorted them to rejoice with him.

2:17. Σπένδομαι is rendered "am to be poured out" (ESV, cf. NLT, "lose my life, pouring it out"), "am being poured out" (NIV, NRSV, NASB, NKJV), or "am poured out" (CSB). The genitive τῆς πίστεως ὑμῶν is usually rendered ambiguously, "of your faith" (ESV, NRSV, CSB, NASB, KJV, NKJV) but also as a genitive of source, "coming from your faith" (NIV) or an attributive genitive, "your faithful service is an offering" (NLT).

2:17. The third section of this paragraph begins with: "But even if" (ἀλλά εἰ καί), which carries the thought beyond that of 2:16, where Paul referred to his apostolic ministry as strenuous running and laboring. Now he spoke of his life and/or potential death as a drink offering to God. He assumed this was true for the sake of

argument (εἰ + indicative, first class condition). "Poured out as a drink offering" (BDAG s.v. "σπένδω" p. 937) uses the imagery of sacrifice, common in both Greco-Roman thought and the Old Testament (*TDNT* 7:528–33). The Philippians may have understood the imagery in terms of a pagan sacrifice to the gods, but Paul was thinking of the Old Testament background of Levitical offerings. It is unlikely that he would refer to his life as a sacrifice to the gods, especially since elsewhere, when he used sacrifice as a metaphor for Christian life and ministry, he alluded to the Old Testament background (Rom. 12:1; 15:16; Eph. 5:2) (Fee, 1995, 251, n. 51). In the Old Testament, a drink offering was sometimes added to the main sacrifice in order to make it total and complete (Exod. 29:40–41; Lev. 23:13, 18; Num. 15:5–10; 28:6–10). Paul pictured his life being poured out as a drink offering added to (ἐπί) the Philippians' sacrifice and service. His offering would complete their sacrifice. "Sacrifice" (θυσία) and "service" (λειτουργία) describe a priest-like offering made by the Philippians. Paul later will call the Philippians' financial gift a "sacrifice" (same word, Phil. 4:18). He was thinking at least of their financial participation with him, but more likely of their comprehensive partnership in ministry (prayer, evangelism, suffering, sending Epaphroditus to help him, and so on), and in fact their whole lives offered to God (Gnilka, 1976, 155). "Of your faith" (τῆς πίστεως ὑμῶν) denotes that their sacrifice and service to God sprang from their faith in him (genitive of source, Silva, 2005, 129.).

With "poured out as a drink offering" Paul had in mind both his present apostolic sufferings, including imprisonment, as well as his potential martyrdom (Flemming, 2009, 136–37). He had fully presented his life (and possible death) to God as an offering (Fowl, 2005, 129).

The conclusion to Paul's conditional statement is: "I rejoice" (χαίρω) and "I rejoice with" (συγχαίρω) "all of you." This implies that the Philippians had joyfully offered their lives in service to God. So he likewise rejoiced in adding his own personal sacrifice to theirs.

2:18. Paul offered one last exhortation to this section (1:27–2:18). "In the same way also" (τὸ δὲ αὐτὸ καί, BDF §154; MHT 3:246; Moule, 1959, 34), "you rejoice and rejoice with me." Paul knew that they had joyfully served God. He did not want the fact of his suffering to dampen their joy. He wanted them to rejoice that he was completing their sacrifice. Even in the midst of pouring out one's life to God through suffering on behalf of Christ, joy is not only possible; it is expected of believers who have experienced new life in him.

Paul's repetition of the verbs "rejoice" (χαίρετε) and "rejoice with" (συγχαίρετε) in 2:17–18 was emphatic. Paul set an example for the Philippians. His joy provided the model for them to rejoice.[5]

THEOLOGICAL FOCUS

The exegetical idea (Paul exhorted the Philippians, as God motivated and empowered them, to strive to become a spiritually mature, holy community as they headed toward the future salvation God would bring to completion, and to rejoice with him in their mutual sacrificial service to God) leads to this theological focus: God motivates and empowers believers to strive to become a spiritually mature, holy community as they head toward the future salvation God will bring to completion.

The basic command (2:12) focuses on the responsibility of believers. The salvation they are to "work out" is the final salvation God is working in them and will consummate at Jesus's return. They are to put forth effort to fully bring about the effects of their justification (past judicial deliverance from the penalty of sin), to cooperate with God in their sanctification (present growth in holiness and deliverance from the power of sin), and to grow in maturity toward their glorification (future resurrection and deliverance from the presence of sin).

The imperative (statement of command) in 2:12 is explained by the indicative (statement of fact) in 2:13. The indicative (what God has already done, is doing, and will yet do) forms the basis for the imperative (what believers are to do in cooperation with God). Believers are able to work out their salvation because God is already working in them. This statement focuses on divine sovereignty, initiation, and empowerment of salvation. God's prior work in believers is what enables them to work out their salvation. He produces both the willingness and the empowerment for them to live out their salvation in the church and in the world until their salvation is consummated. "Work out" implies continuing to work toward the conclusion of what God has already begun by grace and will complete by grace.

PREACHING AND TEACHING STRATEGIES

Exegetical and Theological Synthesis

The clear focus of Philippians 2:12–18 is our partnership with God in becoming more like Jesus. We are unfinished products that must work to align our lives with God's demands. The exegesis draws out allusions to the Old Testament to discourage grumbling among believers and encourage our public witness by morally excellent lives. If the task sounds too heavy,

---

5 The words "joy," "rejoice," and "rejoice with" occur sixteen times in Philippians. Joy is to be the mark of the Christian life—specifically, joy in the midst of trials (1:28–30). Paul was not saying that the Philippians should enjoy pain as if it is "spiritual" to suffer. Rather, they were to patiently endure suffering with joy, knowing that God will complete his work (1:6) and that Christ is returning (3:20–21). They were to rejoice that God has graciously given them the privilege of suffering for the sake of Christ (1:29). Joy does not depend on circumstances; it depends on being joined to Christ.

Philippians 2:13 makes it clear: God helps direct our energies toward becoming spiritually fit.

Sadly, many followers of Jesus plateau in their spiritual development. A complex of doubts, disappointments, failures, and distractions leads to a decline of energy directed toward spiritual growth. Without constant vigilance, our commitment to spiritual growth languishes and our positive testimony wavers. Without focused effort, our once vibrant spiritual pulse slows to a slog. We grow complacent, viewing God's grace as an insurance plan rather than an exercise regimen.

But this is a misunderstanding of grace. Peterson (2010, 5) chides the American church for focusing so intently on getting people "born again" that we've failed to help them "grow up." Grace does not discourage growth (Titus 2:11–12). Grace does not excuse sin (Rom. 6:1). Grace does not exempt us from working (Eph. 2:8–10). No: Grace instructs, inspires, and applauds spiritual fitness. We do not drift into Christlikeness; we keep working toward it.

Preaching Idea
Keep working a plan to become spiritually fit.

Contemporary Connections

What does it mean?
What does it mean to keep working a plan to become spiritually fit? Does moral effort lead to legalism? What is God's role in our spiritual fitness? Not only does God promise to finish the good work he started in his people (Phil. 1:6), he also resources us with his Spirit to live in obedience. Paul hammers home this point in several of his letters, preferring a Spirit-driven life, rather than one enslaved to the flesh (e.g., Rom. 8:1–17; Gal. 5:16–26). While the Holy Spirit distributes diverse spiritual gifts to different people (1 Cor. 12:11), there is no reason to believe he gives more spiritual fervor to a select few. The Holy Spirit is an equal opportunity employer: grieving him or getting our fill is open to every follower of Jesus (Eph. 4:30; 5:18).

While Paul did not explicitly reference the Holy Spirit in 2:12–18, he assumed his readers experienced fellowship in the Spirit (v. 1). The Spirit knits together followers of Jesus as they link arms in telling the world about Jesus. It would be safe to assert the Spirit's role in developing Christlike character (i.e., spiritual fitness), as well.

Unfortunately, the American church has outsourced spiritual development to self-help gurus and leading business thinkers. We understate the redemptive value of suffering and oversimplify how to gain freedom from addiction, low self-worth, personal debt, and sexual struggle. Meanwhile, Scripture recognizes the path to becoming like Jesus—becoming spiritually fit—is long, hard, slow, and painful. Relying on our own efforts or cute strategies severely limits our capacity for growth.

Is it true?
Will God give us the energy and motivation we need to become spiritually fit? Yes, but we must also invest ourselves in the process. There is no way around the paradox of human responsibility and divine initiative. The Scriptures maintain this tension from Genesis to Revelation. In Philippians 2:13 the reminder of God's power supply serves to inspire followers of Jesus to plug into it. It is natural to default to our own strength, which eventually fails. But to depend on God's strength allows the church greater success in becoming spiritually fit.

This of course raises another question: Isn't spiritual fitness too self-focused? Shouldn't we pour our energies into evangelism? It is common to separate evangelism from character development. Western evangelicalism has preferred the former, considering the latter either legalistic or old-fashioned. Revivalism has deep roots in American soil, and "born-again" experiences are much easier to track than advances in spiritual maturity. Of course, this tendency reflects the individualism of the West (i.e., personal salvation), overlooking the corporate nature of most of the New Testament commands (i.e., corporate sanctification).

Throughout Paul's letters (and echoed by other NT writings), the division is not so clear cut. In fact, typically the church as a counter-cultural, character-forming community *was* the witness. Virtue and evangelism were inseparable. Wright (2010, 237) calls this "living Jesus in public," where the church acts as royal priests to the world.

Now what?

What does it look like to keeping working a plan to become spiritually fit? Isn't the goal of becoming like Jesus impossible this side of eternity? Should we feel guilty if we spend time on lesser aims?

First, the impossibility of achieving perfect spiritual fitness should not discourage us from pressing toward it. Paul said as much in Philippians 3:12–16. He recognized God had "laid hold of" him to become like Jesus. Even if his full transformation must wait for Jesus's second coming (v. 21), he made perfection his aim.

Second, we must acknowledge limits to our personal energies. Much recent research has highlighted how self-control is an exhaustible resource. We must experience rhythms of rest, play, leisure, and sleep to recharge. Practicing spiritual disciplines to the point of exhaustion only leads to guilt and burnout. Spiritual fitness does not rule out the occasional warm bath, afternoon nap, or beachside vacation.

Third, we cannot mark any meaningful progress without having a clear goal. Author Stephen Covey (2004) popularized the phrase, "Begin with the end in mind." The principle proves true in the secular world of business, finance, and sports. Excellence grows out of clear aims. Followers of Jesus might celebrate greater strides in maturity if we articulate areas of spiritual fitness we need to grow in.

And before we are overwhelmed by *every* area of our lives, we can focus our attention on Jesus's humility from the Christ hymn or three imperatives from Philippians 2:12–18. We must learn to ask tough diagnostic questions: *How can I abandon my pride and self-centeredness and adopt Jesus's humility at home and work? How can I control my grumbling toward fellow Christ-followers, so it reflects Jesus's gracious attitude? How can I improve my moral testimony among my neighbors, so I shine like Jesus?* The point of self-evaluation is not to lament how out of shape we are spiritually, but to refocus our eyes on Jesus "the author and perfecter of our faith" (Heb. 12:2).

Creativity in Presentation

Most of us are not strangers to making plans. It is working our plans that proves our mettle. I (Tim) have finished three marathons. Each one sapped every ounce of energy from my body, but I crossed the finish line. A marathon requires both perseverance and a plan. Had I failed to train or quit the race at mile twenty (believe me, I was tempted), I would not have achieved my fitness goal. A personal fitness story (e.g., triathlon, loss of twenty pounds, polar plunge) detailing your perseverance and plan may be helpful.

Consider interviewing a physical trainer or nutritionist and asking her what keeps people motivated to "work a plan." Another interview option might be a sports coach, having him share what tactics he uses to keep his athletes improving.

> **Sample Interview Questions**
> **for Physical Trainer**
> 1. What are the essential elements to a personal fitness plan?
> 2. How important are long-term goals to physical fitness?
> 3. What role do short-term wins play in long-term improvement?

4. What is the trainer responsible for? What is the individual responsible for?
5. How often should you tweak your fitness plan?
6. What should you do if you get sidetracked from the plan?
7. What would be essential to a spiritual fitness plan?

Another approach to engage the audience is to propose a daunting, hypothetical goal for them to consider. Saving a million dollars, losing fifty pounds, biking across the country, or completing a master's degree could all suffice. Help them work backward from the goal, asking what it would take to arrive at the destination. *How much time? How much energy? How much of a plan or routine? How much help from others?* Now ask them how will they apply this logic of making plans to becoming spiritually fit. Repeat the same questions from above.

Finally, you might work through a list of daily distractions and exhausting tasks that misdirect our focus. Consider the urgent responses required of emails, text messages, and crying children. Discuss the routine interruptions of coworkers, push notifications, and traffic delays. Admit the deliberate distractions of entertainment, social media, and online shopping. Make the list long, detailed, and personal to convey the overwhelming nature of everyday life. Then ask, "How much energy do you have left to direct toward becoming like Jesus?" To visualize this depletion of energy, make a giant gas tank or stamina bar (like used in video games) that you can lower its level after every distraction or task on the list.

The point you want to emphasize is this: God motivates and empowers believers to strive to become a spiritually mature, holy community as they head toward the future salvation God will bring to completion. Therefore, we should work a plan to become spiritually fit.

- God gives us strength to become spiritually fit (2:12–13).

- A good, not grumbly, attitude toward others is a mark of spiritual fitness (2:14–16).

- A glad, not ungrateful, reception of others is a mark of spiritual fitness (2:17–18).

DISCUSSION QUESTIONS

1. What is the relationship between virtue and evangelism? What happens when we divorce the two?

2. What does a healthy plan for spiritual formation (i.e., discipleship) look like?

3. What is the difference between working *for* your salvation and working *out* your salvation?

4. How is the term "salvation" broader than just referring to "getting saved" at your conversion?

5. What does "fear and trembling" mean (2:12)? How is an attitude of "fear and trembling" appropriate for a believer in Christ—for whom there is no longer any condemnation (Rom. 8:1)? How does your "fear" of the Lord relate to your "trust" in him and your "love" for him?

6. What is God's role and your role in the process of sanctification? What are his responsibilities? What are your responsibilities?

7. Why are "grumbling" and "arguing" so prevalent among God's people in every age? What are their root causes? Why are these considered to be serious sins in Scripture?

8. What does it mean for your life to be poured out as a "drink offering" to God? Why should this be a reason for you to "rejoice"?

Philippians 2:19–30

EXEGETICAL IDEA
The Philippians were to receive and honor two proven, sacrificial servants of Christ from Paul, Timothy, and Epaphroditus.

THEOLOGICAL FOCUS
We should value followers of Jesus who demonstrate sacrificial service for the church.

PREACHING IDEA
Give kudos to those who take risks for Jesus.

PREACHING POINTERS
Paul shifted from moral exhortation to traveling arrangements, sharing with his original readers upcoming plans to see them again. Prior to his arrival, however, the Philippians would receive two familiar ministry partners who had risked their lives: Timothy and Epaphroditus. The exegetical section reveals Paul's reinforcement of the Christ hymn while giving updates on these two commendable servants. Their humility and sacrifice deserve recognition. Moreover, Paul alleviated any worries his first-century readers experienced concerning Epaphroditus's delayed return.

Today we can learn a lesson on commending those who take risks for Jesus. Our world has no shortage of role models. Children exalt heroes from TV and movie screens. Famous athletes and star singers shape cultural trends in dress, language, and politics. Parents, teachers, and coaches serve as personal examples to emulate. The challenge is choosing the right kind of role model, who risks her security, comfort, and reputation to make Jesus famous. Not only does Paul consider himself a risk-taker and worthy role model, but he also gives kudos to two ministry partners who risked their life for Jesus.

TWO CHRISTLIKE SERVANTS (2:19–30)

Following the exhortation section of the letter (1:27–2:18), Paul commended two coworkers, Timothy (2:19–24) and Epaphroditus (2:25–30), both of whom he was sending to Philippi. After that, he would also come.

LITERARY STRUCTURE AND THEMES (2:19–30)

Paul presented them as examples of the Christlike, sacrificial service he encouraged in 2:2–8. They also exemplify a standard of following Jesus that will contrast with the negative examples in chapter 3. He would send Timothy soon so that he (Paul) could be encouraged when he heard how they were doing. He commended Timothy as one who was genuinely concerned for them and who sought the interests of Christ rather than his own. They already knew of Timothy's proven character, how he had served with Paul in the gospel. Paul was confident that afterward he himself would visit them soon. But before Timothy came, Paul was sending Epaphroditus (with the letter), whom they had sent to serve his needs. Epaphroditus had been sick, as they heard, but God had mercy on him. Paul wanted them to welcome Epaphroditus back with joy and to hold him in honor, for Epaphroditus risked his life and almost died for the sake of the mission they sent him on.

Timothy—A Sacrificial Servant to
Respect (2:19–24)
Epaphroditus—A Sacrificial Servant
to Honor (2:25–30)

EXPOSITION (2:19–30)

After the exhortation section (1:27–2:18), Paul revealed his plans for the immediate future, and commended two honorable servants of Christ he was sending to them. He hoped to send Timothy, who would report back to him on how the Philippians were doing. But first Paul was sending Epaphroditus back to them with this letter. Epaphroditus was one of their own, their messenger sent to minister to Paul on their behalf (2:25–30). After Paul finds out about his court case and expected release, he himself would come.

Epaphroditus and Timothy will serve as Paul's apostolic representatives among the Philippians. They can answer any questions concerning what he has written and see how the Philippians respond. Further, they are exemplary servants of Christ the Philippians should honor.

Timothy and Epaphroditus—Two Christlike Servants: Paul commends these men as Christlike sacrificial servants to be honored. As Jesus looked out for the interests of others (2:4–5), so Timothy will genuinely care for them and will seek the things of Christ, not his own interests (2:20–21). As Christ took the form of a lowly slave (2:7), so Timothy has served as a slave with Paul in the gospel (2:22). As Jesus became obedient to the point of death (2:8), so Epaphroditus came near to death in discharging his ministry to Paul (2:27, 30).

Timothy—A Sacrificial Servant to Respect (2:19–24)

Timothy, an exemplary, self-sacrificing servant of Christ who genuinely cares for them, will hopefully come from Paul to them soon so that he can report back to Paul how they have responded to the letter.

Even though Epaphroditus would arrive first (with the letter), Paul began with a commendation of Timothy. Like the opening of the letter, in which Paul gave Timothy the status of coauthor, this paragraph also minded them of Timothy's authority as Paul's representative.

2:19. Εὐψυχῶ is rendered "cheered" (NIV, ESV, NRSV, NLT), "encouraged" (CSB, NASB, NKJV), or "of good courage" (KJV).

2:19. Paul moved from 2:17–18 (δέ) and stated his intent to send Timothy soon. In this context, speaking of travel plans, "I hope" (ἐλπίζω) suggests confidence, but not quite certainty (BDAG s.v. "ἐλπίζω" 2, p. 319; cf. Rom. 15:24; 1 Cor. 16:7; 1 Tim. 3:14; Philem. 22). "In the Lord Jesus" denotes the realm of Paul's expectation. He made his plans "in Christ," knowing that they would be fulfilled if the Lord wills. Paul expected to send Timothy "soon" (BDAG s.v. "ταχέως" 2a, p. 992). He will explain what he means by "soon" in 2:23—as soon as he sees how things go with his court case.

Paul's intent (ἵνα) for sending Timothy was "so that I also may be encouraged when I learn the news about you." "I also" (κἀγώ) implies that Paul expected Timothy's visit to Philippi to be an encouragement to them. Presumably Timothy would be able to give them news of Paul, as well as any further explanation required by what Paul wrote in the letter. Then, when Timothy returns and Paul "learns" (γνούς) "news about you" (τὰ περὶ ὑμῶν)—how the Philippians are doing and how they have responded to the letter, he expects to be "encouraged" (εὐψυχῶ). "Paul expected to be encouraged or heartened with an implication of a release from anxiety (BDAG s.v. "εὐψυχεω," p. 417).

2:20. Paul explained why (γάρ) he wanted to send Timothy, and not someone else: "for I have no one of like mind who will be genuinely concerned for your welfare." "May be encouraged" (εὐψυχῶ) and "of like mind" (ἰσόψυχον) are words unique to Paul and occur only here in the New Testament. "Of like mind" denotes equality of character, one of "like soul," a "kindred spirit" (NASB, BDAG s.v. "ἰσόψυχος," p. 481). Paul and Timothy shared a common mindset in regard to them and to the gospel.

When Timothy arrives, he will be "genuinely" (γνησίως) concerned for your welfare. He shared Paul's "genuine" or "sincere" concern for the Philippians (BDAG s.v. "γνησίως," p. 202). "Concerned" refers to the positive idea of actively caring for someone's welfare (cf. 1 Cor. 7:32–34 [4x]; 12:25) (O'Brien, 1991, 319). The word carries "overtones of the pressure or weight of anxiety that grows out of true concern for the welfare of others" (Martin and Hawthorne, 2004, 154; cf. BDAG s.v. "μεριμνάω" 2, p. 632).

2:21. "Jesus Christ" is read by NIV, ESV, NRSV, CSB, NLT, KJV (Ἰησοῦ Χριστοῦ is found in 𝔓⁴⁶ ℵ A C D F G P Ψ 33 81). The alternate reading in the manuscripts, "Christ Jesus," is reflected in NASB, NKJV (Χριστοῦ Ἰησοῦ is found in B L 0278 104 365 𝔐).

2:21. The reason why (γάρ) Paul had no one of like mind to send except Timothy was because "they all seek their own interests, not those of Jesus Christ." He contrasts Timothy with others he does not identify. "They all seek (ζητοῦσιν) their own interests" marks these individuals as those who do not measure up to the exhortation in 2:4. They "devote serious effort to realize their own objective" (BDAG s.v. "ζητέω" 3b, p. 428). The "things of Jesus Christ" include the spread of the gospel message (1:12–17) and all that Paul had been discussing since 1:27 (cf. Harmon, 2015, 281). Paul was probably using hyperbole to show just how much he esteemed the servant-minded Timothy—especially compared to some of the other preachers in Rome (cf. 1:15, 17).

2:22. The ὅτι clause is understood to be causal, "you know of his proven character because he served" (NIV, CSB), or as epexegetical to "proven character"—"that/how he served" (ESV, NRSV, NASB, KJV, NKJV).

2:22. Paul contrasted (δέ) Timothy with those who seek their own interests: "but you know his proven character." The Philippians already knew Timothy. He had been with Paul on the foundational visit to Philippi (Acts 16:1, 3; 17:14). "Proven character" (δοκιμήν) suggests that Timothy had been tested in ministry and had demonstrated his devotion to Christ and the gospel, his spiritual maturity and integrity (cf. BDAG s.v. "δοκιμή" 2, p. 256). From Timothy's long service with Paul (a decade by this time), they were aware of his character. So he was well qualified to represent Paul at Philippi.

Paul expanded on Timothy's proven character (epexegetical ὅτι). His service with Paul has been "as a child (τέκνον) with a father." Here Paul only indirectly suggested Timothy was his spiritual child (BDAG s.v. "τέκνος" 3b, p. 994; but see 1 Cor. 4:17; 1 Tim. 1:2, 18; 2 Tim. 1:2). The point of the father-son comparison is that Timothy was *like* Paul in spirit and had served *with* Paul in a close ministry relationship (Fee, 1995, 269).

"Served" (ἐδούλευσεν) or "perform the duties of a slave" alludes to the title "bondservants" (δοῦλοι) of Christ Jesus Paul used of himself and Timothy in the opening greeting (1:1), as well as to the example of Christ who took the form of a "slave" (δούλου) in 2:7 (BDAG s.v. "δουλεύω" 2b, p. 259). "In the gospel" denotes the purpose of Paul and Timothy's service to Christ Jesus. They served in the cause of furthering the gospel message—evangelism, church planting, and shepherding the young churches. The picture is of Paul the mentor and Timothy the protégé slaving side by side in birthing the churches and helping them grow. Paul's concern was to emphasize that believers need to have the mind of Christ and take the lowly position of becoming a servant for others (2:5–8). So he commended Timothy as one who had done just that.

2:23. Paul resumed (οὖν) the thought of 2:19: "therefore I hope to send him at once as soon as I see how things go with me." For "I hope" (ἐλπίζω), see 2:19. "As soon as" (ὡς ἄν, BDAG s.v. "ὡς" 8ca, p. 1106; BDF § 455) "I see" (ἀφίδω)

indicates that Paul needed to gain more knowledge about his case before he could send Timothy (BDAG s.v. "ἀφιδάω," 2, p. 158). "How things go with me" (τὰ περὶ ἐμέ) refers primarily to Paul's pending legal case in Rome (cf. 1:12). "At once" (BDAG s.v. "ἐξαυτῆς" p. 346) indicates that Timothy would set out for Philippi as soon as Paul found out about this. Perhaps he expected a verdict to be given shortly, or at least expected to find out more clearly the time frame for his trial (Fee, 1995, 269–70).

2:24. Paul expressed his confidence that the verdict in his trial would be favorable and that he would come to Philippi soon. "I am confident" renders a perfect tense verb (πέποιθα) that denotes Paul was "so convinced," he had become "confident" (BDAG s.v. "πείθω" 2a, p. 792). "In the Lord" (cf. v. 19) identifies the sphere of Paul's confidence. His confidence was in the Lord, not in the courts. He was confident that (ὅτι) he "will come" (ἐλεύσομαι) to them soon. "Soon" (ταχέως) "pertains to a future point in time that is subject to another point of time" (BDAG s.v. "ταχέως," 2a, p. 992; cf. 2:19). Here in verse 24, it refers at best to a matter of months, since Paul was not planning to come until he had (1) seen how things will go with him, (2) sent Timothy, and (3) received a report of their situation once Timothy had returned to him.

Timothy: Paul's Spiritual Son and Trusted Assistant: Timothy is first mentioned in Luke's account of Paul's visit to Lystra on the second missionary journey (Acts 16:1–2). From a Jewish mother who became a believer, Timothy learned the Scriptures as a child (Acts 16:2; 2 Tim. 1:5; 3:15). Paul asked him to accompany him (Acts 16:3) and Paul's trust in him is seen in the important missions he carried out. He represented Paul at Thessalonica (1 Thess. 3:2–6; Acts 17:14–15; 18:5), and co-sent letters to them (1 Thess. 1:1; 2 Thess. 1:1). On the third journey, Paul sent him to Corinth (1 Cor. 4:17; 16:10–11), and Macedonia (Acts 19:22). He was co-sender of 2 Corinthians (1:1) and mentioned to the Romans (Rom. 16:21). He helped take the collection to Jerusalem (Acts 20:4). With Paul during the first Roman imprisonment, he co-sent three prison letters (Phil. 1:1; Col. 1:1; Philem. 1). After Paul's release, Timothy went to Ephesus (1 Tim. 1:3). During Paul's final imprisonment, he asked Timothy to come to him (2 Tim. 4:6–12). Later Timothy himself spent time in prison (Heb. 13:23).

Epaphroditus—A Sacrificial Servant to Honor (2:25–30)

When Epaphroditus—who almost died delivering financial support to Paul, yet completed his mission—arrived home in Philippi with this letter, they were to honor him as an exemplary, self-sacrificing servant of Christ.

In Roman culture, the state's care for prisoners was not intended for health, but "bare survival" (*DNTB*, 829). It was up to family and friends to provide additional food, drink, and care. The Philippians had sent Epaphroditus to Paul with a financial gift and to provide for him in prison (2:25; 4:18). This is the only New Testament text that mentions Epaphroditus. Like Timothy, he serves as an example for the Philippians to honor and emulate.

2:25. The epistolary aorist ἡγησάμην may be rendered as present time, "I think," reflecting Paul's point of view as he is writing (NIV, NRSV), or as past time, "I thought," reflecting the readers' point of view when they receive the letter (ESV, CSB, NLT, NASB, KJV, NKJV).

2:25. Paul moved from Timothy to Epaphroditus (δέ), whom he was sending now. At the time he was writing the letter, Paul "regarded" (ἡγησάμην) or was processing (BDAG s.v. "ἡγέσμαι" 2, p. 434") the necessity (ἀναγκαῖον) of sending Epaphroditus home to Philippi. Paul described him with five titles, three relating to himself and two relating to the Philippians. Hellerman relates this string of five titles to the Roman culture of Philippi, with its focus

on military and civic honors. In contrast to the honors prized by that culture, Paul honors Epaphroditus as a citizen of God's kingdom (2015, 154–58). "My brother" (BDAG s.v. "ἀδελφός" 2a p 18) designates Epaphroditus as a member of the believing community, as well as Paul's close personal relationship with and affection for him (*TDNT* 7:742, n. 29; Collange, 1979, 119–20). "Fellow worker" (συνεργόν) is a term Paul used of close associates in the ministry of the gospel (e.g., Rom. 16:3, 9, 21; 2 Cor. 8:23; Philem. 1, 24) (*TDNT* 7:874–75).

"Fellow soldier" (συστρατιώτην) was typically used of a soldier viewed as equal to the commander-in-chief or a warrior equal to the king (BDAG s.v. "συστρατιώτης," p. 979; *TDNT* 7:704). Here "fellow soldier" denotes a fellow worker, who has faced hardship with Paul in serving the gospel (cf. Archippus in Philem. 2). The Philippians, living in a city originally founded with military veterans, would perhaps especially appreciate this designation of one who was a soldier for the Lord. Fee suggests that Paul was sending Epaphroditus, a wounded comrade, home to rest (1995, 276).

With a mild contrast (δέ) and a change of possessive pronouns (from "my" to "your"), Paul now described Epaphroditus in his relationship to the Philippians. He was their messenger to Paul. "Messenger" (ἀπόστολον) reflects a nontechnical use of the Greek word "apostle," meaning "envoy" (BDAG s.v. "ἀπόστολος" 1, p. 122). The Philippians sent him as their representative and messenger to deliver their financial gift to Paul and perhaps also to stay with Paul and provide for his needs while in prison (Bockmuehl, 1998, 170).

Finally, Epaphroditus was their "minister" (λειτουργόν) to Paul's needs. The term generally refers to all kinds of public servants in the Greek world, but in the LXX refers specifically to the priests and Levites who ministered in the temple (*TDNT* 4:216–21; *NIDNTTE* 3:105). In 2:30, Paul will use a related word ("ministry") to refer to the Philippians' service to Paul through

Epaphroditus. By using "minister" and "ministry," Paul may have been thinking of Epaphroditus's service as a form of *priestly* service (Fee, 1991, 276). "To my need" (τῆς χρείας μου) could refer to anything that might be lacking (BDAG s.v. "χρεία" 2a, p. 1086). In Paul's case, it was a financial ability to purchase the basic necessities of life (food, drink) while in prison.

2:26. The reason (ἐπειδή, "for") Paul believed it was necessary to send Epaphroditus home was because "he was longing for all of you and was distressed because you heard that he was sick." This does not refer to homesickness, but to his emotional "distress" (ἀδημονῶν) because (διότι) they had heard that he was ill (ἠσθένησεν). While Epaphroditus suffered some sort of a "debilitatiing illness" (BDAG s.v. "ασθενέω" 1, p. 142), the exact nature of his illness is unknown. Nor is it clear when he fell ill, or how the Philippians heard of his illness. Perhaps he fell ill on the journey to visit Paul and sent word back to the Philippians by a traveling companion or someone traveling toward Philippi (Fee, 1991, 278). If he did become ill on the way to Rome, his continuing on the journey may have been the risking of his life Paul refers to in 2:30. Or perhaps he did not fall ill until he arrived in Rome. Any reconstruction of events necessarily involves speculation. Paul did not state why Epaphroditus was distressed by the knowledge that they had heard of his illness. Maybe he thought they were still worried about him and did not know he had recovered. This was before the age of instant communication we enjoy. In any case, Paul thought it best to send him home to be with them again.

2:27. Paul explained (γάρ) that Epaphroditus had been sick. "Near [παραπλήσιον] death" reveals how sick he was. "But" (ἀλλα, strong adversative) God "had mercy" (ἠλέησεν) on him. This was Paul's way of saying that God *healed* Epaphroditus. He did not say how God healed him—whether he used means like gifts of healing, prayer with laying on of hands, medical treatment, or a combination of these or other means. Paul's focus was on God's "great concern" about Epaphroditus (BDAG s.v. "ἐλεέω," p. 315) that was evident in God's having enabled Epaphroditus to recover from his illness.

Similarly, Paul himself was also shown mercy when God healed Epaphroditus. With respect to Paul, the purpose/result (ἵνα) of the healing was so he would not experience "sorrow upon sorrow." "Sorrow" (λύπην) could refer to "pain of mind," an afflicted spirit, or a form of grief (BDAG s.v. "λύπη," p. 604). The double use "sorrow upon sorrow" probably emphasizes the idea of overwhelming grief (Harmon, 2015, 293). If Epaphroditus had died, Paul would have been especially grieved; knowing that he was the reason Epaphroditus had made the journey in the first place.[6] But God spared Paul the pain and grief that would have come to him because of Epaphroditus's death. Paul's mention of his own sorrow being spared demonstrated his deep appreciation for Epaphroditus.

From Paul's experience, we are again reminded that following Jesus does not mean the absence of sorrow. It means the ability to rejoice in the midst of sorrow (Fee, 1995, 280), and the ability to be thankful when God's mercy delivers us from sorrow upon sorrow.

---

6   Or the phrase "sorrow upon sorrow" could mean that Paul was thinking specifically of how Epaphroditus's death would add even more sorrow upon (ἐπὶ) the sorrow he was already facing. He did not identify the sorrow to which this would have been added, but besides his sorrow for Epaphroditus's suffering, we could also think of Paul's imprisonment and the rivalry of the preachers with impure motives (Bockmuehl, 1998, 173; Hansen, 2009, 206). The sorrow Paul already felt was connected with his being poured out like a drink offering (2:17).

2:28. The epistolary aorist ἔπεμψα is rendered as present time, "I send," reflecting Paul's point of view as he is writing (NIV, ESV, NRSV, CSB, NLT), or as past time, "I sent," reflecting the readers' point of view when they receive the letter (NASB, KJV, NKJV). Ἀλυπότερος is rendered "less anxious" (NIV, ESV, NRSV, CSB, cf. NASB, NLT) or "less sorrowful" (KJV, NKJV).

2:28. Paul resumed (οὖν) what he said in 2:25 about sending Epaphroditus: "Therefore more eagerly I have sent him." This language resembles that of other Greco-Roman letters that commend their letter carriers, suggesting that Paul was sending Epaphroditus with the letter (Harmon, 2015, 294, n. 47). "More eagerly" (σπουδαιοτέρως) can mean either (1) "with haste" or (2) "being conscientious in discharging a duty or obligation" (BDAG s.v. "σπουδαίως" 2, p. 939). The first meaning would suggest that Paul felt the need to send him back as soon as possible once he recovered (Bockmuehl, 1998, 173). The second would suggest that Paul was zealously and eagerly sending him back—being very glad for Epaphroditus to return home.

Paul purpose (ἵνα) in sending Epaphroditus was twofold. First, "so that when you see him again you may rejoice." The adverb "again" (πάλιν) occurs between the words "see" (ἰδόντες) and "rejoice" (χαρῆτε). It may go with either. Because Paul's style was normally to place the "again" before the word it modified, it may be better to connect it to "rejoice" ("you may rejoice again") rather than "see" (when you see him again") (Fee, 1995, 280). Most English translations put it with "see." Paul wanted the Philippians' joy to be rekindled when they saw their brother alive and well.

Second, Paul's purpose was "so that I may be "less sorrowful" (ἀλυπότερος). The term occurs only here in the New Testament. Most English translations suggest a translation of "less anxious," or "free from all anxiety" (BDAG s.v. "ἄλυπος," p. 48). But in this context where Paul has noted that God's mercy kept him from

adding "sorrow upon sorrow," it may be better to understand it according to the root words from which it is formed (ἀ-λυπή, "without sorrow") (NKJV; Fee, 1995, 281, n. 40). Paul's intent was that when Epaphroditus arrived in Philippi, not only would the Philippians be filled with joy again, but also he would not have to experience the sorrow of Epaphroditus's illness or death.

2:29. Paul concluded (οὖν) his discussion about Epaphroditus's illness and return home with a double exhortation. First, they were to "welcome" (προσδέχεσθε) him—to "receive him in a friendly manner" (BDAG s.v. "προσδέχομαι" 1a, p. 877). "In the Lord" (ἐν κυρίῳ, cf. Rom. 16:2) means that they were to receive him back home as a brother in the Lord, a fellow member of the believing community (Hellerman, 2015, 162). "With (μετά) all joy" expresses the emotion that accompanies their welcome and recalls the previous verse: "that . . . you may rejoice again." "All (πάσης) joy" suggests that he wanted their joy to be unhindered and full as they received him back.

Second, they were to "hold such persons in honor" (ἐντίμους). Epaphroditus and those of like character and service should have the esteem of others in the church. In an honor-based culture, Paul was urging the Philippians to honor such individuals, but not for the normal activities that people were honored (military victories, large civic donations). Service to the Lord is what deserves recognition (cf. Fowl, 2005, 138).

2:30. The participle παραβολευσάμενος is rendered as an adverbial participle, "risking" (ESV, NRSV, CSB, NASB), or "not regarding" (KJV, NKJV), modifying μέχρι θανάτου ἤγγισεν ("came close to death/nearly died"), or as an independent finite verb, "he risked" (NIV, NLT).

2:30. The reason why (ὅτι) the Philippians were to welcome him back with joy and hold him in honor is because "for the sake of the work of

Christ he came near death, risking his life." Paul described Epaphroditus's actions in terms that recall Jesus's example in 2:8, and so presented him as an example of one who has followed the exhortation in 2:4–5. "Work of Christ" refers to participation in spreading the gospel message (cf. 1:5). "Came near death" (μέχρι θανάτου ἤγγισεν) describes the extent of Epaphroditus's selfless service (cf. μέχρι θανάτου in 2:8). In order to serve Paul and so to advance the gospel, Epaphroditus followed Christ's example.

"Risking" (παραβολευσάμενος) occurs only here in the New Testament, and this is its first known occurrence in Greek literature. It may denote the means of his coming near death ("by risking his life"), or the cause ("because he risked his life;" cf. BDAG s.v. παραβολεύομαι, p. 759). "Life" (ψυχῇ) is the Greek word sometimes rendered "soul," and Paul earlier used it to refer to the "mind," "purpose," or "aim" (1:27). But here it refers to the earthly life. Epaphroditus risked his life when he brought the Philippians' gift to Paul, and in fact became deathly ill. In this way, he did not look to his own interests, but to the interests of others (2:4).

The purpose (ἵνα) for which Epaphroditus risked his life was "so that he might supply (ἀναπληρόω) what was lacking (ὑστέρημα) in your service to me." Epaphroditus supplied their lack when he arrived with their gift for Paul. This is not a negative statement about the Philippians, as though they had failed to fulfill a service. Paul was simply noting that because of geographical distance, the Philippians had been unable to provide for Paul's material needs, and Epaphroditus had accomplished his mission. Paul assumed that the Philippians would provide for him, just as all believers should provide for one another. Because Epaphroditus completed his mission, even risking his life, they were to welcome him home with joy and hold him in high esteem.

THEOLOGICAL FOCUS

The exegetical idea (the Philippians were to receive and honor two proven, sacrificial servants

of Christ from Paul—Timothy and Epaphroditus) leads to this theological focus: *We should value followers of Jesus who demonstrate sacrificial service for the church.*

When Paul commended Timothy and Epaphroditus to the Philippians, he was not merely informing the Philippians of the fact that he was sending them, or even why he would send them. He described them in a way that presented them as exemplary, self-sacrificing servants who imitated Jesus. Here are two men who showed what it meant to live according to the exhortations in Paul's letter. They were servants who did nothing according to selfish ambition or empty conceit, but in humility regarded others as more important than themselves. They did not look out for their own interests, but for the interests of others (2:3–4). Timothy served as a slave (2:22; cf. 2:7). Epaphroditus came near death for the sake of the gospel (2:27, 30; cf. 2:8). Paul reinforced the exhortation section through the exemplary service of his two representatives he was sending to Philippi. Paul wanted all of the Philippians to be the kinds of believers Timothy and Epaphroditus represented.

PREACHING AND TEACHING STRATEGIES

Exegetical and Theological Synthesis

In this section, Paul featured two real-life examples of Christlike risk. He carefully chose language—Timothy's *servitude*, Epaphroditus's near-*death*—to echo the Christ hymn (2:5–11). Furthermore, the five titles applied to Epaphroditus reflect the emphasis on status in Philippi, something Paul did not claim for himself (1:1). What Paul readily acknowledged is the partnership between him and the Philippian church in spreading the news of Jesus. Underlying their shared ministry was the mercy of God, which brought healing to a wounded emissary, comfort to a worried church, and imminent release to an imprisoned follower of Jesus.

Earlier in the letter, Paul mentioned positive outcomes of his imprisonment—new routes for God to work. He proclaimed Jesus from prison; others spread news of Jesus, even if to rile him up. Whereas these poorly motivated preachers are unnamed, here Paul shined a light on Timothy and Epaphroditus. They were household names in Philippi. They were model servants of God's church. Paul documented their sacrifices, giving credit for their sense of abandon.

In a few brief verses, Paul surfaced many qualities reflective of Jesus and expected of his followers. He deemed Timothy "selfless" and "proven," like a "child" to Paul, and "likeminded" in his dedication to service. He trusted Timothy not only to represent him, but also report to him happenings in Philippi. He called Epaphroditus "brother," "fellow-worker," "fellow-soldier," "messenger," and "minister." The honorable titles are validated by Epaphroditus's risking death for the cause of Jesus. The description of these two servants is not exhaustive, but makes a compelling case for the kind person worthy of commendation—a person who copies Jesus in choosing risk over reputation.

Preaching Idea

Give kudos to those who take risks for Jesus.

Contemporary Connections

What does it mean?

What are kudos? And isn't taking risks too, well, risky? Kudos is a colloquial way of describing credit, honor, or commendation of others. Sadly, people doing ministry are more prone to hear criticism than praise. We should not confuse real encouragement with flattery. The former speaks truth to a person in a way that diffuses fear and inspires faithfulness (Crabb and Allender, 2013). Flattery, on the other hand, exaggerates the truth to manipulate others or manage their feelings.

The exhortation to take risks must be qualified. To risk for its own sake is folly. It is the pursuit of bored people and adrenaline junkies. These feelings creep into the Western church because following Jesus in a world protected by personal rights and flooded with consumer goods can feel predictable, safe, and unchallenging. Indeed, some elect short-term mission trips to dangerous places for this very reason.

On the other hand, we live in a risk-averse culture. Recalled products, surgeon general's warnings, seat belts, public-service announcements, insurance plans, gun laws, and conservative investment strategies each try to mitigate risk. From womb to tomb we are conditioned to seek comfort and safety over risk. Thus, we must strike a balance in making wise sacrifices to expand the impact of God's kingdom.

Is it true?

Should we really give kudos to others? Won't that lead to an inflated ego? Isn't it just better to reserve our words of praise for Jesus rather than flawed humans? On the surface, these questions sound reasonable, but they use religious jargon to mask God's command for encouragement. It is true that every Christ-follower, however committed or experienced, is flawed; but this does not limit God from commissioning us to represent him.

In fact, many of us have known Jesus most personally through the witness of other believers. Even Jesus acknowledged this fact, praying his followers would reflect him to the world (John 13:35; 17:1–26). Of course, any of our role models is prone to let us down. Churches have been scandalized by pastors who have lied, abused others, or committed adultery. Coaches and parents have let down those who look up to them by poor judgment or broken promises. While we do not give kudos for failure, we may even commend flawed people when we see them confess their sins and make amends.

For many of us, our deepest longing is to hear God someday give us kudos. "Well done, my good and faithful servant," captures the beat of our hearts. This is what theologians call "glorification" or C. S. Lewis describes as "a weight or burden of glory which our thoughts can hardly sustain" (2001, 39). Perhaps, while we wait to receive divine kudos, we could offer some earthly encouragement. Fear of inflating the ego of another is overstated. Moreover, we are commanded to honor those who serve in the church (1 Thess. 5:13; 1 Tim. 5:17).

Now what?

So how should we practice giving kudos and taking healthy risks? Should churches have award ceremonies? First, it is essential to encourage a spirit of encouragement within the church. We must recognize many people serve with low confidence and limited commendation. However, we must resist the urge to institutionalize encouragement. Giving public kudos runs the risk of giving preference to some and overlooking others. And yet, if church leaders make a habit of giving thanks and speaking encouragement, an occasional public display of appreciation from the pulpit only reinforces the need to give kudos.

Second, the types of risk-taking we choose to spotlight go a long way in shaping the people we become. When we draw attention to role models who are selfless, we encourage selflessness. Giving praise to deeply committed people, inspires deep commitment. The Scriptures, church history, and our own stories abound with examples of selfless grandparents, parents, and teachers who risked health, wealth, and personal dreams to emulate kingdom values to their loved ones. We can identify a deeply committed friend who traveled overseas to serve the poor, a deeply committed sibling who traded family comfort to adopt a child with special needs, and a deeply committed coworker who exchanged an impressive salary to pursue vocational ministry. These stories fuel our commitment and fine-tune our selflessness so that we, too, take risks for Jesus.

Creativity in Presentation

Take a minute describing one of your favorite award ceremonies (e.g., Oscars, Golden Globes, Dove, Grammys). Talk about the red carpet, the celebrity performances, comedic emcees, and the anticipation as the presenters open envelope, saying, "And the award goes to. . . ." Then ask a series of questions: *What kind of risks did the winners take? What effort did they put forth? What role did others play in their achievement? What emotions do they display when they receive their kudos?* Finally: *If we had an award ceremony at our church for taking risks for Jesus, would your name be in the envelope? If not you, then who among us?*

Consider staging your own mock awards ceremony as part of the sermon. Roll out red carpet. Buy a bunch of cheap trophies. Fill several envelopes with names of church members. Be sure to involve people in advance, making up silly awards that fit them without offending them. Best Beard, Biggest Bible, Loudest Laugh, Perfect Attendance, and Fullest Quiver, could draw some laughter. Finish by holding an award for "Risk-taking in the name of Jesus," and read the names "Timothy and Epaphroditus."

Personal stories can effectively illustrate the beauty of risk taking. Most pastors can identify a grandparent, parent, or mentor who risked much for Jesus. I (Tim) met weekly with a college professor to discuss matters of theology, ministry, relationships, and family life. Not only did he sacrifice much of his time for me, but he and his wife also opened their home to countless foster children through the years. At this professor's recent funeral, many people commended the way he chose risk over reputation.

The point you want to emphasize is this: We should value followers of Jesus who demonstrate sacrificial service for the church. In other words, we should give kudos to those who take risks for Jesus.

- Kudos for Timothy for risking his reputation to serve Jesus (2:19–24).

- Kudos for Epaphroditus for risking his life in serve Jesus (2:25–30).

DISCUSSION QUESTIONS

1. What Christ-followers have you given kudos to? What was it about their lives that made them worthy of commendation?

2. What about your life is worthy of commendation?

3. What makes a follower of Jesus an effective reflection of Christ?

4. What do you see in Paul's description of Timothy that provides a positive example for believers today?

5. What do you see in Paul's description of Epaphroditus that provides a positive example for believers today?

FOR FURTHER READING

Ellis, E. E. 1993. "Paul and His Coworkers." Pages 183–89 in *Dictionary of Paul and His Letters*. Edited by G. F. Hawthorne, R. P. Martin, and D. G. Reid. Downers Grove, IL: InterVarsity Press.

Gillman, J. L. 1992. "Epaphroditus." Pages 533–34 in vol. 2 of *The Anchor Bible Dictionary*. Edited by D. N. Freedman. 6 vols. New York: Doubleday, 1992.

Gillman, J. L. 1992. "Timothy." Pages 558–60 in vol. 6 of *The Anchor Bible Dictionary*. Edited by D. N. Freedman. 6 vols. New York: Doubleday, 1992.

Grudem, W. 1994. "Sanctification." In *Systematic Theology*. Grand Rapids: Zondervan, 746–62.

Hellerman, J. H. 2013. *Embracing Shared Ministry: Power and Status in the Early Church and Why It Matters Today*. Grand Rapids: Kregel Ministry.

Moore, R. D. 2015. *Onward: Engaging the Culture without Losing the Gospel*. Nashville: B&H Publishing.

Willard, D. 2002. *Renovation of the Heart: Putting on the Character of Christ*. Colorado Springs: NavPress.

Wright, N. T. 2010. *After You Believe. Why Christian Character Matters*. New York: HarperOne.

PURSUING CHRIST, NOT THE LAW: A WARNING AGAINST FALSE TEACHERS (3:1– 4:1)

Following his commendation of Epaphroditus and Timothy, Paul warned the Philippians of the potential threat of false teachers. The identity of the false teachers in 3:2–3 is debated. (1) Some view them as non-Christian Jews advocating circumcision and conversion to Judaism. (2) Others view them as pagan Gentiles seeking to influence the minority Christians. (3) Still others view them as Gentile Christian incorporating Jewish ways into Christianity. (4) The most likely view is that they are Judaizers—Jewish-Christian teachers who advocated not only faith in Christ, but also circumcision and keeping at least parts of the Old Testament law as necessary for justification. The similarities here with Paul's argument in his letter to the Galatians suggest that Paul has in mind false teachers similar to those who earlier had infiltrated the churches of Galatia and those discussed at the apostolic council in Jerusalem (Acts 15). Regardless of their identity, they were adding requirements to the true gospel.

Paul's tone here was not as urgent as in the letter to the Galatians. There is nothing that suggests the false teachers were already present in the church at Philippi. If they were, and if they were having an influence among the believers there, it would be remarkable that Paul only just now brought up the topic. This was more likely a warning for them to keep their heads up and be on the lookout. In any case, Paul presented his own vision of the Christian life as one of pursuing Christ, not the law of Moses. True righteousness is that which comes from God on the basis of faith in Jesus, not on the basis of the law.

This major section, Pursuing Christ, not the Law: A Warning against False Teachers (3:1–4:1), is broken into four preaching units: The True People of God (3:1–6), The Surpassing Value of Knowing Christ (3:7–11), Pursuing the Ultimate Goal (3:12–16), and Imitating Good Examples (3:17–4:1).

Philippians 3:1–6

EXEGETICAL IDEA

Paul's warning against Judaizers emphasized that Christ-followers are God's true people—because they worship and serve God under the power and direction of the Holy Spirit, they trust only in Jesus the Messiah, who secured their justification, and they do not seek justification through keeping the law.

THEOLOGICAL FOCUS

God's true people are those who worship God under the power and direction of the Holy Spirit, who trust only in Jesus the Messiah for justification, and who do not seek justification through keeping the law.

PREACHING IDEA

Don't trust an impressive résumé to secure good standing with God.

PREACHING POINTERS

The tone of Paul's letter takes a turn in chapter 3. The exhortation to copy Jesus's humble, self-giving, sacrificial attitude (as modeled by Timothy and Epaphroditus), contrasts sharply with a warning about Judaizers. Although the original readers may not have directly encountered the legalism Paul criticized, they were no strangers to poorly motivated preachers and cultural pressures. Imminent threat or not, Paul considered it relevant to remind his first-century audience of the happy fact of their new identity in Christ. They don't earn good standing with God by birthright or obedience, but receive it by trusting Jesus.

We are no less affected by moralism in today's church. The specific deeds we deem holy and perverse have a more modern dress, but the tendency to encode some acts as tolerable and others as egregious follows the same line old of logic. We ban certain genres of music (e.g., rap) and make allowances for others (e.g., country). We condemn some content in movies (e.g., sex and language) but justify "lesser" sins (e.g., violence and greed). Moreover, we praise people who take short-term mission trips or practice evangelism, but give little recognition to the volunteer who replaces the trash-can liner or sanitizes the nursery toys. This passage strongly challenges our misplaced trust in an impressive religious resume for good standing with God.

THE TRUE PEOPLE OF GOD (3:1–6)

LITERARY STRUCTURE AND THEMES OF PHILIPPIANS 3:1–6

Paul began this section with an exhortation to rejoice in the Lord, and asserted that to write the "same things" (pointing forward, or perhaps backward) was no trouble for him and was a safeguard for them (3:1). Then he issued the warning: beware the dogs; beware the evil workers; beware the mutilation (3:2). He explained that "we" (those who follow the true gospel), rather than the false teachers, are the (true) circumcision (3:3a). With a threefold relative clause (οἱ plus three participles), Paul described "we": We serve by the Spirit of God, glory in Christ Jesus, and put no confidence in the flesh (3:3b). He qualified the third description by stating that he, more than anyone, had reasons to put confidence in the flesh (3:4). Finally, he provided a list of seven items that would support his confidence in the flesh (3:5–6).

> **Joyful Satisfaction in Jesus (3:1)**
> **Warning against False Teachers (3:2)**
> **God's True People (3:3)**
> **Paul's Former Confidence (3:4–6)**

EXPOSITION (3:1–6)

After the opening exhortation to rejoice (cf. 2:18; 4:4), Paul issued a warning to watch out for false teachers (3:1–2). The heart of this unit is how Paul described the Christian community as God's true covenant people (3:3) and how he made the case for his own Jewish credentials (compared to the false teachers) if that were the way to be righteous before God. But he will go on to say that he regarded all these as loss (3:7). His point was that the Philippians, as believers in Christ, were God's people, and should not

follow any teacher whose "gospel" advocated keeping the Old Testament law, rather than boasting solely in Jesus, who secured their justification.

Joyful Satisfaction in Jesus (3:1)

Paul exhorted the Philippians to find their deep satisfaction in their relationship with Jesus—who he was and all he had done for them—as they endured trying circumstances.

> *3:1.* Τὸ λοιπόν is rendered "finally" (ESV, NRSV, CSB, NASB, KJV, NKLV), "further" (NIV), or "whatever happens" (NLT). Ὀκνηρόν is rendered "trouble" (NIV, ESV, CSB, NASB, cf. NRSV), "grievous" (KJV), or "tedious" (NKJV).

3:1. Turning from his commendations of Timothy and Epaphroditus, Paul moved to a new topic. Most English versions render Paul's introductory word (τὸ λοιπόν) as "finally" (as in, for example, Phil. 4:8; 2 Cor. 13:11). But in this case, Paul will write two more chapters (cf. 1 Thess. 4:1; 2 Thess. 3:1). The word serves, not to announce the conclusion of the letter, but to wrap up one section and move to another (Thrall, 1962, 26; Alexander, 1989, 96–97). So, the NIV rendering "further" is more appropriate (BDAG s.v. "λοιπός" 3b, pp. 602–03).

This is the third of eight occurrences of the affectionate term "brothers" (ἀδελφοί). As before, the masculine form is generic, including "brothers and sisters." The family metaphor emphasizes the close-knit relationships among believers sociologically and theologically (see on 1:12). Paul added the possessive pronoun "my" (μου)—"my brothers"—emphasizing even more his heartfelt connection with them. "Rejoice" recalls the exhortation in 2:18. He will repeat it again twice (4:4). Rejoicing is not merely an emotion. It is an attitude to be chosen and an action to be undertaken. Paul was not calling for a superficial cheerfulness, but for a deep satisfaction with God in the midst of sometimes trying circumstances.

For the first time in the letter, Paul explicitly said that the Philippians were to rejoice "in the Lord" (cf. 4:4). "In the Lord" (ἐν κυρίῳ) denotes the sphere of their existence—the result of having been incorporated into Christ. The fact that they were in the Lord provided the *basis* of their rejoicing (rejoice because of what the Lord has done for you), the *object* of their rejoicing (rejoice at who he is), and the *source* of their rejoicing (rejoice with the joy he supplies) (Fee, 1995, 292). No matter the external circumstances, Christ provides the reasons and resources for joy. Paul did not exhort them to rejoice *in their circumstances,* but to rejoice *in the Lord* in the midst of their circumstances. Their joyful satisfaction was in him.

Paul asserted that to write (γράφειν) the same things was not troublesome, and it was a safeguard for them (BDAG s.v. "γράφω" 2, p. 207). Some scholars argue that "the same things" (τὰ αὐτά) looks backward to the command to rejoice (Martin and Hawthorne, 2004, 173), but it more likely points forward to what he is about to write in 3:2–21. Paul had warned them of these false teachers before. To write the same things was not "troublesome" (ὀκνηρόν). The adjective means that something causes hesitation or reluctance (BDAG s.v. "ὀκνηρός" 2, p. 702; *EDNT* 2:506). Paul was not reluctant to write these same things to the Philippians. In addition, it was a "safeguard" (BDAG s.v. "ασφαλής" 3, p. 147) or "security" (*EDNT* 176, 3) for them. It was in their best interests that he wrote these same things, for it would keep them on firm theological and spiritual ground. Recognizing false teaching, keeping your focus on the pursuit of Christ, and holding to the true gospel of justification by faith provide a strong safeguard to threats to your spiritual life.

Warning against False Teachers (3:2)

Paul exhorted the Philippians to be on their guard against Judaizing false teachers who distorted the gospel about Jesus by adding requirements of circumcision and keeping the law to it.

> *3:2.* Κακοὺς ἐργάτας is rendered "evil workers" (NRSV, CSB, NASB, KJV, NKJV) or "evildoers" (NIV, ESV, cf. NLT). Κατατομήν is rendered "mutilators/mutilation" (NIV, ESV, NRSV, CSB, NLT, NKJV) or "false circumcision" (NASB).

3:2. Paul issued a warning about false teachers He repeated "beware" or "watch out" (βλέπετε) three times for emphasis. The word can mean, more softly, "watch" or "consider" (BDAG s.v. "βλέπω" 5, p. 179). The difference is that of looking at someone and learning versus being on your guard against them. If your daughter walks home from school every day, you warn her to *watch out* for strangers, not merely to cautiously observe them and learn. Some scholars have argued for the softer meaning—"Consider the dogs" (Kilpatrick, 1928). But Paul's emphatic threefold repetition suggests rather that the Philippians were to *look out for* these people, to *be on their guard* against them (Hooker, 2000, 524). The warning sounds urgent, not because the false teachers were already present, but because of the trouble Paul had experienced with them in the past and because of the strong feelings he still had about them (cf. Park, 2007, 54).

We noted above that the identity of the false teachers is debated. We will assume the view that the language Paul used best supports their identity as Judaizers who advocate circumcision and keeping at least parts of the law of Moses in addition to faith in Christ for justification.

Paul used three vivid derogatory terms to refer to the false teachers. All three refer to the same group, not to three different groups. First, he called them "dogs" (κύνας). The view of dogs in ancient societies was mostly negative. Greeks and Romans detested them. Jews considered them unclean (BDAG s.v. "κύνω" 3, p. 579; *TDNT* 3:1101–4). They were not "man's best friend" or lovable pets as they are in the West today. The Judaizers may have thought of those who did not live according to the law of Moses as unclean and so "dogs." If so, Paul ironically turned this label back upon them. As those who distorted the gospel by insisting on adherence to the Mosaic law, they excluded themselves from the covenant and so were unclean "dogs."

Second, Paul called them "evil workers" (κακοὺς ἐργάτας). Elsewhere Paul referred to false teachers as "deceitful workers" (2 Cor. 11:13–15). It may be that he was referring ironically to the Judaizers' self-estimation that by keeping the law they were "good workers" (Martin and Hawthorne, 2004, 174). It is also possible that Paul's use of "workers," reflected the use of this term elsewhere to refer to Christian missionaries (Matt. 9:37–38; 10:10; Luke 10:2, 7). If this is right, because of their Judaizing message, Paul called them "evil workers"—"Christian" missionaries with an evil message consisting of a false gospel that produces evil results (cf. O'Brien, 1991, 355–56). Their "work" turned people away from God.

Third, Paul called them "the mutilation." This is best explained as Paul's play on the word "circumcision." *Circumcision* (περιτομή) means "cut around." *Mutilation* (κατατομή) means "cut to pieces" (BDAG s.v. "κατατομή," p. 528). Paul again ironically turned the false teachers claim to be God's people back on themselves with a word play. Instead of being the circumcision, they were the mutilation. Jews understood circumcision to be the sign of the Abrahamic covenant (Gen. 17:10–11) and a requirement of the law of Moses (Lev. 12:3; cf. Gal. 5:3). The Judaizers were insisting on circumcision probably as both a requirement for justification and as a sign that Gentile converts were now part of the people of God. Paul called their practice mutilation because their teaching perverted the gospel and brought spiritual ruin on their converts (Gal. 5:2–4). Compare his sarcastic comment

about the Judaizers in Galatians 5:12. Ironically, mutilation in the Old Testament was a practice of pagans (Lev. 19:28; 21:5; Deut. 14:1; 1 Kings 18:28). But that was what Paul charged these false teachers with. For Paul, now that Christ had fulfilled the law of Moses, physical circumcision was unnecessary. As a rite of membership in the new covenant, it was no better than pagans lacerating themselves.

God's True People (3:3)

Followers of Christ are the true covenant people of God because they worship and serve God under the power and direction of the Holy Spirit, because they trust only in Jesus the Messiah, who secured their justification, and because they do not seek justification through keeping the Old Testament law.

> *3:3.* Περιτομή is rendered "circumcision" (NIV, ESV, NRSV, CSB, KJV, NKJV) or "true circumcision" (NASB, cf. NLT). Λατρεύοντες is rendered "worship" (ESV, NRSV, NLT, NASB, KJV, NKJV) or "serve" (NIV, CSB). If the genitive form "of God" (Θεοῦ) is original (found in ℵ* A B C D2 F G 1739 𝔐), it qualifies πνεύματι, "who serve/worship in/by the Spirit of God" (NIV, ESV, NRSV, CSB, NLT, NASB). The alternate reading (dative Θεῷ, found in ℵ2 D* P J 365 1175) is taken as the direct object of λατρεύοντες, "who serve/worship God in the Spirit" (KJV, NKJV).

3:3. Paul explained why (γάρ) he referred to the false teachers as the "mutilation" rather than the name they would claim for themselves—the "circumcision." It was because Christ-followers are the "circumcision" (περιτομή). The emphatic "we" (ἡμεῖς) refers to all who embrace the true gospel, whether Jew or Gentile. Peterson calls this statement "the most explicit ecclesiological designation" in the letter (2012, 160). In applying this label to believers who (at least in the case of Gentile converts) had not been physically circumcised, Paul was using "circumcision" in a metaphorical sense to denote those who are related to God through the new covenant (BDAG s.v. "περιτομή" 2b, p. 807). Believers in Jesus Christ are God's covenant people.

Even under the old covenant era, Scripture made it clear that circumcision was primarily a matter of the heart attitude that was to accompany the physical rite (Deut. 10:16; 30:6; Jer. 4:4; cf. Lev. 26:41; Ezek. 44:7). In Romans 2:28–29, Paul had pointed out that a true "Jew" was one who was a Jew inwardly, and that circumcision was a matter of the heart, by the Spirit. Since believers in Christ already *were* the circumcision (an internal matter of the heart), they did not have to *be* physically circumcised as the false teachers argued. Now that the era of the Messiah had dawned, Jesus was reigning, and the Spirit had been poured out. Those who held to the gospel of justification by faith in Christ alone were the true heirs of the covenant—Jew or Gentile (Gal. 3:28). God's people were those who followed the gospel Paul preached rather than the message of the false teachers. For Paul, Israelites who insisted on circumcision (and keeping the law), either for justification or for an identity marker as belonging to God's people, were not the "circumcision." They had forfeited the use of the label through their rejection of the true gospel of salvation by faith in Christ.

"Israel" Designations for the Church: Paul's use of "the circumcision" for the church was similar to his use of other designations for the new covenant people of Jesus Christ (consisting of both Jew and Gentile) that were previously used in the Scripture for the nation of Israel. Theologically, this demonstrates that the church is the fulfillment (not replacement) of Old Testament Israel, the people of God. The ethnic expansion of God's people promised in the Old Testament (e.g., Isa. 2:2–4; 25:6–8; 42:1–4; 45:20–25; 49:6; 52:10; 60:4–22; 66:18–20), in which believing Gentiles were to be incorporated with believing Jews into salvation under the covenant, was fulfilled in Jesus, God's Messiah. Consider these designations: "saints" (Phil. 1:1, etc.), "sons of Abraham" (Gal. 3:7), "Abraham's seed" (Gal. 3:29), "elect" (Rom. 8:33), "the called" (1 Cor. 1:1); "Israel of God" (Gal. 6:16). Paul used these terms (and more) to refer to the new messianic community of Jews and Gentiles together in one body (cf. Hellerman, 2015, 172).

Paul described those who are the circumcision with a threefold relative clause (οἱ plus three participles): "who serve by the Spirit of God and glory in Christ Jesus and put no confidence in the flesh." This description lists three characteristic activities of those who hold to the true gospel and constitutes the reason they are God's covenant people. First, they "serve by the Spirit of God." "Serve" (λατρεύοντες) is used in the LXX of Israel's religious service to God (especially temple service) as his chosen people (Exod. 23:25; Deut. 6:13; 10:12, 20; 28:47; Josh. 22:27; 24:14–15) (*TDNT* 4:58–61; *NIDNTTE* 3:105). Whereas Old Testament Israel had the privilege of worshipping and serving the true God, now that privilege is found and fulfilled in the New Testament church, the covenant community. Service at the Old Testament temple is fulfilled by the service of the whole Christian life, "a life that is oriented toward pleasing God for his eternal glory and our eternal joy" (Harmon, 2015, 314). The translation "worship" (suggesting particular "worship" activities) may be too limiting (Hellerman, 2015, 174).

"By the Spirit of God" denotes the one by whom they serve (πνεύματι, instrumental dative, Varner, 2016, 67). They are empowered and directed by the Holy Spirit (Acts 1:8; 2:33; Rom. 8:9, 14–16; Gal. 4:6). This Spirit-empowered service fulfills the Old Testament promise (Isa. 32:15; 44:3; Ezek. 36:26–27; 37:14; Joel 2:28–29). Possession of the Spirit is the mark of God's people in the new covenant age. They walk in the Spirit rather than keep the law (Gal. 5:18; 2 Cor. 3:6).

Second, those who are the circumcision "boast in Christ Jesus" (cf. 1:26; cf. 2:16). To "boast" (καυχώμενοι) in Christ is to take pride in him (BDAG s.v. "καυχάομαι" 1, p. 536). The idea of boasting in the Lord and not in oneself is encouraged in Jeremiah 9:23–24, and Paul probably intended an echo of that passage here (cf. 1 Cor. 1:31; 2 Cor. 10:17). The boast was "in Christ." This denotes the sphere of believers' boasting, but even more, the object of their boasting, as Paul's use of Jeremiah in the Corinthians references shows (Hellerman, 2015, 174). The "boast" is a joyful exultation because of the one in whom believers put their trust, the one who has secured their justification. As they boast in Christ, "all self-praise disappears" (*NIDNTTE* 2:654). This kind of boasting includes not only glorying in *who* Jesus is, but also glorying in *what* Jesus has done through his death and resurrection, and *what* he continues to do through believers as they serve him. The false teachers' emphasis on circumcision constituted a boasting in keeping the law. But the true gospel excludes such boasting (Rom. 3:27–28).

Third, those who are the circumcision "put no confidence in the flesh." The false teachers' insistence on physical circumcision constituted putting confidence in the flesh. To "put confidence" (πεποιθότες) in the flesh implies that they were depending on or trusting in physical circumcision and law-keeping to make them right with God and to show that they were right with God (BDAG s.v. "πείθω" 2a, p. 792). Paul's use of "flesh" (σάρξ) in this context includes a reference to *physical* circumcision. But theologically, it also refers to the *realm* of the old era outside of Christ, the realm of the Mosaic law. Believers are no longer under the authority of the realm of the flesh. Since believers in Christ are no longer in the flesh (Rom. 8:9), they no longer belong to the old era of the flesh and the law or walk according to it (Rom. 8:4–8). Rather, they belong to and walk according to the new kingdom era of Christ and the Spirit. As a result, their confidence in knowing God necessarily lies there.

Paul's Theological Use of "Flesh": In certain contexts, particularly in discussions of the "flesh" versus the "Spirit," Paul's use of "flesh" (σάρξ) has a theological, or more precisely, eschatological, referent. "Flesh" refers to the human condition outside of Christ and hostile to God (Moo, 2003). The "flesh" is the essential characteristic of the realm of the old era—the realm of bondage to the Mosaic law and to sin.

First Coming of Jesus   Second Coming of Jesus

Adapted from unpublished course notes in John Grassmick's "Seminar in the Theology of Paul" at Dallas Theological Seminary, 1989

The two realms of existence—that of the flesh, law, and sin on the one hand, and that of the Spirit, grace, and freedom on the other—are opposed to one another (Rom. 6:14; 7:6; 8:4–9; Gal. 5:1–6, 16–26). People outside of Christ live in the old era, the present evil age (Gal. 1:4), under the authority of the "flesh." Through his death, resurrection, ascension, and gift of the Spirit, Jesus has brought the era of the flesh and law to an end for believers (Rom. 10:4), and has inaugurated the era of the Spirit and of grace—the new creation. Believers in Christ now live in the Spirit, not the flesh (Rom. 8:9). The new era will be consummated at Jesus's second coming. Believers already belong to the new era (represented by the overlap in the diagram), though they must still live in the old era, which has not yet passed away. They are citizens in the kingdom of the Christ.

In Philippians, the false teachers, still trapped in the old era of the flesh and cut off from salvation in Christ, put their confidence in the powers of the old era. They attempted to keep the law and walk according to the "flesh"—the old human condition. But those in the new covenant age put their confidence not in circumcision or the law, but in Christ through faith. In Philippians 3:4–11, Paul will describe how, as a Jew under the law, he formerly put his confidence in the flesh. But he had cast it all aside in favor of knowing Jesus and receiving God's righteousness. Now that Christ had come, the era of the flesh and the law has come to an end as a way of knowing and walking with God (see Ridderbos, 1975, 64–68; *DPL*, 303–6; Fee, 1994, 816–22; Schreiner, 2001, 140–46; *NIDNTTE* 4:251–62).

Paul's Former Confidence (3:4–6)
Paul pointed out that if being Jewish and keeping the law of Moses were the way to a relationship with God, he would be more qualified than anyone.

3:4. The concessive participle ἔχων is rendered [although I] "have" (NIV, ESV, NRSV), "might have" (NASB, KJV, NKJV), "could have" (NLT), or "once had" (CSB).

3:4. In 3:3 Paul stated that Christians put no confidence in the flesh. Now by switching to the first person singular pronoun ("I"), he qualified that statement with a concession: "although [καίπερ concessive conjunction] I have [good reason for] confidence." If anyone could put confidence in the flesh, Paul could. To "have" (ἔχων) "confidence" (πεποίθησιν) refers to having actual "reason for confidence," not just a subjective thought with no basis in evidence (Martin and Hawthorne, 2004, 183; cf. NIV, ESV, NRSV). Paul had no confidence in the flesh *although he had reason* for having confidence in the flesh. In the list of seven items that follows, while Paul had renounced these as a way to God, he could still claim at least the first four, perhaps five. Some translations try to soften Paul's statement: "might have confidence" (NASB, KJV, NKJV), "could have confidence" (NLT), or "once had

confidence" (CSB). But this softening is unnecessary. Paul's point was that if the false teachers want to discuss Jewishness or righteousness through the law, even though he had grounds for such confidence, as he will say, he regarded this as rubbish in the matter of being right with God.

Paul repeated his point for emphasis and made it more explicit: "if anyone else thinks (δοκεῖ) he has (reason for) confidence in the flesh, I have more." He compared himself specifically with the false teachers; "anyone" refers first of all to them. Paul had "more" (μᾶλλον) empirical reason for confidence than they did. As in 3:3, "confidence in the flesh" refers to trusting in physical circumcision and keeping the law—Jewish credentials—in order to make oneself right with God and to show that one is right with God. Both his Jewish pedigree and his Pharisaic accomplishments gave him more reason for confidence than anyone—if confidence in the flesh was the way to approach God. As in 3:3, flesh (σάρξ) refers to more than physical circumcision and to more than personal achievement. It refers to life in the old order outside of Christ, the realm of the flesh and the law. The old way of approaching God is not compatible with faith in Christ in the present messianic age.

3:5–6. Ἑβραῖος ἐξ Ἑβραίων is rendered "Hebrew of Hebrews" (NIV, ESV, NASB, KJV, NKJV), "real Hebrew" (NLT), or "Hebrew born of Hebrews" (NRSV, CSB). Γένους is rendered "people (NIV, ESV, NRSV), "nation" (CSB, NASB), or "stock" (KJV, NKJV). Ἄμεμπτος is rendered "blameless" (ESV, NRSV, CSB, NASB, KJV, NKJV) or "faultless" (NIV, cf. NLT).

3:5–6. Paul expanded on his claim to have more reason for confidence in the flesh than anyone with a list of seven Jewish credentials. This list demonstrated that none of the false teachers could match his reason for confidence in the flesh. The first four items were privileges of birth. The last three were due to his personal choice—accomplishments that proved his complete dedication to the Mosaic law and the traditions of Judaism prior to his conversion to Christ. Paul listed these honors and credentials, only to show that he now put no confidence in them (3:7–11).

First, "with respect to circumcision (περιτομῇ, dative of reference/respect), an eighth day (person)." By starting with his birth, Paul spoke of circumcision first, appropriate since that was the primary requirement for justification the false teachers added to the gospel. "Eighth day" or "a person-of-eight-days relative to circumcision" (BDAG s.v. "ὀκταήμερος," p. 702) occurs only here in the New Testament. Circumcision was the sign of the Abrahamic covenant (Gen. 17:11) and was to be performed on a male child on the eighth day after his birth (Gen. 17:12; Lev. 12:3). This credential showed first of all that Paul was not a mere proselyte (convert) to Judaism. He was born a Jew. Further, it showed that Paul's parents were law-observant. They fulfilled their covenant obligations with respect to his circumcision.

Second, Paul was "from the nation of Israel." "Nation" (γένους) or "people" denotes Paul's race and bloodline. "Israel" originated with God's name-change of the patriarch Jacob (Gen. 32:28), and came to refer to the nation descended through his twelve sons. "Israel" and "Israelite" were the preferred self-designations of the nation and the Jewish people, drawing attention to their place of privilege as God's covenant people.

Third, Paul was "from/of the tribe of Benjamin" (cf. Rom. 11:1). The fact that Paul could name his tribe showed that he could trace his Jewish lineage, and so demonstrate his Jewishness (O'Brien, 1991, 371). Like the Israelites, the Romans were divided into tribes, and the ability to state one's tribe was an important part of social status in Philippi (Hellerman, 2015, 177).

Fourth, Paul was a "Hebrew ('Εβραῖος) of (ἐξ) Hebrews," that is, a Hebrew from Hebrew parents (ἐξ denotes source). Paul may have

simply meant that there was no Gentile blood in his veins; he was purebred (Fee, 1991, 307). But he may also have meant that, while fluent in Greek language and knowledgeable of Greek culture, he remained a Hebraic Jew (speaking Aramaic, able to read the Hebrew Bible, culturally living according to the law) and had not succumbed to Hellenization (Acts 21:40; 22:2–3).

Fifth, Paul was "in regard to (κατά) the (Mosaic) law, a Pharisee" (Φαρισαῖος). He identified himself with those who were known as 'the separated ones" or "separatists" (BDAG s.v. "Φαρισαῖος," p. 1049; cf. Acts 22:3; 23:6–9; 26:5; Gal. 1:14). With this credential, Paul moved from those advantages that were his by birth to those that were his by choice. Each of these last three advantages begins with "in regard to" (κατὰ) a marker denoting the relationship of one thing to another. Paul claimed to be a member of the sect within Judaism that held to a strict and meticulous interpretation of the law, as applied through its oral tradition. Even as a Christian, Paul still identified as a Pharisee at least in certain doctrinal beliefs, in particular, when among Jews (Acts 23:6). Perhaps he now considered himself a "completed Pharisee" (Martin and Hawthorne, 2004, 186).

Sixth, Paul was "in regard to zeal, persecuting the church." "Zeal" (ζῆλος) denotes "intense positive interest in something" (BDAG s.v. "ζῆλος" 1, p. 427). Paul did not state the object of his zeal, but in addition to a vertical zeal for God and a horizontal national zeal for Israel and her religious institutions, he specifically would have in mind zeal for the law, where the vertical and horizontal were fused (cf. Gal. 1:14) (Ortlund, 2012, 162). It is possible that before his conversion Paul saw himself as a modern-day Phinehas, Elijah, or Mattathias, notable Israelites zealous for God and the law. The Judaizers could not top this.

"Persecuting" (διώκων) refers to harassing individuals or groups because of their beliefs (BDAG s.v. "διώκω" 2, p. 254). Paul referred elsewhere to his persecution of Christians (Gal.

1:13; 1 Cor. 15:9; 1 Tim. 1:13). The Acts narrative suggests that this consisted of breathing threats of murder, seeking official papers from the Jewish authorities with which to arrest believers and bring them to Jerusalem and lock them up, casting his vote against those who were executed, and seeking to get them to renounce Christ (8:3; 9:1–2; 22:4–5; 26:9–11). Luke noted that he was present at the stoning of Stephen and approved of it (Acts 7:58; 8:1). His goal was to destroy the church (Gal. 1:13).

Seventh, the climax of his Jewish résumé, Paul was "in regard to righteousness that is in the law, found blameless." In this context, the "righteousness that is in the law" refers to a particular kind of righteousness (δικαιοσύνην)—the kind that comes through law-keeping. This was an "uprightness" determined by legal standards (BDAG s.v. "δικαιοσύνη" 3c, p. 248). Paul's point was not that this righteousness was legalistic (contra NIV[84]). His point was that he met the demands of the law in terms of an upright life, given his Pharisaic understanding of how to apply the law. It was an *observable* righteousness (Silva, 2005, 152; *NIDNTTE* 3:271). The problem was not that his righteousness in the law was legalistic; it is that (from his new perspective as a follower of Christ) it was incomplete and inadequate.

With regard to this kind of righteousness, Paul had no blemishes on his record. He was "found blameless." "Found" (γενόμενος; NASB) is left untranslated in other popular English versions. Yet the appearance of "found" focuses attention on what other humans could observe according to Pharisaic expectations. "Blameless" (ἄμεμπτος), does not mean " "sinless," for Paul had just stated that he was a persecutor of the church, which he regarded to be sin (1 Cor. 15:9; 1 Tim. 1:13) (Schreiner, 1993, 70; Westerholm, 1988, 161, n. 52). "Blameless" with respect to the righteousness that came from the law was an attainable state for those who kept it meticulously and faithfully (BDAG s.v. "ἄμεμπτος" p. 52; cf. 2:15; Luke

1:6). When a faithful Jew sinned, he could offer the sacrifice prescribed in the law. Paul meant that he followed the law as conscientiously as he could and offered the required sacrifices when he transgressed (Thielman, 1994, 155). He satisfied the external requirements of the law *according to Pharisaic understanding and expectations* (Fee, 1995, 309–10). As a Pharisee, Paul's focus would have been on Sabbath observance, Jewish holidays, food laws, ritual cleanliness, and so on. These are the matters in which he was blameless. He did not mean that he was completely blameless before God. For Paul's judgment (from a Christian perspective) on his pre-conversion life, considering righteousness in a deeper, more appropriate sense before God, see Romans 7:7–25, where he described his very real struggle with sin.

THEOLOGICAL FOCUS

The exegetical idea (Paul's warning against Judaizers emphasized that Christ-followers are God's true people—because they worship and serve God under the power and direction of the Holy Spirit, they trust only in Jesus the Messiah, who secured their justification, and they do not seek justification through keeping the law) leads to this theological focus: God's true people are those who worship God under the power and direction of the Holy Spirit, who trust only in Jesus the Messiah for justification, and who do not seek justification through keeping the law.

Christians must beware false teachers who "add requirements" for salvation to the gospel. In Paul's day false teachers added circumcision and law-keeping to faith in Christ. Any attempt to add requirements to the gospel is a perversion of the gospel and calls for harsh opposition (illustrated by Paul's invective against the false teachers).

Paul's personal story, rich in Jewish credentials, demonstrates that "good works" cannot make one righteous before God. Good works may produce an exemplary life from the perspective of observable behavior. But they are inadequate because they do not deal with the basic issue of justification before God—the sin that has corrupted the human heart.

To be a true heir of God's covenant of salvation, established with Abraham in the Old Testament, faith in Christ alone is required (Gal. 3:26–29). Believers in Christ are God's true people (the "circumcision") and are the ones who serve by the empowerment of the Holy Spirit, whose only grounds for boasting is Christ, and who put no confidence in the flesh—their old identity when they were outside Christ in bondage to sin.

PREACHING AND TEACHING STRATEGIES

Exegetical and Theological Synthesis

What is clear in Philippians 3:1–6 is that a religious resume is not enough to secure a good standing with God. Paul combats the errant notion that we can achieve God's favor by excellent, moral performance. This explains Paul's quick change of tone: from a command to rejoice (v. 1) to a stern warning about false teachers (v. 2). He pulled no punches, combining irony and reversal to expose these heretics, who are not as clean, good, and faithful to God's standard as they think. Contrarily, they are a dirty, evil, corrupt lot. And to add insult to their injury, Paul brandished his impressive resume, seven superior marks, to reiterate the point: birthright and piety do not make us right in God's eyes.

Such appeals to moral performance are nothing new to God. Dating back to Adam and Eve's rebellion in Eden, humans have tried to cover their shame with excuse, blame, and handspun clothing (Coe, 2008, 61). In the Gospels, Jesus combated moral traditions of the Pharisees (e.g., Matt. 5:17–48; Mark 7:1–23). In Acts 15, the Jerusalem Council redirected efforts of Jewish moralists to impose their customs on Gentile believers. And Paul beat the same, antimoralistic drum throughout his epistles (e.g., Gal. 5; Rom. 14).

Moralistic tendencies have continued to crop up throughout church history. Followers of Jesus give greater attention to denominational distinctives, personal disciplines, blue laws, and church traditions than Jesus's saving grace. We often put stock in our giving record, church attendance, hours of service, and biblical intelligence. In addition, we rate certain acts of service—preaching and evangelism—as more important than modest displays of hospitality or nursery duty. These external acts may build an impressive resume to a human audience, but God is not awed. Only the resume of Jesus—humble, self-denying, sacrificial, raised-and-exalted Messiah and Lord—secures our good standing with God.

Preaching Idea

Don't trust an impressive resume to secure good standing with God.

Contemporary Connections

What does it mean?

What does it mean that our impressive resumes do not secure good standing with God? Can God be impressed? If good standing with him is secured through Jesus, do we *ever* need to exert moral effort? While our moral performance may not impress God the same way a show of musical or athletic expertise astounds us, he does express *pleasure* in his people trusting him and working out their salvation (Phil. 2:13 cf. Rom. 12:2). However, we must be clear: there is a great leap from pleasing God to achieving good standing.

Good standing with God does not come from our moral performance. Nor do our spiritual failures and petty rebellions erase our good standing with him. Favor with God is an outgrowth of trust in Jesus. Throughout his letter, Paul referred to followers of Jesus by their new identity: citizens of heaven (not Rome) and members of God's family (not local parentage). Our security stems from our redeemed identity, not our righteous performance. Signs of this

181

new identity include renewed character, spiritual fellowship, bold confidence, and affection for God (Phil. 1:7–11, 27–30; 2:1–4; 3:3).

As discussed in earlier passages (cf. 2:11–18), our character develops in partnership with God. There is tension between human effort and divine unction. Nonetheless, we are responsible to observe his commands. God does not manipulate us like a marionette; he empowers us and partners with us in the process (1:5, 11; 2:13; 4:13). And even if our religious resumes were impressive, we could not boast because God deserves the final credit (1:6).

Is it true?

Is it true we should not trust our impressive resumes to secure good standing with God? Yes, but it is not an easy belief to maintain. We have an unfortunate habit of forgetting grace and forcing people (ourselves included) to conform to a religious mold. Dallas Willard calls this the gospel of "sin management" (1998, 41), which reduces Christian faith to an atonement theory or social ethic. We leverage the message of Jesus to fight off personal guilt or social evils. However, Willard argues, the greater aim of Jesus's kingdom message is life transformation for his followers. If guilt drives our work for Jesus, our trust is lacking. Likewise, if good report in society drives our work for Jesus, we have misplaced our security.

The gospel of sin management is especially hazardous when promoted by people in power. These leaders function like modern-day Pharisees. They flaunt their religious resumes and shame others into imitation. We must beware of people who present personal convictions as community standards. Such people will destroy a church over political opinions, musical styles, programming choices, media usage, and devotional practices. They will guilt others into service by the regular attention they draw to social change. They will equate spiritual maturity with a select list of virtues or practices. They will judge others as

sport. Sadly, too many followers of Jesus have accepted the moral standards of such leaders, thus striving to secure good standing with God on their own efforts.

Now what?

So how do we secure trust in Jesus rather than our impressive (or disappointing) religious resumes? We must first admit our attraction to moralism. Again, from our beginnings in Eden to this passing instant, the desire to set our own moral standards allures us. Moralism provides a sense of control, accomplishment, and superiority over others. The reminder Paul gave on these matters was a "safeguard" we should heed.

Second, we should beware of modern proponents of moralism. Perhaps we would not ape Paul's strong wording (calling moralists "dogs," "evil-doers," and "mutilators"), but we must apply his warning about legalism. We should take caution around parents and church leaders who bully children and congregants into behavior change. We should keep a safe distance from religious authorities whose political rhetoric "in the name of God" lacks civility and humility. At the same time, we must show some leniency to evangelical groups and organizations who make use of a covenant policy, as long as they do not conflate organizational standards with personal holiness.

Finally, like Paul, we need not deny a good upbringing or moral testimony. Our good deeds are a gift from God to bring glory to him (Matt. 5:14–16; Eph. 2:10). Burying them under false modesty may itself be a guise for moralism. On the other hand, if we do have an impressive religious resume, we have greater reason to rejoice in God-given opportunities to obey.

Creativity in Presentation

Anyone who has searched for a job or applied for a scholarship knows the grueling process of building a resume and selling herself in an interview. A video or live skit of a mock interview can illustrate how we try to impress others with our character and accomplishments. While you would have to develop the skit for your congregation, it should run parallel with Paul's resume.

**Sample Interview Questions
for "Good Standing" Scholarship**

What is your name?

What is your family background?

What was your religious upbringing, including church attendance, mode of baptism, communion observation, and VBS involvement?

Do you have any Jesus-inspired t-shirts, tattoos, or piercings?

How many Bibles do you own? Which translations?

How many times have you seen the movies *Fireproof* and *God's Not Dead*?

Did you vote Republican?

What evangelical conferences have you attended or podcasts have you subscribed to?

What fruit of the Spirit are you?

When was the last time you sinned?

Jesus's parable of the Pharisee and tax collector (Luke 18:9–14) is a powerful case study on the folly of basing good standing on moral performance. YouTube hosts several animated versions of this parable. In fact, throughout the Gospels Jesus stands by thieves, prostitutes, adulterers, outcasts, and drunkards; he avoids the religious elite. A reenacted version of any of these stories may visualize Jesus's rejection of moralism.

Christian history is filled with stories of people with wretched moral backgrounds who came to trust in Jesus. Augustine left a life of pride and sexual perversion to serve Jesus. Actor Stephen Baldwin came to know Jesus and overcome drug abuse. Author Rosaria Champagne Butterfield chronicles her conversion from a liberal, lesbian background to Christian faith in *The Secret Thoughts of an Unlikely Convert* (2012). Speaker Annie Lobert broke free from prostitution and launched a rescue mission called Hookers for Jesus. None of these people had an impressive religious resume prior to trusting Jesus. You may also draw from similar testimonies from your personal life or church.

Be sure to stress the main point: God's true people are those who worship God under the power and direction of the Holy Spirit, who trust only in Jesus the Messiah for justification, and who do not seek justification through keeping the law. Therefore, we should not trust an impressive resume to secure good standing with God.

- A happy reminder about right standing with God (3:1).

- Don't trust moralists who equate right standing with certain religious rites (3:2–3).

- Don't trust your own religious resume for right standing with God (3:4–6).

DISCUSSION QUESTIONS

1. What forms of moralism threaten the church today? Why is moralism so attractive?

2. What does your religious resume look like? How can you view it not as a bragging right, but a testimony of God's grace?

3. How can you obey Paul's command to find joyful satisfaction in life's difficult situations when you just don't feel like rejoicing?

4. Why did Paul resort to such harsh name-calling in his warning about the false teachers (3:2)? Is this appropriate for us today?

5. How can Paul call believers in the church (both Jew and Gentile) "the circumcision"?

6. What does it mean to "worship/serve by the Spirit of God," "boast/glory in Christ Jesus," and "put no confidence in the flesh"?

7. How do some twenty-first-century Christians put "confidence in the flesh" as a way to be right before God without necessarily undertaking to keep the Old Testament law? Why is this misguided?

Philippians 3:7–11

EXEGETICAL IDEA

Paul pursued a personal relationship with Jesus as the only way to have a truly right standing before God at the final judgment and to experience the future bodily resurrection.

THEOLOGICAL FOCUS

A personal relationship with Jesus is the only way to have a truly right standing before God at the final judgment and to experience the future bodily resurrection.

PREACHING IDEA

Dump everything that disrupts you from knowing Jesus better.

PREACHING POINTERS

Building off his warning about would-be Jewish moralists, and echoing imagery from the masterful Christ hymn, this passage makes it clear: Intimacy with Jesus was Paul's greatest aim, for it was the only means to right standing with God. Though his religious resume is impressive, Paul deemed it—along with every other accomplishment, comfort, or worldly pursuit—dispensable. The original readers would have heard the edge in Paul's rhetoric, as he crassly threw their cultural values into the garbage heap. They prized social status, religious performance, and family lineage, but he willingly pitched them in the trash.

Our culture does not put a premium on knowing Jesus better. We are conditioned to pursue success, security, and comfort with greater loyalty than knowing him. Busyness in the church can serve as a substitute for knowing Jesus better. Managing our social lives with the myriad of recreational activities, family obligations, and friend groups can distract us from knowing Jesus better. Even all our grandiose (or misguided) thoughts about Jesus may inhibit us from knowing him better. This passage inspires us to dump everything that disrupts us from knowing Jesus better.

THE SURPASSING VALUE OF KNOWING CHRIST
(3:7–11)

LITERARY STRUCTURE AND THEMES (3:7–11)

Paul moved from stating his Jewish credentials to a contrasting assertion: "but whatever were gains to me, these I have regarded as loss." The reason he regarded these and all things as loss is because of the surpassing value of knowing Christ Jesus his Lord (3:7–8a). In fact, he regarded all things to be dung so that he may gain Christ and be found in him (3:8b–9a). Next, Paul expanded on what it meant to be found in Christ: he would not have his own righteousness that was from the law, but rather the righteousness from God that was through faith in Christ (3:9b). Finally, Paul expanded on the purpose for his considering all things to be dung: "that I may know him, that is, the power of his resurrection and the sharing of his sufferings" (3:10a). This would occur by being conformed to his death (3:10b). The ultimate goal was to attain the resurrection from the dead (3:11).

Trading Liabilities for Gain (3:7–9a)
True Righteousness (3:9b–c)
Deeper Relationship through Common Experience (3:10–11)

EXPOSITION (3:7–11)

Having described his Jewish credentials, Paul moved to his decision to abandon his former confidence in the flesh. He described his radical change using the terms of a business accounting ledger with gains and loss columns. Items that in his former life as a Pharisee he considered assets, he now regarded as liabilities. Trusting in his Jewish credentials had left him spiritually bankrupt. This is because there was only one item that belonged in the gains column—knowing Christ. Paul testified that he regarded all things, including Jewish credentials, to be worthless so that he may know Christ, in whom he had the true righteousness from God that was by faith.

This unit contains some of the most "theologically rich" verses in the New Testament (Cohick, 2013a, 169). Paul giving up his Jewish privileges paralleled Jesus giving up his heavenly privileges. Paul spoke of both present and future aspects of knowing Christ. At present he sought to know Christ—specifically, to experience his resurrection power and share his sufferings. In the future he hoped to gain even more of Christ when he was found in him and raised from the dead. By sharing his own passion for knowing Christ, Paul provided a model for the Philippians. He wanted his pursuit of Christ to be the pursuit of every believer. By repudiating his former trust in his Jewish heritage and accomplishments, and by entering into a personal relationship with Jesus Christ instead, Paul achieved a right standing before God that would be proven true at the final judgment.

3:7. Most translations begin with "but" (NRSV, "yet") because of the obvious contrast with 3:6.[1] Διὰ τὸν Χριστὸν is rendered "for the sake of Christ" (NIV, ESV, NASB, cf. KJV, NKJV) or "because of Christ" (NRSV, CSB, cf. NLT).

---

1   The beginning adversative conjunction "but" (ἀλλά), found in ℵ² B D F D L P Ψ 𝔐, may be a later addition by a scribe to make the implied contrast explicit. It is lacking in 𝔓⁴⁶ ℵ* A B 0282 33 81. Fee favors omission (1995, 311, n. 1).

Trading Liabilities for Gain (3:7–9a)

3:7. Paul stated that he regarded "whatever" (ἅτινα = those things listed in 3:5–6 that provided "confidence in the flesh") were "gains" to be "loss." The terms "gains" (κέρδη) and "loss" (ζημίαν) were commonly used as business accounting terms. The plural "gains" depicts a list of assets on one side of a business ledger, namely, the things which are earned profits (BDAG s.v. "κέρδη," p. 541). The singular "loss" suggests that Paul had totaled up all of his past advantages in Judaism one by one and considered the entire sum to be a liability in the matter of being justified before God (Martin and Hawthorne, 2004, 188–89). The "gains" and "loss" terminology may echo Jesus's statement, "What does it profit a man to gain the whole world and forfeit his life?" (Mark 8:36).

Paul considered his Jewish pedigree and accomplishments to be loss "because of Christ" (διὰ τὸν Χριστόν). His new understanding of Jesus as the Christ provided the reason for his determination that the gains were actually a loss. Rendering the preposition (διά) "because of" (NRSV, CSB, NLT) is preferable to "for the sake of" (NIV, ESV, NASB, KJV, NKJV), for Paul was stating the grounds for his change in perspective (Martin and Hawthorne, 2004, 189). "For the sake of" denotes what Paul would stand to gain by his decision. This idea does not occur until the end of 3:8 ("that I may gain Christ").

3:8–9a. The first διά is rendered "because of" (NIV, ESV, NRSV), "in view of" (CSB, NASB), or "for" (KJV, NKJV). Τὸ ὑπερέχον is rendered "surpassing worth/value" (NIV, ESV, NRSV, CSB, NLT, NASB) or "excellence" (KJV, NKJV). Δι᾽ ὅν is rendered "for whose/his sake" (NIV, ESV, NRSV, NLT), "for whom" (NASB, KJV, NKJV), or "because of him" (CSB). The passive voice ἐζημιώθην is rendered "I have suffered loss" (ESV, NRSV, CSB, NASB, KJV, NKJV) or (as an active) "I have lost/discarded" (NIV, NLT). Σκύβαλα is rendered "garbage" (NIV, NLT), "rubbish" (ESV, NRSV, NASB, NKJV), "filth" (CSB), or "dung" (KJV).

3:8–9a. Paul heightened the point he just made in 3:7, beginning with an emphatic combination of conjunctions and particles, "not only this, but even more" (ἀλλὰ μενοῦνγε καί, Thrall, 1962, 15–16; BDF §448[6]). Then he extended the thought of 3:7 in four ways: (1) He changed the tense of the verb "regard" from a perfect to a (continuous) present tense, "I am regarding (still) these things to be loss." (2) Not only did he put the Jewish advantages he listed (3:5–6) in the loss category, he put "all things" there. (3) He expanded the previous phrase "because of Christ" to "because of the surpassing value of knowing Christ Jesus my Lord," specifying what it was about Christ that caused him to regard all things to be loss. (4) He regarded them not merely as "loss," but "dung."

As in 3:7, Paul stated the reason (διά) for his regarding all things to be loss: "because of the surpassing value of knowing Christ Jesus my Lord." "Surpassing value" (τὸ ὑπερέχον) refers to that which is better than something else (BDAG s.v. "ὑπερέχω" 3, p. 1033). Paul could put knowing Christ on one side of the ledger and everything else on the other, and the value of knowing Christ far surpassed the sum of all other things combined.

"Knowing Christ Jesus" (more literally, "the knowledge [γνώσεως] of Christ Jesus" [Χριστοῦ Ἰησοῦ] objective genitive), is the central focus of 3:8–11 (Koperski, 1996, 162). It refers not merely to knowing things about Jesus, but rather to "personal acquaintance" with Christ Jesus (BDAG s.v. "γνῶσις" 2, p. 203).

This is the only place in his letters that Paul called Jesus, "*my* [μου] Lord," expressing the deep, intimate relationship he enjoyed with him. Knowing Christ Jesus consisted of knowing him as his Lord, the one who occupied the position of supreme authority in his life (BDAG s.v "κύριος" 2bγ, p. 578). Christ's lordship over all was the climactic theme of the Christ hymn (2:11), and Paul had accepted his lordship for his own life. The title goes beyond meaning, "owner" or "master" (BDAG s.v "κύριος" 1b and 2a, p. 577). It derives its full significance from the fact that in the LXX, Yahweh is consistently rendered "Lord." The divine Jesus possesses the name of Yahweh and now reigns as Christ the Lord over all.

Christ Jesus was the one "because of (διά) whom" Paul had suffered the loss of all things. For the third time in two verses, this preposition denotes the reason why Paul regarded those things that once gave him confidence in the flesh to be loss. "Suffered loss" (ἐζημιώθην, passive voice) could suggest that the loss was inflicted upon Paul. Hooker suggests that other Jews had stripped him of privileges (2000, 527). But in this context, where the purpose is to "gain" Christ, and where Paul was voluntarily trading his former confidence for the knowledge of Christ, "suffer loss" may well have an active sense, "I have lost" (NIV, NLT, BDF §159[2]). He had willingly renounced all things (Martin and Hawthorne, 2004, 192).

"All things" (πάντα) go beyond the Jewish privileges and accomplishments listed in 3:5–6. They encompass everything that might be considered of value in the present age—possessions, material comforts, status, Roman citizenship—whatever might be thought of as advantageous before God or might encourage confidence in the flesh (Fee, 1991, 317). Because Paul considerd a personal relationship with Christ Jesus to be more valuable than the sum of all other things, he moved everything else to the liability side of the ledger. He willingly set aside all in order to obtain Christ and the righteous standing before God that faith in him provided. Paul might have also been thinking of what his commitment to Jesus had cost him over the years since his conversion—things like family and friends, money or property, perhaps an inheritance (Hellerman, 2015, 184).

Paul regarded all things to be not merely "loss," but "dung" (σκύβαλα), a crude term that occurs only here in the New Testament, and that can refer to (1) excrement, manure, (2) kitchen scraps, garbage, or (3) refuse (BDAG

s.v. "σκύβαλον," p. 932; *TDNT* 7:445–47). Wallace argues that Paul used this term for its "startle effect" somewhere between "crap" and "s**t" (2016).

Paul's point was that the very things he trusted, and that the false teachers still promoted, were dung as far as gaining a right standing before God. Silva thinks Paul was alluding to Isaiah 64:6, "All our righteous deeds are like filthy rags" (2005, 158). Paul had to "lose" his confidence in these things in order to "gain" Christ.

Paul expressed the purpose (ἵνα) for which he had lost all things and now regarded them to be dung: "in order that I may gain Christ and be found in him." Verses 8c and 9a contain two parallel clauses:

(8c) in order that I	may gain Christ
(9a) and	be found in him.

Continuing the accounting terminology, "may gain" (κερδήσω) looks not only at Paul's present relationship with Christ but also ahead to the "day of Christ" (1:6, 10; 2:16). Paul had renounced all other gains, regarding them as loss, in order to acquire by investment in the reign of Jesus now and for the future (BDAG s.v. "κερδαίνω" 1b, p. 541). The "gain" here refers to the personal relationship with Christ that comes through faith (Bockmuehl, 1998, 208). Paul will expand on aspects of this relationship with Christ in 3:10.

"Be found in him" is parallel to "may gain Christ." "Gain" looks at Paul's incorporation into Christ from his perspective; "be found" (εὑρεθῶ) carries the idea of coming upon something either through purpose or accident (BDAG s.v. "εὑρίσκω" 2, 412; *TDNT* 2:769). Here it speaks of someone being found from the perspective of others. At the future judgment ("day of Christ"), Paul's "gain" will consist of his being "found in him." It will be apparent (to anyone) that Paul is "in him"—that he has been incorporated into Christ and now has a personal connection with him (Campbell, 2012, 187–88).

True Righteousness (3:9b–c)

Paul's right standing before God at the final judgment means that he would possess the right standing before God and membership in God's people that came, not from Jewishness and personal achievement in keeping the law, but rather from God, being appropriated through trust in Christ.

3:9b–c. Διὰ πίστεως Χριστοῦ is rendered "through faith in Christ" (NIV, ESV, NRSV, CSB, NLT, NASB, KJV, NKJV) or "by way of Christ's faithfulness" (NET). At the end of the verse, ἐπὶ τῇ πίστει is rendered "on the basis of/based on/depends on faith" (NIV, ESV, NRSV, CSB, NLT, NASB), "by faith" (KJV, NKJV), or "based on Christ's faithfulness" (NET).

3:9b–c. Paul expanded on what he meant by "will be found in Christ" (3:9a) at the final judgment. The participle "not having" (μὴ ἔχων) could denote cause—"found . . . because I do not have my own righteousness," or means—"found . . . by means of not having my own righteousness" (Hellerman, 2015, 185). Probably better is result—"found . . . with the result that I do not have my own righteousness" (Varner, 2016, 76). The double occurrence of "righteousness" (δικαιοσύνην) contrasts *two kinds* of righteousness Paul might be found to possess. At the final judgment, Paul's did not want to be found having the first kind of righteousness, but (ἀλλά) rather having the second. The first kind was the same righteousness that Paul previously said was "in (ἐν) the law" (3:6). This was the righteousness of an upright life achieved by walking blamelessly according to Pharisaic standards. This type of righteousness would have included a nationalistic focus—the perceived Jewish privilege of exclusive membership in the Abrahamic covenant (Wright, 1997, 124–25). Very likely for Paul, it also included a sense of personal achievement. He had achieved "blamelessness" under the Pharisaic interpretation of the law. Now that he had come to know Jesus, Paul considered this first type of righteousness (nationalistic covenant membership and personal achievement under the law) to be inadequate before God and of no benefit at the final judgment.

The second kind of righteousness was what Paul gained when he counted his Jewish credentials loss so that he might gain Christ. This righteousness was a gift from God through faith in Christ. "From God" (ἐκ θεοῦ) denotes God as the *source* of this righteousness. "Through faith in Christ" (διὰ πίστεως Χριστοῦ) indicates the *means* by which the believer receives it. "Faith" refers to "trust, confidence, the active sense of believing" (BDAG, s.v. "πίστις" 2bβ, p. 819). This is the righteousness that will benefit the believer at the final judgment. It consists of a righteous standing (in God's eyes) that is first soteriological (being right with God), but also ecclesiological (being a member of God's people, an heir of the Abrahamic covenant) (Schreiner, 2011). The NET translation "based on Christ's faithfulness" is less likely in this context (see Bird and Sprinkle, 2009 for the debate).

"On the basis of (ἐπί) faith" presents a believer's faith as the grounds for a state of being, the basis upon which he will be found righteous in Christ. Flemming remarks that biblical "faith" is "more than a one-time act of believing in Christ . . . it is a Spirit-enabled, ongoing response of trust, faithfulness, and obedience" (2009, 173).

Deeper Relationship through Common Experience (3:10–11)

Paul's goal was to gain a deeper relationship with Jesus through experiencing both Jesus's power and suffering in ministry, and ultimately to be raised from the dead.

3:10. Τοῦ γνῶναι is rendered "I want to know" (new sentence, NIV, NRSV, NLT, cf. CSB) or "that I may know" (ESV, NASB, KJV, NKJV). The first καὶ is rendered "and" (coordinate), "that I may know him *and* the power" (ESV, NRSV, CSB, NLT, NASB, KJV, NKJV) or "yes" (epexegetical), "know him, *yes* the power" (NIV). If the definite article "the" (τήν) prior to κοινωνίαν is original (found in ℵ² D F G K L P Ψ 𝔐), it can be rendered, "and *the* sharing/fellowship of his sufferings" (NRSV, CSB, NASB, KJV, NKJV). If this article is not original (lacking in 𝔓⁴⁶ ℵ* A B), it can be rendered, "and sharing of his sufferings" (cf. NIV). Κοινωνίαν is rendered "participation" (NIV), "share/sharing" (ESV, NRSV), or "fellowship" (CSB, NASB, KJV, NKJV).

3:10. In Greek, verse 10 continued the sentence begun in 3:8 with a further statement of purpose. Paul's purpose or goal in considering his Jewish heritage and achievements to be loss was to know Christ. "That I may know" (τοῦ γνῶναι) picks up the language of 3:8 ("knowledge of Christ Jesus"), and so returns to the central focus of the text (BDAG s.v. "γνῶσκω" 1b, p. 200). The knowledge of Christ Jesus consists of personal acquaintance (BDAG s.v. "γνῶσις" 2, p. 203). While full knowledge would occur only at the second coming (1 Cor. 13:12), Paul was speaking of knowing Christ Jesus in the present age. He explained what he meant by "that I may know him" (epexegetical καί, Martin and Hawthorne, 2004, 197) with three phrases in the rest of the verse: "that I may know him, that is, (1) the power of his resurrection, and (2) sharing of [his] sufferings, and (3) being conformed to his death."

First, to know Christ Jesus consists of knowing (experiencing) the "power" (BDAG s.v. "δύναμις" 1, p. 262; *NIDNTTE* 2:775–81; *DPL*, 723–25) of his "resurrection" (BDAG s.v. "ἀναστάσεως" 2, p. 71). "Resurrection" describes what "power" Paul was talking about. He meant resurrection power or life-giving power—the kind of power God used when he raised Jesus (BDAG s.v. "ἀνάστασις" 2a, p. 71). The experience of resurrection power was not limited to the future bodily resurrection on the day of Christ (which Paul saved for verse 11), but rather belongs to the present Christian life (cf. Eph. 1:19–20). This is the power of God that establishes the new creation (2 Cor. 5:17), enables newness of life (Rom. 6:4), transforms

the inner person (2 Cor. 3:18; 4:16), and anoints ministry (1 Cor. 2:4; 12:6–7; Gal. 3:5). It is the "full, comprehensive power in its various phases . . . the transforming force that vitalizes the Christian life" (Fitzmyer, 1981, 209). Paul longed to know even more of this power. Silva unnecessarily limits "the power of his resurrection" to the spiritual transformation of believers into the image of Christ (cf. 2 Cor. 3:18) (2005, 164).

Second, to know Christ Jesus consists of "sharing of his sufferings" (παθημάτων, objective genitive), the sufferings that were inflicted upon Jesus (BDAG s.v. "παθημάτων" 1, p. 747). "Sharing" (κοινωνία) is the same word Paul previously used for the Philippians' partnership with him in the gospel (1:5; BDAG s.v. "κοινωνία" 4, p. 553). This "sharing" is an active, not passive, participation in Christ's sufferings. Paul had willingly embraced the suffering that comes with following Christ (Koperski, 1996, 247–48).

Paul already stated that God had granted to believers that they should suffer for the sake of Christ (1:29). He did not mean just any type of suffering, but specifically that which came because one was following Jesus. He already referred to his imprisonment for the gospel (1:7, 12–14, 17), to the conflict that he had experienced (1:30), and to his being poured out as a drink offering (2:17). Elsewhere Paul spoke of his afflictions as an apostle (2 Cor. 1:4–6; 4:7–17; 6:4–10; 11:23–28; Col. 1:24) and of all believers enduring affliction for the gospel (Rom. 8:17; 1 Thess. 1:6; 2:14; 3:3–4; cf. Acts 14:22). These are the afflictions that constitute a "sharing of his sufferings." And they confirm that the sufferings Paul referred to are outward and physical, not just inward, mental, or spiritual. Probably Paul was thinking of all of these (Koperski, 1996, 258–60).

Third, to know Christ Jesus consists of "being conformed [συμμορφιζόμενος] to his death." The passive voice suggests that Paul was being conformed by God. The present tense shows that Paul was talking about his ongoing life of following Jesus and not martyrdom (O'Brien, 1991, 408). He was referring to the theological reality that he had "died and been buried with Christ" (Rom. 6:4–6; Gal. 2:19; Col. 2:12, 20; 3:3). At conversion, through faith he was incorporated into Christ—joined to his death and resurrection, becoming part of Messiah's people. Now as he shared Christ's sufferings, he was more and more being conformed in an experiential way to that theological reality (O'Brien, 1991, 410; *NIDNTTE* 1:325). "Union with Christ in his death is both a past event and an ongoing experience" (Hellerman, 2015, 191). Compare 2 Corinthians 4:10—"Always carrying around the death of Jesus in the body, so that the life of Jesus may also be manifested in our body."

> *3:11.* Eἴ πως is rendered "if somehow" (NRSV), "if by any means" (KJV, NKJV), "that by any means possible" (ESV), "and so somehow" (NIV), "assuming that somehow" (CSB), "in order that" (NASB), or "so that one way or another" (NLT).

3:11. Paul expressed his ultimate goal: "if somehow I may 'attain' (s.v. "καταντάω" 2a, p. 523) the resurrection from the dead." He was speaking of his future resurrection at Jesus's return. Elsewhere, when Paul spoke of the resurrection of believers at the end of the age, his tone was one of certainty (Rom. 8:11–39; 1 Cor. 15:20–23; 1 Thess. 4:15–18). But here the phrase "if somehow" (εἴ πως) may suggest only possibility or contingency: "if somehow, if perhaps" (BDAG s.v. "εἴ" 5nα, p. 279). Compare "if somehow" (εἴ πως) in Romans 1:10; 11:14; and Acts 27:12. Paul appeared hesitant to claim participation in the resurrection.

Rather than suggesting that Paul was entertaining doubts that he would be raised, "if somehow" likely reflects his humility, his unwillingness to presume upon God (Thurston and Ryan, 2005, 125). In a passage where Paul had spoken of his nationalistic privileges and self-attainment to be loss, he realized that

salvation was a gift of God from start to finish (Martin and Hawthorne, 2004, 200). He refused to sound like he was putting any confidence in his own efforts or attainments. His statement may mean something like, "If by the grace of God I might be privileged to participate in the resurrection," recognizing that he was totally dependent upon God (Gundry Volf, 1991, 254–60). Further, "if somehow" reflects that Paul still had to go through the process of dying—the prerequisite (Fee, 1995, 336).

Paul's goal of knowing Christ Jesus included experiencing the resurrection from the dead, which is a *future bodily* event. He will stress in the next passage that he has not yet obtained his goal.

THEOLOGICAL FOCUS

The exegetical idea leads to this theological focus: Paul pursued a personal relationship with Jesus is the only way to have a truly right standing before God at the final judgment and to experience the future bodily resurrection.

Righteousness before God cannot come through good works or your family tree. It cannot come through faith in Christ *plus* works of the law (as the false teachers taught). We cannot attain righteousness through self-effort or religious accomplishment. We can only receive it as a gift from God through faith in Jesus. Paul testified that he traded in his old confidence in the flesh (nationalistic privilege and blamelessness under the law of Moses) for a pursuit of Christ. The pursuit of his old life led neither to the righteousness that is from God nor to an experience of true spiritual power. Righteousness comes through "knowing Christ Jesus"—a personal, experiential relationship with Jesus through faith. Paul wanted to continue to grow in the knowledge of Christ Jesus—by experiencing both his resurrection power and suffering as he became more and more like him in his death. Further, Paul humbly stated his ultimate goal—that after being conformed to Jesus's death, he would experience the resurrection from the dead. This hope drove him and gave meaning and purpose to the sufferings he now experienced as a servant of Christ Jesus.

PREACHING AND TEACHING STRATEGIES

Exegetical and Theological Synthesis

What is clear in Philippians 3:7–11 is that our assets can become liabilities in our relationship with Jesus. Our religious strengths—be it theological understanding, spiritual gifting, church affiliation or ministry involvement—do not secure right standing with God. While they may appear impressive to a human audience, only Jesus's humble, self-giving, sacrificial record impresses God. Putting our trust in religious convictions and accomplishments rather than the faithful Christ, leads to great loss.

Paul assumed faith is more than a casual association with Jesus or one-time confession of his lordship. The kind of faith Paul proposed is intimate. Paul called Jesus "my Lord" (3:8), suggesting a *personal* and *submissive* relationship. Echoing language from the Christ hymn (2:5–11), Paul showed his knowledge of Jesus was *theological.* Paul's desire to partner in Jesus's suffering, be conformed to his death, and feel his resurrection power (3:10), implied that his knowledge of Jesus was *experiential* and *powerful.* Finally, his knowledge of Jesus was *incomplete* and *future-oriented*, anticipating a glorious day when he will be raised, found, and fully known by Jesus (v. 11).

Sadly, when knowledge *about* Jesus becomes a bragging right, it undermines the very purpose it aims to serve: intimacy *with* Jesus. Theological knowledge is no more redemptive than historical trivia or fun facts if not wedded to a relationship with the living God. Indeed, moral training, Bible smarts, and casual knowledge about Jesus are more likely to breed apathy than action in our faith.

Preaching Idea

Dump everything that disrupts you from knowing Jesus better.

Contemporary Connections

What does it mean?

What does it mean to dump everything that disrupts you from knowing Jesus better? Does this idea require us to cloister ourselves and cut off any activity not directly tied to building intimacy with Jesus? What, in fact, does knowing Jesus better even look like? These are good questions, requiring us to clarify terms and caution against new forms of legalism, since a relationship with Jesus is somewhat subjective.

First, knowing Jesus better implies mutuality and trust, cornerstones to any healthy relationship. Time in conversation with Jesus, meditating on his life and redemptive works, remembering him in communion, and longing for his return build our sense of trust. We also know him better by living his kingdom commands with other followers of Jesus (Matt. 18:17; 1 Cor. 12; Eph. 2:20–22; Col. 1:27; 1 John 1:13). Furthermore, intimacy with Jesus grows out of imitation of Jesus—preaching what he preached, serving like he served, loving like he loved, suffering like he suffered. We must be weary of confusing intimacy with physical touch or warm feelings. These external expressions of relational closeness do not apply to all people or all relationships.

Second, we must nuance what disrupts us from knowing Jesus better. *Disobedience* distracts us from greater intimacy. To live in opposition to his commands creates distance, separation, and death. *Disloyalty*—an idolatrous form of thinking that elevates a rival allegiance (e.g., work, politics)—distracts us from knowing Jesus better. In a striking statement, Jesus declared even family loyalties an enemy to true discipleship (Luke 14:23). Finally, everyday *distractions* are not conducive to knowing Jesus better. Distractions run the gamut from video games to household chores to dating relationships to email replies to church meetings to personal hobbies. The person, activity, or responsibility itself may not cause the problem, but the obsessive or disgruntled approach we bring to it can be hazardous.

Here we must practice discernment. We may not need to dump every distracting person, activity, or responsibility. Sometimes a simple break from a distraction keeps it from turning into an area of disobedience or disloyalty. Dumping too many distractions can lead to legalism, as well as rob us of simple joys Jesus allows in our life as reminders of him.

Is it true?

Is knowing Jesus even achievable? Can we know him like a spouse or friend? We are wise to acknowledge that intimacy with Jesus is imperfect and incomplete, but also open to increase. Paul reflected this idea in his prayers (Eph. 3:14–22; Phil. 1:9–11; Col. 1:9–12). Moreover, he confessed it as his chief aim (Phil. 3:7–16). The author of Hebrews presented Jesus as empathetic and approachable (2:18; 4:15–16). While we will not experience perfect intimacy until Jesus's second coming (1 John 3:1–3), we should make the relationship our top priority.

Unfortunately, our intimacy with Jesus is vulnerable. As mentioned above, disobedience, disloyalty, and distractions make knowing him difficult. Added to this list of "relational disruptors" is the devil, whose goal is to rob us of the joys of life and security we find in our Chief Shepherd (John 10:10; 1 Peter 5:8). Thus, aggressive spiritual opposition and negligent spiritual engagement will disrupt us from knowing Jesus better.

Finally, we would be foolish not to recognize how a relationship with Jesus is different than a flesh-and-blood family member or friend. Jesus's earliest followers had the benefit of hearing his laugh or feeling his touch. They inhabited time and space together. Since his ascension, however, knowing him transcends our

five senses. And even though he may not audibly speak or physically touch us, we sense his presence with us through hearing his Word, enjoying his creation, and sharing in his kingdom mission. In fact, being with his people is one of the greatest ways to experience fellowship with him (1 John 1:1–4).

Now what?

What steps should we take to know Jesus better and protect the relationship from disruptions? We might begin by taking an assessment of our relational disruptors, asking what areas of disobedience, disloyalty, and everyday distractions are hindering us from knowing Jesus better.

More specifically we might ask: *What sinful patterns of behavior do I need to turn from so disobedience doesn't reign? Who can hold me accountable in the process? Where should I reprioritize my time, money, energy, and passions to focus on Jesus rather than the people, responsibilities, or goals that disrupt my allegiance to him? What distractions should I take a temporary break from? What distractions deserve tighter controls, so I can know Jesus better?*

Like any relationship, intimacy with Jesus grows from time spent with him. Reading Scripture and prayer both foster intimacy with him, but we must be careful not to limit knowing Jesus to mere formalities. Evangelicals can mistake personal devotions with a personal relationship. We are also guilty of confusing knowledge *of* Jesus with *knowing* Jesus. Good theological understanding aids the relationship, just as accurate information of a coworker or spouse aids allows us to interact better. But thriving relationships go deeper than sharing information and passing time together. We must approach Jesus as a living and powerful, present and empathetic person.

The passage specifically focuses our intimacy with Jesus around three aspects: his suffering, death, and resurrection. We will know Jesus better if we reflect on his sacrificial death.

Confessing false ways of trying to attain right standing with God might be in order. Moreover, any suffering we are currently facing can serve as a window into Jesus's empathy. He understands our pain from firsthand experience. And present opportunities to overcome temptation, advocate for others, or share the gospel might bring a fresh wave of Jesus's resurrection power.

Creativity in Presentation

Consider setting out garbage cans throughout the worship area. Place one beside the preaching area, while positioning several along the perimeter of the room. Stuff the closest one with items to provide imagery for refuse (i.e., *skubala*): a dirty diaper, banana peel, fast-food bag, credit card offers, last week's sermon notes. Later in the message, you might toss into the same trash can items of cultural import—car keys, Nike shoes, cell phone—that lead to disobedience, disloyalty, and distraction. At the close of the message, invite people to write on a scrap of paper something that robs them of intimacy with Jesus. Have them crumple it and dispose of it as they leave.

The dumping imagery plays nicely for dating relationships. While attending a Christian college, I (Tim) recall an impactful chapel series on dating. One of the speakers made a compelling argument to "dump" dating and focus on knowing Jesus better. No single chapel message ever produced such a widespread response. Girlfriends were dumping boyfriends (and vice versa, but to a lesser degree) across the entire campus. Albeit humorous (and bordering on legalistic), the illustration underscores the great loss one might be willing to incur to pursue intimacy with Jesus. "Whom (or what) would you be willing to dump for Jesus?," you might ask.

Personal stories often prove effective. I recently talked with two young men who chose to "dump" college for a year to enter a discipleship residency program where they are sure to know Jesus better. A young lady from my church passed up a full-tuition scholarship to enter a year-long Bible institute. Even my career choice in vocational ministry was met with concern by parents who wanted a more promising financial future for me. Do not hesitate to ask the congregation: *What have you dumped, or would be willing to dump, to know Jesus better?*

Finally, recognize how people hate disruptions while experiencing work flow, enjoying vacation, or eating dinner. Mention the all-powerful "Do Not Disturb" doorhanger available at hotels, allowing the patron a disruption-free stay. Consider adapting the doorhanger sign so it reads: "Praying: Do Not Disrupt," "Reading Bible: Do Not Disrupt," or "Spiritually Occupied: Do Not Disrupt." Make a few available and encourage people to take one and place it in the location they are most inclined to spend time with Jesus.

The point you want to emphasize is this: A personal relationship with Jesus is the only way to have a truly right standing before God at the final judgment and to experience the future bodily resurrection. We should dump everything that disrupts us from knowing Jesus better.

- Earthly gains disrupt us from knowing Jesus better (3:7–8).

- Knowing Jesus better leads to right standing with God (3:9).

- Knowing Jesus's suffering, death, and resurrection power is the greatest gain (3:10–11).

DISCUSSION QUESTIONS

1. What areas of your life lead to disobedience, disloyalty, and distraction in your faith? What can you dump to increase intimacy with Jesus?

2. How do you foster intimacy with Jesus? How has your level of intimacy changed over the years?

3. Using the image of an accounting ledger in the pursuit of right standing before God, what things did Paul have in the "asset" column prior to his conversion to Christ? What did he put there after his conversion?

4. What would you have put in the asset column prior to your conversion? What do you put there now?

5. Explain the difference between "my own righteousness" (3:9b) and "righteousness from God" (3:9c).

6. Explain what "knowing Jesus's resurrection power" looks like practically in your life.

7. What does "sharing Jesus's sufferings" mean, and what does it look like in your life?

Philippians 3:12–16

EXEGETICAL IDEA

The Philippians were to agree with Paul and to pursue the ultimate goal: full intimacy with Jesus in a resurrection body in the age to come.

THEOLOGICAL FOCUS

Believers are to pursue the ultimate goal: full intimacy with Jesus in a resurrection body in the age to come.

PREACHING IDEA

Always take one more step as you strive to become like Jesus.

PREACHING POINTERS

Paul fixed his focus forward in this passage on his forthcoming resurrection and glory. His earthly life was interrupted by a heavenly calling that drove him ever forward. Athletic imagery colors these verses with sweat and vigor, as the exegetical section explains. While the apostle's comments are deeply personal—evident in several first-person pronouns—he invited his original readers to join the marathon. His race was their race; they are spiritual siblings pursuing resurrection and glory together. Perhaps, legalism loomed in the background; however, the passage more clearly encourages followers of Jesus to always take one more step as they strive to become like Jesus.

Today, the idea of striving after Jesus tends toward one of two ends on the human-effort spectrum. On the one hand, followers of Jesus treat salvation as a works-based project. They burn themselves out striving for perfection at home, work, church, and community. On the other hand, an errant understanding of grace discourages some believers from any spiritual effort. The unbreakable promise of heaven renders them of little earthly good. Perfection and passivity constitute the poles of our pursuit of Jesus; his people often pinball between the two. God's calling in our lives embraces the tension of our gritty pursuit and glorious ending.

PURSUING THE ULTIMATE GOAL (3:12–16)

LITERARY STRUCTURE
AND THEMES (3:12–16)

Paul stressed that he had not yet obtained the ultimate goal he spoke of in 3:10–11. The unit consists of two parts—a double disclaimer and a double exhortation. First, with a double disclaimer and use of the verb "press on," Paul emphasized that he had not yet fully received his ultimate goal, but he pressed on toward it. He had not yet obtained it, but he pressed on to take hold of it because Christ took hold of him (3:12). He had not yet taken hold of it, but straining forward he pressed on toward the goal so that he could receive the prize (3:13–14). Second, Paul gave a double exhortation. He exhorted his readers to share his point of view, asserting that if any disagreed with him, God would reveal his point of view to them (3:15), and he exhorted his readers to keep in line with the apostolic teaching to which they had attained (3:16).

Pursuing the Prize (3:12–14)
A Spiritually Mature View of the Christian Life (3:15–16)

EXPOSITION (3:12–16)

In 3:7–11, Paul shared that he regarded all things (including his Jewish credentials) to be worthless so that he might have the righteousness that was from God and so that he might know Christ Jesus in a deeper way, experiencing the power of his resurrection and sharing his sufferings. Ultimately, he wanted to experience intimacy with Jesus in a resurrection body in the age to come. Now, lest his readers misunderstood, Paul made a disclaimer. He clarified that he had not yet reached his ultimate goal. He was still pursuing it on a daily basis, and would continue to do so for the rest of his earthly life. Paul wanted

to head off a potential misunderstanding, lest the Philippians think that because they had become Christians, they had arrived at the goal. He wanted to remind them that they must still pursue the end-time prize. They would not receive it until the resurrection when God would grant them a state of perfection, when they would be fully conformed to the image of Jesus's glorified body (3:20–21). He presented himself as an example of one with the right point of view in this and exhorted the Philippians to share his point of view.

Paul made it clear that the Christian life consists of a disciplined pursuit of a goal: an intimate relationship with Jesus in a resurrection body in the age to come (3:11). He would reach this goal through his present pursuit of knowing Christ more intimately now by experiencing his resurrection power and his sufferings in ministry (3:10). His point was evident from the repetition in these verses:

(12a) Not that I have already obtained [it] . . .
 (12b) But I press on . . .
(13a) Brothers, I do not consider myself to have taken hold of [it].
 (13b) But one thing I do . . .
 (14) I press on . . .
(15a) Let us have this point of view . . .
(16) Let us keep in line . . .

The Christian life is a continual "pressing on" to intimate knowledge of Jesus, which will be fully realized only at the resurrection when he returns.

Pursuing the Prize (3:12–14)

Paul clarified that he had not yet attained his ultimate goal of full intimacy with Jesus in a resurrection body, but this is what he strenuously pursued, and it is what God will give him when Jesus returns.

3:12. Tετελείωμαι is rendered "already arrived at my goal" (NIV, cf. NRSV), "already reached perfection" (NLT), "am already perfect (ESV, NASB, KJV, cf. NKJV), or "am already fully mature" (CSB). Ἐφ' ᾧ is rendered "that for which" (NIV, NASB, KJV, NKJV, cf. NLT) or "because" (ESV, NRSV, CSB).

3:12. With the phrase "not that" (οὐχ ὅτι), Paul began a disclaimer concerning what he had just stated in 3:8–11. "Not that I have already obtained [it]." In this context, "obtained" (ἔλαβον) means, "to enter into a close relationship, receive, make one's own" (BDAG s.v. "λαμβάνω" 8, p. 584). In the Greek text, the verb "obtained" (ἔλαβον) does not have a direct object, so we must fill in what "it" is that Paul had not yet obtained. He must have been referring to his ultimate goal (3:11), which was received only through a process (3:10). The ultimate goal included not merely being raised to physical life again, but also all that came with it—a fuller, more intimate relationship with Jesus in the new heavens and new earth, a state of having been made whole and free from the presence and limitations of sin, a full experience of the spiritual power of the age to come, eternal life in a resurrection body conformed to Jesus's body that is no longer constrained by disease or subject to death, and so on. Later, in 3:14 he will refer to all of this using an athletic metaphor, "the prize" (Hellerman, 2015, 199). The means to obtaining this prize is by seeking the intermediate goal of a deeper relationship with Jesus in the present life through experiencing his resurrection power and suffering in ministry.

The Ultimate Goal (the Prize)

Paul described his ultimate goal as "to attain to the resurrection from the dead" (3:11). This includes an experience of:

Full, intimate relationship with Jesus
State of wholeness—free from sin's presence and limitations
Spiritual power of the age to come
Eternal life in a resurrection body like Jesus's body
No more disease or death
And more!

In a parallel thought (ἤ), Paul stated that he had "not already become perfect" (NASB). This is the only time in Paul's letters that he used this verb (τετελείωμαι), which means "bring to an end, finish, accomplish, bring to a goal, bring to full measure, make perfect" (BDAG s.v. "τελειόω" 2, p. 996). It reflects not merely a state of spiritual maturity, or moral perfection, but rather the consummation of the redemptive process, the attainment of the ultimate goal described above. The time of this consummation is at Jesus's second coming and not before (3:20–21). Paul's use of the passive voice ("be made perfect") suggests that the "perfecting" would be done to him by God. He could not attain this on his own (Witherington, 2011, 209).

In a contrasting assertion (δέ), Paul stated, "But I press on to take hold of." "Press on" (διώκω) carries the sense of "move rapidly and decisively toward an objective" (BDAG s.v. "διώκω" 2, p. 254). The verb can have a negative sense of "persecute," and this is how Paul used it in 3:6. But here the "pressing on" is positive. Perhaps Paul intended a bit of irony between this verse and 3:6. "I used to pursue (persecute) the church; now I pursue the perfection available in Christ." Zealous persecution had become zealous pursuit.

Paul stated the purpose (εἰ)[2] for his pressing on: "to take hold of." "Take hold of" (καταλάβω) is an intensified form of the verb used at the beginning of 3:12, rendered there "obtained." It means, "to make something one's own, win, attain" and may denote a forceful or aggressive seizure (BDAG s.v. "καταλαμβάνω" 1, p. 519) Paul will use this verb twice more in 3:12–13. Together with "press on," Paul's use of this verb suggested a strenuous pursuit of his goal.

The reason (ἐφ ᾧ) Paul pressed on to take hold of the goal was, "because I also was taken hold of by Christ Jesus." The English translations reflect the debate over the meaning of the Greek expression (ἐφ ᾧ), which we understand to mean, "because." (1) It may look forward and express purpose: "But I press on to take hold of (*that*) *for which* I was taken hold of by Christ Jesus" (NASB, NIV, NKJV, NLT, NET). (2) Or it may express cause: "But I press on to take hold of *because* I was taken hold of by Christ Jesus" (ESV, NRSV, CSB). Either way, Paul was emphasizing his continual pursuit to take hold of the goal.

"Was taken hold of" (κατελήμφθην) is a passive form of the same verb Paul just used. He was pressing on to *take hold of* [the goal] because he was first *taken hold of* by Christ Jesus. Christ "took hold" of him at his conversion when he was called to salvation and conscripted into service as an apostle, specifically to go to the Gentiles (Gal. 1:13–17).

3:13. Κατειληφέναι is rendered "taken/laid hold" (NIV, CSB, NASB), "made my own" (ESV, NRSV), "achieved" (NLT), or "apprehended" (KJV, NKJV). NIV and NASB read "not yet" (οὔπω) rather than "not" (οὐ), favored by ESV, NRSV, CSB, NLT, KJV, and NKJV. This reflects a textual variant where the former (οὔπω) is found in ℵ A Dgr* P 33 614; the latter (οὐ) in

𝔓46 B Dc G K Ψ 88 1739 𝔐. The latter is most likely original, since copyists probably softened Paul's statement, changing "not" to "not yet" in order to fit the context. There is little chance copyists would have changed "not yet" to "not" (*TCGNT,* 548; Fee, 1995, 338, n. 5).

3:13. Paul reasserted the disclaimer, but strengthened it in four ways. First, "brothers" (ἀδελφοί) served to get the attention of the readers and to highlight the statement (O'Brien, 1991, 426). For the theological and sociological solidarity suggested by "brothers and sisters," see note at 1:12. Second, Paul expressly added two first-person pronouns, "I" and "myself" (ἐγώ, ἐμαυτὸν), to emphasize what he had determined about himself. Third, he used the stronger verb "taken hold of" (κατειληφέναι) employed twice in 3:12b. Fourth, the verb "consider" or "regard" (λογίζομαι) suggested that Paul had given careful thought to this (BDAG s.v. "λογίζομαι" 3, p. 598; cf. O'Brien, 1991, 427). Like the previous verb "obtained" (ἔλαβον) in 3:12a, "taken hold of" lacks a direct object. We should supply [it], referring to the ultimate goal described above. The state of perfection is available only at the resurrection (3:11), and will only occur after a life of pursuing Christ along with the power of his resurrection and sharing his suffering (3:10).

Paul made a contrasting assertion: "But (δέ) one thing!" Many translations add, "I do" to make the sentence complete, but this is unnecessary and may weaken Paul's rhetoric (Hellerman, 2015, 203). "One thing" (ἕν) highlights that Paul's life consisted of a single pursuit. With two parallel phrases, Paul described how he pressed on:

(1) forgetting   what is behind
(2) straining toward   what is ahead

---

2   Paul expressed his purpose with εἰ + subjunctive verb: "[to see] if/whether I may take hold of." The construction suggests expectancy, not doubt (Fee, 1995, 345, n. 29). Καί may go either with εἰ ("If *indeed*") or with the verb, "If I may *also* take hold of."

The image was of a person running a race: "what is behind" is the course already covered; "what is ahead" is yet to be run. First, Paul stated that he "forgets" what is behind. He did not look back over his shoulder to the past. "Forgetting" (ἐπιλανθανόμενος) means not to have a remembrance of something (BDAG s.v. "ἐπιλανθάνομαι" 1, p. 374). In this context it was not a passive loss of memory, but an active, deliberate, daily choice to move on from the past, not allowing it to hamper his pursuit of the goal.

Paul disregarded his past—"what lies behind" (τὰ ὀπίσω). He was likely referring both to his old life in Judaism and the advantages listed in 3:5–6 and to his (more than twenty-year) apostolic career so far. He knew that his life in Judaism contained many mistakes. But he refused to let the mistakes of the past paralyze him with guilt. Further, he disregarded his past successes as an apostle. He would not rest on his laurels or become complacent with the level of Christlike, sacrificial, self-denying attitude and service he had achieved (Martin and Hawthorne, 2004, 209). He looked forward to new and deeper intimacy with Jesus daily. By his own example, Paul was letting the Philippians know that they must not allow past failures to paralyze them with guilt or "disqualify" them from pursuing a deeper relationship with Christ. Neither should they become complacent, thinking that the level of spiritual maturity or intimacy with Christ they had obtained was "good enough."

Second, Paul stated he strains toward what is ahead. The word "straining toward" (ἐπεκτεινόμενος), "exerting oneself to the uttermost" occurs only here in the New Testament (BDAG s.v. "ἐπεκτείνομαι," p. 361). Again, the picture was of a runner, but now of one who was straining every muscle, stretching out with full concentration toward the finish line as he neared it (Pfitzner, 1967, 140–41). "Reaching forward" (NASB, CSB) may not be strong enough. Perhaps Paul was thinking of

himself as being in the last stages of his earthly race. Still, he refused to be distracted. He put forth the effort to pursue a deeper relationship with Jesus with every fiber of his being. "What is ahead" (τοῖς ἔμπροσθεν) refers to full attainment of the ultimate goal, which Paul will call "the prize" (3:14).

3:14. Σκοπόν is rendered "goal" (NIV, ESV, NRSV, CSB, NASB, NKJV), "end" (NLT), or "mark" (KJV).

3:14. Paul completed the statement begun in 3:13. "Forgetting" and "straining toward" modify the main verb "press on" (διώκω), which Paul repeated from 3:12. The "goal" or "mark" (σκοπόν) refers to Paul's being right on target or in the home stretch (BDAG s.v. "σκοπός," 931). the word could be used as a metaphor to refer to the goal of a person's life (*TDNT* 7:413–14). In this context, Paul had fixed his gaze on the finish line at the end of the race. He did not state precisely what this "finish line" was, but it must have referred to the time of Jesus's return when he would "attain to the resurrection from the dead" (3:11).

Paul pressed on toward the finish line is in order to (εἰς, purpose/intent) get the prize. The "prize" (βραβεῖον) denotes an award for exceptional performance during a competition in the Roman games (BDAG s.v. "βραβεῖον" 1b, 183). In 1 Corinthians 9:24, Paul also used this term, again in a race metaphor, to denote the eschatological prize believers will receive at Jesus's return. The Philippians would have been familiar with the olive branch or celery wreaths given to champions in the games (Reumann, 2008, 556). In 3:11 the prize is "that I may attain to the resurrection from the dead." This is the prize" to which God "called him upward" (lit., "the prize of the upward call of God").

The "upward call" (ἄνω κλήσεως) refers to God's calling of Paul at his conversion. This view of "call" agrees with Paul's normal theological use of the term—denoting God's initial summons of a person to faith. The prize Paul pursued was the one promised by that call or that came as a result of that call ("call," κλήσεως, subjective genitive). God called (summoned) Paul to faith in Christ at his conversion so that ultimately he would receive a resurrection body and eternal life (and all that goes with it; see above) in the age to come.

The call was a heavenly one. "Upward" (ἄνω) indicates its heavenly direction. "Of God" denotes God as the one who calls the believer (subjective genitive). "In [ἐν] Christ Jesus" may denote (1) the sphere of the call, the realm in which God's call of believers is realized—it comes with their incorporation into Christ (O'Brien, 1991, 433); (2) the means by which the call of God is issued—it is mediated through Christ (Silva, 2005, 177); or, (3) the cause or reason of the call—it is issued because of Christ and his work (Campbell, 2012, 138). These options are not mutually exclusive. In, through, and because of Christ Jesus, believers receive the prize, which God has called them to and is reserving for them.

The "Call" of God: Paul frequently spoke of God calling believers into a relationship with himself through faith in Christ (Rom. 4:17; 8:30; 9:11, 24; 11:29; 1 Cor. 1:9, 26; 7:20; Gal. 1:6, 15; 5:8; Eph. 1:18; 4:1, 4; 1 Thess. 2:12; 2 Thess. 1:11; 2 Tim. 1:9). Theologians often refer to this as the "effective call" of God, issued through the human proclamation of the gospel, in which he summons individuals to salvation (Grudem, 1994, 693; Ridderbos, 1975, 235; *NIDNTT* 1:275–76; *EDNT* 2:242–43; *DPL*, 84–85). This is not the general external invitation to all people to respond to the gospel, but the internal summons of the elect that is effective in bringing people to faith (Rom. 8:30). Philippians 3:14 shows that God's call at the beginning of the Christian life ultimately includes the promise of the prize of the resurrection at the end of the age (O'Brien, 1991, 432).

A Spiritually Mature View of the Christian Life (3:15–16)

Paul exhorted the spiritually mature Philippians to agree with him and to likewise pursue the ultimate goal of full intimacy with Jesus in a resurrection body in the age to come.

3:15. Τέλειοι is rendered "mature" (NIV, ESV, NRSV, CSB, NKJV, cf. NLT "spiritually mature") or "perfect" (NASB, KJV).

3:15. Paul transitioned from personal testimony to exhortation with "therefore/then" (οὖν) (omitted by NIV, ESV, NLT). He exhorted the Philippians to share the spiritually mature point of view he just expressed in 3:12–14. The adjective "mature" or "perfect" (τέλειοι) is related to the verb Paul used in 3:12—not that he has already "been made perfect" (τετελείωμαι). It means: mature, fully developed morally, full-grown, adult" (BDAG s.v. "τελειόω" 2, p. 995). In the LXX, "mature" (τέλειοι) is sometimes used of those who are wholly devoted to God and so considered blameless (Gen. 6:9 LXX; Deut. 18:13 LXX) (Flemming, 2009, 193).

Comparison of 3:12 with 3:15 reveals a wordplay:

3:12   Not that I have . . . already been made *perfect* (τετελείωμαι)

3:15   So then, those who are *mature* (τέλειοι), let us . . .

While Paul and the Philippians were not yet "made perfect"—not yet having attained the resurrection with a full, intimate relationship with Jesus—nevertheless he considered himself and them to be "mature" believers who were capable of living in the truth (O'Brien, 1991, 435). Compare Paul's use of "mature" (τέλειοι) in 1 Corinthians 2:6 and 14:20 (cf. Heb. 5:14). All who are "mature" are to press on toward "perfection." When Paul said, "those/all who [ὅσοι] are mature," he referred to the Philippians as a whole. He did not assume that every individual in the church was mature. He left it to each one to decide whether they were. Paul normally included all of his readers (at least potentially) when he used "all who" (ὅσοι, cf. Rom. 6:3; 8:14; 2 Cor. 1:20; Gal. 3:27; 6:16) (O'Brien, 1991, 436–37).

The exhortation, "let us have this attitude" or "let us think this way" (φρονῶμεν) refers to having an opinion with regard to Jesus or to have a particular mindset about how to follow Jesus (BDAG s.v. "φρονέω" 1, p. 1065; for the verb, see note at 1:7). Paul wanted them to share his point of view on this matter. The content of the attitude Paul spoke of should not be limited to what he had just said in 3:12–14 (not yet perfected), but should include all of 3:8–14, for verses 12–14 clarify verses 8–11 (Fee, 1991, 356–57).

Paul added, "And if you think differently/otherwise, this also God will reveal to you." The adverb "differently/otherwise" (ἑτέρως) occurs only here in the New Testament. As in a few other works (Epictetus, *Diatr.* 2.16.16; Josephus, *Ag. Ap.* 1.26; cf. BDAG s.v. "ἑτέρως," p. 400), it may have a negative connotation—not just "differently," but "wrongly, badly"—"If you have the wrong frame of mind" (Silva, 2005, 187–88). Paul considered the possibility (εἴ) that they may not yet fully understand or agree with him in all that he had just said.

If any of the Philippians did not yet share Paul's point of view about following Jesus, he trusted that God would reveal truth to them. "Will reveal" (ἀποκαλύψει) and its associated noun "revelation" are terms Paul used at times to refer to a direct download of information or insight by God to individuals both at their conversion and subsequently during the process of growth in the Christian life (1 Cor. 2:10; 14:6, 26, 30; 2 Cor. 12:1, 7; Gal. 1:12, 16; 2:2; Eph. 3:3, 5; cf. BDAG s.v. "ἀποκαλύπτω" b, p. 112). Paul's comment was not "smug" or arrogant. He was simply encouraging them and trusting that God would, through the Spirit, give them spiritual insight and understanding on matters of the Christian life.

3:16. Τῷ αὐτῷ στοιχεῖν is rendered "let us live up to" (NIV, CSB), "let us hold true/fast/on to" (ESV, NRSV, NLT), or "let us walk/live by the same (KJV, NKJV, NASB). KJV and NKJV add a final exhortation "rule, let us be of the same mind," which reflects a textual variant (κανόνι, τὸ αὐτὸ φρονεῖν) found in ℵᶜ K P Ψ 88 614, but not found in 𝔓¹⁶ 𝔓⁴⁶ ℵ* A B Ivid 6 33 1739. Scribes likely added this variant, with "rule" (κανόνι) explaining "the same" (τῷ αὐτῷ), and "let us be of the same mind" (τὸ αὐτὸ φρονεῖν) reinforcing "let us walk by the same" (τῷ αὐτῷ στοιχεῖν) (*TCGNT*, 549; Fee, 1991, 352, n. 6).

3:16. Paul added another exhortation. "Only" (πλήν) serves to break off the discussion and highlight the exhortation (BDAG s.v. "πλήν" c, p. 826). While there may have been some who did not yet have the right insight or attitude, Paul was confident that there was truth to which all the believers at Philippi had attained. The expression "to what" (εἰς ὅ) underscores Paul's goal (BDAG s.v. "εἰς" 4, p. 290), namely, that "we have attained" (ἐφθάσαμεν) (BDAG s.v. "φθάνω" 3, p. 1053) refers to a basic understanding of the Christian life and what it means to follow Christ in practical Christian behavior (O'Brien, 1991, 440–41). The Philippians had already received instruction on matters of Christian living from Paul and his representatives on their previous visits to the church. They did not have to wait until God gave them more insight before they all could walk in agreement with basic principles.

Paul exhorted all of the Philippians together to "hold to" (στοιχεῖν) or "to keep in line with 'the same' standard of conduct" (BDAG, s.v. "στοιχέω," p. 946). "The same" (τῷ αὐτῷ) refers to the previous clause in 3:16a—"to what we have attained." Paul exhorted the entire community to live in unity, adhering to a common set of basic Christian beliefs, attitudes, and behaviors. This was the Christlike life he was encouraging throughout Philippians.

A Christlike Life according to Philippians: Paul used Jesus as the ultimate example of humility and sacrificial service for Christians (2:2–8). Believers are to pursue imitating Jesus in humility and sacrificial service, striving to become more and more like him in their attitudes and actions—sharing his suffering while at the same time experiencing his spiritual power in ministry (3:10). This pursuit is to continue throughout this life. Through God's grace and working, believers will attain full Christlikeness only at the resurrection (3:11, 14, 21).

THEOLOGICAL FOCUS

The exegetical idea (the Philippians were to agree with Paul and to pursue the ultimate goal of full intimacy with Jesus in a resurrection body in the age to come) leads to this theological focus: Believers are to pursue the ultimate goal, of full intimacy with Jesus in a resurrection body in the age to come.

Conversion to faith in Jesus as the Christ, and the initial blessings from God associated with it—forgiveness of sins, adoption into God's family, new life and relationship with Jesus, and so on—is not the ultimate goal of the Christian life. We have not already arrived, spiritually or physically. Paul's already/not yet view of God's redemptive plan emphasizes that in the present inaugurated kingdom (the "already") we only enjoy an initial foretaste of the blessings of salvation. The full experience ("not yet") awaits the return of Christ, the resurrection from the dead, and the transformation that comes with it (Phil. 3:21; Rom. 8:18–23).

For now, the Christian life consists of a daily "pressing on" with Christ toward that ultimate goal. We are to walk with Jesus, seeking to know him more intimately, learning to walk according to his humility and sacrificial service, and to share his suffering and resurrection power in ministry. This pressing-on must be the "one thing" we do. We should not allow past failures to paralyze us with guilt or "disqualify" us from pursuing this deeper knowledge of

Jesus. Nor should we become complacent, thinking that the level of spiritual maturity or intimacy with Jesus we have obtained is "good enough." John Wesley wrote:

> Remember! You were born for nothing else. You live for nothing else. Your life is continued to you upon earth for no other purpose than this, that you may know, love, and serve God on earth, and enjoy him to all eternity. . . . Therefore let your heart continually say, "This one thing I do." (quoted from a sermon, "What Is Man?" cited in Flemming, 2009, 188)

PREACHING AND TEACHING STRATEGIES

Exegetical and Theological Synthesis

What is clear in Philippians 3:12–16 is the strenuous *process* of pursuing Jesus. God empowers whom he calls (2:13; 3:14). Taking one more step is part of his perfecting process (3:12). He will finish what he started (1:6); his people continue to exert effort (2:12). We believe and repent. We imitate Jesus and exalt him. We work out our salvation with fear and trembling. Running imagery depicts the process as an ongoing pursuit of Jesus until his resurrection becomes a reality. In other words, Paul said, "Until you reach the end, keep reaching for the end."

Paul's language of perfection should not be confused with perfectionism. We must recall the greater context of his discussion. A warning about false teachers (3:2–3) led to related warnings about putting stock in religious resumes (vv. 4–6) or getting caught up in disobedience, disloyalty, and distractions (vv. 7–9). A perfect resume will not impress God. Nor does God give grades based upon earthly goods. Only Jesus—in his humble, self-giving, sacrificial death, and glorious resurrection—guarantees perfection. Intimacy with him is our greatest aim. We pursue the Perfect Christ, not the perfect life.

Recent studies by Beale (2014) and Smith (2016) convey a similar truth: We become what we worship and love. What we love, Smith argues (pp. 7–15), becomes the *telos* point to which our hearts orient themselves. Worshipping sex turns us into perverts. Worshipping power makes us into dictators. Worshipping security morphs us into paranoid control freaks. But aiming our hearts at Jesus Christ conforms us into his image. Until the day we face him—be it our death or his return—our greatest pursuit is to know, love, and worship him into whose image we are being formed.

Preaching Idea

Always take one more step as you strive to become like Jesus.

Contemporary Connections

What does it mean?

What does it mean to always take one more step as you strive to become like Jesus? Can we achieve perfection or Christlikeness? Does the need to always take another step allow for pit stops and days off? To strive means to press on, to move forward, to keep going. Forward motion is further indicated by Paul's phrase, "forgetting what is behind but straining toward what is ahead" (3:13). The Christian life should have directional clarity, ever away from self-centeredness and worldly values, ever toward Christ Jesus and heavenly values.

But we should measure directional clarity over extended periods of time. Every one of us will have miserable days and weeks when sin entangles us, so we stumble backwards. We will have exhausted days and weeks when we cannot muster any spiritual inertia, so we remain idle. We will have discouraging days and weeks when we feel no motivation to move toward Jesus, so we sit in isolation. For such reasons, we suffer lapses in our striving, but these natural breaks do not disqualify us from taking one more step.

Until we die or see Jesus face-to-face, the opportunity to take another step remains.

And our perfect ending of becoming like Jesus requires a disclaimer: We cannot achieve it on our own. Try as we may, we cannot string together enough perfect days to become perfect. We will falter. We will fail. To strive to become like Jesus is to strive for the impossible. Thus we must remember not to lose sight of Jesus—his humility, grace, glory, and ascension—as we strive to become like him.

Is it true?

Does striving even matter if we're not going to receive resurrected bodies until we die or Jesus returns? Doesn't striving lead to busyness and burnout? The answer to both questions is yes, but we must qualify. As already mentioned, our perfection as believers is not a personal achievement, but a Person. The second coming of Jesus (or death) will bring us into the presence of the risen Lord. This is our finish line, our grand finale. Until that day, we may know him in increasing measure, growing in theological understanding, solidarity with his suffering, and dependence on his sustaining power. Such intimacy not only prepares us for our resurrected state, but also improves the quality of our lives in the present. Our love for Jesus makes us more like him in our attitude and actions. Our quality of affection, consistency in sacrifice, ease of humility, and assurance in believing grow as we take one more step. Moreover, as we direct our hearts toward Jesus, we eventually give less attention to bragging rights, pet peeves, bad habits, and decisions that harm self and others.

Of course, we must recognize striving can lead to busyness and burnout. New followers of Jesus often reflect zeal in their newfound faith. They dive into ministry and spiritual disciplines with little regard for pacing. Eventually their zeal wavers. Long-time followers of Jesus develop deep loyalties to their local churches. They volunteer with various ministries and attend all sorts of services. They have little time for intimacy with Jesus because they are busy serving in his name. As cliché as it may sound, we cannot approach serving Jesus as a sprint; it is a marathon. Fortunately, striving after Jesus one step at a time does not exhaust, but invigorates us.

Now what?

How can I strive to become like Jesus without lapsing into perfectionism? What boundaries can I set to guard against busyness and laziness? Peterson (1989, 17–25) observes that busyness and laziness both stem from a self-control deficit. When we fail to set an agenda for ourselves, we let others drive our schedules. His antidote to laziness and busyness is better planning (e.g., master calendar). We all manage limited amounts of time and energy; controlling our calendars helps us maximize both time and energy.

What does this have to do with always taking one more step as we strive to become like Jesus? Simply put: We need to schedule time to pursue him, so the pursuit spills into other aspects of life. It is too easy to compartmentalize our relationship with Jesus to certain segments of the day (e.g., the morning devotional) and hours of the week (e.g., the church service). We must avoid viewing these set aside times as ends to themselves; rather, they are pit stops or check points in our relationship with Jesus. The remainder of the day we pursue him through our work, ministry, family life, relationships, and play.

Paul modeled a spiritual discipline called the prayer of recollection. "Forgetting the past" and "pressing toward the upward call" comprise two steps of recollection. First, we confess false views of ourselves (e.g., finding our identity in our profession or parenting role). Next, we accept God's view of us (e.g., called and empowered by his Spirit). Employing this simple prayer throughout the day serves as a buffer against burnout and maintains intimacy with Jesus between our scheduled times of devotion.

Creativity in Presentation

Consider using contemporary illustrations of racing to visualize Paul's call to strive. The Academy Award–winning film *Chariots of Fire* (directed by Hugh Hudson, 1981), recounts the story of Olympian Eric Liddell, whose faith and athletic achievements tie together. "When I run, I feel God's pleasure," he tells his sister in the film. Another classic image of striving from Hollywood is *Forrest Gump* (directed by Robert Zemeckis, 1994) running with the football, and then running across the country. "Run, Forrest, run," shouts his beloved Jenny, inspiring young Forrest to outpace school bullies. In 2017, Nike recruited Kenyan marathoner Eliud Kipchoge to run the perfect marathon, breaking the two-hour barrier. In spite of his striving, Kipchoge missed the mark of perfection by twenty-five seconds.

Another way to illustrate the striving imagery could include wearing a track suit (or running outfit) for preaching. Moreover, consider setting a treadmill on the stage to reiterate the point of taking one more step. Though it may be difficult to preach while jogging, telling a story about striving while walking at a steady clip would be memorable. An alternative to this idea could include hiking gear and story about a long hike to an uncertain destination. Anyone who has taken a road trip knows the pains of watching a GPS marker inch forward while the destination remains ever in the distance. A personal travel narrative—including missed turns, rest stops, and crying children as you cover one more mile to the destination—will connect with many in an audience.

It is also worth noting Paul used similar racing imagery later in life when writing to his protégé Timothy. "I finished the course," he penned with a sigh of relief (2 Tim. 4:7). We can learn much taking one more step from those who have remained faithful to Jesus for decades and face the end of their lives still pressing forward. D. A. Carson (2014, 120–21) recounts both Bishop Stanway's and Pastor Martyn

Lloyd-Jones's honorable embrace of Jesus at the end of their lives. He summarizes, "Retirement can betray where our hearts really are; so can medical incapacity." Perhaps you can find an example closer to home for your congregation, an end-of-life testimony that radiates with striving to become like Jesus even in its final steps.

Throughout the sermon, be sure to focus on this: Believers are to pursue the ultimate goal of full intimacy with Jesus in a resurrection body in the age to come. Therefore, we should always take one more step as we strive to become like Jesus.

- Paul strived to become like Jesus one step at a time (3:12–14).

- We strive to become like Jesus as long as we have time (3:15–16).

DISCUSSION QUESTIONS

1. What Paul did say you are to pursue in your life (in 3:8–14)?

2. What do you strive after? What is the *telos* point that pulls at your heart?

3. How are busyness and burnout signs you might be striving after the wrong things (or the right things in the wrong way)?

4. Why do Christians become complacent in the pursuit Paul describes in 3:8–14?

5. What past achievements might you need to forget because they lead to nostalgia, not Jesus?

6. How can past failures cause you to "lose heart" in your walk with Christ? Have you experienced this? How can you overcome it?

7. What does being "Christlike" mean? Give some examples of what it looks like in real life.

Philippians 3:17– 4:1

EXEGETICAL IDEA
The Philippians were to follow Paul's pattern of living a Christlike life of humility, self-denial, and sacrificial service while they waited for Jesus to return and complete their redemption by giving them resurrection bodies like his.

THEOLOGICAL FOCUS
Believers should follow the apostolic pattern of living a Christlike life of humility, self-denial, and sacrificial service while they wait for Jesus to return and complete their redemption by giving them resurrection bodies like his.

PREACHING IDEA
Follow in the footsteps of people who align their lives with God's kingdom.

PREACHING POINTERS
Paul capped a series of personal affirmations about striving toward Jesus with an exhortation to imitate the apostle and others who align their lives with God's kingdom. The lifestyle of a believer is described with echoes from the Christ hymn—humility preceding the glory of their resurrection bodies. The exegetical section will show this transformation hinges on Jesus's return. In the meantime, Paul warned his original audience to remain steadfast amid "enemies of the cross," an uncertain group of opponents. In any case, their challenge was to follow Paul's footsteps, not those who aligned their lives with earthly ends.

Today we are swayed by many fads, famous people, and faith options that do not align with kingdom values. We imitate parents and teachers, friends and celebrities, media and marketers whose peddle self-indulgence and shameful gain. We buy sleek products (e.g., MacBooks and Fitbits) to secure social capital. The fear of shame silences our religious convictions (e.g., marriage as a covenant between male and female). We are terribly impressionable people, modifying our behavior based upon our current company. The footsteps we choose to follow become critical in our spiritual formation. This passage appeals to our need to follow in the footsteps of people who align their lives with God's kingdom.

IMITATING GOOD EXAMPLES (3:17–4:1)

LITERARY STRUCTURE AND THEMES (3:17–4:1)

This unit consists of a double exhortation (3:17) followed by two reasons that support it (3:18–19, 20–21), and a concluding exhortation (4:1). Paul exhorted the Philippians to be imitators of him, and to pay attention to those who lived like he and his coworkers lived (3:17). The first reason they should do this was because many did not exhibit a lifestyle that was in keeping with following Jesus. They were enemies of the cross (3:18–19). The second reason was that in contrast to the enemies of the cross, believers belonged to a commonwealth that exists in heaven. And they eagerly awaited a Savior from there, the Lord Jesus Christ. When Christ returns, he will transform their bodies into glorious bodies like his (3:20–21). Consequently, Paul exhorted them to stand firm in the Lord (4:1).

> *Following Good Examples (3:17)*
> *Avoiding Bad Examples (3:18–19)*
> *Citizens of God's Kingdom (3:20–21)*
> *Staying True to Jesus (4:1)*

EXPOSITION (3:17–4:1)

Paul brought the warning against false teachers (3:1–4:1) to a close. He had stressed that he was still pursuing knowing Christ with the ultimate prize of attaining to the resurrection from the dead and all that goes with it. He had urged the Philippians to take the same point of view. Now Paul exhorted them to imitate him and to pay close attention to those who walked according to the model he and his coworkers provided. Imitating good examples was important for two reasons. First, there are many who provided a negative model, whose lifestyles opposed the cross of Christ. Second, believers belonged to a commonwealth in heaven and were awaiting the return of Christ. They were to live according to its values, for they would experience its glory when Jesus returns. This latter emphasis on the certainty of eschatological victory would bring comfort and motivation to believers who, like the Philippians, suffered for their faith.

Following Good Examples (3:17)

The Philippians were to follow the Christlike pattern of a life of humility, self-denial, and sacrificial service (illustrated by Jesus in 2:5–8 and Paul in 3:8–16) that he, his coworkers, and similar examples provided.

> *3:17.* Συμμιμηταί μου γίνεσθε is rendered "join in imitating me" (ESV, NRSV, CSB), "join in following my example" (NIV, NASB, NKJV), or "pattern your lives after mine" (NLT). Περιπατοῦντας is rendered "those who live" (NIV, NRSV, CSB), "those who walk" (ESV, NASB, KJV, NKJV), or "follow" (NLT). Τύπον is rendered "model" (NIV), "example" (ESV, NRSV, CSB, NLT, KJV) or "pattern" (NASB, NKJV).

3:17. Paul exhorted (γίνεσθε) the Philippians to follow his lifestyle in pursuing Christ Jesus and the prize. As their spiritual father, he would naturally be their model of what it meant to follow Jesus's lifestyle (2:5–8). "Fellow-imitators" (συμμιμηταί) never occurs in ancient Greek literature (BDAG s.v. "συμμιμητης," 958). Some suggest that Paul coined the term for this occasion (Bockmuehl, 1998, 228). They were to join themselves together, becoming "co-imitators" of *him* (μου, objective genitive).

Paul was not being arrogant here, nor was he attempting to be "in control." In the ancient world, imitation was a "crucial element in the life of discipleship" (Fowl, 2005, 166). His call to imitation was not egotistical, but pedagogical. He wanted them to imitate his pursuit of a Christlike mindset and being conformed to his death (2:5–8; 3:10). Paul was like a coach who showed them how, and who wanted them to walk the walk, not just talk the talk (Cohick, 2013a, 196).

Paul continued his exhortation by exhorting the Philippians to "pay careful attention to" (σκοπεῖτε) or "notice" (BDAG s.v. "σκοπέω," p. 931) those who "walk" (περιπατοῦντας), that is, live according to the same standard as the example they had in him and his coworkers. He did not want them to focus only on his example.

By "those who walk this way" Paul may have had in mind other itinerant teachers or Christians who might come through Philippi (Fee, 1995, 366). Timothy would be a prime example, though it is better to include him within "us" in the next clause. Epaphroditus may have been an example. Whoever they were, they exhibited the same manner of life as Paul and his coworkers and so were worthy of attention. "Us" (ἡμᾶς) refers to Paul and those on his team. Paul used "example" (τύπον) elsewhere to denote a pattern or model of ethical behavior (1 Thess. 1:7; 2 Thess. 3:9; 1 Tim. 4:12; Titus 2:7 BDAG s.v. "τύπος" 6b, p. 1020).

Imitation in Paul's Letters: Imitating one's teacher was a prominent idea in both the Jewish and Greco-Roman worlds. Imitating teachers allowed you to internalize their teaching and put it into practice (Fee, 1995, 364). In his letters, Paul noted or called for his converts' imitation of himself and his coworkers (1 Cor. 4:16; 11:1; Phil. 3:17; 1 Thess. 1:6; 2 Thess. 3:7, 9), of other churches (1 Thess. 2:14), and of God or Christ (Eph. 5:1; 1 Thess. 1:6). For "imitation," see *TDNT* 4:659–74; *NIDNTTE* 3:304–7; for "imitation" in Paul's letters, see *EDNT* 2:428–30; *DPL*, 428–31.

Avoiding Bad Examples (3:18–19)
The Philippians were to follow Paul's Christlike pattern of life because there were many self-styled "Christians" who did not live according to Jesus's pattern of humility, self-denial, and sacrificial service.

3:18. As in 3:17, περιπατοῦσιν is rendered "live" (NIV, NRSV, CSB) or "walk" (ESV, KJV, NKJV).

3:18. Paul's first reason why (γάρ) it was necessary for them to imitate him and other Christlike examples was because many (πολλοί) "walk" (the same verb he just used in 3:17) in a different way. Paul stated that in the past, when he was with them, he "often" (πολλάκις) or "frequently" (BDAG s.v. "πολλάκις," p. 846) "told" (ἔλεγον) them a number of times about these ones. Now he warned them again, and described the manner of his warning: "even weeping." "Weeping" (κλαίων) or "I say with tears" suggests the intense grief that Paul felt over these individuals (BDAG s.v. "κλαίω" 1, p. 545; cf. O'Brien, 1991, 4511). It may point to the frustration he felt toward them for their hard hearts (considered possible by Martin and Hawthorne, 2004, 222–23), and the grief he felt for the effect they might have on true believers.

The essential characteristic of this "many" was that they were "enemies" (ἐχθρούς), or more pointedly, they were "hostile" to or haters" of (BDAG s.v. "ἐχθρός" 2bγ, p. 419) the cross of Christ. Paul's further description in 3:19 suggests that they opposed the cross and its implications for Christlike living (self-denial, sacrifice, suffering) by their lifestyle.

These enemies were not part of the Philippian church, but rather outsiders, for Paul was warning all of the Philippians about them (Fee, 1995, 367). If they were present in the church, Paul would hardly emphasize that he gave thanks for *all* of the Philippians (1:4, 7). Nor is it likely that they posed an immediate threat to the church. If that were the case, it is doubtful that Paul would only now be mentioning them in the letter. They were probably outsiders who could show up at the church in the future and exert a negative influence primarily through a lifestyle that contradicted the humble, sacrificial lifestyle of Jesus. This group was not the same as the false teachers of 3:2. They were most likely professing "Christians" who served their physical appetites rather than walk the path of Christlike self-denial and sacrificial service. Paul wept because of their opposition to the pattern of authentic Christian living set by Jesus.

3:19. Τέλος is rendered "destiny" (NIV) or "end" (ESV, NRSV, CSB, NASB, KJV, NKJV). Κοιλία is rendered "stomach" (NIV, CSB), "belly" (ESV, NRSV, KJV, NKJV), or "appetite" (NLT, NASB).

3:19. Paul described these enemies of the cross of Christ with four short descriptive phrases. Even with this description, it is difficult to identify them, for the description has been understood in different ways. The Philippians themselves would have known whom Paul was speaking of, for he had often spoken to them about these enemies (3:18).

First, their "end is destruction." "End" (τέλος) denotes their final "outcome" or destiny denotes their final destiny (BDAG s.v. "τέλος" 3, p. 998). "Destruction" (ἀπώλεια) refers to condemnation at the final judgment, as it did in 1:28 (cf. Rom. 9:22; 2 Thess. 2:3; 1 Tim. 6:9). The bottom line is they were going to hell (BDAG s.v. "ἀπώλεια," 2, p. 127; *TDNT* 1:397). Paul may have put this at the head of the list for its shock value (Bockmuehl, 1998, 230–31). In this context, the destruction of these individuals stands in sharp contrast to the final destiny of believers (3:20–21).

Second, their "god is their belly." This description is joined grammatically to the third so that they go together.[3] Paul depicted self-indulgent individuals who served their appetites. If he was using "belly" (κοιλία) more

narrowly as "the body's receptacle for food" (cf. 1 Cor. 6:13), he was thinking specifically of overindulgence at the table—gluttony, or craving particularly fine foods (BDAG s.v. "κοιλία" 1b, 550; Beare, 1969, 136). If he was using "belly" more broadly, he may have been thinking of one's physical "appetites" in general, such as food and sex (Bockmuehl, 1998, 232). For a similar use of "belly," compare Romans 16:18.

"Belly" and Overindulgence: K. O. Sandnes (2002) investigates the use of "belly" (κοιλία) in Greco-Roman moral philosophy and concludes that it is a catchword for a "lifestyle controlled by the desires" and a "code word for gluttony" (57). For Plato, desires were located in the belly and the genitals and had to be mastered (265). For Aristotle, "the passions, including the 'belly' could take control so that men were then enslaved by desires that should be enjoyed only moderately" (46). Moral philosophers used "belly" in their attack against the Epicureans and their indulgence in food, drink, and sex (265–66). Sandnes concludes that the background for Paul's belly-sayings in Philippians 3:19 and Romans 16:18 is the lifestyle that came to be associated with Epicurean philosophy (267).

Third, their "glory is in their shame." As noted above, this is connected grammatically to "god is their belly." "Glory" (δόξα) is honor, prestige, or recognition of status (BDAG s.v. "δόξα" 3, p. 257). It represents what these people delighted and boasted in. They found their honor was that which is actually "shame" (αἰσχύνη) to them. "Shame" in this sense was not their *feelings* of shame, but shame from God's point of view and the *disgrace* that would come to them through divine judgment (BDAG s.v. "αἰσχύνη" 2, p. 30; *TDNT* 1:189). Paul was referring to their indulgence of physical appetites that they delighted in or even boasted about (Bockmuehl, 1998, 232), but which would bring them

---

3   In the Greek text, both phrases are governed by a single relative pronoun, "whose" (ὧν) and are joined by "and" (καὶ).

disgrace. Compare "fornication" coupled with "boasting" in 1 Corinthians 5:1–2. As today, apparently some in the first century gloried in things God finds shameful.

Fourth, "they "set their minds" (οἱ φρονογεια) on earthly things." Their mindset was opposed to Paul's exhortation in 3:15, where he exhorted his readers to share his Christ-centered, upward, and eschatological point of view. "Earthly things" (τὰ ἐπίγεια) denotes the things that are characteristic of the present age, providing personal gratification (BDAG s.v. "ἐπίγειος" 2, p. 369). They are the antithesis of heavenly things that Paul pursues (3:14) and for which believers wait (3:20–21). For a similar contrast of mindsets, see Romans 8:5–8 and Colossians 3:2.

Citizens of God's Kingdom (3:20–21)

The Philippians were to follow Paul's Christ-like pattern of life because they were citizens of God's kingdom waiting for Jesus to return and complete their redemption by giving them resurrection bodies like his.

3:20. Γάρ is rendered "but" (NIV, ESV, NRSV, CSB, NLT) or "for" (NASB, KJV, NKJV). Πολίτευμα is rendered "citizenship" (NIV, ESV, NRSV, CSB, NASB, NKJV) or "commonwealth" (RSV). Ἀπεκδεχόμεθα is rendered "eagerly await/wait for" (NIV, CSB, NLT, NASB, NKJV), "await" (ESV), "are expecting" (NRSV), or "look for" (KJV).

3:20. Some English versions begin 3:20 with a contrastive "but," others with an explanatory "for." This is because the conjunction that begins the statement (γάρ) is explanatory ("for"), yet the content contrasts Paul and his readers with the enemies of the cross. It is best to understand this as a second reason why the Philippians should imitate him (3:17) that at the same time offers a strong contrast between true believers and the "enemies" in 3:18–19 (Fee, 1995, 377–78, n. 13).

Paul's second reason why the Philippians were to follow his pattern of life is because our "citizenship" (πολίτευμα) or "commonwealth" is in heaven" (BDAG s.v. "πολίτευμα," p. 846).

Consider the contrast between Paul and the "enemies of the cross" (adapted from Sandnes, 2002, 142–43):

	Paul	Enemies of the Cross
Orientation	Mind focused heavenward/on Christ	Mind set on earthly things
Self-control	Disciplined straining for goal	Devoted to their belly
Suffering	Sharing Christ's sufferings	Enemies of cross of Christ
Glory	Waiting for resurrection body	Glory is in their shame
End	Prize of the upward call of God	End is destruction

The structure of 3:17–21 looks like this:

(17)	Command	Be imitators of me . . . and pay attention to . . .
(18–19)	Reason #1	For many walk of whom often I used to speak to you . . .
(20–21)	Reason #2	For our citizenship (commonwealth) exists in heaven . . .

"Our" (ἡμῶν) is in the emphatic position to highlight the contrast Paul was making with the enemies of the cross. The Greek term (πολίτευμα) is related to the verb Paul used in 1:27, "live out your citizenship" (πολιτεύεσθε). It occurs only here in the New Testament, and (1) it may mean "citizenship," a meaning only rarely attested (for examples, see *TDNT* 6:519); or (2) it may refer to a political entity: "state, commonwealth," or in some texts, a "colony" of foreigners or relocated veterans (*TDNT* 6:516–35; Lincoln, 1991, 97–101).

Paul meant that the commonwealth to which we belong exists in heaven. We are a heavenly colony planted on earth. For the Philippians, his point was that their commonwealth was God's heavenly kingdom, not the Roman Empire. "Commonwealth" is an active and dynamic term: "the state as a constitutive force regulating its citizens" (Lincoln, 1991, 99). The commonwealth determines and empowers the lives of its citizens.

Without minimizing the privileges of Roman or any earthly citizenship, Paul wanted believers to focus on their ultimate heavenly citizenship. He wanted their orientation to be toward heavenly things not earthly things. Their attitudes and behavior were to be determined by the characteristics and dynamic power of the realm to which they belonged (O'Brien, 1991, 459). Paul made an obvious contrast between believers (3:20–21) and the "enemies of the cross of Christ," who set their minds on earthly things (3:18–19).

Paul's use of "commonwealth" would have special relevance for the Philippians, who lived in a Roman *colonia*. Philippi was considered to be Italian soil. Its citizens enjoyed Roman citizenship, autonomous government, extensive property and legal rights like those in Italy, and exemption from tribute and taxes. So the Philippians enjoyed a "Roman" way of life in Macedonia. In a similar way, the believers in Philippi were to live a "heavenly" way of life on earth. They possessed citizenship in God's kingdom and they had the rights and privileges associated with that citizenship. The commonwealth to which they belonged, God's kingdom, was to determine their values, attitudes, and behaviors.

The present tense verb "is" (ὑπάρχει) emphasizes something that is "really there," that actually "exists" or is "at one's disposal" (BDAG s.v. "ὑπάρχω" 1, p. 1029). Paul's point was that the commonwealth even now exists during this present age. Therefore believers are already citizens of it (O'Brien, 1991, 461). "Heaven" (οὐρανοῖς) denotes the "transcendent abode" where Christ now reigns in his resurrection body at the right hand of God (Eph. 1:20; BDAG s.v. "οὐρανός" 2b, p. 739).

In a phrase modifying heaven, Paul stated that from there, "we also eagerly await a Savior, the Lord Jesus Christ." He was looking to the future when Jesus would come again from heaven (cf. 1 Thess. 1:10). "Eagerly await" (ἀπεκδεχόμεθα) is a verb of intense expectation that Paul used six times in eschatological texts (3x in Rom. 8), to denote believers waiting for the end-time events (BDAG s.v. "απεκδέχομαι," p. 100; *TDNT* 2:56; *EDNT* 1:407). The ultimate hope for the church in the world is end-time deliverance and vindication when Jesus returns.

"Savior" (σωτῆρα), a title Paul seldom used prior to the Pastoral Epistles, occurs here and in Ephesians 5:23 (also of Christ). The title "Savior" typically refers to "one who rescues" or delivers people (BDAG s.v. "σωτήρ" b, p. 985). "Lord Jesus Christ" (cf. 1:2; 2:11; 4:23) specifies which Savior Paul was talking about. For Paul, the background of this term was the LXX, where Yahweh is regularly called "Savior." As with "Lord" in 2:11, Paul took an Old Testament title that referred to Yahweh and applied it to Jesus. For the significance of "Lord" (κύριον), see note on 2:11.

The title "Savior" may have had special significance for those like the Philippians who lived in the Roman Empire. The emperor and other notable statesmen and rulers, as well as Roman gods, were sometimes called "savior." Most often, this had to do with their providing protection or being a benefactor for others. The Caesars were credited for bringing an age of peace, order, and prosperity. Julius Caesar was called "god and absolute ruler and savior of the world" (*TDNT* 7:1010–11; *NIDNTTE* 4:420–2; MM, 621). In the Roman context, the title did not necessarily suggest divinity, and it had nothing to do with salvation from sin, but only benefits in this life. We can't prove that Paul engaged here in a *direct* anti-imperial polemic, but it is reasonable to suppose that by using this designation for Jesus together with "commonwealth," Paul was at least indirectly pointing the Philippians away from Caesar to Christ Jesus. In every age and every culture, Jesus, rather than the state or any individual, provides the ultimate hope and solution to mankind's ills. He alone is Savior.

3:21. Μετασχηματίσει is rendered "transform" (NIV, ESV, NRSV, CSB, NASB, NKJV) or "change" (NLT, KJV). Σῶμα τῆς ταπεινώσεως ἡμῶν is rendered "our lowly body" (NIV, ESV, NKJV) or "body of our humble condition/humble state/humiliation" (CSB, NASB, NRSV). Σύμμορφον τῷ σώματι τῆς δόξης αὐτοῦ is rendered "be like his glorious body" (NIV, ESV, cf. CSB, NLT), "conformed to his glorious body" (NKJV), or "conformed to the body of his glory" (NRSV, cf. NASB),

3:21. Paul asserted what Christ Jesus will do for believers when he arrives. He will transform their natural, physical bodies. This is the final step in believers' redemption provided by the Savior. Paul did not use the term "resurrection" here, but parallels with other Pauline texts (Rom. 8; 1 Cor. 15) show the resurrection is in view. The verb "will transform" (μετασχηματίσει) denotes a change of form (BDAG s.v. "μετασχηματίσει" 1, p. 641; cf. *TDNT* 7:957–58. The change will consist of transforming the "body of our lowliness into conformity with the body of his glory."

"Body" (σῶμα) of our "lowliness" or "humble state" (τῆς ταπεινώσεως) refers to the believer's present mortal body in its state of weakness, frailty, suffering, indignity, and

physical decay ending in death (BDAG s.v. "σῶμα" 1b, p. 984; BDAG s.v. "ταπείνωσις," 2, p. 990). We live in these bodies while in our lowly state due to the effects of sin.

While it is true that at Christ's return a believer's entire being will be transformed, Paul's use of "body" (σῶμα) in this context has a particular focus on the transformation of the *physical* body at the resurrection. In both of its occurrences in this verse, "body" highlights the outward form, the organ through which a person experiences life in the world (cf. Gundry, 1987, 50).

As the opposite of the body of our lowliness, the "body of his glory" refers to Christ's physical resurrection body, the organ in which he now lives in his radiant and glorious position and realm. Paul's use of "glory" (δόξης) here suggests a contrast with the enemies of the cross whose "glory" was in their shame (3:19; BDAG s.v. "δόξα" 1b, p. 257). Their glory was a false glory and would pass. But believers' future glory at the resurrection is a share of Christ's glory and will last forever. "Conformity" (σύμμορφον) or "having a similar form" (BDAG s.v. "σύμμορφος," p. 958) recalls 3:10, where Paul's desire was to "be conformed to" (συμμορφιζόμενος) Christ's death. The bodies of those, who in following Jesus's humility and self-sacrifice seek to be conformed to his death, will be conformed to the body of his glory at the resurrection. Like Paul's use of "form" (μορφή) in 2:6–7, "conformity" (σύμμορφον) specifically refers to the outward appearance and shape of the body (Steenburg, 1988, 85). But this does not mean the transformation will be *merely* external. The change is also from a lowly state to a glorious state, which consists of outward and inward change—a total transformation.

Christ will transform believers' bodies "according to (κατά) the working of his ability also to subject all things to himself." Many English translations have "*by* the outworking of his ability . . ." (NIV, ESV, NRSV, CSB, NASB). But the preposition "according to" (κατά) that tends to be a "marker of norm, similarity, or homogeneity." The phrase does not denote "the means" by which it will be accomplished, but rather "the standard" upon which Jesus will transform believers' bodies. The transformation of their bodies will be "according to" (NKJV) the outworking of his ability to subdue the whole universe (O'Brien, 1991, 465). The norm of similarity may also be merged with *cause* or reason, so Christ's transformation of believers' bodies is also "because of" the outworking of his ability to subdue the whole universe (BDAG s.v. "κατά" 5δ, p. 512).

"All things" (τὰ πάντα) was Paul's way of referring to the entire created order, especially in eschatological or doxological texts (cf. Rom. 11:36; 1 Cor. 8:6 [2x]; 15:27 [3x], 28; Eph. 1:10; 3:9; Col. 1:16 [2x], 17 [2x], 18, 20). "To subject" (ὑποτάξαι) means "to cause to be in a submissive relationship," or "to subordinate" (BDAG s.v "ὑποτάσσω" 1, p. 1042). Elsewhere Paul spoke of *God* subjecting all things to Christ (1 Cor. 15:27; Eph. 1:22; cf. Phil. 2:11, where God exalted Christ above all rational beings). Here it is *Christ himself* who subjects all things (cf. 1 Cor. 15:25[4]). This is another example of Paul's high Christology, where Christ has authority and power to do what God does.

Christ will subject all things by the "working of his power." "Working" (ἐνέργειαν) is the actual operation of "active" power. Paul typically used this term in connection with the working of God's power (Eph. 1:19; 3:7; Col. 1:29; 2:12; cf. BDAG s.v. "ἐνέργεια," p. 335). Here it is the working of *Christ's* power. "Power" or "ability" (substantival infinitive, τοῦ δύνασθαι) is what Christ possesses to transform believers' bodies

at the resurrection. The transformation (whether via resurrection for those who have died, or translation for those still alive) will be in keeping with the working of Christ's power. Paul was arguing from the greater to the lesser (Harris, 1983, 167), and from the cosmic to the individual (Hansen, 2009, 275–76). If Christ Jesus can and will, by the working of his power, subject all things to himself, he certainly can and will also transform the bodies of believers so that they become like his glorious body. He will accomplish believers' glorification. The universal scope of his authority along with his acting specifically on behalf of believers should encourage the Philippians to persevere in following and serving him.

Staying True to Jesus (4:1)
Paul's beloved brothers and sisters in Christ, his joy and source of pride, were to steadfastly follow Jesus in the humble and sacrificial way of life he described in 3:8–21.

4:1. Paul brought the paragraph to a conclusion with an exhortation. As in 2:12, "therefore/so then" (ὥστε) alerted the readers that he would now draw an inference from what he had just written.[5] In light of the fact that their commonwealth existed in heaven, from which they awaited a Savior Jesus, who would give them glorious resurrection bodies like his own, Paul now exhorted the Philippians to stand firm in the Lord. Before he got to the exhortation, he strung together five terms expressing his affectionate feelings for them: (1) my brothers, (2) beloved, (3) longed for, (4) my joy, and (5) crown. Such a string of affectionate terms occurs nowhere else in his letters.

---

4   In the allusion to Psalm 110:1 in 1 Corinthians 15:25, "until *he* has placed all his enemies under his feet," the identity of the subject of the verb "he has placed" is debated. Many think Paul was referring to Christ (Fee, 1987, 756; Thiselton, 2000, 1234; Garland, 2003, 711). This agrees with the flow of subjects in the context leading up to the verb "place." Others think "he" refers to God (Fitzmyer, 2008, 573). This makes 15:25 agree with 15:27 (quoting Ps. 8:6) where God does the subjecting.

5   Paul especially used ὥστε in contexts where he was applying the preceding argument to the local situation (Fee, 1991, 387).

"My brothers" (ἀδελφοί), emphasizes the close-knit relationship Paul had with the Philippians sociologically and theologically (see on 1:12). "Beloved" (ἀγαπητοί) repeated twice in the verse, reminded them of his great affection for them (cf. 2:12). "Longed for" (ἐπιπόθητοι), occurring only here in the New Testament, is the adjectival form of the verb Paul used in 1:8 to express his desire to be with the Philippians (cf. 2:26; BDAG s.v. "ἐπιπόθητοις," p. 377). "My joy" (χαρά, cf. 1:4, 25; 2:2, 29) affirms that *they* were his joy. It means, "You bring me joy." Paul rejoiced as he saw them walking with Jesus and partnering with him in gospel ministry. "(My) crown" (στέφανος) means that they were his adornment or source of pride (BDAG s.v. "στέφανος" 2, p. 944; *NIDNTTE* 4:372). They were the reason for his exultation, the sign of his success in ministry (cf. 2:16).

The exhortation, "stand firm" (στήκετε) recalled 1:27. "Stand firm" suggests the image of a soldier refusing to break rank, holding his ground in battle (BDAG s.v. "στήκω" 2, p. 944). They were to stay true to the gospel, committed to Christ, united through the Spirit, as they awaited the second coming. "In the Lord" (ἐν κυρίῳ) denotes the realm in which believers were to stand firm. This is a variant of Paul's familiar phrase "in Christ."

"In this way" or "so" (οὕτως) denotes the manner in which they were to stand firm. It likely referred backwards to 3:8–21, where Paul described his pursuit of Jesus and exhorted them to imitate him (cf. it pointed backwards in 1 Cor. 7:17; 9:24; 11:28; 15:11; Gal. 6:2; 2 Thess. 3:17) (Fee, 1995, 388). Philippians 4:1 served as a closing exhortation to what he had just been explaining, and so prepared for what was to come.

THEOLOGICAL FOCUS

The exegetical idea (the Philippians were to follow Paul's pattern of living a Christlike life of humility, self-denial, and sacrificial service while they waited for Jesus to return and complete their redemption by giving them resurrection

bodies like his) leads to this theological focus: Believers should follow the apostolic pattern of living a Christlike life of humility, self-denial, and sacrificial service while they wait for Jesus to return and complete their redemption by giving them resurrection bodies like his.

Like Paul, believers are to steadfastly pursue a life of humility and self-sacrifice in ministry. This is a lifestyle committed to knowing Jesus and the power of his resurrection and sharing in his suffering, being conformed to his death (3:10). It consists of having the same mindset that was in Christ when he humbled himself, becoming obedient to the point of the humiliating death on a cross (2:8). This lifestyle contrasts with those who are enemies of the cross, whose gods are their bellies and who glory in their shame, and who set their mind on earthly things.

Living examples (true mentors and coaches) are just as necessary today as they were in the first century. It is important not just to tell people how to act, but to show them. Values (especially the values of self-denial and self-sacrifice) are "caught" more than "taught."

With Paul's call to imitation, he provided substantial motivation. Believers are citizens of God's kingdom, a heavenly commonwealth, and the one whose suffering they presently share will return from heaven as their Savior. He will transform the bodies of their humble existence into resurrection bodies like the body of his own glorious existence.

PREACHING AND TEACHING STRATEGIES

Exegetical and Theological Synthesis

The clear exhortation of 3:17–4:1 is to align one's life with a kingdom of heaven like Paul. In the apostle's day, the call to imitate was a matter of pedagogy, not pride. People learn best through imitation. Unfortunately, no single set of virtues or convictions existed. While there might be dominant cultural values of honor and imperial loyalty in a city like Philippi, lifestyles were not monolithic. Jews, Stoics, Epicureans, and pagans had spokespeople wandering the streets. Even followers of Jesus represented various persuasions, styles, and convictions. Paul made it clear in Philippians 3:17–4:1, his steadfast and hopeful commitment to the kingdom of heaven was preferred.

A closer look at the "enemies of the cross" proves helpful for followers of Jesus in the Western church. Although the enemies are neither identified nor equated with the opponents from earlier (3:2), Paul's descriptive phrase remains relevant to the growing number of godless people today. Research and anecdotal evidence has shown a rise in religiously unaffiliated ("Nones"), as well as atheists. Some fringe religions have witnessed marginal increases; whereas evangelical Christianity may be in decline in the West. Similar to the religious scene in first-century Philippi, atheists and Nones do not all subscribe to the same values or practices. And yet, we can identify clear strains of self-indulgence, self-glory, and earthly thinking (e.g., denial of supernatural), which still lead to a destructive end.

Pastor and author James Emery White has aptly described this shifting religious landscape in *The Rise of the Nones* (2014) and *Meet Generation Z* (2017). In broad strokes, he paints a helpful sketch of Nones. Timothy Keller surfaces many presuppositions of skeptics in his books, *The Reason for God* (2005) and *Making Sense of God* (2016). Not only do these authors expose weaknesses in secular thinking; they model a thoughtful and winsome articulation of the faith. In a post-Christian world, impressionable believers are desperate for leaders who chart a path of bold conviction and Christlike humility.

Preaching Idea

Follow in the footsteps of people who align their lives with God's kingdom.

Contemporary Connections

What does it mean?

What does it mean to follow in the footsteps of people who align their lives with God's kingdom? Isn't it enough to follow Jesus? Sometimes the indirect route to Christlikeness works better than calling people to "be like Jesus." We all pale in comparison to the perfect Christ. His divine nature, powerful works, and sinless life make us feel inept, discouraged, and resigned. However, imperfect imitations of Jesus—fragile and flawed, but faithful nonetheless—make becoming like Jesus seem more achievable.

Earlier in the letter Timothy and Epaphroditus served as implicit models of humble, self-giving, sacrificial living; Paul gave them kudos. Here he presented himself as an explicit model worth copying.

What does it mean to align our lives with the God's kingdom? Aligning our lives with the kingdom of heaven means pursing what Jesus valued and practicing virtues he embodied. The Sermon on the Mount (Matt. 5–7) comprises these values and virtues, ranging from rethinking blessing to living on mission to love of enemy to honesty in speech to sexual purity to secret disciplines (giving, fasting, and prayer) to releasing worry to showing mercy. The dramatic picture of a house withstanding a violent storm underscores the importance of living the kingdom vision of Jesus, not simply paying it lip service. And this kingdom vision seems urgent in a city like Philippi where imperial loyalty spilled into ancient religious worship. Throughout the letter, Paul subverted imperialism, reminding his readers that their greatest loyalty should lie with the Lord Jesus (1:27; 2:11; 3:20).

Is it true?

Is it true we should follow in the footsteps of others? We cannot deny the inborn tendency to emulate others. Babies learn behavior by imitation. Mirror neurons in the brain read and replicate what they see in the world around them.

This may explain why we return a smile or yawn after another person just yawned or smiled. Rather than deny our instinct to copy others, we should leverage it. Paul made the suggestion to imitate him more dogmatically elsewhere (1 Cor. 11:1).

However, we must practice discernment in the role models we choose and the expectations we place upon them. The people we follow will fail us. They will sin. No mentor lacks weaknesses, but the best ones learn from their missteps. Other spiritual leaders collapse beneath the weight of their followers' expectations. They assume a messianic role rather than one of modeling. We should not follow in the footsteps of people who draw more attention to their convictions, opinions, and accomplishments than to God's kingdom. Nor should we follow in the footsteps of people who let others' expectations define them.

Now what?

How do we go about following in the footsteps of people who align their lives with God's kingdom? Is this a formal or informal relationship? Mentoring need not be institutionalized, but a culture of mentoring should exist within the church. Furthermore, the people we follow shape the people we become. Paul presented his passionate, self-denying pursuit of Jesus as an explicit model to follow, in contrast to the "enemies of the cross" (3:18). And their fourfold portrait (v. 19) acted as a litmus test for worldly values.

First, we might ask ourselves: *What is the logical end for the people we follow?* Those who align their lives with God's kingdom will make gains in maturity and intimacy with Jesus. Their definition of the blessed life comes from the Sermon on the Mount, not the American Dream. They will someday see Jesus face-to-face and share in his glory with new bodies. Enemies of the cross face a destructive end. Their self-indulgence, self-glory, and the denial of God lead to a life of despair, inwardness, immaturity, guilt, and distance from God. Hell is their final home.

Second, we may consider the appetites of our role models and mentors. Those who align their lives with the kingdom of God will "hunger and thirst for righteousness" (Matt. 5:6) and understand obedience to their heavenly Father as a food source (John 4:34). In contrast, if we follow the example of enemies of the cross, self-indulgence will define us. We will follow the current of culture that overeats, binges on TV, consumes unnecessary material goods, and even treats relationships like a commodity.

Third, we should evaluate where our role models and mentors find their worth. If their glory is found in physical prowess, superior intellect, financial success, or social connectedness, they may be leading others down a shameful path. These things will not endure unto the resurrection. However, if we follow a path of faithful, hopeful, and humble leaders, we will share in the glory to come.

Finally, we should pay attention to what consumes the minds of our mentors. Enemies of the cross will model a mind devoted to material concerns. Their interest in spiritual reality is overshadowed by gas prices, weather forecasts, sports statistics, tabloids, to-do lists, and countless other trivial matters. The mind worth emulating meditates on matters that please God (see Phil. 4:8).

Creativity in Presentation

Spend a few minutes exposing the copycat tendencies that drive marketing. Advertisers commonly seek out athletes to endorse their products, knowing children will buy what their role models sell. Entertainers likewise endorse a variety of brands (from charge cards to insurance policies), hoping to bump sales by the copycat effect. Present images of several celebrities and encourage the congregation to name the brand they represent. Finish the sequence of headshots with an ancient painting of Timothy, Epaphroditus, or the apostle Paul.

Consider setting a table at the front of the stage or beside the pulpit where you might display two different pairs of shoes. A pair of basketball shoes might represent enemies of the cross. A pair of sandals might stand for the footgear of a faithful follower of Jesus. Throughout the message, refer to the shoes as a symbol for the two paths we can choose to take, aligned with kingdom values or opposed to the cross. You might even pull from the shoes old socks with the words *destruction, indulgence, shame,* and *earthly.*

A variation of this idea is to have two sets of footprints in different colors leading different directions from the stage. Whether you print and laminate your own or buy a set of rubber feet used for dance lessons, consider identifying "kingdom-oriented" steps from "worldly" steps by writing words on them reflective of their diverse set of values. Kingdom values might include humility, love, mercy, generosity, honesty. Worldly values comprise greed, ambition, anger, indulgence, revenge, and dishonesty.

Be sure to make this point: Believers should follow the apostolic pattern of living a Christlike life of humility, self-denial, and sacrificial service while they wait for Jesus to return and complete their redemption by giving them resurrection bodies like his. Indeed, we should follow in the footsteps of people who align their lives with God's kingdom.

- Follow in the footsteps of people like Paul (3:17).

- Avoid the pitfalls of the enemies of the cross (3:18–19).

- Await your new bodies while walking faithfully in your old ones (3:20–4:1).

DISCUSSION QUESTIONS

1. What makes imitation such a critical part to spiritual development?

2. How does your church foster a culture of mentoring? Where can it improve in this area?

3. Can you give an illustration of contemporary Christians, whose lifestyle makes them, practically speaking, an "enemy of the cross of Christ"? Describe what you see that does not fit the lifestyle of Jesus.

4. Why is it important today for us to have living examples of what it means to follow the way of Jesus?

5. What qualities in the lives of Christ and Paul, just from what you have read in Philippians, stand out as worthy of imitation?

6. Who would you consider models for your own walk with Christ? Why?

7. How does the reality of your future resurrection when Jesus returns serve as motivation in the present?

FOR FURTHER READING

Fee, G. 1994. *God's Empowering Presence: The Holy Spirit in the Letters of Paul*. Peabody, MA: Hendrickson. Pages 816–22.

McGrath, A. E. 1993. "Justification." Pages 517–23 in *Dictionary of Paul and His Letters*. Edited by G. F. Hawthorne, R. P. Martin, and D. G. Reid. Downers Grove, IL: InterVarsity Press.

Onesti, K. L. and M. T. Brauch. 1993. "Righteousness, Righteousness of God," Pages 827–37 in *Dictionary of Paul and His Letters*. Edited by G. F. Hawthorne, R. P. Martin, and D. G. Reid. Downers Grove, IL: InterVarsity Press.

Smith, J. K. 2016. *You Are What You Love: The Spiritual Power of Habit*. Grand Rapids: Brazos Press.

FINAL EXHORTATIONS (4:2–9)

Having concluded the warning against false teachers and his call for the Philippians to imitate his example of pursuing the selfless lifestyle of Jesus, Paul gave a series of final exhortations. First he exhorted two women in the church, who had been his co-workers, to be of the same mind, and he asked a "true companion" to help them (4:2–3). Returning to the whole church, he exhorted all to rejoice and to exhibit a humble, gracious spirit toward everyone (4:4–5). Then he exhorted all to be anxious for nothing but to pray with thanksgiving about everything (4:6–7). Finally, he exhorted them to think about things that were excellent and praiseworthy, and to put into practice what they have learned from him (4:8–9).

This major section, Final Exhortations, (4:2–9) is broken into two preaching units: Living Together in Unity (4:2–5) and Experiencing the Peace of God (4:6–9).

Philippians 4:2–5

EXEGETICAL IDEA
The Philippians were to live together in unity, being deeply satisfied with the Lord in every circumstance, exhibiting a humble, gracious spirit to all people.

THEOLOGICAL FOCUS
Believers are to live together in unity, being deeply satisfied with the Lord in every circumstance, exhibiting a humble, gracious spirit to all people.

PREACHING IDEA
Resolve disagreements before they wreak havoc on harmony and happiness.

PREACHING POINTERS
Paul moved toward his conclusion, transitioning from the topic of external opposition to internal tensions. An interpersonal squabble in the church lingered between two women, Euodia and Syntyche (4:2). The nature of their disagreement was not stated, but given the fact Paul addressed them by name in his letter and asked for a mediator (4:3), it suggested that the matter was disruptive to the community. Here, Paul put the unity principle to the test. The original readers surely had awareness of the tension between these important female figures. Resolving their differences would not only prove beneficial to harmony and happiness in the Philippian church; it would also demonstrate Christlike meekness to a watching world.

Settling disagreements in our day is no simple matter. The lack of civility makes tense conversations toxic. People are trigger-happy on social media, willing to lambaste anyone who reflects an opposing view. Political discourse in America has devolved into name-calling and posturing. And under the banner of tolerance, our culture—overly sensitive and quick to take offense—has effectively banned moral disagreement. Followers of Jesus—whose names share a place in the book of life—should resolve their differences with gentleness. Sadly, when tensions arise among believers, we often descend into the same stubborn discord. The passage appeals to our need to resolve disagreements before they wreak havoc on harmony and happiness.

LIVING TOGETHER IN UNITY (4:2–5)

LITERARY STRUCTURE AND THEMES (4:2–5)

Verses 2–9 consist of a series of final exhortations. For preaching purposes, we divide it into two parts. Paul exhorted two women in the church to be of one mind in the Lord (4:2), and asked a "true companion" to help them (4:3a). In a descriptive relative clause, he showed why he appreciated these two: They labored with him in sharing the gospel, along with other coworkers (4:3b). Again showing the importance of his concern, Paul described all of his coworkers as those whose names are in the book of life (4:3c). Next, Paul exhorted everyone to rejoice in the Lord always, repeating it one last time for emphasis (4:4). Then he exhorted them to let their humble, gracious spirits be evident to all (4:5a). The reason for this is that the Lord is near (4:5b).

An Appeal to Two Coworkers (4:2–3)
Joy in Every Situation (4:4)
A Humble, Gracious Spirit (4:5)

EXPOSITION (4:2–5)

Paul began his final exhortations by urging two of the women to be of one mind, to get along and be agreeable toward each other. Apparently there was a rift between them. He also asked the "true companion" to help them come to agreement. Paul's appreciation for these women was evident in his description of them—they contended alongside him in the gospel ministry. He also mentioned Clement and "the rest of my coworkers" in this regard. Again, Paul's long partnership with the Philippian church in the gospel was evident. Then he moved to general exhortations. Twice he commanded them to rejoice in the Lord. Mutual joy in the Lord, not bickering, was to characterize life in the body of Christ. Then Paul exhorted all to let their humble, gracious spirits be evident. This would prevent rifts and promote unity. The motivation he gave for this command was that the Lord was near.

This section has ties with earlier themes in the letter through the repetition of certain terms. Again the theme of "joy" and the command to "rejoice" are present (1:4, 25; 2:2, 17–18, 29; 3:1; 4:1, 4 [2x]). Again he wanted them to "be of the same mind" (2:2, 5; 3:15). Unity and regard for others are prominent themes in this section, as in 1:27; 2:1–5. These exhortations were not random. They summarized and applied some of Paul's main concerns in the letter. He wanted them to rejoice in the Lord as they lived together in unity and exhibited a humble, gracious spirit to all.

An Appeal to Two Coworkers (4:2–3)

Paul urged two ladies in the church, who served with him in spreading the gospel, to humbly be of one mind in their thinking, attitudes, and goals in ministry, and to get along with each other, and he asked an unnamed ministry partner to help them do this.

4:2. Παρακαλῶ is rendered "plead with" (NIV), "entreat" (ESV), "urge" (NRSV, CSB, NASB), "appeal to" (NLT), "beseech" (KJV), or "implore" (NKJV). Τὸ αὐτὸ φρονεῖν is rendered "be of the same mind" (NIV, NRSV, KJV, NKJV), "agree" (ESV), CSB, "settle your disagreement" (NLT), or "live in harmony" (NASB).

4:2. Paul urged Euodia and Syntyche, two women (the Greek names are feminine in form and Paul described them using a feminine relative pronoun), to be of one mind and get along with one another. Apparently, like Lydia (Acts 16), they were prominent in the church (see Malinowski, 1985; Luter, 1996). That Paul called them out publicly suggests their rift was public. Further, the special attention he gave them suggests that (1) they were leaders in the church, and/or (2) their disagreement was having an effect on the whole body. The next verse will describe them as two women who had labored with him, contending by his side in the cause of the gospel. We have no further information about them other than what we read in this text—including whether Paul's public urging had the desired effect.

Paul "urged" (παρακαλῶ) them. This is the term he normally used to entreat or exhort in his letters (Rom. 12:1; 15:30; 16:17; 1 Cor. 1:10; 4:16; 16:15; 2 Cor. 2:8; 6:1; 10:1; Eph. 4:1; 1 Thess. 4:1, 10; 5:14; 2 Thess. 3:12; 1 Tim. 1:3; 2:1; Philem. 9, 10). It can denote a strong urging or a rather strong request (BDAG s.v. "παρακαλέω" 2, p.p. 764). Here, Paul urged each of the women separately, repeating the verb before each name. This showed that he was calling out each one with equal firmness and that (at least in this letter) he was not taking sides (Thielman, 1995, 216). We lack sufficient evidence to say whether the conflict was fundamentally a "ministry" issue (Fee, 1995, 392) or a personal one (Bockmuehl, 1998, 239). Perhaps both factors were present by now.

Paul urged them to "be of the same mind" (τὸ αὐτὸ φρονεῖν). This echoed the command previously given to the whole church in 2:2, "that you (all) be of the same mind." Paul applied that general exhortation to these two individuals specifically. He was not merely saying, "Be friends again." He wanted them to be unified in their thinking, attitudes, and goals in ministry, as well as get along (Fowl, 2005, 178). He wanted each of them to look out for the interests of the other, putting others first. He wanted them to humble themselves, exhibiting the same self-sacrificing mindset that was in Christ (2:3–5), in this way promoting unity and helping the church to be on task.

The sphere of their common mindset was "in the Lord" (ἐν κυρίῳ), suggesting their incorporation into Christ Jesus and the unity they possessed as members of the same body. This also provided the basis of Paul's appeal—be of the same mind because of what the Lord has done for you and who you are in him. Humility, self-sacrifice, and putting the interests of others first—getting along with one another—is necessary because you are joined to Christ; it is part of your submission to him (cf. O'Brien, 1991, 478). Your Christian attitudes and behavior must correspond to your identity in Christ.

4:3. Σύζυγε is rendered "companion" (NIV, ESV, NRSV, NASB, NKJV), "partner" (CSB, NLT), or "yokefellow" (KJV). Συνήθλησάν μοι is rendered "contended at my side" (NIV, CSB), "labored side by side with me" (ESV, cf. KJV, NKJV), "struggled beside me" (NRSV, cf. NASB), or "worked hard with me" (NLT).

4:3. "Yes" (ναί) emphatically confirmed the preceding verse (BDAG s.v. "ναί" c, p. 665) and strengthened the request that followed. With a more polite verb than he used in 4:2, Paul "asked" (ἐρωτῶ) or "requested" an unnamed ministry partner for help with these two women. The use of this verb (a request rather than urging) may imply that Paul considered this person more of a ministry equal, whereas the two women were more subordinate (Fee, 1995, 391, n. 33). At any rate, Paul wanted assistance from a third party to help them reconcile their differences. "Companion" (σύζυγε) refers to a "true comrade," literally "yoke-fellow" (BDAG s.v. "σύζυγος," p. 954). Paul was appealing to a person who had an intimate ministry with him and was someone he trusted. The adjective "true" (γνήσιε) emphasized the legitimacy or validity of the designation "companion" (NRSV "loyal," rather than "true," misses the point).

Though the Philippians would have known whom Paul was addressing, we can only guess at his identity. One plausible suggestion is that Paul was addressing Luke, the author of the Third Gospel and Acts. Luke had spent considerable time at Philippi (suggested by the "we sections" in Acts), and had been with Paul during his current imprisonment (Col. 4:14; Philem. 24). Since Luke is not mentioned at the close of Philippians, it is possible that Paul had earlier sent him to Philippi (Fee, 1995, 394–95). If not Luke, Paul was probably speaking to an otherwise unknown but influential leader of the church at Philippi, perhaps a head overseer.

Paul's request of the true companion to "help" (συλλαμβάνου) suggested taking part in aiding these two women to become of the same mind (BDAG s.v. "συλλαμβάνω" 4, p. 955). The relative clause "who (αἵτινες) contended side by side with me," may be qualitative, describing that they belonged to a certain class—"inasmuch as they belong to those who contended side by side" (Fee, 1995, 395, n. 53). Or it may be causal—"seeing that/because" they contended side by side with me (Robertson, 1934, 727–28). Either way, it shows the appreciation Paul had for them and gives one reason why their dispute matters to him.

"Contended side by side" (συνήθλησαν) occured earlier in 1:27, where Paul stated that he wanted to hear that all of the Philippians were "contending side by side" or "struggling" for the faith of the gospel. The verb suggests a military image of fighting side by side in battle (BDAG s.v. "συναθλέω," p. 964), or an athletic image of a team working together as one (Martin and Hawthorne, 2004, 71), or of gladiators fighting side by side in an amphitheater (Lightfoot, 1953, 106). These women had previously done what Paul encouraged in 1:27, and so demonstrated their bravery alongside Paul (Malinowski, 1985, 62).

As in 1:5, "in the gospel" (ἐν τῷ εὐαγγελίῳ) means something like, "in the spread of the gospel," or "in serving on behalf of the gospel ministry." These two women apparently were with Paul in the beginning.

They had struggled together alongside him as they spread the gospel and planted the church in the somewhat hostile environment of Philippi. He valued them as old friends along with other coworkers, as the next phrase will make clear.

Paul mentioned another coworker, Clement. We know nothing else about him. Presumably he was an early member of the church at Philippi who also labored alongside Paul and the two women for the spread of the gospel in Philippi. When Paul named Euodia, Syntyche, and Clement, he naturally thought of other "coworkers" (συνεργῶν) at Philippi—perhaps too many to name. Epaphroditus was one (2:25). Paul used this term not of believers in general, but of close associates in spreading the gospel (Rom. 16:3, 9, 21; 2 Cor. 8:23; Philem. 1, 24) (*TDNT* 7:874–75).

Paul stated that these coworkers' names were in the "book of life" (βίβλῳ ζωῆς). This refers to God's list of all the saved through history. It is not a literal book on earth, but is figurative, denoting a heavenly registry. Paul mentioned it only here in his letters. This comment provides another reason why Paul wanted these two to get along—because their names, along with the names of other coworkers, are in the registry of the redeemed. The existence of a book of life might have been of special note to the believers at Philippi. In Roman cities, the names of citizens were recorded in the civic register. Even if none of the church members were Roman citizens, they could appreciate the imagery. The book of life, as the civic register of the commonwealth in heaven (3:20), was more important than any Roman registry (Fee, 1991, 397, n. 59). God's kingdom has its own registry, and believers' identification as citizens of God's kingdom supersedes all earthly citizenships. Today we know little about these early Philippian believers. But God knows them. Their names, with those of all believers, are in the book of life.

The Book of Life: The concept of the book of life first occurs in Exodus 32:32–33, and is found in Psalm 69:28. It occurs regularly in apocalyptic literature (Dan. 12:1; 1 En. 47:3; 1QM 12:3), and in the book of Revelation (3:5; 13:8; 17:8; 20:12, 15; 21:27) to refer to the registry of those slated for everlasting life in the age to come. Compare Jesus's saying about rejoicing that "your names are written in heaven" (Luke 10:20), and Hebrews' mention of "the assembly of the firstborn who are enrolled in heaven" (12:23). Compare also Nehemiah 7:5; Psalm 87:6; Isaiah 4:3; Ezekiel 13:9, which may refer to a registry of Israelites in the present age, but supports the idea of a register of God's people. See *TDNT* 1:618–20.

Joy in Every Situation (4:4)

Paul emphatically exhorted the Philippians to have a deep, heartfelt, trusting satisfaction with the Lord in every circumstance.

4:4. This paragraph (4:4–7) and the next (4:8–9) consist of a series of commands in rapid succession. Together they provided a summary exhortation of the things Paul believed to be important for the Philippians in their situation. Witherington writes that in 4:4–9 Paul is "emotively rousing the troops to action one last time" (2011, 242). Note that these commands were not just for believers individually, but for believers living together in unity with one another and serving in the gospel together (Hellerman, 2015, 236).

Paul repeated the exhortation from 3:1 twice, "Rejoice in the Lord." As at 3:1 (cf. 2:18), he called the Philippians to a deep, heartfelt satisfaction with the Lord in the midst trying circumstances. When a writer repeats the same exhortation four times in a short letter like this, it must be something that is on his heart for his readers. If 4:4 was to be read in connection with the situation reflected in 4:2–3, Paul's point was, "Replace bickering with rejoicing." How good and pleasant it is when the brethren dwell in

unity (Ps. 133:1)! As a pastor who had the difficult experience of presiding over a church split years ago, I can tell you that when believers are at odds with one another in the body, joy in the Lord is one of the first things lost. At Philippi there was opposition from without (1:27–30) and contention within (4:2–3). They needed to renew their joy in the Lord.

"In the Lord" (ἐν κυρίῳ) denoted the sphere of their existence, the result of having been incorporated into Christ. Believers are joined to and identified with Christ, who rules over the kingdom to which they belong. The fact that they were in the Lord provided the *basis* of their rejoicing (rejoice because of what the Lord has done for you), the *object* of their rejoicing (rejoice at who he is), and the *source* of their rejoicing (rejoice with the joy he supplies). The qualifier "always" (πάντοτε) or "at all times," after the first exhortation, emphasizes that joy is called for in every circumstance (BDAG s.v. "πάντοτε," p. 755). No matter the situation, Christ Jesus provides the reasons and resources for joy. In this way, joy does not depend on circumstances; it depends on believers' union with the Lord in the midst of circumstances. To be sure everyone got the point, Paul repeated it, "again I will say, rejoice!"

Why Joy Always: Joy is one of the marks of the kingdom of God (Rom. 14:17) and is the fruit of the Holy Spirit (Gal. 5:22; cf. Rom. 15:13). Believers can rejoice even in sufferings, knowing the spiritual benefits they produce (Rom. 5:3–5). Believers can always rejoice, for the Lord is always reigning (Ps. 97:1). The joy of the Lord is to be their strength (Neh. 8:10). Hansen writes, "People caught up in joyful worship of the Lord are united in heart and lifted above the circumstances of life in a vision of the awesome majesty of the Lord" (2009, 288). Throughout the letter, Paul had modeled his own joy in trying circumstances for the Philippians (1:4; 2:17), and had stated that his concern is for their progress and joy in their faith (1:25). This does not preclude the legitimate feelings of lament in trying circumstances (a major theme in the Psalms). But it does mean that for Christians joy ultimately triumphs over lament. Even in sorrow, we can experience a deep, heartfelt, trusting satisfaction with the Lord.

A Humble, Gracious Spirit (4:5)

The Philippians were to exhibit a humble, gracious spirit to all people, for in the scheme of the history of salvation, Jesus's return would soon occur.

4:5. Ἐπιεικές is rendered "gentleness" (NIV, NRSV, NKJV, cf. NASB "gentle spirit"), "reasonableness" (ESV), "graciousness" (CSB), "considerate" (NLT), or "moderation" (KJV). Ἐγγύς is rendered "near" (NIV, NRSV, CSB, NASB), "at hand" (KJV, NKJV), or "coming soon" (NLT).

4:5. Paul moved quickly to another exhortation, "Let your gentleness be evident to all people." Grammatically, this verse stands alone, but there may be a logical connection to 4:4. God's people who rejoice in the Lord in every circumstance can exhibit gentleness to everyone. Or God's people who exhibit a gentle spirit can rejoice in the Lord in every circumstance. The causal effect goes in both directions.

The precise meaning of "gentleness" (ἐπιεικές) is not immediately evident due to the rapid succession of final exhortations. Numerous options exist (BDAG s.v. "ἐπιεικής," p. 371). But the overall context of the letter leads to numerous helpful suggestions: "the opposite to a spirit of contention and self-seeking" (Lightfoot, 1953, 160); "that considerate courtesy and respect for the integrity of others which prompts a person not to be forever standing on his own rights" (Caird, 1976, 150); "a humble patient steadfastness, which is able to submit to injustice, disgrace, and maltreatment without hatred or malice" (O'Brien, 1991, 487); "gentle forbearance with others" (Fee, 1995, 406); "an attitude of contentment with one's state, even when one has not been treated justly" (Silva, 2005, 194). The general idea seems clear—a humble, gracious spirit toward others, regarding their concerns more important than your own (cf. 2:3–4), a spirit that puts up with other peoples' faults and is conciliatory, not insisting on one's own rights. It includes showing others "the sort of leniency and understanding" you would want them to show you, and giving them "the benefit of the doubt" (Witherington, 2011, 246).

Paul's exhortation to let their humble, gracious spirits "be known" (γνωσθήτω) to all meant "let it be evident" or "obvious" to all people (Hellerman, 2015, 237). "To all (people)" shows that Paul meant they were to exhibit this quality not merely to friends or other believers, but to everyone, even enemies—for example, to the unbelievers who opposed them (1:28).

"The Lord is near" provides both motivation and assurance. This is why believers can let their humble, gracious spirits be known to all. This statement may go, not just with the preceding command (4:5a), but also with what follows (4:6), and indeed all of 4:4–7 (Flemming, 2009, 220). As was generally the case in Paul's letters, "the Lord" (ὁ κύριος) refers to Christ, not the Father. "Near" (ἐγγύς) may mean (1) the Lord is near *spatially*—he is spiritually present with us now; or, it may mean (2) the Lord is near *temporally*—his return is near (BDAG s.v. "ἐγγύς" 1 and 2, p. 270).

In support of (1) are several Old Testament statements concerning the Lord's nearness that Paul may have been echoing (Ps. 34:18; 119:151; 145:18). If this is right, Paul encouraged the Philippians that in the midst of every situation, they could rejoice in the Lord (4:4), exhibit a humble, gracious spirit (4:5), and be anxious for nothing (4:6) because Christ was present. Witherington connects 4:5b primarily with 4:6. It is the present spatial nearness of Christ to his people that alleviates anxiety (2011, 246–47). Silva rejects the spatial interpretation, saying that "near" is used spatially in the LXX, but not in the New Testament. The New Testament emphasizes the Lord's direct presence rather than his nearness (2005, 198).

In support of (2) is the context of 3:20–21, where Paul stated that they awaited Christ's return from heaven. Also in support of (2) are the parallels in James 5:8 ("be patient, strengthen your hearts, for the coming of the Lord is near") and Mark 13:29 ("When you see these things taking place, you know that he is near, at the very gates"). Additional support may be found in other statements of the nearness of Christ's return (Rev. 1:3; 22:10) and the cry of the early church, "Come Lord!" (*Maranatha!*, 1 Cor. 16:22; cf. Rev. 22:20). If this is right, Paul encouraged the Philippians that in the midst of every situation, they could rejoice in the Lord, exhibit a humble, gracious spirit, and be anxious for nothing because Christ was coming quickly. In the overall scheme of the history of salvation, we are living in the era in which Jesus's return will occur soon. Reumann writes that Paul "undergirds ethics with eschatology" (2008, 635; cf. Cousar, 2009, 85).

(3) A third possibility is that both ideas are present. Bockmuehl states that each idea (temporal and spatial nearness) implies the other, so it is theologically pointless to choose between the two (1998, 246). Martin and Hawthorne suggest that Paul may have chosen the word "near" because of its ambiguity, and that both ideas are present (2004, 245). While we agree that both ideas are true and relevant, view (2) more likely captures Paul's meaning.

The statement, "The Lord is near," might have been especially relevant to believers in Philippi, a Roman *colonia*, where the emperor cult was prominent and the Roman emperor was seen to be the benefactor of all, providing peace and special privileges to the city. Paul's point would be that they were to find joy, comfort, and peace in their relationship with the Lord Jesus, who is returning soon, rather than the beneficence of the emperor.

THEOLOGICAL FOCUS

The exegetical idea (the Philippians were to live together in unity, being deeply satisfied with the Lord in every circumstance, exhibiting a humble, gracious spirit to all people) leads to this theological focus: Believers are to live together in unity, being deeply satisfied with the Lord in every circumstance, exhibiting a humble, gracious spirit to all people.

Unity had been a prominent theme already in the letter (1:27, 2:2–5; 3:15), and Paul now gave specific directions to the two women, and to an unnamed helper, to get an existing dispute resolved. The theological basis for unity among believers is their common existence in and loyalty to Jesus. Their names are found in God's "book of life" and they are citizens together in God's kingdom.

Practical unity in the church comes by "being of the same mind"—by exhibiting the same humble, self-sacrificing, gracious spirit, and by viewing the Christian life in the same way (according to Paul's description of it in chapters 2–3). This shows the foundational importance of right thinking and a right mindset among believers who are to dwell together in unity. To be of the same mind goes far deeper than merely trying to be friends or to "get along." It consists of believers intentionally cultivating unity in outlook, attitudes, and behavior. This does not mean everyone has the same gifts, aptitudes, areas of interests, or approaches. Unity can thrive in diversity. It takes different parts of a body to make a whole. But within diversity, unity is achieved through believers looking out for the interests of others and humbling themselves, exhibiting the same mindset that was in Christ (2:3–8).

Paul's summary exhortation in 4:5, "Let your humble, gracious spirit be evident to all," while able to stand alone, and not grammatically linked to his admonitions to Euodia and Syntyche, provided a key to their ability to be of the same mind and live in unity. As Lightfoot noted, it is "the opposite to a spirit of contention and self-seeking" (1953, 160). Unity is achieved when believers exhibit a forbearing spirit, when they show leniency and understanding, when they are humble and gracious toward one another, when they extend to others the benefit of the doubt and don't insist on their own rights.

PREACHING AND TEACHING STRATEGIES

Exegetical and Theological Synthesis

In Philippians 4:2–5, Paul addressed a clear disagreement between two notable women in the Philippian church. That Euodia and Synthyche are important women is implied not only by Paul's naming them, but also the designation he applied: "coworkers" who "contended side by side" with him to proclaim Jesus (4:3). Furthermore, the intensity of their disagreement came across in the need for a mediator (an unnamed companion). Finally, that Paul pled with both women by repeating the urgent verb, suggested both had contributed to discord. What remains obscure is the actual content of their conflict, which is often the fate of interpersonal debates: inevitably ideological differences devolve into stubborn, self-righteous friction.

In this brief passage, Paul qualified his exhortations with several references to their partnership in Jesus's mission. They were to agree "in the Lord." They had contended "for the gospel." Their names were written in "the book of life." Their happiness was rooted and found "in the Lord" who "is near." Paul issued these Christ-centered reminders as more than a literary gloss. They are uncontested, theological truths, assuring followers of Jesus their core beliefs are more important than their personal disagreements. Whether the women at Philippi fought over a personal offense or philosophical difference matters less than their meekly moving toward unity for the sake of their gospel witness.

Sadly, the church has a poor record for harmonizing. Divisions and denominational lines testify to the unwillingness of Jesus's followers to knock down their walls and work together. Even in the early church, theological disagreements and philosophical divides appeared. We need to look no further than Paul and Barnabas's split over John Mark (Acts 15:39). More recently churches have battled over music styles, building campaigns, sensitivity toward seekers, Bible translations, and divergent understandings of salvation. Ironically, having our names listed side by side in the book of life does not always provide enough motivation to work side by side in this life.

Preaching Idea

Resolve disagreements before they wreak havoc on harmony and happiness.

Contemporary Connections

What does it mean?

What does it mean to resolve disagreements before they wreak havoc on harmony and happiness? Whose responsibility is it is begin resolving these disagreements: individuals or leaders in the church? Aren't some differences of opinion beneficial for the body of Christ? From the outset, it is critical to note the Spirit did not give birth to a uniform church. Within the body of Christ, individuals play diverse roles, reflect diverse gifts, and express diverse convictions. This diversity is a gift as long as a spirit of gentleness and self-sacrifice undergirds God's people. In fact, diversity often expands our reach and sharpens our understanding of grace.

But followers of Jesus cannot shake off the residue of the old nature. Nor can we erase our personal backgrounds, idiosyncrasies, and perspectives. Thus we do not always see eye to eye with other believers. When we elevate our personal convictions and preferences over others'—driven by ego, insecurity, and stubbornness—our differences may become disagreeable. Left unresolved, interpersonal conflict disrupts harmony and happiness in the church.

In Jesus's teaching in Matthew 18, he envisioned resolution beginning with a conversation between the offended party and his offender. If resolved, the case is closed. If the offense persists, a second and third witness are added to the conversation. Spiritual leaders join the discussion, if necessary. Paul, however, jumped straight to enlisting a moderator and informing the church concerning the disagreement between his feuding, female ministry partners. Perhaps conflict resolution doesn't fit a one-size-fits-all process.

Is it true?

Is it true we should resolve our disagreements? Don't some short-term disagreements lead to long-term harmony and happiness? Are harmony and happiness legitimate aims for believers? God is not opposed to harmony and happiness. His version of harmony and happiness may not align with the Western ideals of self-esteem and pain-free living. He does, however, want unity, maturity, and abounding joy for his people. A less benevolent portrait of God does not do him justice. Moreover, he knows how strained relationships rob us of joy but strong relationships delight us.

Heresy is worth fighting over; however, traditions and differences in ministry philosophy and practice should not divide us. Unfortunately, it is far too easy to brand someone a heretic because they come to the Bible with different experiences, hermeneutics, or theological blinders. Too many earnest followers of Jesus have suffered slander from other believers because they did not agree to disagree on tertiary issues.

We would be wise to note the difference between dogma, doctrine, and tradition. Dogma comprises the core beliefs about the triune God, Jesus being fully God and fully man, salvation by grace, authority of Scripture, and mission of God's people. Dogma deserves a fight. Doctrine unpacks these ideas further, considering the dynamics of creation, mechanics of salvation, extent of our sin nature, and postmortem experience of humanity. Doctrine deserves hearty debate, but probably not the cries of heresy it has so often produced in church history. Tradition, while rooted in doctrine and tied to dogma, is a timely interpretation and expression of Scripture. Followers of Jesus should learn how to resolve disagreements about carpet color, music styles, communion juice, and children's ministry before it wreaks havoc on harmony and happiness in their shared ministry.

Now what?

How do we identify which disagreements need immediately resolved? What practical steps and inner spirit must we bring to conflict resolution to create the best possible outcome? We have all experienced disagreements that combined interlocking issues. One problem leads to another. One offense sparks another. The longer the dissonance remains the more it can become complicated and confusing. One of the greatest challenges in conflict resolution is focusing on the heart of the disagreement. We must work hard at narrowing our focus to the core problem. And we must maintain a humble spirit, knowing we have contributed to the discord.

Paul's double-plea, inviting both women into the resolution process, gives us a meaningful starting point. Conflict cannot resolve without both parties agreeing to participate. And all resolution must begin with an invitation. Since these two women remained in a stalemate, Paul issues the invitation from the outside. Because he is both an authority figure and invested in their well-being, he can take this step. We are wise to recognize that not every interpersonal conflict is our business. But the more relational authority and corporate investment we have in the conflict, the readier we must be to intervene.

Not only does resolving disagreements require us to act meekly, focus on the issue, take responsibility, and accept outside help, but we must also keep in mind the bigger picture. Resolving differences reminds people of a better past and brighter future. "You used to contend side by side with me for the gospel," Paul reminded them. "Now you're just being contentious. Resolve your differences and return to happier days." Our present disagreements pale in comparison to our former joys and future glory.

Creativity in Presentation

Consider illustrating the need for conflict resolution in a couple different ways. First, place two chairs on the stage, turned away from one another. Each chair symbolizes a person. To lighten the mood, set a stuffed animal or doll in either seat. Call chair one Euodia's chair; chair two Syntyche's chair. During the course of the sermon, turn the chairs inward to signify their willingness to resolve the conflict. As you approach the application, reset the chairs to face outward and take a seat. Ask the congregation: *Who's in chair two for you? Whom do you need to turn toward?*

Second, boxing gloves might prove effective in illustrating the idea of conflict (although good luck turning pages in your Bible!). Punctuate each reference to unresolved tensions by hitting your fists together. "Taking off the gloves" becomes a powerful metaphor of ending the fight.

A few examples from church history may show disagreements at different levels, whether hammering out dogma of Jesus's deity (Arius vs. Athanasius), doctrine of tongues (modern rise of Pentecostalism), or tradition over use of icons during the Byzantine Empire. Some fights preserved the purity of the church through councils and creeds; other battles led to bloodshed and excommunication. The Charis Fellowship, with whom I (Tim) associate, has a sad string of uncongenial divisions. My own church suffered a split a few decades before I arrived. But in recent years, my church (and many others in my fellowship) has built partnerships across denominational lines. We recognize we are better when we link arms. We are more than the sum of our differences. Each church and denomination has its stock of similar stories.

In his book *The Emotionally Healthy Leader*, Scazzero (2015, 220) writes about a tool he calls the "ladder of integrity." It walks an individual through ten prompts to clear the air when disharmony lingers. While Scazzero is reluctant to call his ladder a conflict resolution tool, it certainly helps someone articulate the tensions she feels with another. Scazzero's book records an example of the "ladder of integrity"; or you can find a filmed version of it on YouTube. Of course, any personal stories of conflict resolution resulting in harmony and happiness—whether at the workplace, in marriage, on a sports team, or elsewhere—will be relevant.

Ultimately, the point you want to emphasize is this: Believers are to live together in unity, being deeply satisfied with the Lord in every circumstance, exhibiting a humble, gracious spirit to all people. We should resolve disagreements before they wreak havoc on harmony and happiness.

- Contend for the gospel, not against each other, since we're in ministry together (4:3–4).

- Contend for happiness and harmonious witness, since others are watching (4:5).

DISCUSSION QUESTIONS

1. What does "be of the same mind" (NIV, NRSV, KJV, NKJV) or "agree" (ESV, CSB) in 4:2 mean? What does this consist of and how does it promote unity in the church?

2. How does unity among friends, co-workers, and church members promote joy? How does the lack of unity hinder joy? Give personal examples.

3. What are some healthy ways to manage interpersonal conflict?

4. What are lingering conflicts you have seen wreak havoc at home, work, or church?

5. How might a mediator help manage conflict with another?

6. Who is someone in whom you have witnessed a "gentle spirit"? How does this trait promote unity and joy?

7. What does the statement, "The Lord is near" mean? How does it promote joy and a gracious, gentle spirit?

Philippians 4:6–9

EXEGETICAL IDEA
Instead of worrying, the Philippians were to lay out their concerns before God in prayer and to focus on godly virtues, following Paul's sacrificial, Christlike lifestyle, so that they may experience the peace God gives.

THEOLOGICAL FOCUS
A lifestyle of laying out one's concerns before God in prayer, thinking about godly virtues, and following a sacrificial, Christlike lifestyle leads to experiencing God's peace.

PREACHING IDEA
Keep God ever on your mind to calm your restless heart.

PREACHING POINTERS
Having dealt with interpersonal conflict, Paul transitioned to the life of the mind. His awareness of the Lord's nearness serves as a hinge. Paul's original readers had many reasons for anxiety: the apostle's plight, Epaphroditus's health, opposition, suffering, and misguided teaching all threatened them. Until Jesus returned, they were sure to feel tensions as citizens of heaven among Roman enthusiasts. Paul wrote to assure them that a greater peace than Caesar's was available. However, to feel Christ's peace, they would have to fix their minds on God.

Reasons for unrest abound today. Marketers prey on the fear of being left out. Media fuels the fear of disease, crime, and political scandal. Medical talk and research makes people instantly squeemish (just ask people how they feel when searching their symptoms on WebMD!). And followers of Jesus live in a pluralistic society where religious truth claims come across as oppressive. Cries of intolerance and accusations of hate plague the Western church; persecution has pushed the church underground in many other areas. In such a climate, our anxieties take on a life of their own, filling our minds with soul-squelching chatter. This passage implores followers of Jesus to silence the clamor of restless thoughts by keeping our minds ever on God.

EXPERIENCING THE PEACE OF GOD (4:6–9)

LITERARY STRUCTURE AND THEMES (4:6–9)

Continuing his closing exhortations, Paul exhorted the Philippians to be anxious about nothing (4:6a). Rather, they were to make their requests known to God through prayer with thanksgiving (4:6b). The result would be that the peace of God would guard their hearts and minds in Christ (4:7). "Finally" signaled the last closing exhortation. Paul begins with a list of six godly virtues, each highlighted by "whatever," and then listed two qualifying criteria in "if" clauses. He exhorted them to give thought to these things (4:8). Then, in a parallel construction, he exhorted them to do the things they had learned and received and heard and seen in him (4:9a). The result would be that the God of peace would be with them (4:9b).

Prayer, Not Worry (4:6–7)
Virtuous Thought and Practice (4:8–9)

EXPOSITION (4:6–9)

Paul continued his final exhortations, focusing on the thought-life of the Philippians. He focused on how they could experience God's peace (4:7, 9). The exhortation was twofold. First, he exhorted them to be anxious for nothing, but to pray with thanksgiving in everything (4:6). Second, he exhorted them to focus on godly virtues and to put into practice what they have learned from him (4:8–9a). The phrases "peace of God" and "God of peace" verbally unite these two exhortations, which focus on attaining both inner peace of mind (freedom from anxiety) and relational peace within the community (freedom from conflict).

Prayer, Not Worry (4:6–7)

The Philippians were not to worry about any circumstance or issue, but rather lay out their concerns before God in prayer so that as a result, they may experience the peace he gives—inner peace and peace in relationships.

> *4:6.* Γνωριζέσθω is rendered "let be made known" (ESV, NRSV, CSB, NASB, KJV, NKJV) or "present" (NIV).

4:6. Having just stated that the Lord is near (4:5), Paul now exhorted believers to be anxious about nothing. If the Lord is near, there is no need for anxiety. The verb rendered "be anxious" (μεριμνᾶτε) often indicates a positive concern (2:20), but here it is clearly negative indicating apprehensiveness or "being unduly concerned" about something (BDAG s.v. "μεριμνάω" 1, 632). The command echoes the tradition of Jesus's words in Matthew 6:25–34; 10:19. Anxiety indicates a lack of trust in God's sovereign care. Believers must not allow proper concern and diligence about their lives to degenerate into anxious thoughts. They are free from concern *as anxiety* (*TDNT* 4:591). The comprehensive term "nothing" (μηδέν) covers every possible detail or circumstance in life (Fee, 1995, 408–9).

For contrast (ἀλλά), Paul's corresponding positive exhortation provided the alternative to anxiety and was equally comprehensive. "Everything" (παντί) is the opposite of the previous "nothing." "In everything" (ἐν παντί) means in every circumstance or situation (O'Brien, 1991, 492). Worry about nothing; pray about everything. Paul used two synonymous terms for prayer: "prayer" (προσευχῇ), and "petition" (δεήσει). We should not make fine distinctions between them (Martin and Hawthorne, 2004, 245–46). Both express how believers let their requests be made known to God—by means of prayer and petition (datives of means). The third term, "requests" (αἰτήματα), is narrower, denoting the specific items asked for (BDAG s.v. "αἴτημα," p. 30; *TDNT* 1:193; *NIDNTTE* 1:185–89). Note that the third term is "requests," not "demands" (Thurston and Ryan, 2005, 145). Paul wanted the Philippians to talk to God about their concerns.

"Let your requests be made known [γνωριζέσθε] to God" does not suggest that God is unaware of what believers need (see Matt. 6:32). Rather, it has to do with laying out needs and troubles before the Father and casting all anxiety on him (cf. 1 Peter 5:7) (O'Brien, 1995, 493). In humility, believers are to express their complete dependence upon and trust in God. When believers pray, they orient their lives toward God (Hansen, 2009, 291). In this regard, it is important to understand that prayer is not designed to bring God's will into alignment with your will. Instead, through prayer, you bring your heart, mind, and will into alignment with his, as Jesus taught, "Your kingdom come; your will be done" (Matt. 6:10), and as he exemplified in Gethsemane, "Nevertheless, not my will but your will" (Matt. 26:39).

To accompany prayer and petition, Paul added "with thanksgiving" (εὐχαριστίας, *TDNT* 9: 407–15; *NIDNTTE* 2:334–35)." "Thanksgiving" can refer both to the attitude of thankfulness and to the expression of thanks (BDAG s.v. "εὐχαριστία" 1 and 2, p. 416). Paul certainly meant that when they prayed, the Philippians should pray with a grateful attitude. He probably also meant they should verbalize thanks to God. Thanksgiving should accompany all prayers, petitions, and requests (cf. 1 Thess. 5:18). By being thankful believers acknowledge God's goodness and provision even as they pour out their needs and concerns to him. Without thanksgiving, prayer can degenerate into complaining (Hansen, 2009, 291) or to

merely presenting God with a list of demands. With thanksgiving, prayer becomes a means of appreciating, honoring, and glorifying God. Acknowledging his past and present blessings also provides confidence for future blessings. Earlier in the letter, Paul modeled prayer with thanksgiving in his report of his prayers for the Philippians (1:3).

Thanksgiving: In the Old Testament, thanksgiving is a basic expression of worship—acknowledging God's goodness and covenant faithfulness toward his people: "Give thanks to the Lord for he is good; for his steadfast love endures forever" (Ps. 118:1). In the New Testament also, thanksgiving is the proper response when God's people recognize his faithful, active involvement in their lives. It assures that believers have the proper perspective and are thinking rightly about God as their heavenly Father and Provider. For the ungodly, lack of thanksgiving is the first step toward idolatry, leading to foolishness and darkened hearts (Rom. 1:21). And for believers, thanksgiving is to replace filthiness, foolish talk, and crude joking (Eph. 5:4), none of which reflect a thankful heart.

4:7. Ἐν Χριστῷ Ἰησοῦ is rendered "in Christ Jesus" (NIV, ESV, NRSV, CSB, NLT, NASB) or "through Christ Jesus" (KJV, NKJV).

4:7. Paul promised the Philippians a specific provision from God that would follow when they met the condition of offering prayer with thanksgiving. "And" (καί) introduces the result (BDAG s.v. "καί" 1bζ, p. 495). Instead of anxiety, they would experience the "peace of God." This phrase occurs only here in the New Testament (cf. Col. 3:15, "peace of Christ"). Paul presents "peace" (εἰρήνης) as a power from God that guards believers' hearts and minds (BDAG s.v. "εἰρήνη" 2b, 287). As elsewhere in Scripture, "peace" broadly denotes a state of well-being, wholeness, and salvation, corresponding to the Hebrew term *shalom* (*TDNT* 2:411–17;

NIDNTTE 2:111–17; *EDNT* 1:394–96). Peace from God is a fruit of the Spirit (Gal. 5:22).

"Of God" (τοῦ θεοῦ) specifies that Paul is referring to the peace that comes from God and is characteristic of God. "Of God" may denote source, "the peace that 'comes from' God" (Hellerman, 2015, 240), or producer, "the peace produced by God" (*GGBB*, 106), or a characteristic, "the peace that is true of God" (O'Brien, 1991, 496). These are not mutually exclusive. The peace that God provides believers is "the calm serenity that characterizes God's very nature" (Martin and Hawthorne, 2004, 246). God is never anxious, but is serene and tranquil. He exists in perfect harmony. He is a God of well-being and wholeness. He is the "God of peace" (v. 9). God willingly shares this peace that is part of his own character with believers as they pour out their hearts to him in dependence and trust, praying with thanksgiving. The God of peace bestows the peace of God upon his children. In the context of Philippians (4:2–5), Paul is referring not just to the "inner peace" of the individual (removal of anxiety), but also to peace among relationships—peace within the church.

The peace God provides surpasses any other "peace." The Philippians would have been accustomed to thinking of the peace that the Roman emperor provided—*pax Romana* (peace of Rome). The Roman external peace might be able to keep them free from war and conquest for a time, but God's peace, part of his very nature, penetrates to the core of their hearts and minds, and is eternal.

Paul stated that this peace "surpasses all understanding" (ὑπερέχουσα), meaning, "to surpass in quality or value" (BDAG s.v. "ὑπερέχω" 3, p. 1033). He previously used the verb (ὑπερέχουσα) in 2:3 and 3:8. Here he stated that God's peace goes beyond human understanding. "Understanding" (νοῦν) refers to "the faculty of intellectual perception" (BDAG s.v. "νοῦς" 1b, p. 680). God's peace goes beyond the power of the human mind to comprehend it (Bockmuehl, 1998, 248). Further, God's peace is more effective and produces better results than any human thought, insight, or planning for alleviating anxious thoughts (Lightfoot, 1953, 161). It is fully effective.

Paul stated that the peace of God "will guard [φρουρήσει] your hearts and your minds." The idea of "guard" is that of providing security or protection (BDAG s.v. "φρουρέω" 3, p. 1066). This suggests the image of a military outpost guarding an ancient city (2 Cor. 11:32). The Philippians would have been familiar with the detachment of soldiers in their city that guarded the Roman *pax* (peace). In our day, one might think of a strong and effective peacekeeping force sent to a volatile place in the world. With this image, we are to think of God's peace enveloping and securing our hearts and minds, keeping us free from anxiety, fear, and distress. Varner notes that God's peace guards from the inside, rather than the outside (2016, 96).

In the New Testament, the "heart" (καρδία) often denotes the center of one's whole inner life—the center of emotions, desires, passions, and disposition; the seat of understanding, reflection and moral decisions; and the seat of will and resolve (BDAG s.v. "καρδία" 1bη, p. 509; *TDNT* 3:611–12). But since it is paired with "mind" in this context, "heart" is narrower, denoting the emotions (Martin and Hawthorne, 2004, 247), or perhaps the emotions and will (O'Brien, 1991, 498).

"Minds" (νοήματα) can refer either to the "mind" itself (the faculty of processing thought) or to the "thoughts" produced (that which one has in mind as a result of intellectual process) (BDAB s.v. "νόημα" 1 and 2, p. 675). Paul meant something like this: the peace of God will guard both your heart (with its emotions) and your mind (with its thoughts) (Martin and Hawthorne, 2004, 247). This covers the whole inner life of the believer.

God's peace guards believers' inner lives "in Christ Jesus." Because believers have been incorporated into (joined to, united with) Christ through faith, their hearts and minds will be safely guarded in that realm and on that basis. "Through Christ Jesus" (KJV, NKJV), which suggests that Jesus is the means by which God guards believers is true, but it fails to capture the crucial idea of incorporation into Christ—that believers reside in and under Christ as a believing community. Paul's promise was that the very peace of God himself would guard their emotions and thoughts as they resided "in Christ."

Note what Paul promised and what he did not promise. He promised that when believers pray with thanksgiving, God's peace will guard their hearts and minds. They will have peace instead of anxiety. He did not promise that when they pray with thanksgiving, their requests will be answered exactly as they desire. God's peace is not dependent on whether believers receive a "yes" to their requests as asked. It is not dependent on whether their outward circumstances change the way they want them to. It is solely dependent on God granting his peace to guard their hearts and minds.

Virtuous Thought and Practice (4:8–9)

The Philippians were to focus their minds on godly virtues, and to follow Paul in pursuing the self-sacrificing, Christlike life he had taught them, so that as a result, God's peaceful presence would be with them.

4:8. Σεμνά is rendered "noble" (NIV, NKJV), "honorable" (ESV, NRSV, CSB, NLT, NASB), or "honest" (KJV). Δίκαια is rendered "right" (NIV, NLT, NASB) or "just" (ESV, NRSV, CSB, KJV, NKJV). Προσφιλῆ is rendered "lovely" (NIV, ESV, CSB, NLT, NASB, KJV, NKJV) or "pleasing" (NRSV). Εὔφημα is rendered "admirable" (NIV, NLT), "commendable" (ESV, NRSV, CSB), or "of good report" (KJV, NKJV, cf. NASB). Ἀρετὴ is rendered "excellent/excellence" (NIV, ESV, NRSV, NLT, NASB), "moral excellence" (CSB), or "virtue" (KJV, NKJV). Λογίζεσθε is rendered "think about/on" (NIV, ESV, NRSV, NLT, KJV), "dwell on" (CSB, NASB), or "meditate on" (NKJV).

4:8. The word rendered "finally" (τὸ λοιπόν) showed that Paul was now going to wrap up his concluding exhortations (4:1–9) before he proceeded to acknowledge their gift (Martin and Hawthorne, 2004, 248). As before (1:12, 14; 3:1, 13, 17; 4:1), the masculine term "brothers" denotes all of the believers at Philippi ("brothers and sisters"). Philippians 4:8–9 logically connects to 4:6–7. When believers are prone to be anxious, besides talking it over with God, they should also focus on what is good. They must learn to discipline their thoughts and think correctly. Structurally, Paul constructed an eloquent exhortation consisting of two parallel parts—right thinking (4:8) and right doing (4:9).

Paul began with a list of six adjectives describing godly virtues. Before each, the indefinite "whatever" (ὅσα) occurs. This highlights each quality individually, making each one emphatic. It also emphasizes that there are no restrictions, for example, as to the source of a virtue. "Whatever" believers found in the world that measured up to that quality according to the standard of the life and teaching of Jesus, they were to give careful thought to it.

First, they were to consider "whatever is true" (ἀληθῆ). Paul was referring broadly to all truth, whatever its source. "True" refers to that which is in accordance with fact (BDAG s.v. "αληθής" 2, p. 43). It is the opposite of error and falsehood. All truth is God's truth, and truth may come from various sources (e.g., science, history, philosophy). God's truth revealed in Christ Jesus is the ultimate arbiter of what is true ("truth is in Jesus," Eph. 4:21) (*DPL*, 954) and is the greatest, life-altering, truth.

Second, "whatever is noble" (σεμνά) describes that which evokes special respect, that which is honorable, worthy, venerable, holy, and above reproach (BDAG s.v. "σεμνός" bα, p. 919). Paul expected believers to consider things that evoked special respect. In the Pastoral Epistles, Paul used this term to describe deacons (1 Tim. 3:8), women (1 Tim. 3:11), and older men (Titus 2:2) who were dignified, noble, and worthy of respect.

Third, they were to consider "whatever is upright" (δίκαια). Paul was using "upright" in the sense of whatever conforms to the life and teaching of Jesus. In the Greco-Roman world an "upright" person could refer to "one who upholds the customs and norms of behavior, including public service, that make for a well-ordered, civilized society" (BDAG s.v. "δίκαιος" 1, p. 246). But for Paul, Jesus, rather than culture, was the standard of what was upright (see the example in 2:5–8).

Fourth, "whatever is pure" (ἁγνά) referred in the broadest sense to all things that can be morally pure—thoughts, motives, words, and actions (BDAG s.v. "ἁγνός" b, p. 13). Earlier in this letter (1:17) Paul spoke of the motives of certain gospel preachers, who preach "impurely" (the related adverb). But his readers were to dwell on what is pure, not impure.

Fifth, they were to consider "whatever is pleasing" (προσφιλῆ), a term unique to Paul. This refers to that which causes pleasure or delight for others, to what people are favorably disposed toward, what they find lovely or beautiful, attractive or agreeable (BDAG s.v. "προσφιλής," p. 886). For Paul, whether something was pleasing or not depended on whether it conformed to the life and teaching of Jesus.

Sixth, "whatever is winsome" (εὔφημα), another term unique to Paul, most likely refers to speech that is winsome, attractive, or "well-sounding." It speaks of things that will win people and avoid giving offense (Lightfoot, 1953, 161–62; cf. BDAG s.v. "εὔφημος," p. 414; *EDNT* 2:86). This is the Greek word from which we get the English "euphemism."

Having listed six adjectives, each with the all-inclusive "whatever," Paul restricted what he was talking about with two conditional "if" (εἴ) clauses. These two clauses did not merely summarize the preceding six adjectives as umbrella terms, but rather qualified them (Fee, 1995, 416, n. 13). Whatever fell under one of the six virtues must also meet these two criteria. Perhaps Paul added these two further qualifications because some of the six virtues were ambivalent, and could be determined by one's culture (Fee, 1995, 415–16; Bockmuehl, 1998, 251). Specifically, when believers discover from their culture "whatever is true, noble, and so on," if what they find qualifies as "moral excellence" and "worthy of praise" from a Christian point of view, then they should give careful thought to these things. These two qualifications serve as a reminder to believers that they must evaluate what their culture considers to be "true, noble, upright, pure, pleasing, and winsome" according to biblical criteria.

The first qualification, "moral excellence" or "virtue" (αρετή) occurred only here in Paul's letters but was a popular term among the Greeks used to denote the highest good within man (*TDNT* 1:457–61; *NIDNTTE* 1:388–91). Peter used it of God's own moral excellence and puts it first in his list of virtues to be added to believers' faith (2 Peter 1:3, 5). Likewise, Paul had in mind not merely the Greek idea of "virtue," but rather what was distinctively virtuous for the believer who followed Jesus. Particularly for the Philippians, Paul commended a humble, self-sacrificial lifestyle modeled on Jesus to be morally excellent (2:5–8).

The second qualification, "worthy of praise" (ἔπαινος), refers to being worthy of approval or recognition (BDAG s.v. "ἔπαινος" 2, p. 357). Paul used the word to denote both human praise of God (Phil. 1:11; Eph. 1:6, 12, 14) and divine praise of humans (Rom. 2:29; 1 Cor. 4:5). In this context, where it is parallel to the previous "moral excellence," Paul likely had in mind to what was praiseworthy among humans toward one another (cf. Rom. 13:3; 2 Cor. 8:18) (O'Brien, 1991, 507). Especially, Paul would find humble sacrificial service for others (2:5–8) to be worthy of praise. See, for example, his praise of Timothy and Epaphroditus (2:19–30).

Paul exhorted the Philippians to "give careful thought to" (λογίζεσθε) whatever exhibited these six virtues as qualified by the two criteria. They were to let their "minds dwell" on these matters (BDAG s.v. "λογίζομαι" 2, p. 597). Culture may urge people to chase after selfish pleasure, money, power, fame, and so on. Paul exhorted believers to focus on what is truly good and virtuous from God's perspective—humility, self-denial, and self-sacrifice for the sake of serving Christ. As the next verse will make clear, the idea is not merely to think about these virtues, but to put them into practice—to live moral lives characterized by good character and good deeds (*TDNT* 4:289; Martin and Hawthorne, 2004, 250). Christians in a non-Christian culture are not to accept the values of the culture uncritically, nor are they to reject the values of the culture with a blanket condemnation. They are to critically evaluate the highest and best of what their culture offers on the basis of a Christ-centered vision of life, then take the good, and leave the bad.

> *4:9.* Πράσσετε is rendered "practice" (ESV, NASB), "put into practice" (NIV), "keep putting into practice" (NLT), "do" (CSB, KJV, NKJV), or "keep on doing" (NRSV).

4:9. Paul moved beyond the consideration of virtue to putting it into practice. He did not leave the Philippians on their own to figure out what was virtuous. He had already taught them about the virtuous Christian life. He had extolled Christ's humility and selfless service on behalf of others. And he presented himself as a model to imitate. Again using an eloquent structure, Paul listed four ways in which they had received moral instruction from him, either verbally or by example. By adding 4:9 to 4:8, Paul qualified what he had just said. They were to give careful thought to the things that were virtuous in light of what Paul had already taught them and modeled for them. His teaching and example showed them what to practice.

The four ways Paul had given them instruction are divided into two pairs: (1) learned and received; and (2) heard and seen. "What you have learned [ἐμάθετε] and received [παρελάβετε]" likely refers to what Paul verbally taught them about following Jesus during his previous visits, for he paired them with "seen and heard."

"What you have heard [ἠκούσατε] and seen [εἴδετε]" refers to what they previously witnessed about Christian character and behavior from Paul's example, especially when he was with them. Paul specified that he was talking about what you have seen "in me" (ἐν ἐμοί). He knew that values are not just taught; they are caught. He was willing for his own life to be a role model for the Philippians. Earlier he encouraged them to be imitators of him (3:17; cf. 1 Cor. 11:1).

Paul exhorted the Philippians to "practice these things." "These things" (ταῦτα) refers back to "what you have learned and received and heard and seen in me." They were to put into action what they had learned from Paul, either through his instruction or example. "Put into practice," "do," or "accomplish" (BDAG s.v. "πράσσω" 1a, p. 860a) suggested that they were to demonstrate these virtues in their lives.

As in 4:7, Paul promised the Philippians a specific result if they met the condition of 4:8–9a. "And" (καί) introduces a result (BDAG s.v. "καί" 1bζ, p. 495): "The God of peace will be with you." Instead of the "peace of God" (4:7), he promised that the "God of peace" would himself be with them. The "God of peace" means "the God who is characterized by peace and who gives peace" (Martin and Hawthorne, 2004, 254), or "the God who produces peace" (*GGBB*, 106–7). The phrases "peace of God" and "God of peace" are related, the latter denoting producer/source/cause (God), the former product/effect (peace). The peace of God comes through the presence of the God of peace.

"Will be with you" (ἔσται μεθ᾽ ὑμῶν) refers to God's immediate presence through the indwelling Holy Spirit, who produces peace (Rom. 15:13; Gal. 5:22) (Fee, 1995, 420–21). As believers strive to cultivate Christian virtues, exemplified by Paul's instruction and example, the God who himself is peaceful and who gives peace to his people promises to be with them. His presence brings tranquility and serenity in the hearts and minds of believers, as well as harmony among believers' relationships in the church. Here is the solution for the disunity and anxiety that exist among God's people (cf. 4:2–7).

THEOLOGICAL FOCUS

The exegetical idea (instead of worrying, the Philippians were to lay out their concerns before God in prayer and to focus on godly virtues, following Paul's sacrificial, Christlike lifestyle, so that so that they may experience the peace God gives) leads to this theological focus: A lifestyle of laying out one's concerns before God in prayer, thinking about godly virtues, and following a sacrificial, Christlike lifestyle leads to experiencing God's peace.

This section is about how to experience the peace of God in your life. The peace of God is comprehensive, including both inner peace (freedom from anxiety) and relational peace within the Christian community (freedom from conflict). It is the peace that comes with salvation in Christ and the indwelling presence of the Holy Spirit. Deriving from the Old Testament concept of *shalom*, this peace is a sense of well-being—a quiet and tranquil life lived under God's spiritual prosperity and blessing. It comes from the very peace God himself enjoys.

The two exhortations in this section indicate the two responsibilities believers must fulfill in order to experience peace from God. First, they are not to worry about anything, but rather, in every circumstance, talk it over with God. Adding thanksgiving keeps believers from losing perspective of all the good things God provides. Second, they are to focus their minds on virtuous qualities consistent with a life of following Jesus, and put into practice a sacrificial, Christlike lifestyle modeled by Paul. Meeting these two conditions will result in experiencing the peace that God provides.

PREACHING AND TEACHING STRATEGIES

Exegetical and Theological Synthesis

Paul clearly appealed to the life of the mind as a means to God-given peace. In the context of Philippi, this "surpassing" peace goes deeper the socio-political *Pax Romana* enjoyed by Roman citizens. God's peace reaches the heart, which is the center for human knowing, being, and doing. Talking to God (i.e., prayer) and remaining thankful opens the door to this peace. At the beginning of the letter, Paul referenced his gratitude for the Philippians (1:3) and spelled out his prayer for their growth in character (vv. 9–11). Here he called the Philippians to practice prayer and gratitude for themselves.

Notice also, Paul did not divorce thinking from doing. Careful thought is not a sterile, academic exercise but a pathway to virtue. Paul crafted a list of eight, affirming terms worthy of meditation. Pondering leads to practicing, and Paul presented himself as a model (4:9). It is worth repeating that Paul did not deem himself perfect (3:12), but recognized spiritual growth comes out of imitating others (v. 17). A second mention of God-given peace bookends the passage (4:9), reiterating God's nearness and provision in the life of believers.

But as constant as the "fear not" refrain sounds throughout Scripture, God's people suffer fear, anxiety, and unrest due to countless cares. Whether we are like Joshua, who stands at the edge of the Jordan feeling nervous about new responsibilities (1:8), or like Martha, who complains she has too much to do on her own (Luke 10:41), we must learn to cast our cares on our caring God (1 Peter 5:7). Anxiety robs us of peace, filling our minds with problems and frustrations, rather than God-given peace. Throughout Philippians, Paul has affirmed God's sovereignty, Jesus's second coming, and the gospel's ongoing work. Dwelling on thoughts that are true, noble, upright, pure, pleasing, and winsome—rather than rising gas prices, sinking stocks, hepatitis outbreaks, terrorist attacks, and anti-Christian legislation—will make God's ever-present peace feel far less elusive in our fear-mongering world.

Preaching Idea

Keep God ever on your mind to calm your restless heart.

Contemporary Connections

What does it mean?
Are we supposed to deny life's hardships in favor of positivity and overly simplistic God-talk? Earlier in the letter, Paul admonished against complaining and grumbling (2:14). An endless stream of negative talk dulls the witness Jesus wants from his followers. However, Scripture does not advocate for unconditional positivity. Lament psalms (e.g., 3, 51, 88, 137), judgment oracles (e.g., Isa. 5; Amos 2), and epistolary rebukes (e.g., 1 Cor. 5) each speak with a divinely inspired negative tone. Such passages do not endorse negativity, as much as reflect how life is hard (often by our own making), and we don't have to pretend to be happy about it.

On the other hand, all the troubles in life do not erase every good gift given by the heavenly Father (James 1:17). Life is filled with wonders, from the beauties of creation to the ardors of vocation to the joys of friendship to the comforts of home to the sweetness of food to the enticements of story, song, and sport. Even people without faith in God enjoy his gifts. And gratitude offsets anxiety.

Does keeping God ever on our minds simply mean living with gratitude? We don't get off that easy. Gratitude is a starting point to keeping God ever on our minds, but we should also meditate on his lovely character and powerful works. He will finish the good task he started (Phil. 1:6). He turns our trials into his triumphs

(1:12–18). He exalted Jesus who humbled himself (2:5–11). He empowers us to work out our salvation and shine in the world (2:13, 16). He hears our prayers, guards our hearts, and grants us peace (4:6–9).

A steady diet of these thoughts gives encouragement to our hearts. Our trials and cares tend to shrink our focus and increase our heart rate. Keeping God in mind gives us a bigger perspective, awakening our memory to God's past faithfulness, stirring our anticipation of his future deliverance. A calm heart clings to the assurance, even when emotion tries to mislead us.

Is it true?
Is a restless heart a real problem? Is anxiety a sin behavior we can control or a chemical imbalance we should manage? Biblical authors predated the modern obsession with mental health. While Scripture captures the whole range of emotions (e.g., Jonah's rage, Jesus's weeping, David's delight) and hints of disorder (e.g., Elijah's suicidal thoughts, 1 Kings 19:5; Heman's depressive rant, Ps. 88), they do not aim to give clinical advice. In other words, they describe, not diagnose, emotional dysfunction.

Concerning anxiety, it is worth noting contemporary approaches treat it both as a cognitive and chemical issue. Medications help regulate overactive neurotransmitters in the brain. Counseling provides thought-exercises to reduce fear and offer a sense of control. Some Christian counselors may be opposed to medication, thinking it masks a deeper problem related to personal sin. However, there is enough good science to back wise use of medication, as well as respect for the fall's effects on our brain and bodies. When anxiety is treated purely as a sin-response, without any nod to the unconscious or chemical reactions, it may only increase the fear, defeat, and guilt that anxious people already feel.

And yet, medication alone does not expose the issue at the heart of anxiety: control. Followers of Jesus should practice self-control

(Gal. 5:23; 1 Tim. 4:7–10), but understand personal control has its limits. More importantly, we trust our sovereign God will hold the world together, bring justice in his time, and guard our lives with watchful care. Knowing God is in control is the peace-bringing panacea for anxiety. But this truth requires more than glib recitation; prayerful, grateful, regular, honest meditation on God's control gives peace to soothe our restless hearts.

Now what?

How do we make keeping God ever on our minds a habit? As mentioned above, fighting anxiety takes a balanced approach. The more debilitating the battle, the more likely is our need for therapeutic intervention. For situational cares or come-and-go stressors, we may address the issue simply with prayerful, grateful, regular, honest meditation on God's control (Phil. 4:6, 8).

This prayerful, meditative approach goes beyond the "power of positive thinking." Theological reflection requires discipline and diligence. Happy thoughts about God do not bring immediate relief. We must avoid magical thinking. We must also avoid grasping for the gift of peace (v. 7), with no desire for its Giver (v. 9).

A good starting point for addressing anxiety is to identify the presenting fear and trace it to its root. First, take a fear about a work situation or marriage struggle or physical ailment a little deeper. Then, find the underlying concern where your control is tested and proven insufficient. Next, prayerfully and honestly admit the fear to God. Finally, affirm God's perfect character and absolute control: *He is good; he knows my needs; he holds my life together*. Make this process a practice as you reach for the God of peace.

Tracing a Fear to Its Root
1. Presenting Fear: I won't get this sermon done.
2. Digging Deeper: If I don't get this sermon done, I will look like a fool on Sunday.

If I look like a fool on Sunday, I will hear criticism from the congregation.
If the congregation criticizes me, they will realize I am not a great pastor.
If they realize I am not a great pastor, I will be exposed for the failure that I am.
3. Root Fear: I am a failure and everyone knows it.
4. Prayerful Meditation: My poor performance does not decrease God's perfect love for me.

Creativity in Presentation

To help people visualize the capacity of the brain to replace anxieties with affirming thoughts about God, consider having a large glass container filled with orange and white ping-pong balls. The white ones represent God Thoughts; orange stands for Restless Thoughts. Dump a mixture of the two into the container, leaving a little space to add a few more. Explain the process of replacing a fear with an affirmation while physically removing orange ping-pong balls. Make sure to blend general fears with specific ones to increase relevancy.

Hearing testimonials from people in the church who have battled anxious thinking has a dual effect. First, it normalizes the struggle, so those who feel alone in it know they have allies. I (Tim) have watched my wife experience more victory over anxiety the more she shared with others about it. (They have an informal collective I call the "Friends with Anxiety Group.") Second, it provides hope to those whose minds feel controlled by restless thoughts. How they keep God in mind—talking to him, telling him thanks, Scripture reminders—to calm their restless hearts provides a model for the church. Find one or two willing participants to give an interview (live or recorded) about how God is helping them overcome anxiety.

Finally, I am reminded of a sentiment I regularly use to redirect my children's negative thinking. Many a school, church, and social obligation provoke their ranting. My wife and I have canonized the phrase, "Look for the good."

We recognize negativity and stress grow like cancers, but gratitude toward God can replace it. A predisposition toward gratitude reflects a healthy, Christian mind.

The point you want to emphasize is this: A lifestyle of laying out one's concerns before God in prayer, thinking about godly virtues, and following a sacrificial, Christlike lifestyle leads to experiencing God's peace. We should keep God ever on our minds to calm our restless hearts.

- We pour out our restless hearts to experience God's calm (4:6–7).

- We fill our minds with virtuous thoughts to experience God's calm (4:8).

- We give our lives to obedient living to experience his calm (4:9).

DISCUSSION QUESTIONS

1. How do the spiritual and chemical sides of anxiety relate to one another? How should we deal with both causes?

2. Describe some experiences of God's surpassing peace.

3. How does praying to God in every situation reduce anxiety? What happens when you pray?

4. How can being thankful in your prayers reduce anxiety?

5. How is the "peace of God" different from non-Christian concepts of peace and tranquility?

6. For each of the virtues in 4:8 (whatever is true, noble, upright, pure, pleasing, winsome), give an example that meets the criteria—that is worth meditating on. If it is from contemporary culture, how does it need to be filtered through Christ and his Word?

7. Why is focusing your thoughts on positive Christian virtues (as opposed to what is negative, worldly, sinful) such an important spiritual discipline for the Christian life?

8. How is Christ an illustration of each of the virtues in 4:8?

FOR FURTHER READING

Poirier, A. 2006. *The Peacemaking Pastor: A Biblical Guide to Resolving Church Conflict.* Grand Rapids: Baker Books.

Sande, K. 2004. *The Peacemaker: A Biblical Guide to Resolving Personal Conflict.* 3rd ed. Grand Rapids: Baker Books.

Silva, M. 2014. "εἰρήνη" ("peace"). Pages 111–17 of vol. 2 in *New International Dictionary of New Testament Theology and Exegesis.* 5 vols. 2nd ed. Edited by M. Silva. Grand Rapids: Zondervan.

Welch, E. T. 2007. *Running Scared: Fear, Worry, and the Rest of God.* Greensboro, NC: New Growth Press.

PAUL'S JOY BECAUSE OF THEIR GIFT (4:10–23)

After his final exhortations (4:2–9), Paul expressed his joy at receiving the Philippians' gift sent with Epaphroditus. He provided a theological interpretation of the gift, reflecting the three-way partnership in the gospel between God, them, and himself (4:10–20). Then he closed the letter with final greetings and a prayer-wish for the Philippians (4:21–23). For preaching purposes, we will break the unit into two sections, 4:10–13 and 4:14–23.

This section of the letter (1) corresponds to 1:12–26 in that it let the Philippians know how Paul was doing while in prison (cf. Hellerman, 2015, 254); (2) shares terminology and concepts with the opening section (1:3–11) (see Peterman's list, 1997, 91–92); and (3) the closing greetings and prayer-wish balance the opening greeting and prayer-wish (1:1–2). Importantly, the introductory and concluding sections frame the letter with a focus on the themes of partnership in the gospel from the first day (1:5, 7; 4:14–15), of God's work in them for their spiritual progress (1:6, 9–11, 4:17, 19), and of glory to God (1:11; 4:20).

This last major section, Paul's Joy Because of Their Gift, (4:10–23) is broken into two preaching units: Learning to Be Content (4:10–13) and The Meaning of Christian Giving (4:14–23).

Philippians 4:10–13

EXEGETICAL IDEA
While he delighted in their material provision, Paul had learned to be satisfied in life (experiencing spiritual/emotional well-being and peace) in any circumstance (having much or little) through his relationship with Christ and the strength he provided.

THEOLOGICAL FOCUS
Spiritual/emotional well-being and peace comes through a personal relationship with Christ and the strength he provides in every life situation.

PREACHING IDEA
Satisfaction starts by learning to say: "Whatever God gives is good enough!"

PREACHING POINTERS
Thanking the Philippians for their financial support was one of Paul's key purposes for writing the letter. However, his "Thank you" went beyond a word of gratitude. The exegetical section explains how Paul reframed the discussion, turning his appreciation into a theological primer on contentment in God's supply of inner calm and external needs. His first-century audience may have overvalued their financial gift or underestimated how God provides material goods and internal strength in crisis situations. Paul's "Thank you" was not a backhanded rebuke, but another reminder of God's part in the partnership with his people who proclaim Jesus.

Contentment seems less common than entitlement in the Western world. We assume our most basic needs will be met by employers or government aid, giving little credit to God for his abundant supply. Lack of bread and milk sparks a visit to overstocked grocery stores more often than prayer for daily supply. When our old cars, clothes, and computers wear out, we rush to retailers (online or local) to acquire new goods. Whether we pay cash or finance, it is easy to remove God from the receipt. This passage reminds us that all our assets ultimately come from him, so we must find satisfaction in him, learning to say: "Whatever God gives is good enough!"

LEARNING TO BE CONTENT (4:10–13)

LITERARY STRUCTURE
AND THEMES (4:10–13)

In 4:10–13, Paul acknowledged the Philippians' gift they sent with Epaphroditus. He reported his delight that they renewed their concern (4:10a), but clarified this by affirming that their lack of recent material support was due to their lack of opportunity, not to their lack of concern (4:10b). Then he qualified his acknowledgment by stating that he did not speak from need, for he had learned to be content in all circumstances (4:11). Expanding on this contentment, Paul revealed that he had learned the secret of how to how to have a lot or a little, how to be well fed or hungry (4:12). The secret was: he could do all of this in Christ who strengthened him (4:13).

Celebrating God's Provision (4:10)
Satisfaction in Christ (4:11–13)

EXPOSITION (4:10–13)

Now that Paul had discussed the situation at Philippi and given his final exhortations, he formally acknowledged the gift that they sent him through Epaphroditus. This section of the letter is not a mere afterthought, nor is it a mere receipt for their gift. It is an acknowledgment and interpretation of their gift in theological terms that reflects their mutual partnership in the gospel as fellow servants of Christ Jesus. Paul's presupposition was that he and they were part of a three-way partnership with God in the extension of the gospel, and this determined how he and they were to view their financial support (Fee, 1995, 441, 444; Fowl, 2002, 48). God was the Patron (Provider) to whom all praise was due, the Philippians were channels of God's provision, and Paul was the recipient of God's provision through them.

An important part of Paul's acknowledgment in these verses was the teaching he provided regarding contentment. While he let the Philippians know that he rejoiced at receiving their gift, still he underscored that he had learned the secret of being content in every circumstance—whether he had a little or a lot. This was the context in which Paul expresses the well-known statement that he could do all things through Christ who gave him strength.

Celebrating God's Provision (4:10)

Paul expressed the delight he felt when he received their material provision—evidence of their concern for him—through Epaphroditus.

4:10. The aorist ἐχάρην is rendered "I rejoiced" (NIV, ESV, CSB, NASB, KJV, NKJV) or "I rejoice" (NRSV; cf. NLT, "I praise). Ὅτι is rendered "that" (NIV, ESV, NRSV, CSB, NLT, NASB, KJV, NKJV) or "because" (NET). Ἀνεθάλετε is rendered "you renewed" (NIV, CSB), "you revived" (ESV, NRSV, NASB), or "[your care] has flourished" (KJV, NKJV). Ἐφ ᾧ is rendered "for/about me" (= for/about whom) (ESV, NRSV, CSB, NLT), "wherein" (KJV), "though surely" (NKJV), or left untranslated (NIV, NASB).

4:10. Paul moved to the topic of the Philippians' gift and informed them that he "rejoiced in the Lord greatly." Earlier in the letter, he urged the Philippians to "rejoice in the Lord" (3:1; 4:4). Now he reported that this is what he did upon Epaphroditus's arrival. "I rejoiced" (χαίρω) identifies Paul's state of happiness or well-being (BDAG s.v. "ἐχήρην" 1, p. 1075). It most likely refers to the time Epaphroditus arrived from the Philippians with their gift, and is past-time relative both to Paul's writing and their reading (Fee, 1995, 428, n. 17).

"In the Lord" (ἐν κυρίῳ) denotes the sphere and grounds of Paul's delight. He and they had been incorporated into Christ, who is the ultimate basis and source of joy (cf. 3:1; 4:4). "Greatly" (μεγάλως) reveals the intense feeling of delight Paul felt when Epaphroditus first arrived with their gift.

The next phrase denotes either (1) the reason for Paul's delight—"I rejoiced . . . *because* (causal ὅτι) now at length you renewed your concern for me," or (2) the content of his delight—"I rejoiced . . . *that* (declarative ὅτι) now at length you renewed your concern for me." For (1), see NET, O'Brien, 1991, 517; Fee, 1995, 428–29, n. 21; Martin and Hawthorne, 2004, 261. Most English versions support (2). Either way, the force of Paul's statement is much the same. When Epaphroditus arrived with their gift, Paul was delighted.

"Now at length" or "at last" (ἤδη ποτέ) denotes culmination (BDAG s.v. "ἤδη" 2, p. 434; cf. Hellerman, 2015, 255) and implies there had been a lapse of time since their last gift. How long exactly we cannot know. Paul was not sarcastically rebuking them ("Finally you care again!"), as the latter part of the verse demonstrates. "Renewed/revived" (ἀνεθάλετε, lit., "bloomed again," cf. Ezek. 17:24 LXX) occurs only here in the New Testament. By sending Epaphroditus with a gift, they renewed their concern for Paul (4:18). "Concern" (τὸ φρονεῖν) is one of the key words in the letter (see note at 1:7). Paul used it earlier to denote his concern for the Philippians (1:7). Here he referred to their concern on his behalf—"for me" (ὑπὲρ ἐμοῦ) or "on behalf of me" (BDAG s.v. "ὑπὲρ" A1δ, p. 1030). Note that Paul said he rejoiced not because of their gift, but because of what the gift represented—their concern (BDAG s.v. "φρονέω" 1, p. 1065).

Paul clarified (ἐφ᾽ ᾧ)[1] that indeed they were concerned, but they lacked the opportunity to send help. "You were concerned" (ἐφρονεῖτε) emphasized that he knew that at no time did their concern for his welfare wane. "Lacked opportunity" (ἠκαιρεῖσθε) shows that the reason for the hiatus in support was not due to a lack of caring, but to a lack of suitable opportunity to get support to him (BDAG s.v. "ἀκαιρέομαι," p. 34). He did not want them to think that his previous statement ("now at last you renewed") was a rebuke. He meant, "Finally you had the opportunity again to demonstrate your care." We can only speculate as to why they lacked opportunity. Perhaps it was because of distance, lack of someone to send, or circumstances related to Paul's imprisonment in Caesarea, and then Rome. Perhaps they lacked the funds to send (Fowl, 2002: 51). Whatever the reason, Paul made it clear that he understood they were not to blame.

Satisfaction in Christ (4:11–13)

Paul clarified that his delight was in their concern for him, not the gift itself, for he had learned to find complete satisfaction (spiritual/emotional contentment and peace)—no matter his circumstances (having much or little)—in his relationship with Christ through the spiritual strength Christ provided.

> *4:11.* The prepositional phrase καθ᾽ ὑστέρησιν is rendered "because I am in need" (NIV), "of being in need" (ESV, NRSV), "in regard to need" (KJV, NKJV), "out of need" (CSB), or "from want" (NASB).

4:11. Paul offered the first of two qualifications to his acknowledgement of their gift (4:11, 17). Each began with "not that" (οὐχ ὅτι). First, he wanted them to know that he was not saying all

---

1   Ἐφ᾽ ᾧ may be translated "with regard to which [concern]" (Moule, 1959 132; cf. Fitzmyer, 1993a, 331; Reumann, 2008, 650, "on which") or "for whom" (most English versions). The causal (or explanatory) sense "for," as in 3:12, is also possible (BDF §235; BDAG, 365 6c; Varner, 2016, 101), but less likely.

this "because" he was in need (NIV). He wanted them to have the proper perspective on his circumstances and their material support. His rejoicing when Epaphroditus arrived had nothing to do with receiving material provision to cover his need. "Need" (ὑστέρησιν) denotes the condition of lacking what is essential (BDAG s.v. "ὑστέρησις," p. 1044).

Paul explained why (γάρ) he was not speaking on account of need: "for I have learned to be content in whatever [circumstances] I am." If he knew how to be satisfied in every circumstance, their gift was not what brought him joy. "Learned" (ἔμαθον) refers to Paul's gaining a realization, attitude, or skill through experience and practice over time—"learned how" (BDAG s.v. "μανθάνω" 3, p. 615). He was speaking of the many years of personal experience that had taught him to be satisfied in Christ no matter his situation. So their gift, while appreciated, was not essential to his joy. He already stated in 4:10 that it was the renewal of their concern that brought him pleasure. With "I have learned," Paul began a series of verbs—"I have learned" (4:11), "I know" (4:12, [2x]), "I have learned the secret" (4:12)—that climaxes in "I can do" (4:13).

The adjective "content" (αὐτάρκης) occurs only here in the New Testament. The related noun occurs twice (2 Cor. 9:8; 1 Tim. 6:6). This was a favorite term and concept for Stoic philosophers. Stoics, seeking inner peace and contentment, recognized that you can do little about your circumstances. Life happens to you. For them, contentment came through being detached from or indifferent toward circumstances. By mastering anxiety and desire, they could accept whatever fate brought (Fowl, 2003, 52). This "detachment" was the experience of "emotional calm" or what they called being "content" (Peterman, 1997, 136).

Paul's idea of contentment was very different. Contentment came through a relationship with Christ. Paul was not detached from his circumstances or resigned to what fate dealt him. He actively pursued Christ, including the power of his resurrection, participation in his suffering, and being conformed to his death (3:10). Paul willingly participated in God's plan of redemption and fulfilled his role in it. He followed the example of Christ (2:6–8) in sacrificial service and pouring his life out for others (2:17). He did not seek to master himself, but to live for others. He was content not because he was detached, but because Christ strengthened him (cf. Fowl, 2002, 52).

"In whatever [circumstances] I am" (ἐν οἷς εἰμι) denotes when and where Paul could be content. This covered all the very real circumstances he had experienced. He assumed it included those he had not yet experienced or any that may occur.

So Paul revealed one of his spiritual principles for the Christian life, and at the same time emphasized that their provision of his physical need was not what he desired so much as the joy of knowing their concern. Because he had learned to be content in any circumstance through the strength Christ provided, their provision for his physical needs was not the essential thing. He did not love them because they sent him money. Nor did he expect more. That being said, he was grateful for their gift, for their partnership with Paul was one of the means God used to provide for him.

Stoics and Contentment: The idea of contentment was central to Cynic and Stoic philosophy. Cynics focused more on self-sufficiency, Stoics more on inner tranquility (Hellerman, 2015, 258). Being "content" (αὐτάρκης) was the key to happiness, as the Stoic philosopher Seneca (a contemporary of Paul) explains: "The happy man is content with his present lot, no matter what it is, and is reconciled to his circumstances; the happy man is he who allows reason to fix the value of every condition of existence." (De vita beata 6.2)

The idea was to become independent and sufficient within yourself (*TDNT* 1:466), and so able to resist the pressure of outward circumstances by the power of your own innate reason and will. In this way, through inner resolve, your circumstances could not determine your happiness. Contentment did not depend on other people or relationships. You found contentment within yourself, detached from circumstances, independent of others. Again, Seneca:

"The wise man is sufficient unto himself for a happy existence." (*Lucilium* 9.23)

Paul and Contentment: Like the Cynic and Stoic philosophers, Paul did not allow his circumstances to define his actions or thought (Kraftchick, 2007, 202). But that's about all he had in common with them. Paul was decidedly not self-reliant. He was able to be content not by his independence, but by his dependence upon Christ; not by his own strength, but by the one who strengthened him (4:13). He had learned during his career as an apostle to trust in his heavenly Father, to receive the strength extended to him in Christ, and to experience the empowering presence of the Holy Spirit. This was not self-sufficiency. Since Paul was secure in God's love, he was able to receive whatever God brought into his life—whether abundance or lack, success or pain (cf. *NIDNTTE* 1:397). He had learned that God was always with him and was taking him through the role sovereignly prepared for him.

4:12. Ταπεινοῦσθαι is rendered "to be in need" (NIV), "to have little" (NRSV, CSB), "to live on almost nothing" (NLT), "to get along with humble means" (NASB), "to be brought low" (ESV), or "to be abased" (KJV, NKJV). Περισσεύειν is rendered "to have plenty" (NIV, NRSV), "to abound" (ESV, KJV, NKJV; cf. CSB "to have a lot"), "to live in prosperity" (NASB), or "to live with everything" (NLT). Μεμύημαι is rendered "learned the secret" (NIV, ESV, NRSV, CSB, NLT, NASB), "learned" (NKJV), or "am instructed" (KJV). Χορτάζεσθαι is rendered "to be well-fed" (NIV, NRSV, CSB), "to be filled/full" (NASB, KJV, NKJV; cf. NLT, "to be with a full stomach"), or "to face plenty" (ESV). Ὑστερεῖσθαι is rendered "to be in/suffer need" (ESV, NRSV, CSB, NASB, KJV, NKJV), "to be in want" (NIV), or "to be with little" (NLT).

4:12. Paul elaborated on the last part of 4:11 ("I have learned to be content in whatever circumstances I am"). As a result of having "learned," Paul could now say, "I know" (οἶδα). In this context, "I know" means "I know how, I am able" (BDAG s.v. "οἶδα" 3, p. 694). Paul was speaking of the *ability* for living he had gained through experience. He will eloquently describe what he meant by "in whatever [circumstances] I am" (4:11) with a series of contrasts.

To begin, Paul stated that he knew how "to be brought low/be humbled/have little" (ταπεινοῦσθαι). The passive voice of the verb (to be brought low) suggests he was thinking of being humbled by external forces (Witherington, 2011, 276). This could refer to losing prestige or status (being humiliated), to becoming humble in attitude, or to being subjected to deprivation (BDAG s.v. "ταπεινόω" 4, p. 990). Paul was speaking of circumstances beyond his control that had happened to him, rather than intentional self-deprivation.

Paul probably intended an echo of the other occurrence of "humbled" in Philippians: Christ "humbled" (ἐταπείνωσεν) himself (2:8). He saw himself as following the humble lifestyle of his Master. Some interpreters would limit Paul's humbling to economic deprivation (Peterman, 1997, 140). While that seems to be his focus, perhaps he chose this term to allow for a broader reference to any kind of physical or material humbling, especially of the sort he encountered in his ministry (Fee, 1995, 432). "Brought low" aptly describes Paul's account elsewhere of the hardships he experienced in ministry (e.g., 1 Cor. 4:11–13; 2 Cor. 4:8–12; 6:4–5; 11:23–29).

"To have abundance" (περισσεύειν) in this context suggests physical and material abundance (BDAG s.v. "περισσεύω" 1bα, p. 805). Paul did not say much in his letters about his times of material abundance. Nor did he say *how much* abundance he was talking about. For Paul, having abundance probably meant having anything in excess of basic food and clothing (Bruce, 1983, 150). Perhaps he experienced what he considered an "abundance" when Lydia hosted him during his initial visit to Philippi, and when the Philippians had sent him material support previously (Acts 16:15; 2 Cor. 11:8–9; Phil. 4:15–16). Note that Paul said he had to *learn* to cope with having abundance, not just with being humbled. He had to learn to use abundance in a way that was compatible with following Christ in a life of sacrificial service. Calvin's comment is worth quoting:

> He who knows how to use present abundance soberly and temperately with thanksgiving, prepared to part with everything whenever it may please the Lord, giving also a share to his brother according to his ability, and is also not puffed up, that man has learned to excel and to abound. This is an excellent and rare virtue, and much greater than the endurance of poverty. Let all who wish to be Christ's disciples exercise themselves in acquiring this knowledge of Paul's; but yet let them so accustom themselves to the endurance of poverty that it will not be grievous and burdensome to them when they come to be deprived of their riches. (1965, 292)

Next, Paul expanded on the first contrast with a statement containing two more contrasts. "In any and every [circumstance]" (ἐν παντὶ καὶ ἐν πᾶσιν) reiterated and expanded the previous phrase in 4:11—"in whatever [circumstances] I am" (ἐν οἷς εἰμι). "I have learned the secret" (μεμύημαι) occurs only here in the New Testament. Outside the New Testament it was used in a technical sense for being initiated into Greco-Roman mystery religions (BDAG s.v. "μυέω," p. 660). But Paul was not referring to initiation into a mystery religion and probably did not intend a technical sense at all. Rather, he may have used this colorful word as a stylistic variant for "I have learned" (4:11) and "I know" (4:12a) (Schenk, 1984, 32; Silva, 2005, 204). Paul was simply referring to an intimate walk with the Lord through the years, in which he had learned how to be content whether he was well fed or hungry. He did not mean that in Christianity there was an esoteric, hidden secret of contentment to be discovered—a secret key or insight that only a few will obtain. The idea was rather that of becoming experienced in the Christian life—a day-by-day process of gaining an understanding of how to be content with abundance or lack. What Paul had learned was a Christian life principle that is basic and available for all believers. Paul will reveal the secret in 4:13.

We should understand both "being well fed" (χορτάζεσθαι) and "going hungry" (πεινᾶν) in their literal sense of having more than enough or not enough to eat, respectively. In the final contrast, Paul repeated the term from the first, "having an abundance" (περισσεύειν). But instead of using the more general "be brought low/have little" again, this time he contrasted it with "being in need" (ὑστερεῖσθαι), which in this context focuses on material deprivation (BDAG s.v. "ὑστερέω" 5b, p. 1043). "Being in need" for Paul would have meant lacking basic food and clothing.

It is sobering to pause and consider what Paul's decades-long itinerant ministry was really like, and the sacrifices he made. Jesus's words to a would-be follower come to mind, "Foxes have holes, and the birds of the air have nests, but the Son of Man has nowhere to lay his head" (Luke 9:58). But through knowing Christ Jesus, God graciously taught Paul how to find satisfaction and be content in every circumstance.

4:13. Ἐν τῷ ἐνδυναμοῦντί με is rendered "through him who gives me strength/strengthens me" (NIV, ESV, NRSV, CSB, NASB) or "in him who strengthens me" (ASV, RSV). The KJV and NKJV have, "through Christ who strengthens me," reflecting a textual variant in which Χριστῷ occurs after μέ (found in ℵ² D2 F G K L P Ψ 𝔐). If Χριστῷ had been present in the original, it is unlikely that scribes would have omitted it. Probably scribes added "Christ" to make the identity of "him who strengthens me" explicit. The "in Christ" (ἐν Χριστῷ) formula occurs throughout the letter and makes the identification easy (*TCGNT,* 550; Fee, 1995, 426, n. 13).

4:13. Paul summarized and revealed how he was able to be satisfied in any circumstance and brought verses 11–12 to a climax: "All [this] I can do in him who strengthens me." This well-known verse must be interpreted in its context. The "all things" (πάντα) that Paul could do is emphatic (occurring at the beginning of the sentence in Greek) and refers back to and summarizes the content of 4:11–12. It corresponds to "in any and every circumstance" (4:12b) (O'Brien, 1991, 526) and summarizes the series of three contrasts Paul just stated. "All things" refers to *any circumstance* that life brought—whether he was brought low or had an abundance, whether he had much to eat or little. The context does not permit us to interpret this verse (as many have done) to mean that we can do anything we might want or choose to do so long as we depend upon God's strength ("I can run a marathon"; "I can write a best-selling novel"; "I can reach my goal of playing in the NFL"). A better application would be one in which Christ provides peace in the midst of a storm ("I can make it through this stressful day;" "I can face this cancer;" "I can survive this divorce"). It refers not to human accomplishment, but to God's accomplishment in humans in the midst of the ups and downs of life. Paul had learned how to endure the circumstances God brought with contentment (cf. Carson, 1996, 115–16).

"I can do" (ἰσχύω) means "to have the requisite personal resources to accomplish something, to have power, be competent, be able" (BDAG s.v. "ἰσχύω" 2a, p. 484). Paul referred to what he was able to do because he had "learned" (4:11, 12) and because he "knows" (4:12 [2x]). "In him who strengthens" (ἐν τῷ ἐνδυναμοῦντι) makes it clear that Paul's contentment in a situation was not due to Stoic self-sufficiency. The ability did not lie with him. Rather he could do all things "in him who strengthens me." The fact that Paul used the phrase "in Christ," "in the Lord," or "in him" twenty other times in the letter, all with the same preposition (ἐν), suggests that Christ was the one who strengthens him.

Many (mostly) later Greek manuscripts make this clear by adding "Christ" in order to specify who it is that strengthened Paul. These later manuscripts became the basis for the King James Version, so in English we are familiar with the rendering, "I can do all things through Christ who strengthens me." But "Christ" is absent from the earlier manuscripts, and it is unlikely that scribes would drop "Christ" from the text if it were present in the original (*TCGNT,* 550). Whether "Christ" was in the original or not, it is obvious that Paul referred to Christ. Paul used "strengthen" (ἐνδυναμόω) elsewhere of Christ's activity for the believer (1 Tim. 1:12; 2 Tim. 4:17; Eph. 6:10). Because of being joined to Christ, the believer has one who strengthens him. Christ gives all believers the spiritual "strength" or "ability" they need to be content in any and every circumstance (BDAG s.v. "ἐνδυναμόω" 1, p. 333).

Technically, it is probably best to understand the preposition (ἐν) to denote *sphere* as it normally does in numerous "in Christ" texts in Philippians. Paul meant, "All this I can do *in* him" (O'Brien, 1991, 527). Most translations render the preposition to specifically denote *agency*: "All this I can do *through* him."

To translate the statement, "All this I can do *through* the one who strengthens me" is very true and probably more understandable to the average reader, but it lacks the incorporation aspect, which is also present. Paul meant that he found his strength in the personal relationship he enjoyed with Christ by virtue of having been incorporated into him. His strength came from being *in* Christ. The idea of incorporation into Christ suggests, of course, that Paul was strengthened *through* Christ, the one he was joined to.

THEOLOGICAL FOCUS

The exegetical idea (while delighted with their material provision, Paul had learned to be satisfied in life [experiencing spiritual/emotional well-being and peace] in any circumstance [having much or little] through his relationship with Christ and the strength he provided) leads to this theological focus: Spiritual/emotional well-being and peace comes through a personal relationship with Christ and the strength he provides in every life situation.

Christian contentment is the inner satisfaction, sense of security, well-being, and peace that come through trusting a loving heavenly Father, receiving the strength he extends in Christ, and experiencing the empowering presence of the Holy Spirit. It is the sense ("It is well with my soul") that comes through an intimate relationship with Christ in any circumstances life brings.

Christian contentment is not stoicism—being sufficient within yourself. It does not come through detachment from outward circumstances by the power of your own reason and will. Nor does it come by attempting to deny your emotions or desires. It comes not through independence, but through utter dependence on Christ as you willingly embrace all that God brings into your life. It is not passive acceptance, but active faith and participation in God's plan.

The theological presuppositions of contentment are that (1) God is all-loving, all-good, and

for you; (2) God is completely, powerfully sovereign and is working his plan; and (3) God has a role you to play in his plan and is always with you, fulfilling his purposes for you.

PREACHING AND TEACHING STRATEGIES

Exegetical and Theological Synthesis

Paul circled back around to the partnership the Philippians forged with him in proclaiming Jesus. From the outset, he praised the way they linked arms with him (1:5, 7), made personal in the gift sent by Epaphroditus (2:25–30). At the epistle's closing, he restated his appreciation for their partnership. While a cursory reading of the passage makes Paul look deferential to their offering, and even a bit boastful in his contentment, it is critical not to overlook his steady emphasis on the three-way partnership between God, himself, and the Philippians. The work of the church comprises many hands but does not move forward without God's providential resourcing.

In fact, God is easy to miss in the context. First- and second-person verbs and pronouns abound in Philippians 4:10–13. Paul wrote: "I rejoiced . . . you revived your concern for me . . . you were concerned . . . you lacked opportunity . . . *I* speak . . . *I* have learned . . . *I* know . . . *I* also know . . . *I* have learned . . . *I* can do all things through Him who strengthens me" (NASB, emphasis added). And yet, as prominent as Paul appears in this passage, the source of his joy, contentment, and strength is clearly the Lord Jesus Christ (vv. 10, 13).

We must avoid naivete in understanding God's supply. He does not grant his strength through our passive resignation, but he builds it like a muscle as we trust him. Likewise, he does not financially bless us because we lobbed a prayer for wealth, but he tends to channel it through employers, clients, gifts, or grants as an award for our hard work. God has no restrictions in how he supplies for the needs of his people—he placed a coin in the mouth of a fish for Peter to find! But Scripture repeatedly cautions against putting our trust in wealth (Matt. 6:19–34; 1 Tim. 6:6–10). Money will corrupt us if we make it a replacement for God. He is our provider.

Preaching Idea

Satisfaction starts by learning to say: "Whatever God gives is good enough!"

Contemporary Connections

What does it mean?

What is satisfaction? How do we know what we have was given by God? Should we expect pennies from heaven? God provides for people in many standard ways. Pensions, paychecks, honorariums, cash awards, Social Security benefits, and other monetary contributions supply us with the money to meet our basic needs. Behind these contributions are institutions—business, finance, government, benefactors, church, nonprofit—responsible for resourcing us. Typically, God supplies our needs through these channels, rather than raining pennies from heaven.

But God is not limited to supplying through predictable means. He may bless through a spontaneous love offering, random cash gift, found twenty-dollar bill, or class action suit. We can certainly pray to *find* a winning lottery ticket, but we are wiser to work hard at living within our means and stewarding our assets wisely.

Satisfaction springs from accepting our lot and realizing we may not have everything we *want*, but God gives what we *need*. This is a learned behavior, where we regularly take stock of every good gift God has given to us. Appreciation grows when we consider the job, food, shelter, and social connections God has provided. We are happier when we acknowledge our God-given access to people or institutions (e.g., church) that help us in a bind. Much dissatisfaction comes from envying others' stuff, wanting nonessential goods, or devaluing what we already have.

Is it true?

Is it true that what God gives is good enough? Absolutely! But again, we must not limit God's provision to miracles of money. He meets our needs through hard work more often than timely, occasional gifts. The apostle Paul was no slouch. He modeled hard work, not wanting to burden others with constant love offerings (1 Thess. 2:9; 2 Thess. 3:8). Moreover, Paul advocated for letting the indolent rabble of Thessalonica taste dust for their laziness (v. 10).

On the other hand, God does not delight in our hoarding. We must steward our money conscientiously, neither stockpiling nor wasting. Even Jesus supports shrewd use of money to secure friendships (Luke 16:1–15). God does not oppose personal savings. Nor does he have a problem with wealth. Stories of wealthy stewards—Joseph in Egypt and Boaz in Bethlehem—demonstrate the way someone's overstock can bless others. We must not reduce what God gives to in-the-moment gifts or week-to-week income, but also along-the-way savings.

Of course, it is easy to lapse into a reliance on money rather than God. When making financial decisions we trust our bank accounts, credit scores, and investment advisors to guide us. When paying bills and feeding mouths, we trust our purses, grocers, and pantries to supply for us. The notion that most Americans live paycheck to paycheck explains the low-grade anxiety affecting their lives. Greater trust in God could calm our financial worries: He does provide.

Now what?

How do we learn satisfaction? Is it a matter of simply saying: "What God gives is good enough!"? No. Clever scripts will not produce satisfaction, but it's not a bad starting point. Every believer would benefit from regularly reciting: "Whatever God gives is good enough!"

And yet, in a materialistic world, cluttered with constant marketing, we are conditioned to be dissatisfied. We must be cautious, however, of running to the opposite end of materialism: minimalism. If we reread Paul's comment to the Philippians, he did not advocate for minimalistic living. His contentment was framed in terms of theology, not material wealth. The Lord supplied him with the strength to accept his lot, for richer or poorer, better or worse. It takes no more of God's grace to learn satisfaction as a rich businessman than a poor single mother.

The route to satisfaction begins with repenting of twin evils related to material wealth: envy and self-sufficiency. The former wants all the goods others have acquired; the latter takes all the credit for all the goods he has earned. Paul had to "learn" contentment by having envy and self-sufficiency beaten out of him in his roller-coaster career as an apostle. We learn it from our economic and emotional ups and downs as followers of Jesus.

We continue to nurture satisfaction by looking back at the myriad ways God has provided for us in the past. We may have experienced seasons of plenty or seasons of poverty, but God sustained us in either case. We may have received help from friends or been the benefactor for someone. It behooves us to remember God's history of provision.

Creativity in Presentation

Steve Martin's debut movie, *The Jerk* (1979), is a rags-to-riches-to rags story with a poignant closing scene. Martin's character, Navin Johnson, tries to come to terms with his financial losses while writing check after check (for $1.09) to people who won a class action suit against him. He feigns contentment, saying, "I don't need any of this. I don't need this stuff . . . . Just this ashtray . . . and paddle game . . . and remote control. . . ." As the scene progresses, Navin stumbles out of the house with an armload of

just one more "need," humorously capturing the challenge of satisfaction with material stuff.

That God will provide whenever and however he deems fit has several examples. My (Tim's) wife and I finalized our adoption without debt through God's supply in the form of personal savings, a second job, an envelope fundraiser, coffee sales, anonymous gifts, and grants, totaling more than $40,000. One of my former professors told our theology class about his "poor days" while pursuing his doctoral degree. On a particularly tight week, his wife found an unexpected envelope with money in their freezer! Jim Cymbala writes about a timely donation slipped anonymously under his doorway in the early days of his church plant. He also acknowledges the sparse, weekly offering as a regular means of God's supply. Stories like these, personal or secondhand, illustrate ways God takes care of us financially.

To drive home the idea that God provides, consider printing hundreds of labels stating: "A Gift Supplied by God." Place small labels on the back of pews or chairs, on coffee pots and milk jugs, on classroom doors and toilet stalls. Put them on your Bible, wallet, and cell phone to display during the sermon. Set large labels on distant focal points: pulpit, projector screen, music stage, and parking lot. Throughout the sermon, point out different items and read the label. Then proclaim, "God gave this and it's good enough." (Don't be afraid to have the congregation repeat the phrase: "Whatever God gives is good enough!") Print extra labels to pass out to congregants as they leave the service, so visual reminders of God's provision can stick with them throughout the week.

The main point is this: Spiritual/emotional well-being and peace comes through a personal relationship with Christ and the strength he provides in every life situation. Satisfaction starts by learning to say, "Whatever God gives is good enough!"

- What God gives through others makes us grateful (4:10).

- What God gives in all circumstances teaches us satisfaction (4:11–12).

- Strength God gives in all things builds our confidence (4:13).

DISCUSSION QUESTIONS

1. How would you describe your biblical philosophy of stewardship?

2. When was a time when you were on the receiving end of a significant financial gift? How did God supply the gift? How did it make you feel?

3. When have you experienced contentment (sense of peace, serenity, satisfaction, well-being) and can attribute it only to the strengthening presence of Christ?

4. What factors in your environment tend to sow feelings of discontent? How do you overcome those factors?

5. Would you find it more difficult to find true contentment *from the Lord* when having abundance or when lacking material provisions? How are the dynamics different in those two situations?

6. Why should true contentment not depend on how much stuff you have?

Philippians 4:14–23

EXEGETICAL IDEA

The Philippians' material aid to Paul was a spiritual investment and act of worship that would bring spiritual reward and provision from God.

THEOLOGICAL FOCUS

Christian giving is a spiritual investment and act of worship that brings spiritual reward and provision from God.

PREACHING IDEA

God stamps his seal of approval on generous living.

PREACHING POINTERS

Paul continued to convey his appreciation for the Philippians' generosity. Their most recent gift through Epaphroditus—one of many previous donations—showed revived concern for Paul and the expansion of the gospel. The exegetical section will demonstrate how Paul looked beyond the material side to the spiritual, seeing their offering as a God-pleasing sacrifice. If the original readers had mistaken his comments about contentment as a slight, Paul assured them of his gratitude, magnified by the apostle's understanding of their future reward. Paul closed his letter with a final reminder to his readers that their gracious heavenly Father has riches in store for them. Glory is the stamp of approval awaiting generous followers of Jesus.

Generosity should mark today's church, as well. There is no shortage of causes and needs to give to: building programs, short-terms trips, homeless shelters, camp scholarships, clean water wells, utility relief, and the general church budget. Followers of Jesus will give an account for how they steward, spend, and share their monetary resources. Our wallets are windows into our worship; sacrificial giving pleases God. And knowing the Western church comprises the wealthiest people on the planet only adds to the urgency of giving to good causes and clear needs. This passage speaks directly to the financial opportunities knocking at the doors of the church.

THE MEANING OF CHRISTIAN GIVING (4:14–23)

LITERARY STRUCTURE AND THEMES (4:14–23)

Philippians 4:14–20 continues 4:10–13; we divided the unit only for preaching purposes. Paul began with a mild contrast to 4:13 commending them—they had done well to share with him in his distress (4:14). He strengthened this commendation by reminding them that after his foundational visit, they were the only church to partner materially with him (4:15), explaining that they sent money to him in Thessalonica more than once (4:16). He qualified this by clarifying that he did not seek their gift, but rather the profit that increased to their account (4:17). Then Paul officially acknowledged that he had received their gift and that he was now "paid in full" (4:18). He promised that in return God would fill their every need according to his riches in glory in Christ (4:19). He ended the unit climatically with a doxology to God (4:20). In 4:21–23, Paul closed the letter with an exhortation to greet the saints (4:21a), sent greetings from those with him (4:21b–22), and offered a prayer-wish for them (4:23).

> ### A Good Investment (4:14–17)
> ### An Act of Worship Pleasing to God (4:18–20)
> ### Closing Greetings and Prayer-Wish (4:21–23)

EXPOSITION (4:14–23)

Continuing to acknowledge the Philippians' gift, Paul provided a theological interpretation of their giving. He assumed that they were part of a three-way relationship in the gospel between God (Provider), them (channels of God's provision to Paul), and himself (recipient of God's provision through them). Because of their faithful partnership and willingness to be channels of God's provision, Paul was fully supplied. He let them know that their giving was not merely a transfer of material goods between friends. It was an investment that yielded spiritual return for them in the present and future. It was also an offering to God, for which in return he would provide their every need. In all of this, God was the one who received glory.

A Good Investment (4:14–17)

The Philippians material aid was a sign of partnership and identification with Paul in his imprisonment and apostolic ministry, a partnership that they alone shared with him, which would bring spiritual blessing to them in this age and the age to come.

> *4:14.* Πλήν is rendered "yet" (NIV, ESV), "in any case" (NRSV), "still" (CSB), "even so" (NLT), or "nevertheless" (NASB, NKJV). Θλίψει is rendered "trouble/s" (NIV, ESV), "distress" (NRSV, NKJV), "affliction" (NASB, KJV), "hardship" (CSB), or "difficulty" (NLT).

4:14. Paul did not want the Philippians to get the wrong idea from his qualification in 4:11–13—that he was asserting his independence from them, or that they should not have sent Epaphroditus with the gift. To make sure they understood, he commended them: "Yet you did well." "Yet" (πλήν) is a mild adversative that adds a contrasting idea to what precedes (BDAG s.v. "πλήν" 1c, p. 826). "You did well" (καλῶς ἐποιήσατε) is a formula that affirms they had acted appropriately (BDAG s.v. "ποιέω" 5d, p. 841). To assist a friend in need is a basic part of friendship.

Rather than focusing on their gift, Paul commended them for sharing with him in his trouble. By sending their gift through Epaphroditus, they had identified with Paul in his imprisonment. "Share with" (συγκοινωνήσαντες) is another occurrence of "partnership" language in the letter (1:5, 7; 2:1; 3:10; 4:15; cf. BDAG s.v. "συγκοινωνέω" 1b, p. 952). Paul cared deeply about what their gift represented—their partnership in the ministry of the gospel, particularly in his present situation. "Trouble" (θλίψει) refers to any affliction that inflicts distress (BDAG s.v. "θλίψις" 1, p. 457). In Paul's case, it referrred to his imprisonment for the cause of Christ (Martin and Hawthorne, 2004, 268). They had done well to identify with Paul in his imprisonment, and could potentially have brought trouble upon themselves by so identifying with him.

> *4:15.* Ἐν ἀρχῇ τοῦ εὐαγγελίου is rendered "in the beginning of the gospel" (ESV, KJV, NKJV), "in the early days of the gospel" (NRSV, CSB; cf. NIV, "early days of your acquaintance with the gospel"), or "at the first preaching of the gospel" (NASB; cf. NLT, "when I first brought you the Good News"). Ἐκοινώνησεν is rendered "shared with" (NIV, NRSV, CSB, NASB, NKJV) or "entered into partnership with" (ESV).

4:15. Paul strengthened his commendation by reminding them what they "knew" (οἴδατε)—that (ὅτι) after his foundational visit, they were the only church to partner materially with him. Their history of financial partnership with him had been unique. He addressed them, "Philippians" (Φιλιππήσιοι), perhaps to capture their attention on this point.

"In the beginning [ἀρχῇ] of the gospel" refers to the time when they became believers during his foundational visit on the second missionary journey (BDAG s.v. "αρχῆ" 1a, p. 138; cf. Acts 16:11–40). *For them* this was the beginning of the gospel—the beginning of their reception of the gospel and participation with Paul in spreading its message. Compare 1:5, where Paul spoke of their partnership in the gospel *from the first day* until now.

"When I went out [ὅτε ἐξῆλθον] from Macedonia" joins the previous phrase to specify the time Paul was speaking of. He might have been referring more broadly to the general time period after he left Berea for Athens (Acts 17:14–15), including the time of his eighteen-month stay in Corinth (Acts 18: 1–18) (O'Brien, 1991, 533, n. 129). Or he may have been referring more narrowly to the time of his departure from Philippi and stay in Thessalonica (Acts 16:40–17:9) (Peterlin, 1995, 171–75). Either way, Paul's point was that their latest gift was a renewal of their exclusive support in the earliest days.

Paul reminded the Philippians that at this time, "not one church [οὐδεμία ἐκκλησία] partnered" with him "except" (εἰ μὴ, BDAG s.v. "εἰ" 6ια, p. 278) them only. "Partnered" (ἐκοινώνησεν) is the verb form of the noun Paul used in 1:5 (because of your "partnership" in the gospel) and is related to the participle Paul just used in 4:14 (BDAG s.v. "κοινωνέω" 2, p. 552). The Philippians had a unique partnership with Paul in the matter of financial support during that time.

They alone partnered with Paul "in the matter 'of giving' [λόγον δόσεως] and 'receiving' [λήμψεως]." Paul used commercial accounting terms to express their partnership. The word λόγον frequently refers to a financial account (BDAG s.v. "λόγος" 2b, p. 600). Together with "of giving [δόσεως] and receiving" (λήμψεως), the phrase refers to financial transactions of credits and debits on two sides of a ledger (BDAG s.v. "δόσις," p. 259; s.v. "λήμψις," p. 593). Paul's unique partnership with the Philippians included their sending support and his receiving it. Paul was not talking about an official or legal partnership, as though they had drawn up a business arrangement. He was using a business metaphor to express their participation together in spreading the gospel. While "the matter of giving and receiving" refers first to financial transactions, for Paul it was also an expression of the partnership, friendship, and spiritual unity in Christ Jesus he had enjoyed with them.

Paul's Financial Support Policy: By acknowledging their gift, Paul was speaking first about the financial aspects of their partnership. Some have understood Paul's language to refer *only* to the financial details of their relationship—expenditures and receipts (Martin and Hawthorne, 2004, 270). But Greek and Roman authors also used "giving and receiving" terminology to describe the giving and receiving of gifts and services between friends, and the mutual obligations that friends owe to one another (Marshall, 1987, 160–64; Peterman, 1997, 51–89).

At several places in his letters, Paul noted that he refused support from those to whom he ministered so that he might offer the gospel free of charge (1 Cor. 4:12; 9:3–18; 1 Thess. 2:9; 2 Thess. 3:6–12; cf. Acts 20:33–35). He worked as a tentmaker (Acts 18:3). This policy prevented accusations of his being a traveling evangelist who was after people's money. Working also allowed Paul to set an example of hard work and discipline for his converts and to not be a burden on them. This suggests that Paul's partnership with the Philippians (accepting money) was an exception to his general practice. Also, he would apparently at times accept a one-time gift for travel expenses (Rom. 15:24; 1 Cor. 16:6; 2 Cor. 1:16) (cf. Flemming, 2009, 236).

4:16. Καὶ ἅπαξ καὶ δὶς is rendered "more than once" (NIV, NRSV, NLT, NASB), "once and again" (ESV, KJV, NKJV), or "several times" (CSB).

4:16. Paul explained (ὅτι) his statement that in the beginning of the gospel only they partnered with him: "For indeed in Thessalonica more than once you 'sent' [ἐπέμψατε] for my need." Even before Paul left Macedonia, while he was staying in Thessalonica (Acts 17:1–9), the Philippians sent financial support more than once (BDAG s.v. "πέμπω" 2, p. 795). The idiomatic expression "more than once" (καὶ ἅπαξ καὶ δίς) suggests several occasions, perhaps two or three times (BDAG s.v. "ἅπαξ," 1, p. 97; cf.

1 Thess. 2:18). Their latest gift through Epaphroditus was a renewal of their partnership with Paul that began before he even left Macedonia on the second missionary journey.

4:17. Καρπὸν is rendered "fruit" (ESV, CSB, KJV, NKJV), "profit" (NRSV, NASB), "more" (NIV), or "reward" (NLT). Πλεονάζοντα is rendered "increases" (ESV, CSB, NASB), "accumulates" (NRSV), "be credited" (NIV), or "abounds" (KJV, NKJV).

4:17. For the second time in his acknowledgement, Paul added a "not that" (οὐχ ὅτι) qualification (cf. 4:11): "Not that I seek the gift." As in 4:11, he did not want them to misunderstand his acknowledgement. "I seek" (ἐπιζητῶ, BDAG s.v. "ἐπιζητέω" 2, p. 371) expresses the idea of serious interest or strong desire. "Gift" (δόμα) refers to their recent material aid sent by Epaphroditus. It was a gift between friends and partners, not a "payment." He was not focused on their money. Nor were his comments about their history with him (4:15–16) a request for more money. Paul was guarding against their feeling pressured to provide more support. He was assuring them that his delight over them (4:10) was not dependent on their gifts.

In contrast (ἀλλά, strong adversative, BDAG s.v. "ἀλλά" 4, p. 45) to what he did not seek, Paul told them what he did seek: "But I seek the profit that increases to your account." "Profit" (καρπὸν) suggests the image of an investment portfolio (BDAG s.v. "καρπός" 2, p. 510). However, the gain was not material, but spiritual. "Increases" (πλεονάζοντα) depicts the gain accruing to the portfolio as they gave (BDAG s.v. "πλεονάζω" 1, p. 824). Paul viewed financial giving as spiritual investing. Investing financially in the cause of the gospel leads to reception of a spiritual and heavenly reward. Compare Jesus's saying, "Lay up for yourselves treasures in heaven" (Matt. 6:20). It is unnecessary to decide if by "profit" Paul was thinking exclusively of future rewards as opposed to present blessings also. He probably had both in view (O'Brien, 1995, 539). When believers give, they increase their capacity to give. When they love, they increase their capacity to love. When they serve, they increase their capacity to serve. These present blessings continually multiply. And on the day of Christ, the joy and blessing will be the fullest for those who have invested the most.

An Act of Worship Pleasing to God (4:18–20)

The Philippians material aid to Paul was an act of worship that pleased God, who would in return supply their needs.

4:18. Ἀπέχω is rendered "received full payment" (NIV, ESV, cf. NRSV), "received everything in full" (CSB, NASB), or "have all" (KJV, NKJV). Περισσεύω is rendered "have more than enough" (NIV, NRSV, cf. ESV), "have an abundance" (CSB, NASB, cf. KJV, NKJV, "abound"). Πεπλήρωμαι is rendered "am amply/well/fully/generously satisfied" (NIV, ESV, NRSV, CSB, NLT, NASB), or "am full" (KJV, NKJV).

4:18. Paul officially acknowledged that he had received their gift. "I have received full payment" (ἀπέχω πάντα) contains a verb (ἀπέχω) that was used in commercial contexts as a technical term meaning, "paid in full" (BDAG s.v. "ἀπέχω" 1, p. 102; cf. Deissmann, 1978, 110–12; more fully, Ogereau, 2014a, 105–18). Silva suggests that we should imagine Paul with a warm smile as he sent his friends this "receipt," and that his tone was not one of coldness or aloofness but playfulness (2005, 206).

"I have more than enough" (περισσεύω) lets them know that because of their gift, Paul now considered himself well supplied and then some. He was extravagantly blessed by their generosity (BDAG s.v. "περισσεύω" 1b, p. 805). Paul reasserted the idea of "I abound" for emphasis using a different verb: "I am full" (πεπλήρωμαι) or "I am fully supplied" (BDAG s.v. "πληρόω" 1b, p.

828). The passive voice of the verb indicates that his "fullness" was not due to his own doing, but to their generous giving as channels for God's blessing. He had been filled up by what they had sent and so now was full. Paul will use this word again in 4:19 to promise the Philippians that God will "fill up/fully supply" their every need.

Paul explained the means by which or reason why he had been filled up: "having received [δεξάμενος] from Epaphroditus the things you sent." He already alluded to Epaphroditus bringing the gift in 2:25 ("your messenger and minister to my need") and 2:30 ("risking his life so that he might supply what was lacking in your service to me"). "The things" (τὰ) refers to their material gift. Paul did not state exactly what they sent him, but it was some form of material/financial aid, including perhaps food and clothing (Ogereau, 2014a, 266).

Paul moved away from business terminology and described their gift using terminology from the Old Testament sacrifices. By doing this, he helped the Philippians understand the true significance and value of their gift from God's point of view. All Christian giving is ultimately giving to God. Their gift is "a fragrant aroma, an acceptable sacrifice, pleasing to God." This was not merely a business transaction. It was not merely an act of friendship toward Paul. It was an act of worship. "Fragrant aroma" (ὀσμὴν εὐωδίας) depicts an image of sacrifice as a fragrance arising to God's nostrils and pleasing him (BDAG s.v. "ὀσμή" 2b, p. 463).

In the LXX, "sacrifice" (θυσίαν) describes a variety of sacrifices offered to God (BDAG s.v. "θυσία" 2b, p. 463). In Ephesians 5:2, Paul used these same terms, *fragrant aroma* and *sacrifice*, to describe Christ's offering himself for us. Earlier Paul described himself as being poured out for a "sacrifice" (Phil. 2:17). "Acceptable" (δεκτήν) described their sacrifice as being approved by God (BDAG s.v. "δεκτός" 2, p. 217). "Pleasing (εὐάρεστον) to God" reiterated and emphasized that God had taken pleasure in their gift sent to Paul (BDAG s.v. "εὐάρεστος" p. 403).

Together these phrases lifted the status of the Philippians' aid to Paul. His explanation of the spiritual value of their gift helped them understand his qualification in 4:17—that he did not seek the gift (the financial help he received); he sought the profit accruing to their account. Their reward with God was built up through their spiritual act of worship that pleased him. When believers give financially or materially toward the progress of the gospel, they should understand the value of such gifts in God's eyes. Rather than measuring their gift according to it earthly financial value, they should measure it according to its value before God as a sacrificial act of worship that pleases him.

4:19. Tὸ πλοῦτος αὐτοῦ ἐν δόξῃ is rendered "his riches *in* glory" (ESV, NRSV, CSB, NASB, KJV, NKJV), "the riches *of* his glory" (NIV), or "his glorious riches" (NLT, NET). Ἐν Χριστῷ Ἰησοῦ is rendered "in Christ Jesus" (NIV, ESV, NRSV, CSB, NLT, NASB, NET), or "by Christ Jesus" (KJV, NKJV).

4:19. Paul made a promise to the Philippians and tied it to the gift they had sent: "And my God will fill up every need of yours according to his riches in glory in Christ Jesus." "And" (δὲ) connects the promise with 4:18. They had given a gift that had filled up Paul and pleased God— *and* this was what God would do in return. "My God" identified Paul's close, personal relationship with the Father. Since Paul personally could not bless the Philippians for their gift, his God would. Paul's long history with God, in which he had experienced God meeting his needs time and again, gave him the confidence to assure the Philippians that God would meet theirs. "Will satisfy" (πληρώσει), "will make full," "will meet," will fill up," or "will supply" (BDAG s.v. "πληρόω" 1a, p. 828) is the same verb Paul used in 4:18 to describe the effect their gift had on him. God would reciprocate by filling up their every need.

"Every need of yours" (πᾶσαν χρείαν ὑμῶν) has been understood to refer exclusively to present *material* needs (Martin and Hawthorne, 2004, 273–74). It certainly applies to physical and material needs. This is obvious from the fact that Paul had just stated that their gift filled up his (physical and material) needs. But there is no good reason to limit this promise only to physical and material needs (O'Brien, 1991, 546; Fee, 1995, 449). Paul's letter raised issues in which they had spiritual, emotional, and relational needs as well. They could count on God to provide strength, endurance, joy, and encouragement—whatever was needed.

Paul did not provide a timetable for God's provision of their need. His timing is perfect, though it may not agree with what believers desire (cf. Hansen, 2009, 326). Also, Paul was speaking of God providing *needs* and not necessarily everything believers might *want*. He alone knows what they truly need. When applying this verse to our own lives, we should remember that God's provision is wise, appropriate, sufficient, and timely.

The standard (κατά with the accusative, BDAG s.v. "κατά" 5a, p 512) by which God would fulfill their every need was "according to his riches in glory in Christ Jesus." "Riches" (πλοῦτος), "wealth," or "abundance" refers to the abundance of both material and spiritual resources God possesses (BDAG s.v. "πλοῦτος" 2, p. 832). Since God possesses an abundance of riches—everything belongs to him—he will have no trouble providing for every need. And his provision of their every need would be in keeping with all the riches he possesses. God's provision would be "on a scale worthy of his wealth" (Michael, 1928, 226).

God's Spiritual Riches for Believers: When Paul spoke of the riches (πλοῦτος) of God, he normally spoke of the *spiritual* riches he possessed by virtue of his being God with all of his divine attributes—the "riches of his kindness" (Rom. 2:4), "riches of his glory" (Rom. 9:23; Eph. 3:16), "riches of the wisdom and knowledge of God" (Rom. 11:33), "riches of his grace" (Eph. 1:7; 2:7). He also spoke of the "riches of the glory of his [God's] inheritance" (Eph. 1:18), the "riches of Christ" proclaimed to the Gentiles (Eph. 3:8), the "riches of the glory of this mystery in the Gentiles, which is Christ in you" (Col. 1:27), "riches for the world" and "riches for the Gentiles" (Rom. 11:12), and all the "riches of full assurance of understanding" (Col. 2:2). Paul used this term to describe God's glorious attributes and the blessings of salvation he gives believers in Christ. The riches that God possesses by virtue of his being God is the storehouse from which he shares an abundance of riches with those who are in Christ.

"In glory" (ἐν δόξῃ) probably refers to the transcendent sphere or realm in which God dwells (Fee, 1995, 453; cf. ESV, NRSV, CSB, NASB, KJV, NKJV) and the storehouse out of which God's blessing and provision are poured. Elsewhere Paul stated that Christ was taken up "in glory" (1 Tim. 3:16) and that we will appear with him "in glory" (Col. 3:4), similar uses of the same phrase (preposition ἐν + dative δόξῃ). An alternative is to understand "in glory" to denote an attribute of "riches"—"glorious riches" (Martin and Hawthorne, 2004, 274; NIV, NET, NLT). But when "glory" modifies riches this way elsewhere, it occurs in the genitive case (Rom. 9:23; Eph. 1:18; 3:16; Col. 1:27), rather than the dative as here.

"In Christ Jesus" (ἐν Χριστῷ Ἰησοῦ) denotes believers' incorporation into Christ, the sphere in which believers live and relate to God. Some understand this phrase to denote the agent through whom God will supply believers' needs ("through/by Christ Jesus," O'Brien, 1991, 549; KJV, NKJV), but Paul's normal use of the "in Christ" phrases in Philippians argues for understanding "in Christ Jesus" to denote sphere. As in 4:13, the instrumental idea ("through Christ") is true, but incomplete. Paul began the letter writing, "to all the saints 'in Christ Jesus'" (1:1). Now he ended the letter in the same way. The riches with which God will fill up believers' every need are those that are found with him "in glory," and he will provide them to believers in as much as they are "in Christ Jesus."

4:20. Paul's promise of God's provision according to his riches in glory led into a closing doxology: "Now to our God and Father [is, be] the glory [ἡ δόξα] forever and ever. Amen." God and his limitless riches dwell "in glory" (4:19). Now Paul ascribed "glory" to him. The thought of God lavishing his riches on believers should cause them to praise him.

Paul called him "God and Father" (θεῷ καὶ πατρί). The God who provides so abundantly for his own is not only "God," he is also "Father." In 4:19, Paul referred to his own intimacy with God (*my* God). Now he included the Philippians with him in joint praise—*our* God and Father. Jesus reminded his disciples that God was a good Father who gave good things to his children (Matt. 7:11), in particular, the Holy Spirit (Luke 11:13).

"Forever and ever," literally, "to the ages [αἰῶνας] of the ages" denotes that God's glory will never end (BDAG s.v. "αἰών" 1b, p. 32. "Amen" (ἀμήν) is a transliteration of a Hebrew term taken from the Old Testament and the Jewish synagogues (BDAG s.v. "ἀμήν," 1a, p. 53; *TDNT* 1:335–38). It means "surely" (*HALOT* 1:64; *TDNT* 1:335), adding a "Yes!" to the doxology Paul just pronounced. "Glory to our God and Father forever always—yes, so be it!"

Closing Greetings and Prayer-Wish (4:21–23)

Paul sent final greetings and wished upon the Philippians God's favor that comes to believers in Christ.

4:21–22. Ἅγιον is rendered "saint" (ESV, NRSV, CSB, NASB, KJV, NKJV) or "God's people" (NIV; cf. NLT, "holy people"). Ἀδελφοί is rendered "brothers/brethren" (ESV, CSB, NLT, NASB, KJV, NKJV), "brothers and sisters" (NIV), or "friends" (NRSV).

4:21. Paul closed his letter with final greetings. He instructed the Philippians to "greet" (ἀσπάσασθε, BDAG s.v. "ασπάζομαι" 1a, p. 144) "every" (πάντα) "saint" (ἅγιον). Paul might have been addressing this command to a specific group within the church (perhaps the "overseers and deacons" mentioned in 1:1 (O'Brien, 1991, 552), or he might have been addressing the church as a whole (Fee, 1991, 457).

It is possible that Paul wrote, "*every* saint in Christ Jesus" (not "all" as in NIV) because of the budding disunity within the congregation. If he sent greetings to every individual, he would not appear to be taking sides. This could also be why Paul did not single out any individuals by name for greetings as he did in a few of his letters (Martin and Hawthorne, 2004, 280). For "saint" (ἅγιον), see comment on 1:1. It refers not so much to the ethical character of believers as to the fact that they are God's elect, called into a covenantal relationship with him.

Paul sent greetings from "the brothers (ἀδελφοί) with me." He did not identify who these "brothers" are. Presumably they were coworkers who were with him at the time he wrote the letter—for example, Timothy, whom he hoped to send (2:19). Like the other uses of "brothers" in the letter, it could be generic ("brothers and sisters"). It is not clear if Paul had any female coworkers with him.

4:22. Paul sent greetings from a wider circle, from "all the saints." This probably referred to all the believers in the Roman house churches. "Caesar's household" (οἰκίας, BDAG s.v. "οἰκία" 3, p. 695) referred not to Nero's family, but to the large number of slaves and freedmen who worked for him, serving in various areas—domestic affairs, business, medicine, education, literary and secretarial assistance (*DPL*, 83–84; *DNTB*, 1001; BDAG s.v. "Καῖσαρ," p. 499; *TDNT* 5:133; Reumann, 2008, 729–30). The phrase corresponds to the modern "civil service" (*DPL*, 83). These individuals were not necessarily aristocratic. The phrase did not include

the praetorian guard of 1:13, the elite military (Reumann, 2008, 739), but to lower-level civil service. "Caesar's households" were found not only in Rome, but also at headquarters in the imperial provinces. Paul was sending greeting from some of these civil servants who had become believers. This would be an encouragement, for it would demonstrate that the gospel was penetrating the very heart of the empire. If the Philippians were being threatened because their faith in Christ Jesus (1:29), it would be good news that some in Caesar's household in Rome had become believers (Fee, 1991, 460). Some in the emperor's own service did not proclaim him to be Lord. Rather, they affirmed that Christ was Lord!

4:23. NIV, ESV, NRSV, CSB, NLT, NASB read, "with your spirit" (μετὰ τοῦ πνεύματος ὑμῶν), attested by 𝔓46 ℵ* A B D F G P 075. Alternately KJV and NKJV read, "with you all" (μετὰ πάντων), attested by ℵ2 K L Ψ 𝔐. It is possible that a scribe might change Paul's "with you all" (μετὰ πάντων) to "with your spirit" (μετὰ τοῦ πνεύματος ὑμῶν), influenced by Gal. 6:18 or Philem. 25. Or perhaps a scribe might change Paul's "with your spirit" (μετὰ τοῦ πνεύματος ὑμῶν) to "with you all" (μετὰ πάντων), influenced by 1 Cor. 16:23–24; 2 Cor. 13:13; 2 Thess. 3:18; Titus 3:15. NIV, KJV, and NKJV close with "amen" (ἀμήν), supported by 𝔓46 ℵ A D K L P Ψ 𝔐. Omission is supported by B F G 6 1739*vid 1836. If "amen" were original, it is hard to see why a scribe would omit it. But it was common for scribes to include "amen" according to liturgical practice (*TCGNT*, 551).

4:23. Paul closed with a prayer-wish/blessing: "The grace of the Lord Jesus Christ [be] with your spirit." "Grace" (χάρις) is the unmerited favor that comes to believers from God through Jesus Christ in the gospel (BDAG s.v. "χάρις" 2c, p. 1079). The opening greetings of Paul's letters typically mentioned, "grace and peace from God our Father and the Lord Jesus Christ." But his closing blessings typically mentioned only "the grace of the Lord Jesus Christ." With both his openings and closing blessings, Paul's letters showed that believers' lives were to be completely Christ-centered, beginning and ending with grace through Christ.

Normally Paul's closing prayer-wish/blessing was for the grace of Christ to be "with *you*" (Rom. 16:20; 1 Cor. 16:23; 2 Cor. 13:14; Col. 4:18; 1 Thess. 5:28; 2 Thess. 3:18; 1 Tim. 6:21; Titus 3:15). In four letters, including here, he said, "with *your spirit*" (Gal. 6:18; 2 Tim. 4:22; Philem. 25). Paul sometimes used "spirit" (πνεύματος) to refer to the immaterial part of man (2 Cor. 7:1), or the inner human life (1 Cor. 2:11; 2 Cor. 2:13; 7:13). But here he designated the whole person, the very self (BDAG s.v. "πνεῦμα" 3c, p. 833). This makes the formula "with your spirit" equivalent to "with you" found in the other letters (*TDNT* 6:435). While the pronoun "your" (ὑμῶν) in Greek is plural, the noun "spirit" is singular. As with the singular "saint" in 4:21, the singular "spirit" (= "self") focuses attention on each of the believers at Philippi. Paul wanted each of them to experience the grace of Christ (O'Brien, 1991, 555). Less likely, Flemming suggests that the singular "spirit" stands "collectively for the whole church" (2009, 254). Paul's point was, "May the grace of the Lord Jesus Christ be with each one who follows Christ as Lord!"

THEOLOGICAL FOCUS

The exegetical idea (the Philippians' material aid to Paul was a spiritual investment and act of worship that brought spiritual reward and provision from God) leads to this theological focus: Christian giving is a spiritual investment and act of worship that brings spiritual reward and provision from God.

Paul revealed the theological significance of Christian giving. First, using the image of an investment portfolio, he pictured it as a spiritual investment that yields spiritual dividends—not only spiritual fruit in this life, but also eternal reward in the age to come. When believers give, they grow spiritually and increase their capacity to give (2 Cor. 9:6–11). When Jesus returns, the joy and blessing will be the fullest for those who have invested the most.

Second, using sacrificial terms from the Old Testament, Paul pictured the Philippians' giving as a fragrant aroma, an acceptable sacrifice, pleasing to God. All Christian giving is ultimately to God, and is an act of worship. Using a word play, Paul stated that he was "filled" by their gift, and that in return God will "fill up" their every need. Believers cannot outgive God. Together these images lift the status of the Philippians' aid to Paul, and show believers how God views Christian giving. Generous giving glorifies God (2 Cor. 9:12–15).

When believers give financially or materially toward the progress of the gospel, they should understand the value of such gifts in God's eyes. Rather than measuring their gift according to its earthly financial value, they should measure it according to its value before God as a sacrificial act of worship that pleases him.

PREACHING AND TEACHING STRATEGIES

Exegetical and Theological Synthesis

Philippians 4:14–23 provides a clear, theological framework for generosity. Financial bonds form a partnership; the Philippians gave so Paul could go forward with the gospel message. Their giving expanded his reach beyond Philippi to Thessalonica (v. 17) and, presumably, Rome (v. 18). Generosity not only showed their support of Paul's gospel cause, but also established solidarity between the apostle and Philippian church. Of course, Paul was quick to point out the divine player in the financial arrangement: All riches originate with God (v. 19). As such, God received the final, doxological emphasis in the letter (vv. 20, 23).

Paul's theology of generosity likely stemmed from Jesus; teaching on giving and reward flow regularly from his lips. He encouraged almsgiving in the Sermon on the Mount (Matt. 6:2–4). He assumed apostles would earn their keep when he sent out the Twelve (10:5–42). His parable of the faithless steward cautioned against stinginess (25:14–30). His praise of the woman with an alabaster jar served as a timeless example of extravagant giving (26:6–13). Paul aptly summarized Jesus's teaching on giving and reward to the Ephesian elders: "It is more blessed to give than to receive" (Acts 20:35).

Paul's commentary on generosity gravitates toward the concept of heavenly reward. He reframed the discussion, coloring it with liturgical terms. He assured the Philippians of God's current pleasure and future payoff for their generosity (4:18–19). This perspective proves especially helpful when money is a common cause of stress, greed, abuse, and politicking. Reclaiming God's role as our chief benefactor and ourselves as his vessels undercuts the tendency to misuse money.

Preaching Idea
God stamps his seal of approval on generous living.

Contemporary Connections

What does it mean?
What does it mean that God stamps his seal of approval on generous living? Do we earn God's favor by being generous? Throughout the letter to the Philippians, Paul disabused his readers of the belief that they can earn right standing with God. Righteousness is the believers' inheritance, a gift received on the basis of Christ's sacrifice. Nonetheless, salvation does not exempt Christ-followers from good works (1:6; 2:13–17). Generosity—sacrificial giving—is a good work that receives God's seal of approval. Moreover, many people will admit to being generous with more than money; they give time and talent, too.

How do we determine which causes and needs we sacrificially give to? They key to generosity is discernment, both looking at the cause and our motives. The list of causes is endless: crisis relief, sex trafficking, clean water, Bible translation, orphan care, and church building projects. These can easily result in guilt and "giving fatigue." Sometimes small contributions, given via text or online (called "click-activism"), simply relieve us of a sense of responsibility. Giving to assuage guilt does not fit God's design. DeYoung (2013, 49) stresses that Christians can care about many issues without feeling compelled to give to all of them.

Is there a single standard for Christian generosity? The earliest followers of Jesus practiced a "give-it-all-away" mentality in Jerusalem. Later, Paul suggested collecting money on the first day of the week (1 Cor. 16:2). He did not set an amount, but since the days of the Old Testament, congregational leaders have proposed 10 percent as a tithe. The New Testament makes a case for radical generosity but never codifies a percentage. It does, however, specify that God loves a consistent, cheerful giver, and will reward such a person with ample supply (2 Cor. 9:6–12).

Is it true?
Is it true that God stamps his seal of approval on generous living? How is giving affected when our financial circumstances change? Are we sure to receive a rich reward for our generosity? Indeed, God's people should be generous; cheerful giving delights him.

Followers of Jesus should learn to view all their assets as God-given gifts. We should hold our finances with open hands. We have likely experienced times of plenty or the pinch of debt. In either season, it is important to nurture both contentment and generosity. Perhaps, rising medical bills or periods of unemployment force Christ-followers to reduce their giving amounts. Do we show equal eagerness to increase giving when new streams of income appear?

Finally, we should beware of interpreting God's "reward" as financial blessing. The "prosperity gospel" perverts the true gospel. When we primarily give to get a greater material reward—promotion, clean bill of health, annual bonus, free cruise—we misunderstand the ways of God. Televangelists have prospered from this bait-and-switch tactic, but Scripture makes no promise of material blessing for those who sacrifice monetarily. Our sure reward is heavenly blessings (Eph. 1:3–14), not earthly ones.

Now what?

How do we make generosity part of our lives? How do we guard ourselves against poorly motivated giving? A healthy starting point for any talk on giving or spending begins by recalling our role as stewards. Every asset we have belongs to God. If we donate 20 percent, we steward the other 80 percent for his glory. This mindset loosens our grip on our goods.

Second, we should give with purpose. It is too easy to practice spontaneous generosity, which often devolves into little generosity. Paul kept track of the Philippians' giving record. They were his first donors—and regular donors—who had recently refreshed their financial link with him (Phil. 4:10, 15–16). This brief account underscores their practice of intentional, repeated generosity.

Finally, we should view our giving as an act of worship. Paul reminded the Philippians of the sacrificial nature of their offerings. Our donations to good causes are a fragrant aroma to God. Sadly, we can pollute this smell by making our giving more about us than God. We may give for the tax credit or donor's plaque. Having one's name inscribed as a beneficiary of a local fountain or statue was all too common in Philippi (Hellerman, 2013, 89–100). We give to exalt Jesus, not ourselves.

Creativity in Presentation

To give the sermon practical application, consider taking a special offering the week of the message. Advertising a person, ministry need, or charitable organization in advance will allow for people to come prepared to give. Depending on the size of the church, this lesson may require extra coordination. Use a special container to gather the money (as well as online options). Give a total before the service closes. Some churches with larger resources may be able to capitalize on the opportunity by giving away a minivan to a single parent or large check to a local school (for playground equipment) or nonprofit organization (for their food pantry) as a follow up to the service. My (Tim's) church uses the proceeds from an investment account to award an annual "Pay It Forward Grant," designed to launch a new ministry or push a ministry partnership to the next level of effectiveness.

Many great Christian organizations have developed tools to illustrate the power of generosity and stewardship. Dave Ramsey's Financial Peace University features video clips and articles related to generosity. Author Eugene Cho, founder of One Day's Wages, encourages followers of Jesus to donate a day's wage to end global poverty. His family took the challenge, and his moving testimony is available on YouTube or www.onedayswages.org. Samaritan Ministries is a health-sharing network, an alternate to health insurance based upon the idea of bearing one another's burdens (Gal. 6:2). Their website (www.samaritanministries.org) has a library of illustrated video clips. I (Tim) personally experienced an outpouring of generosity from other Samaritan members to help pay my ER bill following a frightening dog attack. (Paul did say, beware of dogs!)

Giving people a chance to assess their giving may shed light on their generosity. Consider providing a personal generosity assessment to help people think through their giving. Be sure questions do not simply measure numbers, but also surface their attitude in giving. Contrast the personal assessment with an evaluation of corporate giving in the church. (Note: This may require the help of a church treasurer or budgeting team.)

Sample Personal Generosity Assessment

1. What percentage of your earnings do you consistently give?
2. Where do you charitably allocate your money?
3. How has your generosity changed in the last three months? Year? Five years?
4. When you receive an unexpected cash gift of more than $100, what do you do with it?
5. Where do you fritter away the most amount of money?
6. What area of your budget could you tweak to increase generosity?
7. What goes through your mind when you receive a phone call from a charity?
8. How well do you tip at restaurants?
9. How much control or accountability do you like related to your tithing?
10. On a scale of 1 to 10, how cheerful is your giving? (1 = Bah Humbug; 10 = Hallelujah)

The big idea to reiterate is this: Christian giving is a spiritual investment and act of worship that brings spiritual reward and provision from God. God stamps his seal of approval on generous living.

- Generous living helps others (4:14–17).

- Generous living makes God happy (4:18–20).

- Final greetings recall God's generosity (4:21–23).

DISCUSSION QUESTIONS

1. How do you determine which causes to give to and how much to give to them?

2. In addition to financial giving, what are other forms of generosity?

3. Why is giving to gospel ministry a spiritual investment?

4. How have you thought of your Christian giving until now? What difference will it make to view it as spiritual investing?

5. What difference will it make to view your giving as a sacrificial offering that is pleasing to God?

6. If you give sacrificially to God, what can you trust him to do in return? How can you grow in this kind of trust?

FOR FURTHER READING

Alcorn, R. 2005. *The Treasure Principle: Unlocking the Secret of Joyful Giving.* Colorado Springs: Multnomah Books.

Burroughs, J. 2002. *The Rare Jewel of Christian Contentment.* London: Banner of Truth Trust. First published 1648.

Powell, M. A. 2006. *Giving to God: The Bible's Good News about Living a Generous Life.* Grand Rapids: Eerdmans.

Swenson, R. A. 2013. *Contentment: The Secret to a Lasting Calm.* Colorado Springs: NavPress.

REFERENCES

Aland, B. et al. 2014a. *The Greek New Testament.* 5th rev. ed. Stuttgart: Deutsche Bibelgesellschaft/United Bible Societies.

_____. 2014b. *Novum Testamentum Graece.* 28th ed. Stuttgart: Deutsche Bibelgesellschaft/ United Bible Societies.

Alcorn, R. 2001. *The Treasure Principle: Discovering the Secret of Joyful Giving.* Special ed. Colorado Springs: Multnomah Books.

Alexander, L. 1989. "Hellenistic Letter-Forms and the Structure of Philippians." *Journal for the Study of the New Testament* 37:87–101.

Allen, D. M. 2010. "Philippians 4:2-3: To Agree or Not to Agree? Unity Is the Question." *Expository Times* 121:533–38.

Arzt-Grabner, P. 2010. "Paul's Letter Thanksgiving." In *Paul and the Ancient Letter Form,* edited by S. E. Porter and S. A. Adams, 129–58. Leiden, Brill.

Ash, A. L. 1994. *Philippians, Colossians & Philemon.* College Press NIV Commentary. Joplin, MO: College Press.

Baesvi, C., and J. Chapa. 1993. "Philippians 2.6-11: The Rhetorical Function of a Pauline Hymn." In *Rhetoric and the New Testament.* Edited by S. Porter and T. H. Olbricht, 338–56. Sheffield: JSOT Press.

Balz, H., and G. Schneider, eds. 1990–93. *Exegetical Dictionary of the New Testament.* 3 vols. Grand Rapids: Eerdmans.

Barclay, J. M. G. 1987. "Mirror-Reading a Polemical Letter: Galatians as a Test Case," *Journal for the Study of the New Testament* 31:73–93.

_____. 1988. *Obeying the Truth: Paul's Ethics in Galatians.* Vancouver: Regent College Publishing.

_____. 2015. *Paul and the Gift.* Grand Rapids: Eerdmans.

Barnet, J. 2006. "Paul's Reception of the Gift from Philippi." *St. Vladimir's Theological Quarterly* 50:225–53.

Barrett, C. K. 1998. *Acts 15-28.* International Critical Commentary. London: T&T Clark.

Barth, K. 1962. *Epistle to the Philippians.* Translated by J. W. Leitch. Richmond: John Knox.

Bateman IV, H. W. 1998. "Were the Opponents at Philippi Necessarily Jewish?" *Bibliotheca Sacra* 155:39–61.

Bauckham, R. 1998. *God Crucified: Monotheism and Christology in the New Testament.* Grand Rapids: Eerdmans.

_____. 2009. *Jesus and the God of Israel: "God Crucified" and Other Studies in the New Testament's Christology of Divine Identity.* Grand Rapids: Eerdmans.

Bauer, W. 2000. *Greek-English Lexicon of the New Testament and Other Early Christian Literature.* 3rd ed. Revised and edited by F. Danker. Chicago: University of Chicago.

Beale, G. K. 2014. *We Become What We Worship: A Biblical Theology of Idolatry.* Downers Grove, IL: IVP Academic.

Beare, F. W. 1969. *A Commentary on the Epistle to the Philippians.* 2nd ed. London: Black.

Becker, E. 1997. *The Denial of Death.* New York: Free Press.

Berry, K. L. 1996. "The Function of Friendship Language in Philippians 4:10-20." In *Friendship, Flattery, and Frankness: Studies on Friendship in the New Testament World.* Edited by J. T. Fitzgerald, 107–24. Supplements to Novum Testamentum 82. Leiden: Brill.

Best. E. 1955. *One Body in Christ.* London: SPCK.

Bird, M. 2007. *The Saving Righteousness of God: Studies on Paul, Justification and the New Perspective.* Paternoster Biblical Monographs. Eugene, OR: Wipf & Stock.

Bird, M. F., and P. M. Sprinkle, eds. 2009. *The Faith of Jesus Christ: Exegetical, Biblical, and Theological Studies.* Peabody, MA: Hendrickson.

Black, D. A. 1995. "The Discourse Structure of Philippians: A Study in Textlinguistics." *Novum Testamentum* 37:16–49.

Blass, F., and A. DeBrunner. 1961. *A Greek Grammar of the New Testament and other Early Christian Literature.* Translated and revised by R. Funk. Chicago: University Press.

Bloomquist, L. G. 1993. *The Function of Suffering in Philippians.* Journal for the Study of the New Testament Supplements 78. Sheffield: JSOT Press.

_____. 2007. "Subverted by Joy: Suffering and Joy in Paul's Letter to the Philippians." *Interpretation* 61:270–82.

Bock, D. 2007. *Acts.* Baker Exegetical Commentary on the New Testament. Grand Rapids: Baker Academic.

Bockmuehl, M 1997. "'The Form of God' Phil 2:6: Variations on a Theme of Jewish Mysticism." *Journal of Theological Studies* 48:1–23.

_____. 1998. *The Epistle to the Philippians.* Black's New Testament Commentary. Peabody, MA: Hendrickson.

Bond, L. S. 2005. "Renewing the Mind: Paul's Theological and Ethical Use of Φρόνημα and Cognates in Romans and Philippians." PhD diss., University of Aberdeen. *Tyndale Bulletin* 58:317–20.

Bonhoeffer, D. 1954. *Life Together.* New York: Harper & Row.

_____. 1973. *The Cost of Discipleship.* New York: Macmillan.

Bormann, L. 1995. *Philippi: Stadt und Christengemeinde zur Zeit des Paulus.* Supplements to Novum Testamentum 78. Leiden: Brill.

Bornkamm, G. 1971. *Paul.* New York: Harper & Row.

Botterweck, G. J. and H. Ringgren, eds. 1974–2001. *Theological Dictionary of the Old Testament.* 12 vols. Grand Rapids: Eerdmans.

Boyer, J. L. 1981. "First Class Conditions: What Do They Mean?" *Grace Theological Journal* 2:75–114.

Brewer, R. R. 1954. "The Meaning of *politeuesthe* in Philippians 1:27." *Journal of Biblical Literature* 7:376–83.

Briones, D. 2011. "Paul's Intentional 'Thankless Thanks' in Philippians 4.10-20." *Journal for the Study of the New Testament* 34:47–69.

Bromily, G. W., ed. 1979–1988. *The International Standard Bible Encyclopedia.* 4 vols. Rev. ed. Grand Rapids: Eerdmans.

Brooks, D. 2016. *The Road to Character.* New York: Random House.

Brown, C., ed. 1975–78. *The New International Dictionary of New Testament Theology.* 3 vols. Grand Rapids: Zondervan.

Brown, R. 1997. *Introduction to the New Testament.* Anchor Bible Reference Library. New York: Doubleday.

Bruce, F. F. 1977. *Paul: Apostle of the Heart Set Free.* Grand Rapids: Eerdmans.

_____. 1983. Philippians. New International Biblical Commentary. Peabody, MA: Hendrickson.

_____. 1985. *The Pauline Circle.* Grand Rapids: Eerdmans.

_____. 1988. *The Canon of Scripture.* Downers Grove, IL: InterVarsity Press.

_____. 1990. *The Acts of the Apostles. Greek Text with Introduction and Commentary.* 3rd rev. and enlarged ed. Grand Rapids: Eerdmans.

Bultmann, R. 1951. *Theology of the New Testament.* Vol. 1. Trans. K. Grobel. New York: Charles Scribner's Sons.

Burk, D. 2004. "On the Articular Infinitive in Philippians 2:6: A Grammatical Note with Christological Implications." *Tyndale Bulletin* 55:253–274.

_____. 2008. "Is Paul's Gospel Counterimperial? Evaluating the Prospects of the 'Fresh Perspective' for Evangelical Theology." *Journal of the Evangelical Theological Society* 51:309–37.

Burnham, G. 2010. *In the Presence of My Enemies.* Carol Stream, IL: Tyndale Momentum.

Burroughs, J. *The Rare Jewel of Christian Contentment.* London: Banner of Truth Trust, 2002. First published in 1678.

Butler, P. 2006. *Well Connected: Releasing Power, Restoring Hope through Kingdom Partnerships.* Colorado Springs: Authentic.

Butterfield, R. 2012. *Secret Thoughts of an Unlikely Convert: An English Professor's Journey into Christian Faith.* Pittsburgh: Crown & Covenant.

Byrne, B. 1997. "Christ's Pre-Existence In Pauline Soteriology." *Theological Studies* 58:308–30.

Caird, G. B. 1976. *Paul's Letters from Prison.* New Century Bible. Oxford: University Press.

Calvin, J. 1965. *The Epistles of Paul the Apostle to the Galatians, Ephesians, Philippians, and Colossians.* Calvin's Commentaries. Edited by D. W. Torrance and T. F. Torrance. Translated by T. H. L. Parker. Grand Rapids: Eerdmans.

Campbell, C. 2012. *Paul and Union with Christ: An Exegetical and Theological Study.* Grand Rapids: Zondervan.

Carson, D. A. 2014. *Praying with Paul: A Call to Spiritual Reformation.* 2nd ed. Grand Rapids: Baker Academic.

_____. 1992. *A Call to Spiritual Reformation: Priorities from Paul and His Prayers.* Grand Rapids: Baker.

_____. 1996. *Exegetical Fallacies.* 2nd ed. Grand Rapids: Baker Books.

Carson, D. A. and D. J. Moo 2005. *An Introduction to the New Testament.* 2nd ed. Grand Rapids: Zondervan.

Cassidy, R. J. 2001. *Paul in Chains: Roman Imprisonment and the Letters of St. Paul.* New York: Crossroad.

Castelli, E. A. 1991. *Imitating Paul: A Discourse of Power.* Literary Currents in Biblical Interpretation. Louisville: Westminster/John Knox.

Chilcoat, B. 2009. *Nobody Tells a Dying Guy to Shut Up: An Account of God's Faithfulness.* Columbus, OH: Corban Productions.

Claiborne, S. 2016. *The Irresistible Revolution, Updated and Expanded: Living as an Ordinary Radical.* Grand Rapids: Zondervan.

Clarke, A. D. 2008. *A Pauline Theology of Church Leadership.* Library of New Testament Studies 362. London: T&T Clark.

Coe, J. 2008. "Resisting the Temptation of Moral-Formation: Opening to Spiritual Formation in the Cross and the Spirit." *Journal of Spiritual Formation and Soul Care* 1:54–78.

Cohick, L. H. 2013a. *Philippians.* The Story of God Bible Commentary. Grand Rapids: Zondervan.

_____. 2013b. "Philippians and Empire: Paul's Engagement with Imperialism and the Imperial Cult." In *Jesus Is Lord, Caesar Is Not: Evaluating Empire in New Testament Studies.* Edited by S. McKnight and J. B. Modica, 166–82. Downers Grove, IL: InterVarsity Press.

Collange, J. F. 1979. *The Epistle of Saint Paul to the Philippians.* Translated by A. W. Heathcote. London: Epworth.

Cousar, C. B. 2007. "The Function of the Christ-Hymn 2.6-11 in Philippians." In *The Impartial God: Essays in Biblical Studies in Honor of Jouette M. Bassler.* New Testament Monographs 22. Edited by C. J. Roetzel and R. L. Foster, 212–20. Sheffield: Phoenix.

_____. 2009. *Philippians and Philemon.* The New Testament Library. Louisville: Westminster John Knox.

Covey, S. 2004. *Seven Habits of Highly Effective People: Powerful Lessons in Personal Change.* New York: Free Press.

Crabb, L. and Allender D. 2013. *Encouragement: The Unexpected Power of Building Others Up.* Grand Rapids: Zondervan.

Craddock, F. 1985. *Philippians.* Interpretation: A Bible Commentary for Preaching and Teaching. Atlanta: John Knox.

Crouch, A. 2017. *The Tech-wise Family: Everyday Steps for Putting Technology in Its Place.* Grand Rapids: Baker Books.

Croy, N. C. 2003. "'To Die Is Gain' Philippians 1:19-26: Does Paul Contemplate Suicide?" *Journal of Biblical Literature* 122:517–31.

Cullmann, O. 1963. *The Christology of the New Testament.* Rev. ed. Translated by S. Guthrie and C. Hall. Philadelphia: Westminster.

Dalton, W. J. 1979. "The Integrity of Philippians." *Biblica* 60:97–102.

Davids, P. 1982. *Commentary on James.* New International Greek Testament Commentary. Grand Rapids: Eerdmans.

Davies, W. D. 1980. *Paul and Rabbinic Judaism.* 4th ed. Philadelphia: Fortress.

Davis, C. W. 1999. *Oral Biblical Criticism: The Influence of the Principles of Orality on the Literary Structure of Paul's Epistle to the Philippians.* Journal for the Study of the New Testament Supplements 172. Sheffield: Sheffield Academic Press.

DeSilva, D. A. 1994. "No Confidence in the Flesh: The Meaning and Function of Philippians 3:2-21." *Trinity Journal* 15 NS:27–54.

_____. 2000. *Honor, Patronage, Kinship, and Purity: Unlocking New Testament Culture.* Downers Grove, IL: InterVarsity Press.

De Vos, C. S. 1999. *Church and Community Conflicts: The Relationship of the Thessalonian, Corinthian, and Philippian Churches with Their Wider Civic Communities.* Society of Biblical Literature Dissertation Series 168. Atlanta: Scholars Press.

Deissmann, A. 1978. *Light from the Ancient East.* Translated by L. R. M. Strachan. Grand Rapids: Baker. First published in English in 1910.

Denton, D. R. 1982. "Ἀποκαραδοκία." *Zeitschrift für die neutestamentliche Wissenschaft und die Kunde der älteren Kirche* 73:138–40.

Doble, P. 2002. "'Vile Bodies' or Transformed Persons? Philippians 3.21 in Context." *Journal for the Study of the New Testament* 86:3–27.

Dodd, B. 1999. *Paul's Paradigmatic "I": Personal Example as Literary Strategy.* Library of New Testament Studies 177. Sheffield: Academic Press.

Droge, A. J. 1988. "*Mori Lucrum:* Paul and Ancient Theories of Suicide." *Novum Testamentum* 30:262–86.

Dunn, J. D. G. 1983: "The New Perspective on Paul." *Bulletin of the John Rylands Library* 65:95–122.

_____. 1988. *Romans.* Word Biblical Commentary. 2 vols. Dallas: Word,.

_____. 1989. *Christology in the Making.* 2nd ed. Philadelphia: Westminster.

_____. 1993. *The Epistle to the Galatians.* Black's New Testament Commentaries. Peabody, MA: Hendrickson.

_____. 1998. *The Theology of Paul the Apostle.* Grand Rapids: Eerdmans.

Eastman, S. 2008. "Imitating Christ Imitating Us: Paul's Educational Project in Philippians." In *The Word Leaps the Gap: Essays in Honor of Richard B. Hays.* Edited by J. R. Wagner, C. K. Rowe, and A. K. Grieb, 427–51. Grand Rapids: Eerdmans.

_____. 2011. "Philippians 2:6-11: Incarnation as Mimetic Participation." *Journal for the Study of Paul and His Letters* 1:1–22.

Edsall, B., and J. R. Strawbridge. 2015. "The Songs We Used to Sing? Hymn 'Traditions' and Reception in Pauline Letters." *Journal for the Study of the New Testament* 37:290–311.

Edwards, M. J. 1999. *Galatians, Ephesians, Philippians.* Ancient Christian Commentary on Scripture. Downers Grove, IL: InterVarsity Press.

Engberg-Pederson, T. 2003. "Radical Altruism in Philippians 2.4." In *Early Christianity and Classical Culture: Comparative Studies in Honor of Abraham J. Malherbe.* Edited by J. T. Fitzgerald, T. H. Olbricht, and L. M. White, 197–204. Leiden: Brill.

Esler, P. F. 2005. "Paul and the Agon: Understanding a Pauline Motif in Its Cultural and Visual Context." In *Picturing the New Testament in Visual Images: Studies in Ancient Visual Images.* Edited by A. Wissenrieder, Wendt, and P. Gemünden, 356–84. Wissenschaftliche Untersuchungen zum Neuen Testament 2. Reihe, 193. Tübingen: Mohr Siebeck.

Evans, C. A., and S. E. Porter. 2000. *Dictionary of New Testament Backgrounds.* Downers Grove, IL: InterVarsity Press.

Erickson, M. J. 2013. *Christian Theology.* 3rd ed. Grand Rapids: Baker Academic.

Fabricatore, D. J. 2010. *Form of God, Form of a Servant: An Examination of the Greek Noun μορφή in Philippians 2:6-7.* Lanham, MD: University Press of America.

Fanning, B. M. 1990. *Verbal Aspect in the Greek New Testament.* Oxford: University Press.

Fantin, J. D. 2011. *The Lord of the Entire World: Lord Jesus, A Challenge to Lord Caesar?* New Testament Monographs 31. Sheffield: Sheffield Phoenix.

Fee, G. D. 1987. *The First Epistle to the Corinthians.* New International Commentary on the New Testament. Grand Rapids: Eerdmans.

_____. 1991. *Gospel and Spirit: Issues in New Testament Hermeneutics.* Grand Rapids: Baker Academic.

_____. 1992: "Philippians 2:5-11: Hymn or Exalted Pauline Prose?" *Bulletin for Biblical Research* 2:29–46.

_____. 1994. *God's Empowering Presence: The Holy Spirit in the Letters of Paul.* Peabody, MA: Hendrickson.

_____. 1995. *Paul's Letter to the Philippians.* New International Commentary on the New Testament. Grand Rapids: Eerdmans.

_____. 1999. *Philippians.* IVP New Testament Commentary Series. Downers Grove, IL: InterVarsity Press.

_____. 2006. "The New Testament and Kenosis Christology." In *Exploring Kenotic Christology: The Self-Emptying of God.* Edited by C. S. Evans, 25–44. Oxford: University Press.

Fewster, G. P. 2015. "The Philippians 'Christ Hymn': Trends in Critical Scholarship." *Currents in Biblical Research* 13:191–206.

Fikkert, B., and S. Corbet. 2009. *When Helping Hurts: How to Alleviate Poverty without Hurting the Poor . . . and Yourself.* Chicago: Moody Press.

Fisk, B. N. 2006. "The Odyssey of Christ: A Novel Context for Philippians 2:6-11." In *Exploring Kenotic Christology: The Self-Emptying of God.* Edited by C. S. Evans, 45–73. Oxford: University Press.

Fitzmyer, J. A. 1981. *To Advance the Gospel: New Testament Studies.* New York: Crossroad.

_____. 1988. "The Aramaic Background of Philippians 2:6-11." *Catholic Biblical Quarterly* 50:470–83.

_____. 1993a. "The Consecutive Meaning of *eph' hō* in Romans 5.12." *New Testament Studies* 39:321–39.

_____. 1993b. *Romans.* Anchor Bible. New Haven, CT: Yale University Press.

_____. 1998. *The Acts of the Apostles.* Anchor Bible. New Haven: Yale University Press.

_____. 2008. First Corinthians. Anchor Yale Bible. New Haven: Yale University Press.

Flemming, D. 2009. *Philippians: A Commentary in the Wesleyan Tradition.* New Beacon Bible Commentary. Kansas City: Beacon Hill.

_____. 2011. "Exploring a Missional Reading of Scripture: Philippians as a Case Study." *Evangelical Quarterly* 83:3–18.

Fowl, S. F. 1990. *The Story of Christ in the Ethics of Paul: An Analysis of the Function of the Hymnic Material in the Pauline Corpus.* Journal for the Study of the New Testament Supplements 36. Sheffield: JSOT Press.

_____. 2002. "Know Your Context: Giving and Receiving Money in Philippians." *Interpretation* 56:45–58.

_____. 2003. "Philippians 1:28b, One More Time." In *New Testament Greek and Exegesis: Essays in Honor of Gerald F. Hawthorne.* Edited by A. Donaldson and T. Sailors, 167–79. Grand Rapids: Eerdmans.

_____. 2005. *Philippians.* Two Horizons New Testament Commentary. Grand Rapids: Eerdmans.

Foxe, J. 2001. *Foxe's Book of Martyrs.* Newberry: Bridge-Logos.

Freedman, D. N. 1992. *The Anchor Bible Dictionary.* 6 vols. New York: Doubleday.

Fung, R. Y. K. 1988. *The Epistle to the Galatians.* New International Commentary on the New Testament. Grand Rapids: Eerdmans.

Furnish, V. P. 1984. *II Corinthians.* Anchor Bible. Garden City, NY: Doubleday.

Garland, D. E. 1985. "The Composition and Unity of Philippians: Some Neglected Literary Factors." *Novum Testamentum* 27:141–73.

_____. 2006. "Philippians." In *The Expositor's Bible Commentary.* Rev. ed. Edited by T. Longman III and D. E. Garland. Vol. 12, 175–261. Grand Rapids: Zondervan.

_____. 2003. *1 Corinthians.* Baker Exegetical Commentary on the New Testament. Grand Rapids: Baker Academic.

Geiger, S. 2010. "Philippians 2:12-13: Work Out Your Own Salvation with Fear and Trembling." *Wisconsin Lutheran Quarterly* 107:284–95.

Geoffrion, T. C. 1993. *The Rhetorical Purpose and the Political and Military Character of Philippians: A Call to Stand Firm.* Lewiston, NY: Mellen Biblical Press.

Gnilka, J. 1976. *Der Philipperbrief.* Herders Theologischer Kommentar zum Neuen Testament. Freiburg: Herder.

Gorman, M. J. 2007. "'Although/Because He Was in the Form of God': The Theological Significance of Paul's Master Story Phil 2:6-11." *Journal of Theological Interpretation* 1 2:147–69.

_____. 2009. *Inhabiting the Cruciform God: Kenosis, Justification, and Soteriology in Paul's Narrative Soteriology.* Grand Rapids: Eerdmans.

_____. 2015. *Becoming the Gospel: Paul, Participation, and Mission.* Grand Rapids: Eerdmans.

Grayston, K. 1967. *The Letters of Paul to the Philippians and to the Thessalonians.* Cambridge Bible Commentary. Cambridge: University Press.

Greenlee, J. H. 2001. *An Exegetical Summary of Philippians.* Dallas: SIL International.

Grindheim, S. 2005. *The Crux of Election: Pauls' Critique of the Jewish Confidence in the Election of Israel.* Wissenschaftliche Untersunchungen zum Neuen Testament 2. Reihe., 202. Tübingen: Mohr Siebeck.

Grudem, W. 1994. *Systematic Theology.* Grand Rapids: Zondervan.

Gundry, R. 1987. *Sōma in Biblical Theology with an Emphasis on Pauline Anthropology.* Grand Rapids: Zondervan.

_____. 1994. "Style and Substance in 'The Myth of God Incarnate' according to Philippians 2:6–11." In *Crossing the*

Boundaries: Essays in Biblical Interpretation in Honour of Michael D. Goulder. Edited by S. E. Porter, P. Joyce, and D. E. Orton, 271–93. Leiden: Brill.

Gundry Volf, J. M. 1990. *Paul and Perseverance: Staying In and Falling Away.* Wissenschaftliche Untersuchungen zum Neuen Testament 2. Reihe, 37. Tübingen: Mohr Siebeck. Louisville: Westminster John Knox.

Gupta, N. K. 2008. "'I Will Not Be Put to Shame:' Paul, the Philippians, and the Honourable Wish for Death." *Neotestamentica* 42:253–67.

———. 2010. "To Whom Was Christ a Slave Phil 2:7? Double Agency and the Specters of Sin and Death in Philippians." *Horizons in Biblical Theology* 32:1–16.

———. 2012. "Mirror Reading Moral Issues in Paul's Letters." *Journal for the Study of the New Testament* 34:361–81.

Guthrie, D. 1970. *New Testament Introduction.* Downers Grove, IL: InterVarsity Press.

Guthrie, G. H. 1995. "Cohesion Shifts and Stiches in Philippians." In *Discourse Analysis and Other Topics in Biblical Greek.* Edited by S. M. Porter and D. A. Carson, 36–59. Journal for the Study of the New Testament Supplement Series 113. Sheffield: Sheffield Academic.

Hagner, D. A. 2012. *The New Testament: A Historical and Theological Introduction.* Grand Rapids: Baker Academic.

Hansen, G. W. 2009. *The Letter to the Philippians.* Pillar New Testament Commentary. Grand Rapids: Eerdmans.

Harmon, M. S. 2015. *Philippians.* Mentor Commentary. Ross-shire, Scotland: Christian Focus.

Harris, M. J. 1983. *Raised Immortal: Resurrection and Immortality in the New Testament.* Grand Rapids: Eerdmans.

———. 2001. *Slave of Christ: A New Testament Metaphor for Total Devotion to Christ.* New Studies in Biblical Theology 8. Downers Grove, IL: InterVarsity Press.

———. 2005. *The Second Epistle to the Corinthians.* New International Greek Testament Commentary. Grand Rapids: Eerdmans.

———. 2012. *Prepositions and Theology in the Greek New Testament.* Grand Rapids: Zondervan.

Harrisville, R. A., III. 2010. "Πιστις Χριστον and the New Perspective on Paul." *Logia* 19:19–28.

Harvey, J. D. 1998. *Listening to the Text: Oral Patterning in Paul's Letters.* ETS Studies. Grand Rapids: Baker Books.

Hawthorne, G. F., R. P. Martin, and D. G. Reid, eds. 1993. *Dictionary of Paul and His Letters.* Downers Grove, IL: InterVarsity Press.

Hays, R. B. 1989. *Echoes of Scripture in the Letters of Paul.* New Haven, CT: Yale University Press.

———. 2000. "Galatians." In *The New Interpreter's Bible.* Edited by L. Keck. Vol. 12, 181–348. Nashville: Abingdon.

———. 2002. *The Faith of Jesus Christ: The Narrative Substructure of Galatians 3:1-4:11.* 2nd ed. Grand Rapids: Eerdmans.

Heen, E. M. 2004. "Phil 2:6-11 and Resistance to Local Timocratic Rule: *Isa theō* and the Cult of the Emperor in the East." In *Paul and the Roman Imperial Order.* Edited by R. A. Horsley, 125–53. Harrisburg, PA: Trinity Press International.

Heil, J. P. 2010. *Philippians: Let Us Rejoice in Being Conformed to Christ.* Society of Biblical Literature Early Christianity and Its Literature. Atlanta: SBL Press.

Heilig, C., C. J. T. Hewitt, and M. F. Bird, eds. 2017. *God and the Faithfulness of Paul: A Critical Examination of the Pauline Theology of N. T. Wright.* Minneapolis: Fortress.

Hellerman, J. H. 2003a "The Humiliation of Christ in the Social World of Roman Philippi, Part 1." *Bibliotheca Sacra* 160:321–36.

_____. 2013. *Embracing Shared Ministry: Power and Status in the Early Church and Why It Matters Today*. Grand Rapids: Kregel Ministry.

_____. 2003b "The Humiliation of Christ in the Social World of Roman Philippi, Part 2." *Bibliotheca Sacra* 160:421–33.

_____. 2005. *Reconstructing Honor in Roman Philippi: Carmen Christi as Cursus Pudorum*. Society for New Testament Studies Monograph Series. New York: Cambridge University Press.

_____. 2009a. "ΜΟΡΦΗ ΘΕΟΥ as a Signifier of Social Status in Philippians 2:6." *Journal for the Evangelical Theological Society* 52:779–97.

_____. 2009b. "Brothers and Friends in Philippi: Family Honor in the Roman World and in Paul's Letter to the Philippians." *Biblical Theology Bulletin* 39:15–25.

_____. 2010a. "Vindicating God's Servants in Philippi and in Philippians: The Influence of Paul's Ministry in Philippi upon the Composition of Philippians 2:6-11." *Bulletin for Biblical Research* 20:85–102.

_____. 2010b. *When the Church Was a Family: Recapturing Jesus' Vision for Authentic Christian Community*. Nashville: B&H.

_____. 2015. *Philippians*. Exegetical Guide to the Greek New Testament. Nashville: B&H.

Hemer, C. J. 1989. *The Book of Acts in the Setting of Hellenistic History*. Edited by C. H. Gempf. Wissenschaftliche Untersuchungen zum Neuen Testament 2. Reihe, 49. Tübingen: Mohr Siebeck.

Hengel, M. 1974. *Judaism and Hellenism: Studies in Their Encounter in Palestine during the Early Hellenistic Period*. Translated by J. Bowden. Philadelphia: Fortress.

_____. 1977. *Crucifixion*. Philadelphia: Fortress.

_____. 1979. *Acts and the History of Earliest Christianity*. Trans. J. Bowden. London: SCM.

Hofius, O. 1976. *Der Christushymnus Philipper 2,6–11 : Untersuchungen zu Gestalt und Aussage eines urchristlichen Psalms*. Wissenschaftliche Untersuchungen zum Neuen Testament 17. Tübingen: Mohr Siebeck.

Holloway, P. A. 1998. "Notes and Observations *Bona Cogitare:* An Epicurean Consolation in Phil 4:8-9." *Harvard Theological Review* 91:89–96.

_____. 2001. *Consolation in Philippians: Philosophical Sources and Rhetorical Strategy*. Society for New Testament Studies Monograph Series 112. Cambridge: University Press.

_____. 2006. "Thanks for the Memories: On the Translation of Phil 1.3." *New Testament Studies* 52:419–32.

_____. 2008. "*Alius Paulus:* Paul's Promise to Send Timothy at Philippians 2.19-24." *New Testament Studies* 54:542–56.

Hooker, M. D. 1975. "Philippians 2:6-11." In *Jesus und Paulus. Festschrift für Werner Georg Kümmel zum 70. Gegurtstag*. Edited by E. E. Ellis and E. Grässer, 151–64. Göttingen.

_____. 1989. "ΠΙΣΤΙΣ ΧΡΙΣΤΟΥ," *New Testament Studies* 35:321–42.

_____. 2000. "Philippians." In *The New Interpreter's Bible*. Edited by L. Keck. Vol. 11, 469–549. Nashville: Abingdon.

Hoover, R. W. 1971. "The Harpagmos Enigma: A Philological Solution." *Harvard Theological Review* 56:95–119.

Horrell, D. G. 2005. "Introduction." *Journal for the Study of the New Testament* 27:251–55.

Horsley, R. A., ed. 1997. *Paul and Empire: Religion and Power in Roman Imperial Society*. Harrisburg, PA: Trinity Press International.

_____. 2000. *Paul and Politics: Ekklesia, Israel, Imperium, Interpretation: Essays in Honor of Krister Stendahl*. Harrisburg, PA: Trinity Press International.

_____, ed. 2004. *Paul and the Roman Imperial Order*. Harrisburg, PA: Trinity Press International.

Houlden, J. L. 1977. *Paul's Letters from Prison.* Westminster Pelican Commentaries. Philadelphia: Westminster.

Hurtado, L. W. 1984. "Jesus as Lordly Example in Philippians 2:5-11." In *From Jesus to Paul: Studies in Honour of Francis Wright Beare.* Edited by P. Richardson and J. C. Hurd, 113–26. Waterloo: Wilfred Laurier.

_____. 2003. *Lord Jesus Christ: Devotion to Jesus in Earliest Christianity.* Grand Rapids: Eerdmans.

_____. 2005. *How on Earth Did Jesus Become God? Historical Questions about Earliest Devotion to Jesus.* Grand Rapids: Eerdmans.

Jeremias, J. 1971. *New Testament Theology.* New York: Macmillan.

Jervell, J. 1998. *Die Apostelgeschichte.* Kritisch-exegetischer Kommentar über das Neue Testament (Meyer-Kommentar) 3. Göttingen: Vandenhoeck & Ruprecht.

Jewett, R. 1970a. "The Epistolary Thanksgiving and the Integrity of Philippians." *Novum Testamentum* 12:40–53.

_____. 1970b. "Conflicting Movements in the Early Church as Reflected in Philippians." *Novum Testamentum* 12:362–90.

Jowers, D. W. 2006. "The Meaning of ΜΟΡΦΗ in Philippians 2:6-7." *Journal of the Evangelical Theological Society* 49:739–66.

Justnes, Å. 2012. "Un-Pauline Paul? Philippians 2.6-11 in Context." *Symbolae Osloenses* 86:145–159.

Kärkkäinen, V.-M. 2013. *Christ and Reconciliation: A Constructive Christian Theology for the Pluralistic World.* Grand Rapids: Eerdmans.

Käsemann, E. 1968. "A Critical Analysis of Philippians 2:5-11." *Journal for Theology and the Church* 5:45–88.

Keller, T. 2010. *The Freedom of Self-Forgetfulness: The Path to True Christian Joy.* Leyland, Lancashire: 10Publishing.

Keown, M. J. 2009. *Congregational Evangelism in Philippians: The Centrality of an Appeal for Gospel Proclamation to the Fabric of Philippians.* Paternoster Biblical Monographs. Eugene, OR: Wipf & Stock.

_____. 2015. "Did Paul Plan to Escape from Prison? Philippians 1:19-26." *Journal for the Study of Paul and His Letters* 5:89–108.

Kilpatrick, G. D. 1928. "ΒΛΕΠΕΤΕ, Philippians 3:2." In *In Memoriam Paul Kahle.* Edited by M. Black and G. Fohrer, 146–48. Berlin: Töpelmann.

Kim, S. 1984. *The Origin of Paul's Gospel.* 2nd ed. Grand Rapids: Eerdmans.

_____. 2002. *Paul and the New Perspective: Second Thoughts on the Origin of Paul's Gospel.* Grand Rapids: Eerdmans.

_____. 2008. *Christ and Caesar: The Gospel and the Roman Empire in the Writings of Paul and Luke.* Grand Rapids: Eerdmans.

_____. 2017. "Paul and the Roman Empire." In *God and the Faithfulness of Paul: A Critical Examination of the Pauline Theology of N. T. Wright.* Edited by C. Heilig, J. T. Hewitt, and M. F. Bird, 277–310. Wissenschaftliche Untersuchungen zum Neuen Testament 2. Reihe, 413. Tübingen: Mohr Siebeck.

Kittle, G., and G. Friedrich, eds. 1964–76. *Theological Dictionary of the New Testament.* 10 vols. Grand Rapids: Eerdmans.

Koehler, L., and W. Baumgartner. 2001. *Hebrew and Aramaic Lexicon of the Old Testament.* 2 vols. Leiden, Brill.

Koester, H. 1961–62. "The Purpose of the Polemic of a Pauline Fragment Philippians III." *New Testament Studies* 8:317–34.

_____. 1982. *Introduction to the New Testament.* 2 vols. Philadelphia: Fortress.

Koperski, V. 1992. "Textlinguistics and the Integrity of Philippians: A Critique of Wolfgang Schenk's Arguments for a Compilation Hypothesis." *Ephemerides theologicae lovanienses* 68:331–67.

_____. 1996. *The Knowledge of Christ Jesus My Lord: The High Christology of Philippians 3:7-11.* Kampen: Kok Pharos.

Koukouli-Chrysantaki, C. 1998. "Colonia Iulia Augusta Philippensis." In *Philippi at the Time of Paul and after His Death.* Edited by C. Bakirtzis and H. Koester, 5–35. Harrisburg: Trinity Press International.

Kraftchick, S. 2007. "Abstracting Paul's Theology: Extending Reflections on 'Death' in Philippians." In *The Impartial God: Essays in Biblical Studies in Honor of Jouette M. Bassler.* Edited by C. J. Roetzel and R. L. Foster, 194–211. New Testament Monographs 22. Sheffield: Phoenix.

Kraftchick, S. J. 2008. "Self-Presentation and Community Construction in Philippians." In *Scripture and Traditions: Essays on Early Judaism and Christianity in Honor of Carl R. Holladay.* Edited by P. Gray and G. R. O'Day, 239–62. Supplements to Novum Testamentum 129. Leiden: Brill.

Krentz, E. 1993. "Military Language and Metaphors in Philippians." In *Origins and Methods: Toward a New Understanding of Judaism and Christianity: Essays in Honour of John C. Hurd.* Journal for the Study of the New Testament Supplements 96. Edited by B. H. McLean, 105–27. Sheffield: Academic.

———. 2000. "Civic Culture and the Philippians." *Currents in Theology and Mission* 35:258–63.

———. 2003. "Paul, Games, and the Military." In *Paul in the Greco-Roman World: A Handbook.* Edited by J. P. Sampley, 344–83. Harrisburg, PA: Trinity Press International.

Kümmel, W. G. 1975. *Introduction to the New Testament.* Rev. English ed. Nashville: Abingdon.

Lambrecht, J. 2007. "Paul's Reasoning in Philippians 2,6-8." *Ephemerides Theologicae Lovanienses* 83:413–18.

———. 2003. "The Identity of Christ Jesus Philippians 2,6-11." In Jan Lambrecht, *Understanding What One Reads: New Testament Essays.* Edited by V. Koperski, 245–62. Leuven: Peeters.

Lewis, C. S. 1996. *Mere Christianity.* New York: Touchstone Books. First published 1952.

Lewis, C. S. 2001. *The Weight of Glory.* San Francisco: HarperSanFrancisco. Originally published 1941.

Llewelyn, S. R. 1995. "Sending Letters in the Ancient World: Paul and the Philippians." *Tyndale Bulletin* 46:337–56.

Liddell, H. G., R. Scott, and H. S. Jones. 1996. *A Greek-English Lexicon with Revised Supplement.* 9th ed. Oxford: Clarendon Press.

Lightfoot, J. B. 1953. *St. Paul's Epistle to the Philippians.* Grand Rapids: Zondervan,.

Lincoln, A. T. 1991. *Paradise Now and Not Yet: Studies in the Role of the Heavenly Dimension in Paul's Thought with Special Reference to His Eschatology.* Grand Rapids: Baker.

Loh, I. J., and E. A. Nida. 1977. *A Translator's Handbook on Paul's Letter to the Philippians.* Helps for Translators. Stuttgart: United Bible Societies.

Lohmeyer, E. 1961. *Kyrios Jesus: Eine Untersuchung zu Phil. 2,5-11.* 2. Auflage. Sitzungsberichte der Heidelberger Akademie der Wissenschaften, Philosophisch-historische Klasse, Jahrgang 1927/28. 4. Abhandlung. Heidelberg: Carl Winter-Universitätsverlag.

Lohse. E. 1976. *The New Testament Environment.* Translated by J. Steely. Nashville: Abington.

Lucas, A. J. 2014. "Assessing Stanley E. Porter's Objections to Richard B. Hays's Notion of Metalepsis." *Catholic Biblical Quarterly* 76:93–111.

Luter, A. B. and M. V. Lee. 1995. "Philippians as Chiasmus: Key to the Structure, Unity, and Theme Questions." *New Testament Studies* 41, 89–101.

———. 1996. "Partnership in the Gospel: The Role of Women in the Church at Philippi." *Journal for the Evangelical Theological Society* 39:411–20.

MacDonald, G. 2010. *Who Stole My Church: What to Do When the Church You Love Tries to Enter the 21st Century*. Nashville: Tommy Nelson.

MacLeod, D. J. 2001. "Imitating the Incarnation of Christ: An Exposition of Philippians 2:5-8," *Bibliotheca Sacra* 158:308–30.

Malinowski, F. X. 1985. "The Brave Women of Philippi." *Biblical Theology Bulletin* 15:60–64.

Marrow, S. B. 1982. "Parrēsia and the New Testament." *Catholic Biblical Quarterly* 44:431–46.

Marshall, I. H. 1990. *The Origins of New Testament Christology*. Updated ed. Downers Grove, IL: InterVarsity Press.

_____. 1991. *The Epistle to the Philippians*. Epworth Commentaries. London: Epworth.

_____. 1993. "The Theology of Philippians." In K. P. Donfried and I. H. Marshall, *The Theology of the Shorter Pauline Letters*, 115–74. Cambridge: University Press.

_____. 2004. *New Testament Theology: Many Witnesses, One Gospel*. Downers Grove, IL: InterVarsity Press.

Marshall, P. 1987. *Enmity in Corinth: Social Conventions in Paul's Relations with the Corinthians*. Wissenschaftliche Untersuchungen zum Neuen Testament 2. Reihe, 23. Tübingen: Mohr Siebeck.

Martin, M. W., and B. W. Nash. 2015. "Philippians 2:6-11 as Subversive *Hymnos*: A Study in the Light of Ancient Rhetorical Theory." *Journal of Theological Studies* 66:90–138.

Martin, R. P. 1976. *Philippians*. New Century Bible Commentary. Grand Rapids: Eerdmans.

_____. 1987. *Philippians*. Tyndale New Testament Commentaries. Downers Grove, IL: InterVarsity Press.

_____. 1988. *James*. Word Biblical Commentary. Waco, TX: Word.

_____. 1997. *A Hymn of Christ: Philippians 2:5-11 in Recent Interpretation and in the Setting of Early Christian Worship*. Downers Grove, IL: InterVarsity Press.

Martin, R. P., and B. J. Dodd, eds. 1998. *Where Christology Began: Essays on Philippians 2*. Louisville: Westminster John Knox.

Martin, R. P., and G. W. Hawthorne. 2004. *Philippians*. Rev. ed. Word Biblical Commentary. Nashville: Thomas Nelson.

McKnight, S., and J. B. Modica, eds. 2013. *Jesus Is Lord, Caesar Is Not: Evaluating Empire in New Testament Studies*. Downers Grove, IL: InterVarsity Press.

Melick, R. R., Jr. 1991. *Philippians, Colossians, Philemon*. New American Commentary. Nashville: B&H.

Metzger, B. M. 1994. *A Textual Commentary on the Greek New Testament*. 2nd ed. Stuttgart: Deutsche Bibelgesellschaft.

Meyer, H. A. W. 1928. *Critical and Exegetical Handbook to the Epistles to the Philippians and Colossians*. 4th ed. Translated by J. C. Moore and W. P. Dickson. London: Hodder & Stoughton.

Michael, J. H. 1928. *The Epistle of Paul to the Philippians*. Moffatt New Testament Commentary. New York: Harper and Brothers.

Miller, C. 2010. "The Imperial Cult in the Pauline Cities of Asia Minor and Greece." *Catholic Biblical Quarterly* 72:314–32.

Miller, E. C. 1982. "Πολιτεύεσθε in Philippians 1.27: Some Philological and Thematic Observations." *Journal for the Study of the New Testament* 15:86–96.

Miller, J. C. 2011. "Paul and His Ethnicity: Reframing the Categories." In *Paul as Missionary: Identity, Activity, Theology, and Practice*. Edited by T. J. Burke and B. S. Rosner, 37–50. Library of New Testament Studies 420. New York: T&T Clark.

Moessner, D. P. 2009. "Turning Status 'Upside Down' in Philippi: Christ Jesus' 'Emptying Himself' as Forfeiting Acknowledgment of His 'Equality with God' Phil 2:6-11." *Horizons in Biblical Theology* 31:123–143.

Moo, D. J. 1983. "Law, 'Works of Law,' and Legalism in Paul." *Westminster Theological Journal* 45:73–100.

_____. 2000. *The Letter of James.* Pillar New Testament Commentary. Grand Rapids: Eerdmans.

_____. 2003. "'Flesh' in Romans: A Problem for the Translator." In *The Challenge of Bible Translation: Communicating God's Word to the World: Essays in Honor of Ronald F. Youngblood.* Edited by G. S. Scorgie, M. L. Strauss, and S. M. Voth, 365–79. Grand Rapids: Zondervan.

_____. 2013. *Galatians.* Baker Exegetical Commentary on the New Testament. Grand Rapids: Baker Academic.

Moore, R. D. 2015. *Onward: Engaging the Culture without Losing the Gospel.* Nashville: B&H Publishing.

Moore, T. S. 2015. *Translating Philippians Clause by Clause: An Exegetical Guide.* Ebooks for Translating the New Testament. Leesburg, IN: Cyber-Center for Biblical Studies.

Morris, L. 1956. "ΚΑΙ ΑΠΑΞ ΚΑΙ ΔΙΣ." *Novum Testamentum* 1:205–8.

Moule, C. F. D. 1959. *An Idiom Book of New Testament Greek.* Cambridge: University Press.

_____. 1970. "Further Reflexions on Philippians 2:5-11." In *Apostolic History and the Gospel: Biblical and Historical Essays Presented to F. F. Bruce on His 60th Birthday.* Edited by W. W. Gasque and R. P. Martin, 264–76. Grand Rapids: Eerdmans.

_____. 1972. "The Manhood of Jesus in the NT." In *Christ, Faith, and History.* Edited by S. W. Sykes and J. P. Clayton, 95–110. Cambridge: University Press.

Moule, H. C. G. 1981. *The Epistle to the Philippians.* Thornapple Commentaries. Grand Rapids: Baker. First published in 1879.

Moulton, J. H., W. F. Howard, and N. Turner. 1906–76. *A Grammar of New Testament Greek.* 4 vols. Edinburgh: T&T Clark.

Moulton, J. H., and G. Milligan. 1972. *The Vocabulary of the Greek Testament Illustrated from the Papyri and Other Non-Literary Sources.* Grand Rapids: Eerdmans.

Müller, J. J. 1955. *The Epistles of Paul to the Philippians and to Philemon.* New International. Commentary on the New Testament. Grand Rapids: Eerdmans.

Müller, U. B. 2002. *Der Brief des Paulus an die Philipper.* 2nd ed. Theologischer Handkommentar zum Neuen Testament. Leipzig: Evangelische Verlagsanstalt.

Nanos, M. D. 2009. "Paul's Reversal of Jews Calling Gentiles 'Dogs' Philippians 3:2: 1600 Years of an Ideological Tale Wagging an Exegetical Dog?" *Biblical Interpretation* 17:448–48.

_____. 2011. "'Judaizers'? 'Pagan' Cults? Cynics?: Reconceptualizing the Concerns of Paul's Audience from the Polemics in Philippians 3:2, 18-19." Accessed December 1 2016. http://www.marknanos.com/Cynics-In-Phil3-May11.pdf.

_____. 2013. "Paul's Polemic in Philippians 3 as Jewish-Subgroup Vilification of Local Non-Jewish Cultic and Philosophical Alternatives." *Journal for the Study of Paul and His Letters* 3:47–91.

Nash, B. 2016. "Philippians 3:4-11 as Subversive Enconium." *Stone-Campbell Journal* 19, 85–93.

Nebreda, S. R. 2011 *Christ Identity: A Social-Scientific Reading of Philippians 2.5-11.* Forschungen zur Religion und Literatur des Alten und Neuen Testaments 240; Göttingen: Vandenhoeck & Ruprecht.

Newton, P. 2017. *The Mentoring Church: How Pastors and Congregations Cultivate Leaders.* Grand Rapids: Kregel Ministry.

Neyrey, J. H. 2009. "Lost in Translation: Did It Matter If Christians "Thanked" God or "Gave God Glory"? *Catholic Biblical Quarterly* 71:1–23.

Novenson, M. V. 2010. "God Is Witness" A Classical Rhetorical Idiom in Its Pauline Usage." *Novum Testamentum* 52:355–75.

Oakes, P. 2001. *Philippians: From People to Letter.* Society for New Testament Studies Monograph Series 110. Cambridge: University Press.

_____. 2002. "God's Sovereignty Over Roman Authorities: A Theme in Philippians." In *Rome in the Bible and the Early Church.* Edited by P. Oakes, 126–41. Grand Rapids: Baker Academic.

_____. 2005. "Re-Mapping the Universe: Paul and the Emperor in 1 Thessalonians and Philippians." *Journal for the Study of the New Testament* 27:301–22.

O'Brien, P. T. 1977. *Introductory Thanksgivings in the Letters of Paul.* Supplements to Novum Testamentum 49. Leiden: Brill.

_____. 1980. "Thanksgiving within the Structure of Pauline Theology." In *Pauline Studies in Honour of Professor F. F. Bruce.* Edited by D. A. Hagner and M. J. Harris, 50–66. Grand Rapids: Eerdmans.

_____. 1991. *The Epistle to the Philippians.* New International Greek Testament Commentary. Grand Rapids: Eerdmans.

_____. 2004. "Was Paul Converted?" In *Justification and Variegated Nomism.* Vol. 2. Edited by D. A. Carson, P. T. O'Brien, and M. A. Seifrid, 361–91. Grand Rapids: Baker Academic.

O'Collins, G. 2009. *Christology: A Biblical, Historical, and Systematic Study of Jesus.* 2nd ed. Oxford: University Press.

Oden, T. C. 1998. *Life in the Spirit: Systematic Theology: Volume Three.* Peabody, MA: Prince Press.

Ogereau, J. M. 2014a. *Paul's Koinonia with the Philippians: A Socio-Historical Investigation of a Pauline Economic Partnership.* Wissenschaftliche Untersuchungen zum Neuen Testament 2. Reihe, 377. Tübingen: Mohr Siebeck.

_____. 2014b. "Paul's κοινωνία with the Philippians: Societas as a Missionary Funding Strategy." *New Testament Studies* 60:360–78.

Ortlund, D. 2012. *Zeal Without Knowledge: The Concept of Zeal in Romans 10, Galatians 1, and Philippians 3.* Library of New Testament Studies 472. London: T&T Clark.

Osiek, C. 2000. *Philippians, Philemon.* Abingdon New Testament Commentaries. Nashville: Abingdon.

Palmer, D. W. 1975. "'To Die Is Gain' Philippians 1:21." *Novum Testamentum* 17:203–18.

Pao, D. W. 2002. *Thanksgiving: An Investigation of a Pauline Theme.* New Studies in Biblical Theology 13. Downers Grove, IL: InterVarsity Press.

Park, M. S. 2007. *Submission within the Godhead and the Church in the Epistle to the Philippians.* Library of New Testament Studies 361. London: T&T Clark.

Peppard, M. 2008. "'Poetry', 'Hymns' and 'Traditional Material' in New Testament Epistles or How to Do Things with Indentations," *Journal for the Study of the New Testament* 30:319–42.

Perriman, A. 1991. "The Pattern of Christ's Sufferings: Colossians 1:24 and Philippians 3:10-11." *Tyndale Bulletin* 42:62–79.

Perkins, P. 1987. "Christology, Friendship, and Status: The Rhetoric of Philippians." *Society of Biblical Literature Seminar Papers:* 509–20.

_____. 1991. "Philippians: Theology for the Heavenly Politeuma." In *Pauline Theology Volume 1: Thessalonians, Philippians, Galatians, Philemon.* Edited by J. M. Bassler, 89–104. Minneapolis: Fortress.

Pervo, R. I. 2009. *Acts.* Edited by H. W. Attridge. Hermeneia. Minneapolis: Fortress Press.

Peter-Ben, Smit. 2014. "Paul, Plutarch and the Problematic Practice of Self-Praise περιαυτολογία: The Case of Phil 3.2-21." *New Testament Studies* 60:341–59.

Peterlin, D. 1995. *Paul's Letter to the Philippians in the Light of Disunity in the Church.* Supplements to Novum Testamentum 79. Leiden: Brill.

Peterman, G. W. 1997. *Paul's Gift from Philippi: Conventions of Gift Exchange and Christian Giving.* Society for New Testament Studies Monograph Series 92. Cambridge: University Press.

Peters, J. 2015. "Crowns in 1 Thessalonians, Philippians, and 1 Corinthians." *Biblica* 96:67–84.

Peterson, E. 1989. *The Contemplative Pastor: Returning to the Art of Spiritual Direction.* Grand Rapids: Eerdmans.

Peterson, J. 2012. "'In the Churches of Macedonia': Implicit Ecclesiology in Paul's Letters to the Thessalonians and Philippians." In *The New Testament Church: The Challenge of Developing Ecclesiologies.* Edited by J. Harrison and J. D. Dvorak, 148–63. Eugene, OR: Pickwick.

Pfitzner, V. C. 1967. *Paul and the Agon Motif: Traditional Athletic Imagery in the Pauline Literature.* Supplements to Novum Testamentum 16. Leiden: Brill.

Pilhofer, P. 1995–2000. *Philippi.* 2 vols. Wissenschaftliche Untersuchungen zum Neuen Testament 87 and 119. Tübingen: Mohr Siebeck.

Platt, D. 2010. *Radical: Taking Back Your Faith from the American Dream.* Colorado Springs: Multnomah Books.

Plummer, A. 1919. *A Commentary on St. Paul's Epistle to the Philippians.* London: Scott.

Poirier, A. 2006. *The Peacemaking Pastor: A Biblical Guide to Resolving Church Conflict.* Grand Rapids: Baker Books.

Poirier, J. C. 2012. "The Meaning of Πίστις in Philippians 1:27." *Expository Times* 123:334–37.

Polhill, J. B. 1999. *Paul and His Letters.* Nashville: Broadman & Holman.

Pollard, T. E. 1966–67. "The Integrity of Philippians." *New Testament Studies* 13:57–66.

Porter, S. E. 1993. "Word Order and Clause Structure in New Testament Greek: An Unexplored Area of Greek Linguistics Using Philippians as a Test Case." *Filología neotestamentaria* 6:177–206.

Powell, M. A. 2006. *Giving to God: The Bible's Good News about Living a Generous Life.* Grand Rapids: Eerdmans.

Poythress, V. S. 2002. "'Hold Fast' versus 'Hold Out' in Philippians 2:16." *Westminster Theological Journal* 63:45–53.

Punch, J. D. 2014. "Σκύβαλα happens: Edification from a Four-Letter Word in the Word of God?" *Bible Translator* 65:369–384.

Punt, J. 2009. "A Biblical Death-wish: Paul Celebrating Dying in Phil 1:21." *Verbum et Ecclesia* 30:202–20.

Ramsaran, R. A. 2002. "Living and Dying, Living Is Dying Philippians 1:21: Paul's Maxim and Exemplary Argumentation in Philippians." In *Rhetorical Argumentation in Biblical Texts: Essays from the Lund 2000 Conference.* Edited by A. Eriksson, T. H. Olbricht, and W. Übelacker, 325–38. Emory Studies in Early Christianity. Harrisburg: Trinity Press International.

Rapske, B. 1994. *The Book of Acts and Paul in Roman Custody.* Book of Acts in Its First Century Setting 3. Grand Rapids: Eerdmans.

Reed, J. T. 1991. "The Infinitive with Two Substantival Accusatives: An Ambiguous Connection?" *Novum Testamentum* 33:1–27.

———. 1997. *A Discourse Analysis of Philippians: Method and Rhetoric in the Debate over Literary Integrity.* Journal for the

Study of the New Testament Supplement Series 136. Sheffield: Academic Press.

Reicke, B. 1970. "Caesarea, Rome, and the Captivity Epistles." In *Apostolic History and the Gospel: Biblical and Historical Essays Presented to F. F. Bruce on His 60th Birthday.* Edited by W. W. Gasque and R. P. Martin, 277–86. Grand Rapids: Eerdmans.

Reumann, J. 2008. *Philippians.* Anchor Yale Bible. New Haven, CT: Yale University Press.

Richardson, P. 1969. *Israel in the Apostolic Church.* Cambridge: University Press.

Ridderbos, H. 1975. *Paul: An Outline of His Theology.* Grand Rapids: Eerdmans.

Robertson, A. T. 1934. *A Grammar of the Greek New Testament in the Light of Historical Research.* Nashville: Broadman Press. First published in English by Hodder & Stoughton in 1914.

Robinson, J. A. T. 1952. *The Body: A Study in Pauline Theology.* Philadelphia: Westminster.

_____. 1976. *Redating the New Testament.* Philadelphia: Westminster.

Sampley, J. P. 1980. *Pauline Partnership in Christ: Christian Community and Commitment in Light of Roman Law.* Philadelphia: Fortress.

Sande, K. 2004. *The Peacemaker: A Biblical Guide to Resolving Personal Conflict.* 3rd ed. Grand Rapids: Baker Books.

Sanders, E. P. 1977. *Paul and Palestinian Judaism.* Philadelphia: Fortress.

_____. 1983. *Paul, the Law, and the Jewish People.* Philadelphia: Fortress.

Sandnes, K. O. 2002. *Belly and Body in the Pauline Epistles.* Society for New Testament Studies Monograph Series 120. Cambridge: University Press.

Scazzero, P. 2015. *The Emotionally Healthy Leader: How Transforming Your Inner Life Will Deeply Transform Your Church, Team, and the World.* Grand Rapids: Zondervan.

Schenk, W. 1984. *Die Philipperbriefe des Paulus: Kommentar.* Stuttgart: Kohlhammer.

Schnabel, E. J. 2004. *Early Christian Mission.* 2 vols. Downers Grove, IL: InterVarsity Press.

Schoeps, H. J. 1961. *Paul: The Theology of the Apostle in the Light of Jewish Religious History.* Translated by H. Knight. Philadelphia: Westminster.

Schreiner, T. R. 1993. *The Law and Its Fulfillment.* Grand Rapids: Baker Books.

_____. 1998. *Romans.* Baker Exegetical Commentary on the New Testament. Grand Rapids: Baker Books.

_____. 2001. *Paul, Apostle of God's Glory in Christ: A Pauline Theology.* Downers Grove, IL: InterVarsity Press.

_____. 2011. "The Saving Righteousness of God in Christ." *Journal of the Evangelical Theological Society* 54:19–34.

Schubert, P. 1939. *Form and Function of the Pauline Thanksgivings.* Berlin: Töpelmann.

Schürer, E. 1973–86. *The History of the Jewish People in the Age of Jesus Christ.* Revised and edited by G. Vermes, et al. 3 vols. Edinburgh: T.&T. Clark.

Silva, M. 2005. *Philippians.* 2nd ed. Baker Exegetical Commentary on the New Testament. Grand Rapids: Baker Academic.

_____. ed. 2014. *New International Dictionary of New Testament Theology and Exegesis.* 5 vols. 2nd ed. Grand Rapids: Zondervan.

Smit, P. B. 2013. *Paradigms of Being in Christ: A Study of the Epistle to the Philippians.* Library of New Testament Studies 476. London: Bloomsbury T&T Clark.

_____. 2014. "Paul, Plutarch, and the Problematic Practice of Self-Praise περιαυτολογία: The Case of Phil 3.2-21." *New Testament Studies* 60:341–59.

Smith, J. K. 2016. *You Are What You Love: The Spiritual Power of Habit.* Grand Rapids: Brazos Press.

Snyman, A. H. 1993. "Persuasion in Philippians 4.1-20." In *Rhetoric and the New Testament*. Edited by S. E. Porter and T. H. Olbricht, 325–37. Journal for the Study of the New Testament Supplement Series 90. Sheffield: Academic Press.

_____. 2005a. "A Rhetorical Analysis of Philippians 1:27-2:18." *Verba et Ecclesia* 26:783–809.

_____. 2005b. "Philippians 2:19-30 from a Rhetorical Perspective." *Acta Patristica et Byzantina* 16:289–307.

_____. 2006a. "A Rhetorical Analysis of Philippians 3:1-11." *Neotestamenica* 40:259–83.

_____. 2006b. "A Rhetorical Analysis of Philippians 3:12-21." *Acta Patristica et Byzantina* 17:327–48.

_____. 2007a. "Philippians 4:1-9 from a Rhetorical Perspective." *Verbum et Ecclesia* 28:224–43.

_____. 2007b. "Philippians 4:10-23 from a Rhetorical Perspective." *Acta Theologica* 27 (2):168–85.

_____. 2007c. "A New Perspective on Paul's Rhetorical Strategy in Philippians." *Acta Patristica et Byzantina* 18:214–30.

Stearns, R. 2010. *The Whole in Our Gospel: What Does God Expect of Us? The Answer That Changed My Life and Might Just Change the World.* Nashville: Tommy Nelson.

Steenburg, D. 1988. "The Case Against the Synonymity of *Morphe* and *Eikon*." *Journal for the Study of the New Testament* 34:77–86.

Stegman, T. D. 2011. "Paul's Use Of *Dikaio*-Terminology: Moving Beyond N. T. Wright's Forensic Interpretation." *Theological Studies* 72:496–524.

Steindl-Rast, D. 1984. *Gratefulness, The Heart of Prayer: An Approach to Life in Fullness.* Ramsey, NJ: Paulist.

Still, T. D. 2012. "More Than Friends? The Literary Classification of Philippians Revisited." *Perspectives in Religious Studies* 39:53–66.

Stott, J. 2007. *The Living Church: Convictions of a Lifelong Pastor.* Downers Grove, IL: InterVarsity Press.

Stowers, S. K. 1991. "Friends and Enemies in the Politics of Heaven: Reading Theology in Philippians." In *Pauline Theology Volume 1: Thessalonians, Philippians, Galatians, Philemon.* Edited by J. M. Bassler, 105–21. Minneapolis: Fortress.

Strimple, R. B. 1979. "Philippians 2:5-11 in Recent Studies: Some Exegetical Conclusions." *Westminster Theological Journal* 41:247–68.

Sweney, C. 2011. *A New Kind of Big: How Churches of Any Size Can Partner to Transform Communities.* Grand Rapids: Baker Books.

Swenson, R. A. 2013. *Contentment: The Secret to a Lasting Calm.* Colorado Springs: NavPress.

Swift, R. C. 1984. "The Theme and Structure of Philippians." *Bibliotheca Sacra* 141:234–54.

Tellbe, M. 1994. "The Sociological Factors Behind Philippians 3:1-11 and the Conflict at Philippi." *Journal for the Study of the New Testament* 55:97–121.

Thielman, F. 1994. *Paul and the Law: A Contextual Approach.* Downers Grove, IL: InterVarsity Press.

_____. 1995. *Philippians.* The NIV Application Commentary. Grand Rapids: Zondervan.

_____. 2003. "Ephesus and the Literary Setting of Philippians." In *New Testament Greek and Exegesis: Essays in Honor of Gerald F. Hawthorne.* Edited by A. M. Donaldson and T. B. Sailors, 205–23. Grand Rapids: Eerdmans.

_____. 2005. *Theology of the New Testament: A Canonical and Synthetic Approach.* Grand Rapids: Zondervan.

Thiselton, A. C. 1978. "Realized Eschatology at Corinth." *New Testament Studies* 24:510–26.

———. 2000. *The First Epistle to the Corinthians.* New International Greek Testament Commentary. Grand Rapids: Eerdmans.

Thrall. M. 1962. *Greek Particles in the New Testament.* Linguistic and Exegetical Studies. Grand Rapids: Eerdmans.

Thurston, B. B., and J. M. Ryan 2005. *Philippians and Philemon.* Sacra Pagina. Collegeville, MN: Liturgical Press.

Tobin, T. H. 2006. "The World of Thought in the Philippians Hymn Philippians 2:6-11." In *The New Testament and Early Christian Literature in the Greco-Roman Context: Studies in Honor of David E. Aune.* Edited by J. Fotopoulos, 91–104. Supplements to Novum Testamentum 122. Leiden: Brill.

Tsang, S. 2011. "Are We 'Misreading' Paul?: Oral Phenomena and Their Implication for the Exegesis of Paul's Letters." *Oral Tradition* 24:205–25.

VanGemeren, W. A., ed. 1997. *New International Dictionary of Old Testament Theology and Exegesis.* 5 vols. Grand Rapids: Zondervan.

Varner, W. 2016. *Philippians: A Handbook on the Greek Text.* Baylor Handbook of the Greek New Testament. Waco, TX: Baylor University Press.

Verhoef, E. 2005. "The Church of Philippi in the First Six Centuries of Our Era." *Hervormde Teologiese Studies* 61:565–92.

———. 2013. *Philippi: How Christianity Began in Europe: The Epistle to the Philippians and the Excavations at Philippi.* London: Bloomsbury T&T Clark.

Vincent, M. R. 1897. *A Critical and Exegetical Commentary on the Epistles to the Philippians and to Philemon.* International Critical Commentary. Edinburgh: T&T Clark.

Wagner, J. R. 2007. "Working Out Salvation: Holiness and Community in Philippians." In *Holiness and Ecclesiology in the New Testament.* Edited by K. E. Brower and A. Johnson, 257–74. Grand Rapids: Eerdmans.

Wallace, D. B. 1996. *Greek Grammar Beyond the Basics.* Grand Rapids: Zondervan.

———. 2016. "A Brief Word Study on Σκύβαλον." Accessed Bible.org December 12, 2016. http://www.bible.org/article/brief-word-study-skuvbalon.

Waltke, B. K. 1992. "The Fear of the Lord: The Foundation for a Relationship with God." In *Alive to God: Studies in Spirituality Presented to James Houston.* Edited by J. I. Packer and L. Wilkinson, 17–33. Downers Grove, IL: InterVarsity Press.

Walton, S. 2011. "Paul, Patronage and Pay: What Do We Know about the Apostle's Financial Support?" In *Paul as Missionary: Identity, Activity, Theology, and Practice.* Edited by T. J. Burke and B. S. Rosner, 220–33. London: Bloomsbury T&T Clark.

Wanamaker, C. A. 1987. "Philippians 2:6-11: Son of God or Adamic Christology?" *New Testament Studies* 33:179–93.

Wansink, C. S. 1996. *Chained in Christ: The Experience and Rhetoric of Paul's Imprisonments.* Journal for the Study of the New Testament Supplement 130. Sheffield: Sheffield Academic Press.

Ware, J. P. 2005. *The Mission of the Church in Paul's Letter to the Philippians in the Context of Ancient Judaism.* Supplements to Novum Testamentum 120. Leiden: Brill.

———. 2011. "'The Word of Life': Resurrection and Missions in Philippians." In *Paul as Missionary: Identity, Activity, Theology, and Practice.* Edited by T. J. Burke and B. S. Rosner, 209–19. Library of New Testament Studies 420. New York: T&T Clark.

Watson, D. F. 1988. "A Rhetorical Analysis of Philippians and Its Implications for the Unity Question." *Novum Testamentum* 30:57–88.

_____. 2003. "A Reexamination of the Epistolary Analysis Underpinning the Arguments for the Composite Nature of Philippians." In *Early Christianity and Classical Culture: Comparative Studies in Honor of Abraham J. Malherbe.* Edited by J. T. Fitzgerald, T. H. Olbricht, and L. M. White, 157–77. Leiden: Brill.

_____. 2007. *Paul, Judaism, and the Gentiles: Beyond the New Perspective.* Rev. and expanded ed. Grand Rapids: Eerdmans.

Welch, E. T. 2007. *Running Scared: Fear, Worry, and the Rest of God.* Greensboro, NC: New Growth Press.

Westerholm, S. 1988. *Israel's Law and the Church's Faith.* Grand Rapids: Eerdmans.

_____. 2004. *Perspectives Old and New: The "Lutheran" Paul and His Critics.* Grand Rapids: Eerdmans.

White, J. E. 2017. *Meet Generation Z: Understanding and Reaching the New Post-Christian World.* Grand Rapids: Baker Books.

_____. 2014. *The Rise of the Nones: Understanding and Reaching the Religiously Unaffiliated.* Grand Rapids: Baker Books.

White, J. L. 1986. *Light from Ancient Letters.* Philadelphia: Fortress.

White, L. M. 1990. "Morality between Two Worlds: A Paradigm of Friendship in Philippians." In *Greeks, Romans and Christians: Essays in Honor of Abraham J. Malherbe.* Edited by D. L. Balch, E. Ferguson, and W. A. Meeks, 201–15. Minneapolis: Fortress.

Whitenton, M. R. 2010. "ΠΙΣΤΙΣ ΧΡΙΣΤΟΥ: Neglected Evidence from the Apostolic Fathers." *Journal of Theological Studies* 61:82–109.

Wiles, G. P. 1974. *Paul's Intercessory Prayers: The Significance of the Intercessory Prayer Passages in the Letters of St. Paul.* Cambridge: University Press.

Willard, D. 1998. *The Divine Conspiracy: Rediscovering Our Hidden Life in God.* San Francisco: Harper Collins.

_____. 2002. *Renovation of the Heart: Putting on the Character of Christ.* Colorado Springs: NavPress.

Williams, D. K. 2002. *Enemies of the Cross of Christ: The Terminology of the Cross and Conflict in Philippians.* Journal for the Study of the New Testament Supplement 223. New York: Sheffield Academic Press.

Willis, W. 2012. "The Shaping of Character: Virtue in Philippians 4:8-9." *Restoration Quarterly* 54:65–76.

Winter, B. W. 1994. *Seek the Welfare of the City: Christians as Benefactors and Citizens.* First Century Christians in the Graeco-Roman World. Grand Rapids: Eerdmans.

Winter, S. F. 2015. "Obedient to Death: Revisiting the Rhetorical Function of Philippians 2:6-11." *Australian Biblical Review* 63:1–13.

Witherington, B., III. 1994. *Paul's Narrative Thought World: The Tapestry of Tragedy and Triumph.* Louisville: Westminster/John Knox.

_____. 2011. *Paul's Letter to the Philippians: A Socio-Rhetorical Commentary.* Grand Rapids: Eerdmans.

Wong, T. Y.-C. 1986. "The Problem of Pre-Existence in Philippians 2,6-11." *Ephemerides Theologicae Lovanienses* 62:267–82.

Wright, N. T. 1993. *The Climax of the Covenant: Christ and the Law in Pauline Theology.* Minneapolis: Fortress.

_____. 1997. *What Saint Paul Really Said: Was Paul of Tarsus the Real Founder of Christianity?* Grand Rapids: Eerdmans.

_____. 2000 "Paul's Gospel and Caesar's Empire." In *Paul and Politics: Ekklesia, Israel, Imperium, Interpretation: Essays in Honor of Krister Stendahl.* Edited by R. A. Horsley, 160–83. Harrisburg, PA: Trinity Press International.

_____. 2010. *Justification: God's Plan and Paul's Vision.* Downers Grove, IL: IVP Academic.

_____. 2011. "Justification: Yesterday, Today, and Forever." *Journal of the Evangelical Theological Society* 54:49–63.

_____. 2013a. *Paul and the Faithfulness of God.* 2 vols. Minneapolis: Fortress.

_____. 2013b. *Evil and the Justice of God.* Downers Grove, IL: IVP Books.

Wurmbrand, R. 1998. *Tortured for Christ.* Bartlesville, OK: Living Sacrifice.

Yarbro Collins, A. 2003. "Psalms, Philippians 2:6-11, and the Origins of Christology." *Biblical Interpretation* 11(4):361–72.

Zerbe, G. 2009. "Citizenship and Politics According to Philippians." *Direction* 38:193–208.